COMMUNITY AND IDENTITY IN ANCIENT EGYPT

This book examines a group of twelve ancient Egyptian tombs (ca. 2300 BCE) in the elite Old Kingdom cemetery of Elephantine at Qubbet el-Hawa in modern Aswan. It develops an interdisciplinary approach to the material – drawing on methods from art history, archaeology, anthropology, and sociology, including agency theory, the role of style, the reflexive relationship between people and landscape, and the nature of locality and community identity. A careful examination of the architecture, setting, and unique text and image programs of these tombs in context provides a foundation for considering how ancient Egyptian provincial communities bonded to each other, developed shared identities within the broader Egyptian world, and expressed these identities through their personal forms of visual and material culture.

Deborah Vischak currently teaches at Parsons the New School for Design and Queens College in New York. She was a Mellon Postdoctoral Fellow in the Department of Art History and Archaeology at Columbia University and a Postdoctoral Research Associate and Lecturer in the Department of Art and Archaeology at Princeton University. She has traveled throughout Egypt, working on excavations and conducting field research from Giza to Aswan. Vischak has been published in the *Journal of the American Research Center in Egypt* and in an Internet-Beiträge zur Ägyptologie und Sudanarchäologie (IBAES) volume examining methodological approaches to Old Kingdom tombs.

COMMUNITY AND IDENTITY IN ANCIENT EGYPT

The Old Kingdom Cemetery at Qubbet el-Hawa

DEBORAH VISCHAK

CAMBRIDGE
UNIVERSITY PRESS

CAMBRIDGE
UNIVERSITY PRESS

32 Avenue of the Americas, New York, NY 10013-2473, USA

Cambridge University Press is part of the University of Cambridge.

It furthers the University's mission by disseminating knowledge in the pursuit of education, learning, and research at the highest international levels of excellence.

www.cambridge.org
Information on this title: www.cambridge.org/9781107027602

First published 2015

Printed in the United States of America

This publication is made possible in part from the Publication Fund, Department of Art and Archaeology, Princeton University.

A catalog record for this publication is available from the British Library.

Library of Congress Cataloging in Publication data
Vischak, Deborah, 1971–
Community and identity in ancient Egypt : the Old Kingdom cemetery at Qubbet el-Hawa / Deborah Vischak
pages cm
Includes bibliographical references and index.
ISBN 978-1-107-02760-2 (hardback)
1. Qubbat al-Hawa' Site (Egypt) 2. Cemeteries – Egypt – Qubbat al-Hawa' Site. 3. Tombs – Egypt – Qubbat al-Hawa' Site. 4. Aswan (Egypt) – Antiquities. 5. Community life – Egypt – Aswan – History – To 1500. 6. Group identity – Egypt – Aswan – History – To 1500. 7. Visual communication – Egypt – Aswan – History – To 1500. 8. Material culture – Egypt – Aswan – History – To 1500. 9. Egypt – History – Old Kingdom, ca. 2686–ca. 2181 B.C. 10. Social archaeology – Egypt – Aswan. I. Title.
DT73.Q72V57 2014
932′.3–dc23 2014020944

ISBN 978-1-107-02760-2 Hardback

For my mom

Contents

List of Figures		*page* ix
List of Plates		xii
List of Tables		xiii
Acknowledgments		xv
	Introduction	1
1	People and Place: Historical and Social Context	19
2	Tombs in Context: Description of Cemetery and Overview of Tombs	38
3	Figure, Panel, Program: Form and Meaning	133
4	Individuals, Community, Identity: Summation and Interpretation of Program Content	179
	Conclusion: Monuments of a Community	216
Appendix A Chronology and the Two Heqaibs		225
Appendix B Text Translations		239
Notes		295
Bibliography		309
Index		325

Figures

1.	Map of Egypt in the Old Kingdom	*page* xvii
2.	Overview of Aswan area	xviii
3.	Panoramic view of Aswan area	39
4.	View from the townsite at Elephantine to Qubbet el-Hawa	39
5.	Plan of the cemetery at Qubbet el-Hawa	40
6.	View of the courtyard of the tomb of Mekhu and Sabni1	59
7.	Plan of QH25/26, tomb of Mekhu and Sabni1	60
8.	View of interior columns in the tomb of Mekhu and Sabni1	61
9.	View of the false door of Sabni1 showing offering panels along the niche (MS28, MS29)	65
10.	View to the north from tomb of Sobekhetep	68
11.	Plan of QH90, tomb of Sobekhetep	69
12.	View from entrance to false door in tomb of Sobekhetep	70
13.	Relief of a *ka*-priest and his family in the tomb of Sobekhetep (SH2)	71
14.	Façade of tomb of IiShemai	72
15.	Plan of QH98, tomb of IiShemai Setka	73
16.	Plan of QH102, tomb of Khwin-Khnum	76
17.	Interior view of the tomb of Khwin-Khnum	76
18.	Plan of QH103, tomb of Tjetji	79
19.	Column in the tomb of Tjetji (Tj3, 3a)	81
20.	View south from the courtyard of tomb of Khui	82
21.	Plan of QH34e, tomb of Khui	83
22.	View of the interior of the tomb of Khui	84
23.	Detail of relief of Khnumhetep in the tomb of Khui (Ku2)	85
24.	View of the façade of the tomb of Khunes	87

25.	Plan of tombs QH34h–i, of Khunes and Ankhes	89
26.	View of the interior of the tomb of Khunes	89
27.	Diagram of the south wall in the tomb of Khunes (Kh5–7)	92
28.	Relief of Khunes (Kh19)	93
29.	Relief of offerers in the tomb of Khunes (Kh25, 26)	94
30.	Relief of offerers in the tomb of Khunes (Kh20)	94
31.	Diagram of the west wall in the tomb of Khunes (Kh8–18)	95
32.	View of tomb group including tomb of Harkhuf	98
33.	View of the façade of the tomb of Harkhuf	99
34.	Detail of the façade of the tomb of Harkhuf (H2)	100
35.	Plan of QH34n, tomb of Harkhuf	100
36.	View of the tomb group QH35, QH35d, and QH35e	103
37.	Detail of the façade of Pepynakht Heqaib1 (Pn2)	106
38.	Plan of QH35, tomb of Pepynakht Heqaib1	106
39.	Relief of offerers in the tomb of Pepynakht Heqaib1 (Pn8)	108
40.	View of the shared façade of tombs QH35d and QH35e	108
41.	Plans of the tombs QH35d of Pepynakht Heqaib2 and QH35e Sabni2	110
42.	Interior view of the tomb of Pepynakht Heqaib2	110
43.	Diagram of the entrance thicknesses in the tomb of Pepynakht Heqaib2 (PnH3–7)	113
44.	Relief of Pepynakht Heqaib2 on the upper section of the south entrance thickness (PnH3)	114
45.	Middle section of the north entrance thickness in the tomb of Pepynakht Heqaib2 (PnH6)	115
46.	Lower section of the south entrance thickness in the tomb of Pepynakht Heqaib2 (PnH4)	116
47.	Detail of relief of Pepynakht Heqaib2 on the north entrance thickness (PnH7)	116
48.	Detail of relief of offerers on the north entrance thickness (PnH7e–f)	118
49.	Diagram of the east wall in the tomb of Pepynakht Heqaib2 (PnH8–21)	119
50.	East wall, south of the entrance in the tomb of Pepynakht Heqaib2 (PnH8–14)	120
51.	Relief Panel K in the tomb of Pepynakht Heqaib2 (PnH17)	121
52.	Relief Panel O in the tomb of Pepynakht Heqaib2 (PnH21)	122
53.	Diagram of the internal "west wall" in the tomb of Pepynakht Heqaib2 (PnH24–28)	122

54. Diagram of the façade of the tomb of Sabni2 (Sb1–9) 125
55. Relief of Sabni2 on the façade of his tomb (Sb7) 126
56. Relief of offerers on the façade of the tomb of Sabni2 (Sb6) 127
57. Diagram of the entrance thicknesses in the tomb of Sabni2 (Sb10–13) 128
58. East entrance thickness in the tomb of Sabni2 (Sb10–11) 129
59. View of the interior northeast area in the tomb of Sabni2 (Sb14, 15 visible) 130
60. Fishing and fowling scene in the tomb of Sabni2 (Sb15) 130
61. Bull-fighting scene in the tomb of Sabni2 (Sb17) 132

Plates

Color plates follow page 78

I	View of southern end of Qubbet el-Hawa
II	View of northern end of Qubbet el-Hawa
III	a. View south from Qubbet el-Hawa b. View north from Qubbet el-Hawa
IV	East wall in the tomb of Mekhu (MS7, 7a)
V	Fishing and fowling scene in the tomb of Sabni1 (MS27)
VI	Sobekhetep with *ka*-priest (SH3)
VII	IiShemai with two *ka*-priests (IiS4)
VIII	*Ka*-priest and family in the tomb of Sobekhetep (SH4)
IX	Khwin-Khnum with *ka*-priest (KK6)
X	Offering figures in the tomb of Tjetji (Tj4)
XI	a. Offering figures with animals in the tomb of Khwin-Khnum (KK2) b. *Ka*-priest and family in the tomb of Khwin-Khnum (KK4)
XII	Interior view of the tomb of Harkhuf (H9–12 visible)
XIII	Lower portion of the north entrance thickness in the tomb of Pepynakht Heqaib2 (PnH7)
XIV	North section of the east wall in the tomb of Pepynakht Heqaib2 (PnH15–21)
XV	Panel F in the tomb of Pepynakht Heqaib2 (PnH13)
XVI	a. Detail of Panel C in the tomb of Pepynakht Heqaib2 (PnH10) b. Detail of Panel E in the tomb of Pepynakht Heqaib2 (PnH12) c. Detail of offering figure in the tomb of Tjetji (Tj3a)
XVII	Panel I in the tomb of Pepynakht Heqaib2 (PnH15)
XVIII	Panel T in the tomb of Pepynakht Heqaib2 (PnH28)
XIX	Schematic plan of the distribution of styles among the Old Kingdom tombs at Qubbet el-Hawa

Tables

1. Style distribution by tomb, tomb owners, and subsidiary figures *page* 287
2. Scene identification with figure references and concordance with Edel, Seyfried, and Vieler 289

Acknowledgments

I have many people to thank for their generous help on this project. First and foremost to my graduate advisor, David O'Connor, for all his relentless support, his unparalleled insights, and the hours and hours of his life he lost talking with me about this material. To Donald Hansen for his creative ideas and unending kindness, to Ogden Goelet for his help with confounding inscriptions and so many other things, to John Baines for many inspiring conversations and exceedingly productive editing, and to Tally Kampen for her sense of humor and selfless behind-the-scenes support. At Cambridge University Press, thanks to Beatrice Rehl, Isabella Vitti, and especially Anastasia Graf.

My research in Egypt was facilitated by many people; I traveled to numerous sites, and at each place I was met with thoughtful inspectors going out of their way to help however they could. I would like to thank Dr. G. A. Gaballah and Dr. Zahi Hawass, former heads of the Supreme Council of Antiquities. I need to especially thank Osama Fahmi Mahmoud el-Amin in Aswan, for his extensive knowledge and for the time he took with me in the tombs talking over the material. Even more than that, for his friendship; he welcomed me in Aswan, introduced his family, and shared far too many treats from Dandash. My experience in Egypt would not have been the same without him, and he continues to be a valued friend and colleague.

Thanks to the American Research Center in Egypt for research support and especially for the exceptional help. Amira Khattab and Mr. Amir Abdel Hamid helped in my on-site research. A USAID fellowship through ARCE enabled my work in Egypt, and a dissertation fellowship from the American Association of University Women facilitated a crucial phase of writing.

I owe a special thanks to Karl-Joachim Seyfried who has been exceptionally generous with his extensive knowledge of Qubbet el-Hawa over many years. Thanks to Rachel DeLue at Princeton for her thoughtful help, and thanks to Alejandro Jimenez Serrano who was incredibly kind to offer a tour of their work and conversations about the site in the midst of a very busy 2012 season.

Also in Egypt, thanks to my good friend Matthew Adams, for being helpful on my initial research trip (including a memorable trip to Qasr wa es-Sayyad), for sharing his knowledge and experience, and for being a kindred spirit in the provincial world. To my friend Michael Jones for his shared sensibility and productive critiques, and to Kara Cooney for being an invaluable friend and colleague on our mutual 2001 research trips. And to Michelle Marlar, for the 2003 season, Hali Balak, and many other things.

I owe many personal thanks. To my cousins and good friends Jessica Lewis and Matthew Patterson, for their dealing with my chaotic lifestyle and obsession with the Red Sox; my academic allies Michelle Berenfeld, Edward Powers, and Meredith Martin; to my dear friend Jacob Radford for too many things to list; to Klea Simakis, for her humor and wisdom; to my brother Michael for baseball games, football games, and magic tacos; and to my sister Robyn Hamaguchi, a lifeline throughout. To my grandparents Robert and Virginia Lewis for their valuing of education, and to my parents, George and Barbara Vischak, for so many things, but especially generosity and tolerance.

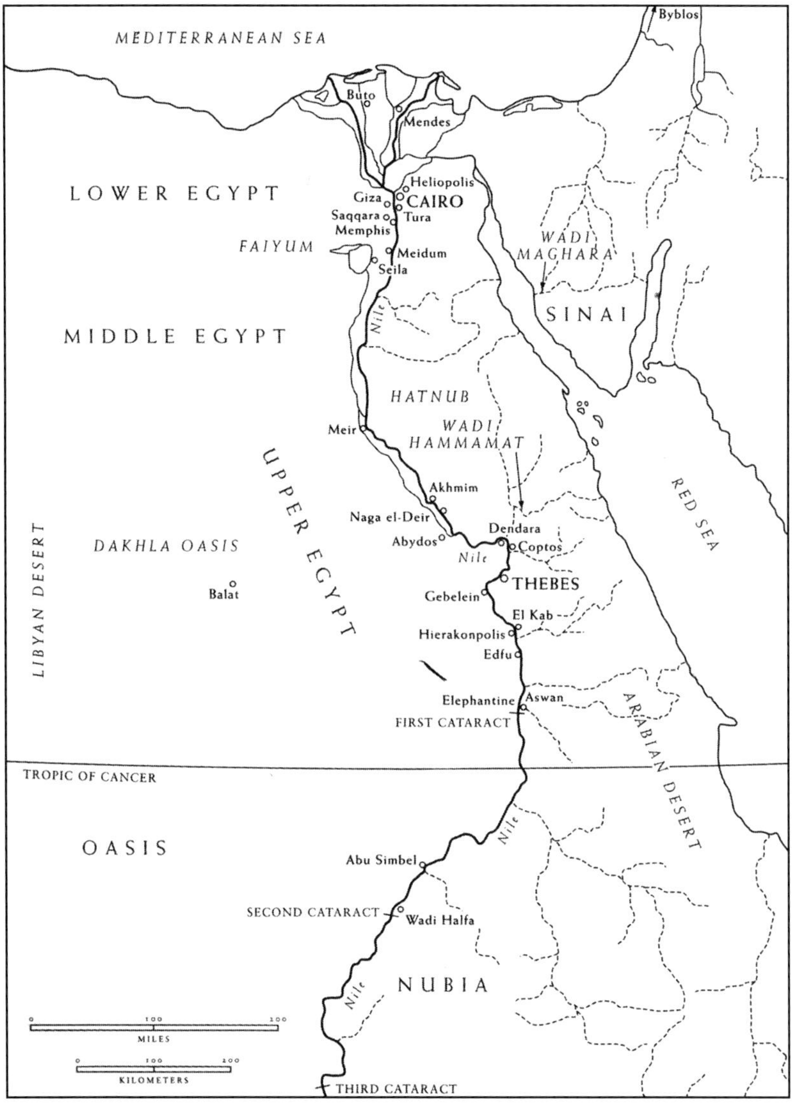

1. Map of Egypt in the Old Kingdom

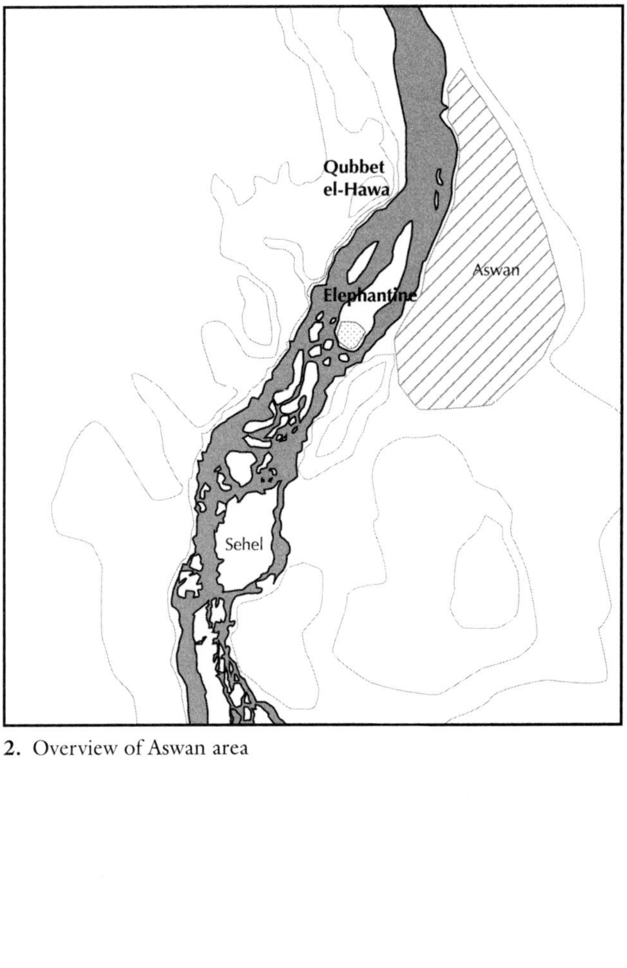

2. Overview of Aswan area

Introduction

It was like the nature of a dream, like a Delta (man) seeing himself in Elephantine.[1]

In southern Egypt, 500 miles from Cairo, the Nile River courses through the islands of the First Cataract, flanking the northernmost island of Elephantine before returning to a single, smooth current flowing northward to the Mediterranean Sea (Figures 1, 2). The high desert escarpment running along the west bank rises to a peak where the reunified river bends toward the north. This peak, today called Qubbet el-Hawa, is home to rock-cut tombs built by the elite citizens of the ancient town on Elephantine Island (Figure 3, Plates I, II). The elite tomb owners residing in this unique environment at the boundary of the Egyptian Nile valley founded the cemetery during the late Old Kingdom (c. 2300–2150 BCE), a period of sociopolitical change characterized by the expansion of provincial elite cemeteries that transformed the landscape of Egypt.

For much of the Old Kingdom, the standard for an elite burial meant having a tomb in one of the preeminent cemetery sites at Giza and Saqqara, where massive royal pyramids transformed the open desert into a sacred landscape of the afterlife. The statement of predominance made by these pyramids and their surrounding elite cemeteries near the ancient capital at Memphis has long shaped our approach to the study of Egypt in the Old Kingdom. This emphatic expression of cultural and political unity has encouraged scholars to construct a linear narrative focused on the king and the central government, from the origins of unification through phases of the administration's evolution and the eventual disintegration of central control. Material from provincial sites is drawn into this project, bringing additional data to help flesh out the narrative. Titles from provincial tombs bolster studies of the structure and development of the Egyptian administration, and lengthier texts, like autobiographies, provide insight into the country's interests and activities over the course of the Old Kingdom.[2] With feet firmly planted in Memphite sand, scholars have viewed provincial material culture, in particular the art of the provincial elite, mainly as variably successful reproductions of Memphite models. Formal similarities are favored, while differences are rationalized so as not to disturb the smooth curve of the central narrative arc.

This linear history provides an essential framework for the study of all aspects of Egyptian society and culture, but it also limits our ability to seek meaning in the differences found in provincial material culture. A smaller number of studies concerning individual provincial sites illustrate the informative potential in examining provincial material in its original context.[3] These studies have elicited indications of a much richer diversity of local experiences and forms of material culture than are typically visible in the broader histories. This study focuses on a group of twelve elite tombs created during the late Old Kingdom in the cemetery at Qubbet el-Hawa in Aswan, examining their text and image programs and architectural space. This analysis of the tombs in their original context seeks to demonstrate that their unique character is the meaningful product of a living community that created and used the tombs, and in so doing to identify additional narrative and cultural threads within the complex fabric of Egyptian society in the Old Kingdom.

Data and Context

The interest of Western scholars first turned to Qubbet el-Hawa in the late nineteenth century.[4] In 1883, with an awareness of the longstanding importance of Aswan/Syene as a border town, the presumption that an important cemetery must be nearby led the local British commander Francis Grenfell to the cliff, which, though heavily sanded over, still showed visible signs of an ancient presence. Grenfell recruited the renowned Egyptologist E. A. Wallis Budge to bring his expertise to their first discoveries, and the process of uncovering, examining, and recording the tombs began. A number of other interested parties contributed to this process, including Ernesto Schiaparelli, who discovered the tomb of Harkhuf, and Lady William Cecil, who uncovered, among others, the double tomb of Mekhu and his son, Sabni. In the early twentieth century, most local archaeology was devoted to the townsite on Elephantine, beginning with German, French, and Italian teams. Following World War II, Egyptian teams led by Labib Habachi excavated the Sanctuary of Heqaib in the townsite, and following this work, Habachi briefly turned his attention to Qubbet el-Hawa. From 1946 to 1951, Habachi focused on tombs 35, 35d, and 35e, in search of the Heqaib who was later deified and honored by the sanctuary. Issues surrounding this work and the identity of these tomb owners are discussed in **Appendix A**.

More systematic excavations of the entire site, including a return to many of the previously found (and in some cases, previously lost) tombs were begun in 1957 under the auspices of the Bonner Ägyptologisches Institut, led by Elmar Edel.[5] These excavations continued until 1981. Throughout his many years of work at Qubbet el-Hawa Edel wrote numerous articles, but ultimately he focused primarily on the corpus of offering pottery recovered from the cemetery. As Edel discovered, the tomb owners at Qubbet el-Hawa performed a unique practice, inscribing their offering vessels to identify both the food being offered and the individual responsible for the offering.[6] Discovery of this local practice substantiates the search for other localized sociocultural traditions, in particular at Elephantine. This tradition's emphasis on the identity of the elite tomb owners and their connection to and support of each other affords an instructive parallel to the unique programs in their tombs.

Edel passed away before completing the collation and analysis of the many years of work at the site; however, his materials were left in the capable hands of Karl-Joachim Seyfried and Gerd Vieler. Their final publication of the remaining materials came out in 2008, making available all collected data regarding the architecture, images, and texts, and finds from the entire excavated cemetery.[7] This exceedingly thorough work comprises three volumes, as well as eighty-eight plates of drawings and fifty-five plans and sections. Along with the full publication of the collected data, the editors focus heavily on analyzing the architecture of the monuments, including dimensions, structural concerns, and building processes; with regard to these issues, their work should be considered the authoritative analysis. Any detailed analysis of the images is of less concern to their work; it is one goal of this publication to contribute a more thorough discussion of these aspects.

Following the conclusion of Edel's excavations, a number of small projects were undertaken at the site, including the discovery of a mud-brick *mastaba* at the base of the hill by Mohi el-Din, as well as the clearing of several smaller tombs by members of the Supreme Council of Antiquities, led by Osama Fahmi Mahmoud el-Amin.[8] An Italian team worked briefly at Qubbet el-Hawa surveying for additional tombs in the early 2000s. In addition, a collection of finds from Edel's excavations currently housed in the Ägyptische Museum der Universität Bonn are undergoing renewed investigation by Dr. Martin Fitzenreiter and his staff.

In 2008, a team from the Universidad de Jaén, led by Alejandro Jiménez Serrano, began work at Qubbet el-Hawa.[9] They have undertaken both conservation and excavation projects, focusing most recently on the large Middle Kingdom tomb QH33. This complex excavation has already yielded significant information about the reuse of the cemetery site into the New Kingdom, Third Intermediate, and Late Periods, as they approach the phase of initial use in the reign of Senwosret III. Dr. Mari Paz Saéz and members of the Jaén team have also conducted an extensive study of the mountain's geologic structure, which will allow the team to stabilize tombs potentially at risk and preserve the site into the future. Their continued work is sure to uncover vital information about Qubbet el-Hawa, and about provincial sites and communities more broadly.

Over the years, isolated elements from the tombs at Qubbet el-Hawa, mainly texts, have been analyzed in some detail, either individually or as part of a general study of provincial material.[10] The autobiographies of several tomb owners, most notably that of Harkhuf, have drawn particular interest for their illumination of Egyptian relations with the neighboring Nubians, as well as for details of the Egyptian administration of expeditions.[11] The reliefs carved into the tombs have received significantly less attention, but in a similar manner only isolated pieces of relief, or in a few cases larger parts of single programs, are mentioned.[12]

These analyses inevitably separate the selected text or image from other materials at Qubbet el-Hawa in order to consider it within the whole of Egyptian history and culture. Egyptian artifacts often stand against such a wide backdrop, as many have been removed from their original context of creation or use. In the case of the Qubbet el-Hawa programs, as with most provincial elite tombs, these artifacts remain in situ; therefore, the images and texts of the programs can be recontextualized – removed from isolation and connected to each other and their architectural context as well as to their environmental setting in a specific landscape and location in the country.

The physical context of the tombs and their programs plays an important role in investigating their many layers of meaning. The placement of images and texts within the tombs impacts their visibility, their prominence, and their relationship to elements of the tomb's architecture and to other images and texts. The tombs exist in a real space, and in their shape, size, and construction they engage their surrounding environment – the desert cliffs, the river, the sunlight, and the island of Elephantine itself. The cemetery visually impacts the environment as an important part of the local landscape inhabited by the tomb owners who built them.

The attention to context also underlies the analysis of the material. Although the whole of Egyptian Old Kingdom material culture provides a comparative basis for interpreting these tombs, the cemetery itself is the primary context in which the tombs and all their constituent elements are analyzed. Relationships among the images, texts, and architecture of the tombs in this cemetery provide fundamental data for an analysis of their meaning as products of material culture. Similarities and connections among the tombs are highlighted, particularly as their shared qualities contrast with the standards of other Old Kingdom elite tombs. Within this narrower framework, variations among the Qubbet el-Hawa tombs provide nuance to the broader picture of the cemetery. Each individual tomb provides a secondary context for examining the images and texts. Relationships within a program have a special status, distinct from the relationships among images and texts throughout the cemetery, which provide another source of contextually based data.

The physical context of the material examined herein thus establishes the limitations of the available data to be studied, the setting for the examination of the material, and the basis for its analysis. This emphasis rests upon the presumption that contexts of the material are meaningful. The recognition and interpretation of context lies at the heart of modern standard archaeological work, both in process and interpretation. Establishing a context for material culture is the work of the interpreter, and thus unavoidably subjective, yet the investigation of meaning in material culture involves the search for patterns of similarity and difference, which requires the setting of boundaries. Contexts are not static; boundaries can be reasonably shifted like lenses on a camera, expanding, contracting, and changing focal points to gain different views of the material. Examining material culture in multiple, altered contexts can lead to nuanced and varied forms of understanding.

In the case of ancient Egyptian tombs, because we understand each tomb to be an integrated monument with a particular function and connected to an individual, we see all the components, from architecture to text and image programs, working together toward a shared goal that is both functional and expressive. The importance of the monument to the tomb owner includes its successful expression of his identity, and thus we presume his guiding hand behind its final form. In the context of the cemetery, a basis for meaningful connections exists in the shared circumstances of tomb building, for example the environment of the cemetery (the use of high desert cliffs, thus rock-cut tombs, the quality of the stone) and available technology (including number and skill of local workers.)

The tomb owners' shared association with the town on Elephantine and membership in its community would have provided a basis for interwoven experiences that can be linked to the form of the tombs. In the case of Qubbet el-Hawa, the survival of the townsite provides an especially rare form of context for understanding the monuments. Elephantine is one of very few townsites throughout Egypt that has been extensively excavated, and one of an even smaller group that provides settlement information from the Old Kingdom period. Following sporadic work at the site through the first half of the twentieth century, the site has been under systematic excavation by a joint German and Swiss team since 1969.[13] The highly skilled, in-depth work conducted by numerous teams over the years – currently led by Stephan Seidlmayer of the German Archaeological Institute – has provided invaluable insight into life in an Egyptian provincial town, uncovering information about the structure and organization of the townsite, local administrative and religious activities, and the transformation of the site over time, including through the various phases of the Old Kingdom under investigation here. This work provides a window onto the lived experiences of the elite officials who built their tombs at Qubbet el-Hawa, and onto those of the larger community of which they were an important part. At the core of the emphasis on context as meaningful is recognition of the people behind the creation of the monuments and of their actions as a source of meaning. The role played by the people, in this case the tomb owners, artisans, and a wider community of supporters, on the form of the tombs and their programs constitutes a central concern of this study.

Agency and Material Culture

Centering the people who created the tombs at Qubbet el-Hawa concurs with my interpretive approach to the material, which is informed to a great extent by agency theory. Agency-based methodologies appear in both art historical and archaeological scholarship; however, in the past decade or so, agency has been a more specific focus of theoretical discussion in archaeology. Despite this attention, the complexity of the concept renders a universally accepted definition elusive.[14] In a volume of essays published in 2000, editors Marcia-Anne Dobres and John E. Robb endeavored to pull together two decades of archaeological work on agency in order to begin theorizing the concept with greater rigor.[15] Their overview includes a brief discussion of two sociologists, Anthony Giddens and Pierre Bourdieu, whose work provided the springboard for most current agency theory.[16]

Though Giddens's theory of structuration and Bourdieu's theory of practice differ to some degree, the two scholars shared a view of the potential of people to determine, and change, the world they lived in. Bourdieu's key concept of habitus emphasizes the unconscious, routine aspects of daily life that structure institutions, while Giddens's slightly broader theory focuses on the duality of agency and structure, in which structure refers to the diffuse and long-standing traditions that provide a framework for a society, while agency refers to the creative force of the people constituting the society that can both continue and sometimes transform these elements of structure.

A key element of agency theory and an essential aspect of this study is the recognition of agents as knowledgeable. H. Martin Wobst's summary of Giddens's theory brings this out well: "Humans are envisioned as entering contexts informed by experience and by their knowledge of history and social structure; they are taken to have a sense of what is or is not habitual, appropriate, opportune, painful, or rewarding in those contexts, and their actions are assumed to be informed by this sense."[17] As this quotation touches on, most initial agency theory equated "agent" with "individual," in part because the disciplinary shift from prioritizing institutions (processual) to recognizing the individuals who comprised them (post-processual) contributed to archaeology's embrace of agency theories. This search for "individuals" has brought its own problems; for example, how the concept of the individual exists cross-culturally, the nature of individual agency, and the importance of the agency of larger groups – communities. Elizabeth DeMarrais investigates "group dynamics," and her interests lie outside the more traditional concern with power struggles in the realm of "shared, numinous experience," both in ritual and more secular daily activities.[18] She discusses resources available to social groups, and states: "These resources ... can also be drawn upon by the group to materialize a shared presence in the world.... Likewise, collective agency and organizational capacities can be managed communally with significant implications for socio-political change."[19]

This analysis of Qubbet el-Hawa prioritizes the role of agency, both of individuals and of the local community at Elephantine. Often, studies of Egyptian culture, in particular Old Kingdom provincial culture, focus on aspects of structure; religious concepts, the ideology of the society, and the power of the king are seen as determining much of what occurs, including the production of material culture, and the Egyptians themselves are viewed as having little sense of varying possibilities and little option for engaging them. Yet even in a society like that of Old Kingdom Egypt, which was characterized by a dominant, consistent, and enduring worldview, the Egyptian people were aware of the world they lived in and understood their monuments to be meaningful. Religious traditions, work, and visual and spoken language were learned and engaged by active, informed agents whose acquired knowledge and meaningful actions carried these Egyptian traditions forward in time.

From this perspective, a provincial cemetery such as Qubbet el-Hawa is not simply evidence of the endurance of Egyptian ideas about death or of general changes in the government of the Old Kingdom. The tombs attest to a group of people living in Elephantine who identified and functioned as part of the elite, who understood the purpose of the tomb monument and recognized its value, and who brought a tradition previously associated with the capital out into new territory. The local elite's comprehension of the value of the tradition is evident in the significant investment of resources required for these elaborate rock-cut tombs. As participators in this tradition, the elite owners relied on the tombs to function successfully for ritual and social purposes alike. This group of tomb owners and artisans created these tombs and these programs to achieve important functional and expressive goals. An agency methodology is especially productive when examining the visual culture of the provincial tombs, which will be discussed next.

Agency theories are continually evolving as scholars confront new questions they elicit, or consider key aspects in greater depth. For example, Giddens's theory insists upon the interdependent relationship of agency and structure: structure provides the "field of possibilities"[20] within which agency acts, and the actions of the agents form, perpetuate, and transform structure. In an article published in 2005, Rosemary A. Joyce and Jeanne Lopiparo push this view further. They argue against seeing agency and structure as separate, theorizing instead a "structured agency," in which structure only comes into being over a long view, the result of continuous agency at work.[21] In the same 2005 volume of the *Journal of Archaeological Method and Theory*, Dobres and Robb clarify the role of material culture in any agency-based analysis: "Thus, from an agency perspective, the relationship between material culture and people is complicated, context specific, and dialectical."[22]

Recognition of the dialectical relationship between people and material culture, and between agency and structure, is especially important when addressing a body of material culture created over a span of time, such as the tombs comprising the cemetery at Qubbet el-Hawa. Because each tomb exists due to the actions of thinking agents (tomb owners and artisans) who are aware of and respond to the structural conditions of their environment, the point in time of the creation of the tomb or program has relevance to its interpretation. Structural changes occur even in a relatively stable society such as ancient Egypt, which is apparent from a diachronic view of the Old Kingdom. While the smaller degrees of transformation may be mostly hidden from our view, the material culture created during the Old Kingdom gives concrete form to the reality of constant change. Each object of material culture, especially a large, complex monument such as a tomb, once created and existing in the Egyptian world transforms that world. A (new) tomb takes form based upon not only religious ideas or class ideology, but also on the form of existing tombs. Thus, each tomb becomes part of the "field of possibilities," the environment in which later tombs are built, as an active contributor to the structural conditions that the tomb owners and artisans who come after will see, interpret, and learn from. The agents and the field are continuously enmeshed.

Even when we can no longer see modifications of rituals, evolution of religious ideas, the ebb and flow of trends, we know that the consistent building of new elite tombs continued to change the conditions in which tomb building occurred. At a cemetery such as Qubbet el-Hawa, for example, the first tomb took shape under highly different circumstances than a tomb built 100 years later in the same cemetery. The first tomb owner broke from a long-established, ideologically supported tradition, while the tomb owner 100 years later was taking part in an established practice, one that emerged in response to the transforming actions of the previous generations of tomb builders. Aspects of the structure in which the tomb owners created tombs had been altered, therefore the monuments they created might have embodied different shades of meaning. This aspect of an agency approach especially affects the interpretation of the tomb programs in how they both share similarities and differ to small degrees.

Any agency methodology engaging visual culture, particularly outside the Western canon, owes a degree of debt to the work of Alfred Gell, especially his book *Art and Agency*.[23] Gell's desire to break away from what he perceived as a limiting hierarchy of art led him to develop his argument for the "social agency" of objects. He focused on modes of reception, showing how artworks are active participants in social process through their affective properties. This perspective coincides with the broader conversation of agency theory that highlights the reflexive relationship between people and material culture; however, Gell's resistance to the importance of cultural context, rejection of aesthetics, and rather outdated view of style have proven problematic for many scholars. Irene Winter engages Gell's theories in a discussion of ancient Near Eastern art, arguing for a more nuanced view of object agency that requires attention to the cultural context: "For anthropology no less than art history, a larger set of dimensions within which agency is imputed to artworks seems called for: dimensions that consider not only 'social relations in the vicinity of objects,' but also underlying authority structures, systems of belief, notions of history, and systems of value – symbolic, material, and aesthetic."[24]

This analysis of the tombs at Qubbet el-Hawa equally values a "larger set of dimensions"; the affective properties of the material culture at this site are essential to this discussion; however, they cannot be disentangled from the network of contexts – physical, historic, cultural, communal, and so forth – within which they functioned. In addition, like Winter and many other art historians considering the mediating of agency by objects and images, this analysis engages more deeply with the role of style than does Gell, and anthropologists and archaeologists more generally.

Style and Visuality

Archaeologists and art historians both use style as a tool for interpreting visual and material culture; yet traditionally, the concept of style has differed in the two disciplines. In a fundamental discussion of style, Meyer Schapiro begins by identifying a clear division between how it is conceived and utilized in archaeology, in contrast to art history: "For the archaeologist, style is exemplified in a motif or pattern.... Style here is a symptomatic trait.... To the historian of art, style is an essential object of investigation ... style is, above all, a system of forms with a quality and a meaningful expression."[25] In the fifty years since Schapiro wrote these words, debates in both disciplines have led to more complex ideas of style, often leading to more aligned perceptions, yet differences still remain. The concept of style used in this analysis draws upon ideas from both disciplines.

Because style is, as Schapiro notes, so essential to the history of art, the concept has received more extensive attention in this field. The modes of interpretation informed by textual analysis that were so influential in the humanities from the mid-century on made a great impact in art historical work of the 1980s and 1990s, especially in the form of semiotic theories of art.[26] While this analysis is not (strictly speaking) semiotic, many aspects of these theories find voice here, particularly in the communicative role of visual culture and of style in particular. Keith Moxey writes that in a semiotic approach to a social art history "the work of art will be read as if its surface were part of the social fabric of which it was once an organic whole.... The focus [is] on the function of the work within a broader pattern of social communication."[27] Style is not simply a result, but an active element in creating meaning: "A semiotic view would ascribe to art the same function as social custom and view it as actively engaged in the construction of culture."[28] This analysis is concerned less with attributing specific meaning to each style, focusing instead on the meaning of the use of styles by the artists and patrons at Qubbet el-Hawa.

Another popular theme of art historical discourse important to this discussion is visuality, which refers to, in essence, the relationship between viewers and monuments of material and visual culture. It characterizes the act of viewing as not simply a biological sensory process, but rather as a socially constructed one – that individuals see with knowledge and experience that mediates the process. As phrased by Norman Bryson, "The visual field we inhabit is one of meanings and not just shapes, that is permeated by verbal and visual discourses, by signs; and that these signs are socially constructed, as are we."[29]

Reconstructing such a culturally constructed visual field is challenging, and only more so for ancient Egypt, not only because of the limited textual material we have, in comparison to later historic eras, but also because of the lack within these texts of a significant discussion about the visual aspects of their monuments. Furthermore, the discussion of visuality within art history is grounded largely in the European Renaissance discourse about art, itself connected to a particular aspect of the Classical tradition: that which concerns works of naturalistic art. Thus, the nature of this self-consciously constructed discourse (in the Western tradition) is in many ways at odds with Egyptian visual culture. At its heart, despite the numerous naturalistic aspects of Egyptian art, it is not a visual tradition concerned with naturalism; and, as is often noted, the Egyptians had a distinctly different concept of "art." Ancient Egyptians perceived their material and visual monuments, and discussed them, in a much different way than did citizens of other cultures, especially those identifying as part of a "Western" tradition.

Despite these apparent complications, and despite the fact that we could never conclusively define an ancient Egyptian visuality, interrogating their concepts of form and meaning is essential. Much of what survives as evidence of the lives and ideas of ancient Egyptians is material and visual, and the sophisticated elite monuments speak to a profound concern with the visual. By developing ways to consider how the visual aspects of these monuments constructed and communicated meaning, it is possible to create frameworks for integrating the visual aspects of the monuments into the broader discussions of meaning. Considering how the denizens of Old Kingdom Elephantine might have seen their world is important in an agency methodology, and also opens up interpretive possibilities.

In general, archaeological scholarship has been less concerned with investigating the meaning of style, with important exceptions, especially the 1993 publication, *The Uses of Style in Archaeology*. The essays in this volume reflect an important change in archaeology, from conceiving style as a passive indicator of process to an active contributor in communicating meaning. As stated by the editor, Margaret Conkey, "Style is not just a medium for description but a medium of social practice,"[30] a view paralleling Moxey's discussion of a semiotics of social art history, focusing on the use of style in a social and communicative context.

This evolving view of style coincides with the trend toward post-processual archaeologies, which, though comprising a wide range of concerns (identity, gender, performance, and so forth), share generally a view of material culture as active in the construction of meaning in human society. This shift has brought archaeological and art historical scholarship into closer dialogue, and though many areas of interest provide important insight for this analysis, investigations of landscape and space have been especially influential. The rich body of literature considers landscape in a way very similar to material culture, looking at how landscapes shaped society, how communities conceived landscapes, how people moved through space, and the effects movement had. Many of these analyses consider, in essence, the "style" of landscape, its forms, and the relationship between them and the people inhabiting them, seeing them, moving through them, and experiencing them. This analysis of Qubbet el-Hawa highlights the integral role played by the unique landscape of Elephantine and its environs in the construction of meaning at the cemetery.

The agency-informed approach, outlined here, which is rooted largely in archaeological scholarship also influences the conception of style held here. An agency methodology is especially productive when examining the visual culture of Egyptian provincial tombs. Most archaeological work tends to draw on visual material for content and as chronological markers, which is frequently the path Egyptian art history follows as well, the result being an emphasis on structural aspects of the society. The seeming formal consistency of much Egyptian art, especially that of the Old Kingdom, may also heighten our reliance on structure, as agency-based methods tend to engage variation in material culture rather than similarity. The relief-carved and painted images in provincial tomb programs, such as those at Qubbet el-Hawa, often show the strongest stylistic contrast to customary Old Kingdom forms. When agency is not considered, only broad circumstances rooted in economics and power enter analyses that are typically limited to one aspect – why the style of the image does not conform to Old Kingdom/Memphite standards. If instead we recognize that considerable resources were invested in the images and that they have a central role in important monuments constructed by and for people living with knowledge of their cultural traditions, we can then consider many more aspects of the images, and their informative potential expands greatly. A close examination of all of the images in the Qubbet el-Hawa programs and an identification of their unique qualities is an important facet of this study.

Debates around agency methodologies have led to a number of related perspectives that also have relevance to the conceptualizing of style. Theories of embodiment emerged in part from a desire to more fully express the nature of "agents," and were initially developed in feminist archaeologies as a way to recover ancient women often lost under the gloss of social structures.[31] In response to the mind/body divide traditionally presumed in Western discourse, and to the elevation of the mind as the true (sole) source of agency, archaeologies of embodiment locate the physical body and its lived, sensory experiences as essential sources of and for agency.[32] These perspectives draw on phenomenology and link to post-processual emphases on materiality, seeing the body as material as well. While this analysis does not engage in embodiment theories in-depth, it does assume the importance of embodied agents. Their sensory experiences, especially vision and movement through space, are presumed in the discussion of light and shadow, access to the cemetery, the sizes of doorways and courtyard, the visibility of the cemetery from the townsite and vice versa, and of course in the reception of style in the architecture and images.

In a 2005 article discussing agency and style in archaeology, Richard Lesure addresses the different ways archaeology and art history conceive of style, summing up the approaches as two dichotomies: in archaeology it is style versus function, whereas in art history it is style versus content.[33] Yet in this gap Lesure identifies a connection in their shared relevance to theories of embodiment. This turn toward embodiment has become pervasive in discussions of visual and material culture, leading to emphases on materiality and "thing theory" in both archaeology and art history.[34] The concept of style used in this analysis was developed in this context, drawing on ideas from both disciplines and with a view of embodied agents creating and consuming their visual culture. Style here is considered within the wider realm of visual experience, and this discussion argues for linking all experiences of seeing, whether of relief-carved images or landscapes, and the innumerable layers in between.

Locality and Community

A focus on the physical context of the material and an agency-based approach are the twin pillars of this study's overarching interest in the intertwined themes of locality and community identity. Archaeological attention to ancient communities has increased in the past few decades, in efforts to bridge the gap between individuals and the larger culture.[35] Defining "community" has proven to be as complex as defining "agency," and in many ways it is similarly ubiquitous and unarticulated in much archaeological scholarship. Michael Kolb and James Snead developed a definition based upon three factors: "We therefore consider the community to be a minimal, spatially defined locus of human activity that incorporates social reproduction, subsistence production, and self-identification."[36]

Their assertion of the role of shared space in communities differs from sociological theories that argue for defining community as a mental construct, related specifically to identity. As expressed by A. Bernard Knapp, "Communities therefore should be seen as social constructs, not necessarily tied to a specific place, and providing an important source of identity for their inhabitants."[37] Despite this assertion, as an archaeologist Knapp does not fully leave the role of shared space behind, "and yet communities undeniably have a strong association with a 'sense of place.'"[38] Jason Yaeger and Marcello A. Canuto similarly address the issue of location as a necessary element of defining a community, via a perspective informed by *practice* as conceived by sociologists such as Bourdieu: "We do not neglect the spatial aspects of the community because there must exist physical venues for the repeated, meaningful interaction needed to create and maintain a community, but we reject notions of the community as solely a socio-spatial unit."[39] Canuto and Yaeger describe their approach, which is heavily informed by agency methodologies, as "interactionalist," emphasizing the continuous interactions of agents as determining the existence of the community: "We advocate conceiving of the community as a dynamic socially constituted institution that is contingent upon human agency for its creation and continued existence."[40]

Building upon the work of Canuto and Yaeger, Naoíse Mac Sweeney also attempts to tackle the divide between "relational communities" and "geographic communities," while maintaining a view of both as dynamic and socially constructed. She focuses ultimately on geographic communities as they relate to archaeological work.

> The geographic community is no longer thought to be a natural social structure.... Rather, it is now understood as a conscious mental construct, built both on and through social practice and lived experience, which is itself facilitated by residential proximity and regular direct interaction. The intellectual, the environmental, and the social all have their part to play in its construction.[41]

This analysis of Qubbet el-Hawa shares a similar view. The community at hand is comprised of the people who lived in Elephantine, presuming the island site to be the primary settlement but also allowing for inhabitation of the adjacent (though less well understood) settlement on the east bank. This Elephantine community bonded through shared experiences and social practice, and it is intimately connected to the location they inhabited. As noted previously, the cemetery at Qubbet el-Hawa is the primary context in which the tombs and programs are studied, but the proper full context includes the wider environs of the river, the cataract, and the east and west banks flanking the island. The focus on the people who created and used the tombs necessitates this broader context, as these people inhabited a space greater than that bounded by the cemetery. Their learning of and response to structural conditions occurred mainly where they lived, in the town on Elephantine, where they grew up, learned the language, practiced their religion, fulfilled professional responsibilities, and played a part in their community. These spatial boundaries are somewhat subjective, as it is certain many of the tomb owners (and perhaps others) spent time in the capital at Memphis; they also traveled often into Nubia, and even at home their daily activities may well have taken them beyond the immediate environs of the town. Nonetheless, their connection to the town and the cemetery is certain, as is the connection between the two.

The defining of spatial boundaries in a meaningful connection to the boundaries of a group of people rarely occurs in Egyptological studies. We tend to identify social and cultural boundaries only along the same lines as political ones, emphasizing a unified Egyptian identity in contrast to that of a foreign people, rather than separate, inter-Egyptian identities. Yet the significance of land in general with regard to the Egyptian culture, both in terms of the agricultural economy and religious and national identity, is a common theme. Elizabeth Frood notes that a "sense of place" appears as a theme in texts dating back to the Old Kingdom,[42] and examples of local landscapes (especially Abydos, Amarna, and the Qurna mountain on the west bank in Luxor) holding powerful meaning during Egyptian history suggests the Egyptians' sense of the significance of specific locations, rooted in the landscape. [43] Perhaps most importantly, the enduring division of Egypt by the ancient Egyptians themselves into "Upper" and "Lower," which are geographically based designations, provides a solid basis for investigating the importance of landscape and conceived spatial boundaries within Egyptian culture.[44]

A layered view of community that incorporates both shared space and active social practice coincides well with an agency-based approach by placing the creation of meaning, both of a community identity and of a sense of place, in the hands of people. Emphasizing the importance of the construction of identity by the community allows the inclusion of other types of communities that are defined not by space but by other aspects of identity; at Qubbet el-Hawa, for example, the identity of the tomb owners as part of the (Egypt-wide) elite community. In this analysis, both types of community play a role in the form of the monuments: the community defined by their shared connection living and working at Elephantine (their sense of locality), and the smaller community within defined by their identification with the elite.

The Elephantine community's recognition of themselves as a community powerfully influenced the creation of their tombs, in particular the unique nature of their tomb programs. The distinctive experiences of members of the Elephantine community, including their professional work, their cultural environment, and their physical distance from the king and Memphite traditions, are all rooted in the landscape and location of their town. These unique experiences in this place during a particular time became manifest in the complex and unique tombs created by the people who inhabited it.

This book will present an analysis of the architecture, images, and texts of a group of twelve Old Kingdom tombs in the cemetery. Chapter 1 draws on archaeological and textual data to situate the structure, organization, and experiences of the local Elephantine community within ancient Egyptian culture and history of the period. Chapter 2 brings the reader into the necropolis at Qubbet el-Hawa, beginning with an overview of the cemetery and moving into a more detailed review of the text and image programs. Next, the setting, architecture, and the images and texts of the twelve tombs are discussed in order to bring out the material and visual relationships among the tombs, the architecture, the images, and the texts. Chapter 3 explores how form and visuality contribute to the function and meaning of the monuments. Chapter 4 considers in greater depth the significance of the thematic focus of the text and image programs on identified subsidiary, primarily offering, figures and discusses how this unusual aspect of the tombs relates to the theme of identity, particularly of the community as a whole. Having analyzed in detail the various material, visual, and textual elements of the tombs at Qubbet el-Hawa, the conclusion reintegrates these pieces, examining their formal and functional interrelationships.

1

People and Place: Historical and Social Context

The tombs cut into the cliff along the west bank of the Nile at the site called Qubbet el-Hawa belonged to the elite citizens of the ancient town of Abu, modern Elephantine, which was located on an island in the Nile river just north of the First Cataract (Figure 2). Throughout the Old Kingdom, Elephantine played a unique role in the Egyptian state due in large part to its geographic setting and consequent situation within the political and cultural map of Egypt. The ancient capital of Memphis occupied a strategic position more than 500 miles north of Elephantine at the mouth of the Delta, nearer the Mediterranean Sea. Elephantine was the southernmost town in Old Kingdom Egypt, far from the capital and much closer to the Nubians living along the Nile Valley upstream of the First Cataract (Figure 1). Given Elephantine's proximity to Nubia, it became Egypt's base for trade with and expeditions into Nubia, and by the Sixth Dynasty the local citizens were largely occupied with these major interests of the king. This valuable function of the local town combined with the relatively limited local agriculture created a unique set of circumstances in which the local citizens, elite and nonelite alike, lived and worked. The titles and autobiographies of the Qubbet el-Hawa tomb owners reveal their distinctive experiences, which clearly distinguished them from the rest of the elite (and nonelite) in Egypt during this time.

The natural setting of Elephantine Island influenced the shape and development of the settlement on it and its connection to its broader environs. The town of Abu occupied the southern part of the island, with the earliest settlement based along the southeastern rise[1] (Figure 3). The island's geography provided natural boundaries for the expansion and organization of the town. The locally distinct granite boulders that may have given Abu ("elephant") its name also provided the town with a unique temple for their local god. The community selected a natural niche between two partially contiguous boulders as the sacred spot of the god, providing offerings before it and ultimately enclosing the surrounding area with mud brick walls, creating a ritual space unlike any other known in Egypt.[2] The native community's adaptation to their environment endured over the course of the Old Kingdom, even with both aggressive and more subtle forms of central administration activity at the site: the initially intrusive fortress wall of the First Dynasty was eventually reshaped to suit the town, and throughout the Old Kingdom the unique temple space never disappeared into the form of more traditional temple architecture.[3]

The community's connection to their environment extended beyond the island itself. Evidence for a second settlement of some kind on the nearby east bank of the river suggests a local presence there from the middle of the Old Kingdom.[4] Rock inscriptions also appear throughout the area, on the rocky islands as well as both banks of the river, clarifying the local community's active interaction with the broader space. The various uses of the name Abu supports the implication of this material evidence, that the Egyptians perceived Abu as more than just the town on the island. The term appears to have referred to the whole island, as well as lands along the east and possibly west banks, as well. Furthermore, the waters surrounding the island were an integral part of the identity of Abu, as references to the "water of Elephantine" occur as early as the Pyramid Texts. Although sometimes during the Old Kingdom the written name of the town was determined with the city wall or "fortress" sign, which apparently specified the settlement and its associated fortress wall, the town and the region were never differentiated through the use of different names. The physical setting of the island and its geographic environment may have provided reason for this practice. The island of Elephantine is one among many clustered here in the Nile River, together manifesting the changing geology of the riverbed at the First Cataract (Figure 2). Moving upstream from the rest of Egypt, Elephantine is the first visible part of the First Cataract, by itself an indication of the entire feature. As the part that stands for the whole, the island is a sort of material synecdoche for the First Cataract, the place where the calm Nile and easier travel ends, the edge of the ordered world of Egypt, all of which, for the Egyptians, was expressed in the name Abu.

The natural boundary of the First Cataract became a political boundary as well between the emerging Egyptian state and the Nubian civilization to the south. The fortress wall constructed by kings of the First Dynasty indicates the deeply rooted Egyptian sense of ownership over Elephantine and of its need for protection from potentially hostile forces.[5] Although little evidence exists to indicate Nubian aggression against the Egyptian state during the Early Dynastic and Old Kingdom periods, a sense of them as *other* than Egyptian and thus potential competition for land and resources as well as a potentially chaotic threat is clear.[6] During the same period in which the fortress was built, Lower Nubia appears to have been purposely cleared of its indigenous population, a process that the town of Elephantine likely supported. Through the first half of the Old Kingdom, Lower Nubia remained largely unsettled, occupied instead by widely scattered Egyptian towns with fortresses similar to that on Elephantine, as far south as Buhen. In the latter half of the Fifth Dynasty, the process is reversed, and the Egyptian towns in Nubia disappear, followed by the subsequent reappearance of Nubian material culture of the (so-called) C-Group.[7]

In the later Old Kingdom, including the Sixth Dynasty period in which the Qubbet el-Hawa tomb owners lived and worked, the Egyptian government sought to maintain dominance over Lower Nubia, but with resident populations of Nubians this process was more complicated, and the town at Elephantine formed an important strategic base. The autobiographies of Harkhuf, Pepynakht Heqaib1, Sabni1, and Sabni2 provide a picture of generally stable relations between Nubia and Egypt that nonetheless became antagonistic at times.[8] Harkhuf's description of three separate trips he led into Nubia suggests that by the third trip, his dealings with the leader of the Lower Nubian communities had become more insecure.[9] The autobiography of Pepynakht Heqaib1, who likely followed soon after Harkhuf, begins with a description of his aggression against regions of Lower Nubia, including the capture and killing of many Nubians. In addition, an inscription of Merenre in the temple of Satet indicates the king himself took several of the Nubian leaders prisoner.[10] A later trip by Pepynakht Heqaib1 was apparently meant to stabilize relations with the Nubians.[11] In Sabni1's autobiography he writes of his efforts to retrieve his father Mekhu's body from Nubia, but does not indicate Mekhu died in any type of military conflict.[12] Sabni2 writes of successfully building barges in Wawat with no mention of conflict, but he does point out the many soldiers who accompanied his expedition.[13]

Earlier scholars have suggested the possibility that Elephantine was originally an Egyptian outpost in Nubian territory, based in part on the writing of the town name and on its not being integrated into the early system of designating Egyptian nomes.[14] In addition, the presence of Nubian material culture as far north as Kubaniya, eleven miles north of Aswan, was interpreted as evidence of a non-Egyptian cultural context.[15] More recent excavation of the town site of Elephantine by the German and Swiss Archaeological Institutes has corrected and nuanced this earlier perception. Distinctively Egyptian material culture appears in contexts reaching back to the Naqada II period at least; there is also evidence of the founding of the local Egyptian temple of Satet during the same period.[16] The groups of finds from most early Elephantine contexts include pottery typical of both Egyptian sites to the north and Nubian sites to the south. While during the Old Kingdom proper Egyptian forms dominate the find groups, Nubian material is always present in the mix. Dietrich Raue views this mixed character of material culture as characteristic of Elephantine, resisting a more direct reading of a mixed population.[17] As Seidlmayer describes it, Elephantine existed within a "zone of contact" between the Nubian and Egyptian people, likely combining both people and material culture, the way many such border towns do.[18]

In contrast to Elephantine, other Egyptian towns and villages were located along the banks of the river, surrounded by extensive, cultivable fields that provided their wealth and contribution to the state in the form of agricultural products. The limited fields on the island of Elephantine and along the nearby east and west banks of the Nile were not comparable to those of the river valley further north, but the town provided other natural resources, primarily in the form of granite and other valued stones. Along with these resources, Elephantine's historic importance in Egypt's relationship with Nubia determined its continued significance to the Old Kingdom state. During the Sixth Dynasty, as Lower Nubia was repopulated by indigenous groups, Elephantine's importance grew not only for its strategic significance but also as the primary and most proximate base for trade and expeditions into Nubia. The luxury goods such as ivory and gold that Nubian trade provided remained especially important to the king during the Sixth Dynasty.

Although tombs were first cut into the cliff at Qubbet el-Hawa most likely toward the end of the Fifth Dynasty, these early monuments did not survive later tomb construction. Instead, tombs cut and decorated in the second half of the Sixth Dynasty became sacred monuments of the community, maintained even as the cemetery became more intensely populated.[19] This timing coincides with the period of both Lower Nubian repopulation and increased trade with Upper Nubia in the Sixth Dynasty. This phase of the Old Kingdom was characterized by changes not only in the administration of expeditions into Nubia and elsewhere, but also to the overall structure of the provincial administration. The changes are evident in the titularies of the provincial officials, in the biographies from their tombs, in a handful of other resources such as royal decrees, and most vividly in the widespread increase in elite cemeteries throughout the provinces of Upper Egypt. Elite burials had occurred outside of the Memphite cemeteries from the earliest stages of the Old Kingdom; however, the proliferation of elite decorated tombs during the Sixth Dynasty related to transformations of provincial administration and represented a shift in the relationship between the king and the provincial elite.

The king's interest in the provinces had always been rooted in agriculture, and the administration of the provinces throughout the Old Kingdom reveals this focus. Many early provincial leaders were called *ḥḳꜣ ḥwt*, "chief of the estate," and they were involved in managing land as well as raising cattle and organizing workers.[20] Administrative restructuring in the late Fifth and Sixth Dynasties occurred in response to the increasingly complex process of managing the extensive exploitation of provincial land and to the king's desire to more effectively integrate provincial leaders into the state system.

During the Sixth Dynasty, the typical title of the provincial elite was *ḥry tp ꜥꜣ n spꜣt,* "great overlord of the nome," traditionally shortened to *nomarch* by Egyptologists.[21] This general title implied oversight over a wide range of responsibilities, and in fact the increasing complexity of the provincial administration further distanced the provincial leaders from hands-on management of local land. Nonetheless, the emphasis on agriculture remained; in particular, collection and redistribution of its products through the state structure, as is evident through common titles such as *imy-rꜣ šnwty*, "overseer of the granaries," and the continued use of chief of the estate. Nomarchs often held titles related to the judiciary, such as *sꜣb ꜥḏ-mr,* "juridical official," and *mdw-rḫyt*, "staff of the commoners or herdsmen," befitting their roles as community leaders and the highest local authorities representing the king.[22] In addition, many nomarchs held high-ranking titles in the priesthoods of their local gods.

Given the lack of significant agriculture in the region of Elephantine, the absence of many typical provincial elite titles at Qubbet el-Hawa is not surprising; the titularies of the tomb owners at Qubbet el-Hawa reveal the unique situation of these individuals within the Old Kingdom Egyptian state. They incorporate some titles typical of all provincial elite during this period, but include many other titles distinct to their region. Like those of most elite tomb owners, their titularies were divided between honorific titles, which indicated primarily the tomb owner's status within the internal hierarchy of the elite, and official titles, which more directly indicated the tomb owner's function on behalf of the country's administration.[23] The other divide among their titles, between those they shared with other provincial elite and those distinct to this cemetery, closely follows the pattern of the honorific/official split.

The honorific titles held by the twelve Qubbet el-Hawa tomb owners examined in this study place the majority of them just below the highest tier of the national elite hierarchy. Only one tomb owner, Pepynakht Heqaib2, held the highest ranking title *ỉry pˁt,* "hereditary prince," in the inscription on the façade of his tomb, while nine of the remaining eleven tomb owners held the title *ḥ3ty-ˁ*, "count" or "mayor." The very common string of ranking titles *ḥ3ty-ˁ, ḫtmty bỉty, smr wˁty, ẖry-ḥbt,* "count, sealer of the king of Lower Egypt, sole companion, lector priest," appears in eight of the twelve titularies, and all twelve tomb owners have at least two of those four ranking titles. The presence of these common honorific titles firmly places these Qubbet el-Hawa tomb owners at an elevated status within the structure of the administration during this time.

A number of titles related to the royal mortuary cults of the Sixth Dynasty further indicate the connection of these tomb owners to the other provincial elite and to the king. Pepynakht Heqaib2 (35d) and Sabni2 (35e) were both "inspector of *ḥm-nṯr* priests" (i.e., low level priests in the mortuary cult) at the pyramids of Pepy I and Merenre, and Khwin-Khnum (102) held the same position at the pyramid of Pepy II. Pepynakht Heqaib1 (35) held four different titles at pyramids of the last three kings of the Sixth Dynasty. Membership in the administration or priesthood of a king's pyramid had long been an indicator of high status that also entailed financial rewards and provided means for the king to support his officials, and thus create further bonds of loyalty. Royal cult-related titles were especially common among the provincial elite, where the resulting relationships helped stabilize the country under the king and integrate the local elite into the state structure.[24]

These honorific and royal cult titles indicate that the tomb owners at Qubbet el-Hawa shared the same status among the elite as their colleagues in the other provinces; however, they did not share their characteristic official titles. As noted previously, the title "great overlord of the nome" was the standard title of the provincial elite during the Sixth Dynasty, and provincial leaders often held titles related to agriculture and judicial matters. Priests of the local god's temple comprised another common group of officials in almost all other provincial elite cemeteries. Yet at Qubbet el-Hawa no such nomarchs are buried, few references to the management of land or agriculture are made, and the priests of the local temple are absent.

Instead, the tomb owners at Qubbet el-Hawa hold titles related to conducting expeditions into the neighboring lands of Nubia. Three tomb owners, Sobekhetep (90), Harkhuf (34n), and Tjetji (103), as well as one of the subsidiary figures buried in Mekhu's chapel (Metjenw), hold the title *ḫtmty nṯr,* "god's sealer." Though the specific meaning of this title as "expedition leader" can be ascertained only in the Middle Kingdom, the context of its use in the Old Kingdom strongly indicates the same. Eichler suggests that in the earlier part of the Old Kingdom, the responsibility of the "god's sealer" related to transporting goods over a distance, a natural basis from which to expand into expedition leader. [25] Additional titles held by Khui and Khwin-Khnum, *ỉmy-r3 sšw ʿprw*, "overseer of the scribes of the crews," and *ỉmy-ḫt wỉ3 ʿ3*, "attendant of the Great bark," also indicate jobs related to expeditions.[26] All of these titles frequently appear in elite titularies during the Old Kingdom, as the expeditions for raw materials and precious goods that were long an important element of the Egyptian economy took officials into the Sinai and the eastern desert as well as Nubia.

Two other titles occur more frequently in Qubbet el-Hawa and are less common outside of it: *ỉmy-r3 ḫ3swt*, "overseer of foreign lands," and *ỉmy-r3 ỉʿ3w*, "overseer of Egyptianized Nubians." The first title appears during the Sixth Dynasty only among the tombs at Qubbet el-Hawa,[27] and two variations on this title, "overseer of all foreign lands of Yam, Irtjet, and Wawat" and "overseer of all foreign lands of the northern and southern regions" from rock inscriptions in the Wadi Hammamat and Tomas designate two officials who are buried at Qubbet el-Hawa.[28]

Given the geographic limitations of this title, Müller-Wollermann argues that foreign lands in this instance refers specifically to Nubia.[29] "Overseer of foreign lands" implies greater responsibility, and hence higher status, than the more restricted "expedition leader", an interpretation supported by the apparent status of the relative titleholders.

The second title, *ỉmy-r3 ỉʿ3w*, "overseer of Egyptianized Nubians," has engendered extensive discussion as to its exact nuance and has been variously translated as overseer of mercenaries, scouts, or interpreters. In his 1976 dissertation, Lanny Bell investigated the term *ỉʿ3w* in detail, and although his final summary implies that the *ỉʿ3w* referred only to Egyptianized Nubian soldiers, his earlier discussion accommodates a broader interpretation that includes Egyptianized Nubians who were not only soldiers, but other types of workers, as well as Egyptians who functioned as interpreters.[30] Bell's research into the linguistic origins of the word *ỉʿ3w* reveals its root meaning as "babbler," a reference to the unfamiliar speech of those so identified. As such, his initial broad interpretation that incorporates both Egyptian interpreters and "Egyptianized" Nubians seems plausible. His ultimate emphasis on these *ỉʿ3w* as soldiers seems to result from "the many occasions when Nubians are mentioned in contexts appropriate to fighting men."[31] The context of use of *ỉʿ3w* has led most scholars, including Bell, to agree on its frequent connection to expedition activities.[32] Soldiers populated most expeditionary forces, but as many expeditions focused on trade and the retrieval of raw materials, they necessarily incorporated other types of workers, as well. Edel identified the *ỉʿ3w* as both soldiers and interpreters, and Eichler calls the *ỉʿ3w* "Hilfstruppen" (i.e., auxiliary or backup troops), and suggests they were not only paramilitary troops, but likely mining workers, as well.[33] Ultimately, we can determine, at a minimum, that *ỉʿ3w* refers to individuals of Nubian ethnicity who lived in Egypt and who worked on expeditions, never as leaders but rather as part of the labor force. Although the title "overseer of *ỉʿ3w*" was more widely distributed during the Fifth Dynasty, during the Sixth Dynasty the great majority of examples in tomb inscriptions appear at Qubbet el-Hawa.[34]

These titles indicate the tomb owners' responsibilities for managing expeditions into Nubia, the purposes of which are clarified by various epithets inscribed in their tombs. Along with several variations of the essential *ỉm3ḫw*, "honored before," and examples of the common *n(y) st-ỉb nb.f*, "favorite of the king," the remaining epithets refer to the foreign lands. Most of the epithets refer to bringing back products from the foreign lands, meaning Nubia, as is clarified in Tjetji's epithet *ỉnn ẖrt ḫ3śwt rs(ywt) n nswt*, "he who brings back products from the southern foreign lands to his lord." Another common epithet hints at the fluctuating relationship between Nubia and Egypt during this time: *dd nrw ḥr m ḫ3swt*, "he who places the dread of Horus in the foreign lands," which implies a more aggressive posture on the part of the Egyptian state. One unique epithet from the interior of the tomb of Sabni2 (35e) may reinforce that aggression: *3myt m Ḥrw m ḫ3śwt*, "the throw-stick of Horus (i.e., the king) in the foreign country/Nubia."[35]

The tomb owners also emphasize their expedition work in the lengthy autobiographies carved into the facades of three tombs (Sabni1 26, Harkhuf 34h, Pepynakht Heqaib1 35), and in the interior of a fourth (Sabni2 35e). These texts detail expeditions into Nubia and make no mention of other types of work done on behalf of the king or the state (i.e., related to the administration of the nome or town). Harkhuf's text emphasizes "all sorts of perfect and luxury items" that he brought back from various parts of Nubia, "the likes of which had never before been brought back to this land."[36] In discussing his third trip to Nubia, the text notes that the leader of Yam sent numerous troops with Harkhuf to help his passage through Irtjet, Wawat, and Setju, suggesting their awareness of potential conflict with some of the Nubian groups, but it does not include reference to military action.[37] In contrast, Pepynakht Heqaib1's autobiography begins, "The majesty of my lord sent me, to devastate the land of Wawat and Irtjet," where he "killed a great number there,"[38] making clear the military aspect of the expedition leaders' responsibilities. Both Harkhuf and Pepynakht Heqaib1 discuss efforts to "satisfy" and "pacify" Nubian leaders, thus implying a political role for these tomb owners, as well. Sabni1's text discusses Sabni's retrieval of the body of his father Mekhu, who was also an expedition leader and apparently died on his own expedition into Nubia. Upon return from Nubia, Sabni1 journeyed north to Memphis, to bring to the king the many goods collected by his father.[39] Sabni2 also emphasizes products over conflict, briefly describing his efforts to build boats in Wawat in order to transport obelisks to the king.[40]

These autobiographies contribute to a picture of increased royal interest in Nubian trade during the Sixth Dynasty. During this phase of restructuring in the provincial administration, it appears that the administration of expeditions was also transformed, indicated by the change in burial place of the expedition leaders, in particular the "god's sealers", from Memphite cemeteries to cemeteries located in the provinces.[41] In the Sixth Dynasty, the number of god's sealers/expedition leaders buried in the capital dropped, while many more appeared in provincial cemeteries, especially southern cemeteries located near common expedition routes. Furthermore, the god's sealers/expedition leaders in the provinces were of lower rank than those in the capital. In his discussion of expeditions during the Old Kingdom, Eichler suggests that those in the capital with expedition-related titles dealt with the results of expeditions (i.e., managing the distribution of goods, building materials, and so forth), while those who held the title "god's sealer" in the provinces carried out the actual expeditions. Both Eichler and Müller-Wollermann agree that at all times orders for the expeditions came only from the king, but during the Sixth Dynasty the organization and management of expeditions occurred in the towns nearest the expedition goal points.[42] El-Dissouky and O'Connor also support the view that the expedition leaders resided at Elephantine and that their expeditions began there, contra Edel, who argues that all expeditions originated in Memphis.[43] Eichler does agree with Martin-Pardey's view that the officials involved in expedition work were separate from those managing local nome business.[44]

This emphasis on official responsibilities in Nubia went hand in hand with limited reference to local administrative duties. As noted previously, the most characteristic titles of the provincial elite do not appear in the titularies of the Qubbet el-Hawa tomb owners, and the titles that do indicate local duties refer specifically to the location of their hometown on the southern border of Egypt, rather than to the First Nome as a whole. Three tomb owners have at least one version of a title beginning *ḥry sšt3*, a common designation in the Old Kingdom often held by nomarchs. Translated as "secretary" or "he who is privy to the secrets," the title seems generally related to record keeping or other aspects of bureaucracy.[45] Two of the four versions of the titles here refer to the *tp-rśy/tp-šmꜥw* or the "Head of the south," which is a designation for the settlement at Elephantine.[46] A third title specifies the "narrow doorway of the south," which is also a reference to the town of Elephantine and which clarifies the Egyptian perception of Elephantine as the border town through which foreign people and things enter and Egyptian people and things leave. El-Dissouky discusses a fragment of a papyrus found on Elephantine that mentions a *wḏt* or official document relating to the arrival of Nubians from upstream, an indication of the special types of administrative duties that would logically be conducted in Elephantine.[47]

Specifying the location at the southern border of Egypt characterizes another title at Qubbet el-Hawa, held by both Sabni1 (26) and Sabni2 (35e). Beginning, *mḥ ỉb n nśwt*, "confidant of the king," the title has several variations, but the version at Qubbet el-Hawa concludes with the designation "in the head of the south."[48] The function of this official position remains vague, but it emphasizes the close connection between the official and the king. Several other titles at Qubbet el-Hawa that do not concern expeditions appear to reinforce the close connections between the officials buried here and the king. Khui was an *ỉmy-rꜣ ẖnw*, "overseer of the Residence," which indicates he lived and worked in the capital for a period of time and thus had a closer relationship to the king than other provincial officials who never worked there. That he includes this title in his tomb at Qubbet el-Hawa suggests he felt this connection an important one to convey. Khwin-Khnum holds the higher ranked title, *ẖry tp nśwt*, "royal chamberlain," which although primarily honorific, again emphasizes the connection between the official and the king.[49]

Another title (thus far) unique to Qubbet el-Hawa, *ḥry tp ꜥꜣ n nśwt*, "great overlord of the king," is a variation on the standard nomarch title, discussed previously, that is absent from the cemetery. The replacement of the word "nome" or the name of a particular nome with "of the king" proclaims an apparently special interest of the king in this part of Egypt and on the responsibilities of the officials located there. Although Edel read an inscription on a fragment of pottery from a funerary offering that belonged to one of the officials, IiShemai Setka, as the standard nomarch title *ḥry tp ꜥꜣ n śpꜣt*, Seyfried and others who subsequently examined the same fragment feel confident this reading was incorrect.[50]

Seyfried, following Lorton, suggests the best interpretation of the title as "great representative of the king", and argues that this official marked a direct connection between the king and, here in Elephantine, the work of the expedition leaders.[51] Given the overall lack of exploitable land throughout the First Nome, it would be reasonable to envision the king's focus on Elephantine as the region's center of economic value based upon the twin aspects of border control and expeditions. Combined with the long-standing strategic importance of the town of Elephantine, its isolation from its nome in the administrative structure would not be surprising.

The limited references among the titularies of the Qubbet el-Hawa tomb owners to administration of their local town raises the question of who then *was* responsible for its administration. El-Dissouky points out that given the nature of their work as expedition leaders, these local elite were often gone for months on end and thus not in a position to be running the local administration.[52] He notes as well several examples of individuals buried outside of Elephantine who had titles related to administrative duties there, including Tjetjw in Saqqara, Qar in Edfu, and Djaw in Deir el Gebrawi.[53] Although it seems reasonable that high elite officials in other nomes may have had a hand in managing the local business of Elephantine, the titles held by these individuals are all variations on the *ḥry sšt3 mdt* titles, which as noted previously are also held by three tomb owners at Qubbet el-Hawa: Harkhuf, Khwin-Khnum, and Sabni2. This evidence suggests that the local elite of Elephantine perhaps shared administrative responsibilities with select, high-ranking officials based outside of their town, but it does not seem to support a view that the administration of Elephantine was entirely removed to other nomes. Ultimately, the limited reference to local administration may have been determined by its unique nature. Without significant agricultural institutions, large sections of the typical provincial administrative structure would have been unnecessary in Elephantine. The town's economic contribution to the state was likely fulfilled through the extensive trade goods collected on expeditions and perhaps stone quarried in the region as well. Thus, much of the typical administration in other towns may have fallen under the administration of expeditions in Elephantine. The presence of seal impressions with the title *imy-r3 iʿ3w* found in the administrative building in the town itself might support this view.

The structure of the administration of the rest of the First Nome is uncertain, as there is little surviving information. Martin-Pardey suggests that the capital of the First Nome was not at Elephantine, but rather at Kom Ombo, based upon information from the Middle Kingdom.[54] The area of Kom Ombo provided the most cultivable land in the nome, and thus could have been the primary source for food for the entire nome whether or not it was the capital. Lacking evidence, one may hypothesize that the supply of food to the town of Elephantine was integrated into the administration of expeditions. Moreno García discusses the supplying of expeditions as an important function of many agricultural institutions spread throughout the country.[55] In Pepy II's letter to Harkhuf, carved into the façade of Harkhuf's tomb, the king refers to orders he has sent to the *ḥkꜣ niwt mꜣwt*, "chief of the new towns," to "command that supplies be taken which are in his charge from every estate storeroom and from every temple; I make no exemption therefrom."[56] Although this letter apparently refers to supplies necessary for Harkhuf to get to Memphis, and Moreno García's discussion refers to the supplying of the expeditions specifically, perhaps the supplying of the town of Elephantine with food and other necessities fell into the same category of administration, as the town itself was so closely connected with expeditionary business. Unfortunately, no evidence survives regarding this aspect of the administration of Elephantine.

The last title to be noted from among the tombs at Qubbet el-Hawa is *imy-rꜣ šmꜥw*, "overseer of Upper Egypt," found throughout Upper Egypt during the Sixth Dynasty. The true nature of this position during the Sixth Dynasty is still debated.[57] Whether viewed as primarily honorific or in fact entirely functional, scholars generally agree that the "overseer of Upper Egypt" was an official working in the provinces on behalf of the central administration, thus even without clearly understood responsibilities, the title indicates a direct connection to the central administration. Although it was held by many members of the Upper Egyptian provincial elite, taken together with the other local titles at Qubbet el-Hawa, it contributes to an overall emphasis here on the king's interest in the local elite.

In summary, the titularies of the tomb owners at Qubbet el-Hawa can be divided into the typical categories of honorific and official. The honorific titles are common to all provincial elite from the same time period, while the official ones are distinctive to this cemetery.[58] Titles related to expeditions and other engagement with Nubia are far more frequent here than anywhere else in the country. No reference to agriculture management or the local priesthood appears in the Qubbet el-Hawa titularies, and all the official titles connected to the local administration refer specifically to the location of the town in which the tomb owners lived, at the "head of the south." The titles, epithets, and autobiographies all emphasize the tomb owners' work as expedition leaders, and several of the official ones, especially the local version of the nomarch title, "great overlord of the king", seem to emphasize the close connection between these officials and the king.

Because Elephantine was so strongly identified with the business of expeditions into Nubia, both the limited reference to local administration and the highlighting of the close connections between the Qubbet el-Hawa tomb owners and the king is not surprising. Unlike at other sites where expedition leaders were buried (for example in Thebes, modern Luxor) and nome officials were also present, the emphasis at Qubbet el-Hawa is clearly on expedition business, which had special strategic and economic significance to the king.

What then was the relationship of the Qubbet el-Hawa tomb owners to their local community? In his analysis of the development of provincial government during the Old Kingdom, Moreno García sees the provincial elite as locally powerful families who become integrated into the state system through connections to the king, and in return, through these connections to the king gained power and status within their communities.[59] These connections are formed primarily through the establishment by the king of royal funerary domains in the nome, which provide management roles for the local elite who function essentially as intermediaries between the local community members who conduct the agricultural work and the king. This analysis incorporates a view of a patrimonial-type village structure, in which larger households headed by wealthier and more powerful families support not only their immediate families, but an extended network of workers of all types, evidence of which appears throughout Egyptian history.[60]

At Elephantine, the absence of typical provincial elite offices, especially those related to the management of agriculture, is linked not only to the border location of the town, but also to the lack of cultivable land in the region and the resulting absence of royal funerary domains in the area, which in turn would have affected the economic base of the local elite and the rest of the local community.[61] Though farming, fishing, and hunting for subsistence occurred, the local people were most likely involved in the business of expeditions and border control: the business of their town. Eichler states that workers from the provinces were probably called upon for expeditions.[62] This view can be supported by several Old Kingdom texts, including a handful of rock inscriptions left by expeditions. An inscription from Hatnub mentions workers called up from three separate places.[63] Other inscriptions specify detachments "from the

Residence," which implies that not all workers were from the Residence but from many different towns throughout the country.[64] In Weni's autobiography he speaks of the army that he leads, made of "many tens of thousands from all of Upper Egypt," and also, "companions, overseers of foreigners, overseers of priests of Upper and Lower Egypt, overseers of the workroom in charge of troops of Upper and Lower Egypt and the rulers of their estates and towns."[65] Although Weni leads a military expedition, it is likely that large groups of workers for quarrying or trading expeditions would be similarly assembled. Furthermore, trade with Nubia during the Old Kingdom often had a military element, and several of the Qubbet el-Hawa tomb owners also held the title *ỉmy-rꜣ mšʿ*, "overseer of troops," which indicates the presence of military troops on the expeditions, as well.[66]

It is thus reasonable to assume that during the Sixth Dynasty, people from Elephantine were among those called upon to work on expeditions. The limited local agriculture would have meant a large available workforce in contrast to other populations occupied with an agricultural economy. In addition, given the Nubian-influenced cultural context of Elephantine, there is a strong possibility that many Nubian-speaking Egyptians lived in Elephantine, and they were no doubt relied upon for expedition work. If in fact these Nubian-speaking Egyptian "translators" formed part of the *ỉʿꜣw*, then the presence of so many overseers of *ỉʿꜣw* at Qubbet el-Hawa further suggests that many of these people were based in Elephantine. If instead *ỉʿꜣw* referred only to the Egyptianized Nubians who worked on expeditions (soldiers or otherwise), it is equally possible that settlements of such Nubians were located in the region. The limited evidence for Nubian settlements locates an early settlement in Dahshur,[67] but the Nubian material culture recovered in the area of Elephantine (down to Kubaniya) supports a logical assumption, that Egyptianized Nubians who worked on expeditions would be located close to the starting point of these expeditions. The recent discovery of a Nubian cemetery at Hierakonpolis, though largely dated to the Middle Kingdom, provides further support for this hypothesis.[68] In addition, perhaps the movement of overseers of *ỉʿꜣw* out of Memphis and to the provincial sites, in particular to Elephantine, is connected to the relocation or additional development of Nubian settlements in those areas. Perhaps the tomb owners' responsibilities as overseers of these *ỉʿꜣw* included work not only on expeditions, but to some degree at home, as well.

Given the titles that refer to "secrets of the south" and other indications of border-control work, some portion of the local population must have been involved in this aspect of the administration.[69] This emphasis on expedition and border-related work does not imply a complete absence of agricultural work in the town; small areas of cultivable land on the island and along the east bank of the river were surely exploited for farming.[70] Due to the small scale of the enterprise and the relative lack of royal interest, perhaps the management of local agriculture fell into the hands of lower-ranked officials, if not simply local workers, who left no records.

In sum, despite the lack of a typical agriculture-based economy in Elephantine, and despite the lack of agriculture-related titles among the local elite, they (likely) functioned in a similar manner, as intermediaries between the local working population, who they oversaw, and the king. The absence of titles indicating their responsibility for the nome does not change their status as the wealthiest and most powerful people in the town of Elephantine. Helck suggested that even though the tomb owners at Qubbet el-Hawa lacked the nomarch titles, they nonetheless functioned essentially as such. Martin-Pardey disagrees, given the apparent division between the administrative branches dealing with expeditions on the one hand and nome administration on the other.[71] Both are likely correct, in a sense. From the perspective of the central administration, these Qubbet el-Hawa tomb owners were expedition leaders first and foremost, and they were not involved in the typical responsibilities of nomarchs. Yet to the local community, these elite individuals were leaders, "head men" of the town, which is made clear by the establishment of a separate cemetery for them. A cemetery existed on the island of Elephantine from the earliest phase of the settlement; during the Fifth Dynasty it moved to the southwestern part of the island, separated from the town site on the southeastern part by a river channel that flooded during the inundation.[72] The establishment of the cemetery at Qubbet el-Hawa during the Fifth Dynasty and its expansion during the Sixth, physically separated from the traditional burial areas still in use and comprised of significantly larger and more elaborate rock-cut tombs, implies a local awareness of the distinct, elevated status of these tomb owners. The construction of the tombs and more significantly the conducting of the *ka*-cults at these tombs would have required the participation of a segment of the local population, and the secure existence of these elaborate tombs so close to the town suggests that the local community at least accepted, and more likely supported, their presence.

As we currently understand the basic social structure of a town, a small group of larger, wealthier households supported a range of both family members and non-blood-related people connected to the household often through work. These supported people were then themselves responsible for their own smaller households, in a sort of nesting pattern of extended kin.[73] As Eyre describes this structure:

> The personnel were in the same way dependent on the favour, patronage and provision of the official as he was on the king.... They [i.e., the elite] stressed constantly the performance of their public duties, to the king and to the populace at large ... the general picture ... is of patronage and provision working downwards through society from the king, in return for labour and service working up from the lowest peasant.[74]

Although most scholars base their analyses on the agricultural economy of the majority of the Egyptian provinces, this kind of social structure does not require such an economic base, and even though land ownership was most likely always a basis of wealth and status, it was the *use* of wealth and status that characterized this structure. As Kemp suggests, "Their [Egyptian mayors'] power must have lain in the respect and influence they commanded by virtue of local landownership and *family ties and a network of patronage and obligation.*"[75] The wealthiest people living in a town were inextricably connected to the rest of the community through this pattern of the social structure.

In any community such as Elephantine, there are many points of disparity such as wealth, education, gender, age, profession, even perhaps ethnicity. Yet within the larger context of the Egyptian nation, the community at Elephantine was shaped by a range of factors, many of which were tied to the space they inhabited. This is evident in the physical and material reality of the town where they lived, the island beneath all of them, and their surrounding environment. They shared a local god and cult, with a unique ritual space tightly bound with their distinctive geography. The cultural context in their "zone of contact" with Nubia encompassed them all, and many were likely engaged with Nubian people and culture through expeditions and trade, and perhaps nearby settlements of Egyptianized Nubians. Their lack of local cultivable land combined with the keen interest of the king in their trading business meant they relied on the state to support them with grain from other sources. While economic activity may well have occurred outside of the state structure during this period, trade or expeditions being undertaken without the directive of the state seems unlikely. As such, the community at Elephantine would have relied heavily on the success and stability of the central administration to ensure continued resources for expeditions seeking luxury goods and raw materials.[76]

Along with a shared environment, culture, and professions or sources of subsistence, a community has some form of shared self-identity, and although little evidence exists that overtly expresses to us this Elephantine shared self-identity, it is possible to hypothesize external factors that would have encouraged its development, beyond the material and social aspects given. As Seidlmayer states, "Clearly, the settlement gained its *character* as a town through the functions it took over on the national level.... It is equally clear, however ... the *identity* of the local community expresses itself in more subtle ways."[77] Identity, especially among a community, often crystallizes most vividly when the community is confronted by a group of people who do not share their specific cultural traits in religion, language, traditions, and in particular for the Egyptians, stylistic qualities such as hairstyles and clothing. For the community at Elephantine, their close proximity to and constant engagement with the Nubian people just south of them (and most likely in their town or region itself) would have highlighted the cultural traits they shared and their desire to claim them. Some of these traits would have been closely tied to their local traditions, while others belonged to their larger identity as Egyptian. Yet the quintessence of their Egyptian identity, the king and the elite culture at Memphis, remained hundreds of miles away. The few visits of the king to Elephantine, while no doubt dramatic, would not have provided a consistent model of "Egyptian-ness" due to their infrequency. The local elite individuals, with their more frequent visits to Memphis, close connections to the king and the elite structure expressed through their titles and other forms of reward, and especially their participation in elite material culture in their construction of decorated tombs, represented this Egyptian identity most powerfully and reliably for the local community. Thus, a desire to support and be connected to the local elite and the cemetery at Qubbet el-Hawa was based not only on the universally Egyptian elements of the innate social structure and the ideology of order, but also for both groups (the elite and the rest of the population) on a local reliance on each other for an identity and place in their world. Given their close contact with non-Egyptian, Nubian people and places, they may have felt this desire more strongly than in other provincial towns. The elite tomb owners buried at Qubbet el-Hawa, as local head-men, both belonged to this local community and provided an important source of stability for it. In constructing their tombs, they helped define their community's identity and integrate it into the Egyptian state structure.

2

Tombs in Context: Description of Cemetery and Overview of Tombs

Qubbet el-Hawa in Arabic means "windy dome," a reference to the shrine to Muslim saint Ali Abu-l'Hawa built atop the mountain into which the ancient tombs are cut. The construction of this small shrine continued a 3,000-year-old tradition of the local community's perception of this mountain's spiritual and social significance. During the era of Coptic dominance in the region, the site had been adapted for use as a small monastery. In choosing Qubbet el-Hawa, the Coptic monks followed in the footsteps first left by their ancient predecessors, as it was the elite of ancient Elephantine who, in the Fifth Dynasty, first came to the mountain and transformed it from a natural to a man-made monument in their landscape.

This "mountain" is in fact a section of the desert escarpment, which here in Aswan and throughout the region of the First Cataract hugs the edges of the Nile River until it completes its course around the cataract's rocky outcrops to continue flowing downstream. At the point where the river reunites, the escarpment rises to a high, convex ridge that forms an especially distinctive feature in the landscape (Figure 3). The recognizable aspect given this feature via the natural form of the cliff, together with the visibility of it throughout the region of Elephantine, surely played an important role in its selection as the site of the new elite cemetery. Of likely equal value was its location within the environs, downstream from the settlement and marking a natural boundary of the area.

The encroachment of the desert cliffs upon the river's edge is relatively rare. In much of the Nile Valley, the cliffs recede behind the flood plain of the river and a swath of low desert, a pattern which begins to emerge just north of Qubbet el-Hawa, where narrow bands of cultivable land appear. The unusual nature of this local topography allowed the

3. Panoramic view of Aswan area.

4. View from the townsite at Elephantine to Qubbet el-Hawa.

Elephantine elite to establish their cemetery of rock-cut tombs not only in a setting highly visible from the town site and the river, but also in a theologically ideal west bank site, in contrast to the numerous Upper Egyptian provincial cemeteries situated on the east bank for reasons of access and community connection (Figure 4).

The unusual landscape also allowed the elite to separate their cemetery from that of the remaining population not only spatially, but typologically, as well. From the beginning of the Old Kingdom, the local cemetery shared the southern section of the island with the town site, and consisted of built mastabas, albeit of slightly unusual types.[1] Evidence of a hierarchy among the mastaba tombs in the cemetery indicates the presence of elite burials from earlier periods; the movement to Qubbet el-Hawa further heightened the status of the local elite, in both life and death.

The tombs are cut side by side into the Nubian sandstone of the mountain, creating horizontal rows of tombs running from south to north along the convex curve of the cliff, which here mirrors the bend of the river from slightly northeast to slightly northwest (Figure 5, Plates I, II). The majority of tombs form two tiers along the mountain's east face; a handful of tombs from a third, lower tier have also been uncovered. The top tier of tombs is situated roughly halfway up the face of the mountain, and it runs approximately 400 meters from the southernmost to northernmost tombs. The bend in the cliff marks the approximate midpoint of this continuous span of tombs, effectively dividing the cemetery into northern and southern sections. The

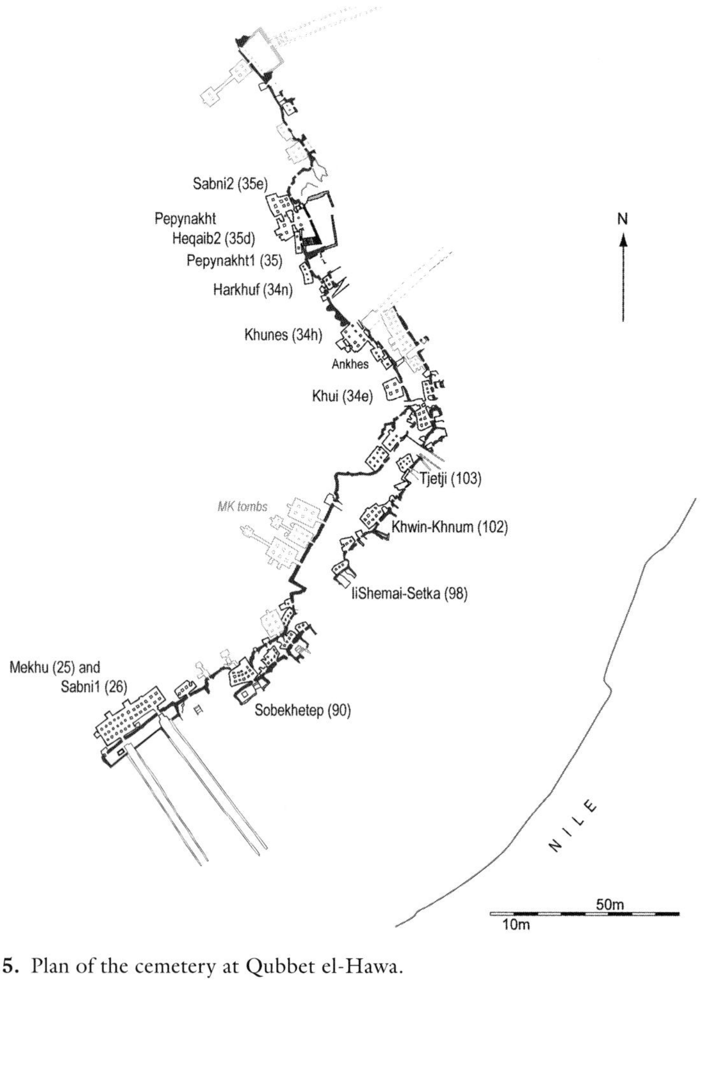

5. Plan of the cemetery at Qubbet el-Hawa.

second tier runs about half the length of the top tier, and the tombs are concentrated around the bend of the cliff and in the southern section of the cemetery.

Edel et al. underscore the religious significance of the setting of Qubbet el-Hawa in their detailed analysis of tomb architecture, pointing out the religious "ideal" the site offered, being on the west bank and allowing the tombs to face east, directly toward the rising sun.[2] Beyond the religious significance, the site's location has visual, and by extension social, implications, as well, as the location of each tomb determines its relationship to the broader environment; tombs in the southern section of the cemetery are visible from the settlement site at Elephantine, while tombs in the northern section are blocked from view by the projection of the cliff. The northern tombs are visible from the river north and east of the cliff, particularly to boats heading toward Elephantine from the rest of Egypt. Because of the angle of the cliff, the southern tombs face back toward the settlement site, and from their forecourts the whole island and its environs in the First Cataract are visible, while a view of the river heading downstream is blocked by the cliff. From the forecourts of the northern tombs, only the tip of the island of Elephantine may be visible, but they offer an unimpeded view of the river and both of its banks extending northward (Plate IIIa and b).

The earliest surviving tomb with texts and images dates to the Sixth Dynasty, though evidence of even earlier, though apparently simpler, tombs remains, as well. Why the earlier tombs were not maintained is not clear, but from the beginning of the reign of Pepy II, the cemetery expanded with many more and larger, now preserved, monuments. The site was used through the end of the Old Kingdom and beyond, with tombs still being cut in the Middle and New Kingdoms, and multiple intrusive burials in the Late Period and Greco-Roman eras.

Tombs: General

The Old Kingdom tombs at Qubbet el-Hawa present an especially diverse array of architectural forms, influenced in part by the setting, the available technology, and the transformation of the site over time. In the final publication of the excavation of the cemetery, Edel et al. present a thorough analysis of the tomb architecture, assessing the possible origins and development of the local forms, as well as the architectural processes.[3] What follows here engages this material but provides a more descriptive discussion of the specific tombs being considered.

In creating tombs for the Elephantine elite, the ancient workmen cut into the slope of the cliff to create a flat, vertical façade, approached from a roughly horizontal surface of a forecourt. Depending upon the angle of the cliff's slope, the forecourt could be entirely cut from the living rock and enclosed by rock-cut walls, such as the one shared by the tombs of Mekhu and Sabni1 (Figure 7). Alternately, in areas where the cliff's slope is gentler, the forecourt was only partially enclosed by rock-cut walls connected to the façade of the tomb, with the remaining area enclosed by walls built from the broken stone excavated during the construction of the tomb, such as those of Sobekhetep and Harkhuf (Figures 10, 32). These forecourts provided important ritual space for the processes of the funeral and mortuary cult, as well as for subsidiary burials,[4] which appear in the forecourt of every tomb discussed here, accessed via shafts sunk into the forecourt's surface with burial chambers underground. The size and elaboration of the forecourt varies with each individual tomb, but in all cases they expand the exterior aspect of the tomb and designate a piece of the mountain as belonging to the tomb owner. Although most of these forecourts have been transformed from their original state through reuse, intentional damage, excavation, and blown sand, enough material survives to give a strong impression of the overall shape of the forecourts and their role within the tomb complexes.

Access to the tomb chapels was through doorways cut into their smoothly dressed façades. Most doorways were surrounded by rectangular recesses that created a narrow "lintel" above and a "jamb" to either side of the doorway, and many of the doorways also had drums, the cylindrical stone feature representing a rolled reed mat, set underneath their lintels, similar to most tomb entrances of the Old Kingdom. While the majority of these doorways were a standard height, several reached monumental scale; for example, the entrances to the tombs of Mekhu, Sabni1, Khunes, and Pepynakht Heqaib2, each of which reached more than 4 meters (Figures 7, 24, 36). The height of these entrances related in each case to the high interior space of the tomb, but they also affected the exterior appearance of the tombs, as the tall doorways created dark, unnatural rectangles against the pale cliff, making them especially visible from a distance.

Along with the dimensions of the façade and doorway, the embellishment of the façade surface also varies from tomb to tomb. The lengthy autobiographies of Sabni1, Harkhuf, and Pepynakht Heqaib1, for which Elephantine is most famous, are all carved into the façade of their respective subject's tomb together with relief-carved images of the celebrated tomb owners. Other façades bear relief-carved images of offering figures (Pepynakht Heqaib2), while many others have no relief or inscriptions of any kind. Edel et al. note the unusual presence of obelisk-shaped stele flanking the entrances of at least twelve different tombs, a tradition unknown, with one exception, outside of the capital-area cemeteries.[5] Only one tomb, that of Pepynakht Heqaib2, had a portico outside its entrance, defined by two tall columns cut from the cliff (Figure 36).

The tombs range from small, single chambers with floors nearly filled with tomb shafts, to the 270m^2 floor area of the double tomb of Mekhu and Sabni1. Unsurprisingly, most of the larger tombs occupy the top tier in the cemetery. Among the Old Kingdom tombs, most are "broad halls," that is they are wider (north-south) than deep (east-west) in plan, although there are exceptions (that may in part anticipate the more typical Middle Kingdom form of long hall tombs, as exemplified by the tombs of Sirenput I [QH36] and II [QH31]). Like many larger rock-cut tombs throughout the provinces, nearly all of the tombs at Qubbet el-Hawa have internal pillars cut from the rock and arranged in rows. While most of these internal supports are rectangular pillars, a handful of tombs have rounded columns, most prominently the tomb of Mekhu (Figure 8). Brunner identified these columns as being the earliest example of true columns in an Upper Egyptian provincial tomb. The tomb of Tjetji also utilizes columns, while tomb QH35i interestingly pairs two columns with two rectangular pillars.

Greater architectural consistency appears in the relationship between the chapel entrance and the false door, the focal point of Egyptian mortuary cult activity. Very often, the false door is set opposite the entrance, creating a "cult axis" from doorway to primary ritual place. In some cases, for example in the smaller tombs of Harkhuf and Pepynakht Heqaib1, the entrance to the horizontal, or slightly sloping, tunnel leading to the burial chamber is set directly across from the chapel entrance, leaving little wall surface area for the false door; here the false door is carved adjacent to the shaft entrance (Figures 35, 38). In later tombs this conflict was resolved by having the tunnel entrance cut either fully into the floor, or partially into the west wall and partially into the floor, leaving sufficient room for the false door to be carved above it, and thus directly across from the entrance. This arrangement occurs in the tombs of Sobekhetep and Pepynakht Heqaib 2 (Figures 11, 41).

In spite of the shared formal elements, the variations in size, shape of the plan, height of the ceiling, and the size, number, and arrangement of pillars give each tomb, and in particular its internal space, a distinctive character. For example, the volume of Mekhu's tomb is more than 80 cubic meters greater than that of the tomb of Khunes, but because of the many large columns placed closely together and the lower ceiling, Mekhu's tomb chapel gives the impression of being much more compact and cramped than the open, soaring space created by the high ceiling and fewer, narrow pillars in the tomb chapel of Khunes (Cf. Figures 8, 26). The tomb of Khwin-Khnum is both deeper and higher than that of Harkhuf, but its two rows of irregular pillars and the shafts cut into its floor create a small, awkward space that contrasts with the much simpler, less crowded environment created by the long narrow plan and single row of pillars in Harkhuf's tomb. While it was characteristic of Old Kingdom Egyptian tomb builders to resist replicating tomb plans or designs, the builders at Qubbet el-Hawa exploited the potential of the formal tools available to them to create a particularly rich diversity of ritual spaces.

Text and Image Programs

The most distinctive aspects of these architecturally diverse Old Kingdom tombs at Qubbet el-Hawa are their programs of texts and images. When visiting the site, the beauty of the cemetery's setting and the diversity and drama of the architecture, along with the Coptic and Islamic remains testifying to its long and complex history, often dominate the viewer's senses, powerfully overshadowing the role of the images and texts. Especially in comparison to the large Memphite mastabas with extensive programs that have a variety of detailed imagery, or to the nearer New Kingdom painted tombs in Luxor that overwhelm with colorful and well-preserved imagery, the programs at Qubbet el-Hawa indeed make a much subtler visual statement. Those seeking to find parallels, or examples, of such Memphite and Theban models typically perceive these unusual programs as simple provincialism, and thus disengage from further visual inquiry. But, in fact, these programs of texts and images have much to say, and it is their unified visual language that makes them so compelling.

There are three main elements shared by the programs in these Qubbet el-Hawa tombs that differentiate them as a unified group from the programs in the majority of Old Kingdom elite tombs in Egypt, including those in other provincial cemeteries. The first element is their mode of decoration; that is, the composition and placement of groups of images and texts within the space of the tomb chapel. The second element is their thematic focus on offering figures, and the third element is the diversity of style apparent among the images comprising the programs.

In most Old Kingdom elite tombs, both built mastabas and rock-cut tombs, the text and image programs cover the interior walls of the chapel. As the chapel spaces expanded over the course of the Old Kingdom, so, too, did the repertoire of scene types. Even in those tomb chapels left unfinished, the completed sections comprise images and texts laid out over the full surface of a wall (usually leaving a low dado the bottom 0.5 meter or so of the wall). Whether the design consisted of a single scene or a series of scenes organized in registers, it is clear the artists conceived of a full wall surface as the basic component of a tomb's program. In contrast to this widespread standard, in the tombs at Qubbet el-Hawa the programs were composed of independent scenes or figures carved or painted onto a section of a wall or pillar. Unlike most elite tomb chapel walls, which were fully smoothed, these walls were not so thoroughly treated. The workmen dressed the walls and pillars to create relatively flat, vertical surfaces that remained rough, and the great percentage of these surfaces were left in this state. Only the area intended to receive an image was finished to a smooth surface, and the prepared area was filled with the scene (though there are examples of small, prepared areas that were not ultimately used, whether through design or lack of time). The result is a program consisting of a series of "panels," separate and independent scenes distributed within the tomb and surrounded by the rough, untreated surface of the wall. The single exception to this pattern is found in the tomb of Khunes, in which two walls are covered with low raised relief in a manner more similar to traditional Memphite design.

These panels appear throughout the tombs, but almost entirely in areas that received light. The artists' need for light when creating the images may have contributed to the intentional location of the panels, but this locational patterning also implies the presence of an audience and thus a sense of display in the conception and execution of the programs. This perceived audience and its role in the formation of the programs will be discussed in subsequent chapters. Pillars were especially popular for panels, due perhaps to their convenient size and potential for receiving light, as were entrance thicknesses. In some cases a single wall or pillar held several scenes, but they were still executed in this panel mode, with each scene having its own distinct limits, separated from another by the blank, rough surfaces of the untreated wall (for example, Figures 50, 59, Plate XIV).

The second defining element of the Qubbet el-Hawa programs is their thematically limited content. Most tomb programs created during the second half of the Old Kingdom incorporated a diverse array of scene types – agricultural activities; musicians and dancers; the production of funerary goods such as furniture, statuary, and jewelry; extensive offering figures, and so forth – that had by that time become traditional. The lack of this material at Qubbet el-Hawa is extremely unusual, but it is important to note that the images they *did* utilize were selected from this longstanding tradition. Every Qubbet el-Hawa tomb program includes at least one image of the tomb owner; these are commonly located on the entrance thicknesses and less often on an internal wall or pillar, or the façade (Harkhuf, Pepynakht Heqaib1). The at-this-time iconic fishing and fowling scene appears in three tombs: Sabni1, in Plate V; Khunes; and Sabni2, in Figure 60. The provincial favorite fighting bulls scene appears in the tomb of Sabni2 (Figure 61), and also as a brief "vignette" in the tomb of Khunes. One relatively large panel in the tomb of Mekhu includes elements of scenes showing workers engaged in agricultural activity (Plate IV). Isolated examples of other workers engaged in activities such as grinding grain or brewing beer appear in three other tombs, but in these cases the active figures are not part of scenes devoted to the activity; rather, they are incorporated into the kinds of scenes that dominate these programs: groups of offering figures (Plate XVIII).

These isolated references to the traditional iconographic repertoire represent only a small part of the Qubbet el-Hawa Old Kingdom programs; the vast majority of the images depict subsidiary figures, identified with names and often titles, almost entirely engaged in carrying offerings for the cult of the tomb owner. A small percentage of these figures do not carry offerings; instead, they stand with their hands by their sides or one hand to the chest in a posture of humility. Although in some cases a meaningful difference seems intended, overall these figures are analogous to those carrying offerings: rather than being active and engaged with other figures, they stand as individuals in direct relationship to the tomb owner.[6] For convenience, in this description of the tomb programs all such figures are referred to as "offering figures," although distinctions of posture will be noted. The figures may be alone, in pairs, or in groups that are often clearly identified as families by the accompanying text.

The third characteristic element of the programs is the conspicuous diversity of style among the figures and scenes. This diversity stands in stark contrast to the stylistic uniformity common in Memphite and other provincial tombs. Although every image in the program of a Memphite tomb was not stylistically identical, the evidence suggests that a *seemingly* uniform style throughout the tomb was traditionally a goal of the artists. For example, the majority of the decorative program in the double tomb of Niankh-Khnum and Khnum-Hetep at Saqqara is executed in low raised relief; however, in the outer, built section of their tomb, high above the doorway leading to the interior courtyard, a large section was painted rather than carved.[7] Nonetheless, by depicting the figures at the same scale and with the same proportions as the others and by organizing them in registers consistent with those on the rest of the wall, the artists smoothly integrated this painted section into the relief-carved majority, so that the difference is not obvious.

The artists at Qubbet el-Hawa made no such effort to integrate the images. Each panel is usually executed in a single style, but panels within one tomb or even on the same wall are very often in different styles. Individual offering figures surrounding an image of the tomb owner on an entrance thickness or pillar are often in a different style from the tomb owner and from the other subsidiary figures in the same area. This evidence strongly suggests that even an *effect* of stylistic consistency throughout the image program of a tomb was not a concern of the tomb owners and artists at Qubbet el-Hawa.

These three elements – composition and placement, thematic content, and stylistic diversity – are interrelated formally and functionally. They form a unique system that is used consistently throughout the tombs, knitting them together to create a similar impression on the viewer and a unified expression from this elite community. The tombs are further interwoven through the use of the different styles, most of which appear in at least several of the tombs, albeit in varying combinations.

The material examined in this study comes from twelve tombs in the cemetery, those that have the most extensive use of images and text that have survived well. Two pairs of tombs are connected: those of Mekhu and Sabni1 share a largely continuous façade and internal space; those of Pepynakht Heqaib2 and Sabni2 have clearly distinct internal chapels yet share a forecourt and internal connecting passageway; in addition, a thirteenth tomb is considered – the small chapel of Ankhes – that has only one decorated pillar and is largely an appendage to the much larger chapel of her husband Khunes. The complete list of tombs and their owners[8] is: 1./2. Mekhu and Sabni1 (double tomb), QH 25, 26; 3. Sobekhetep, QH 90; 4. Ii-Shemai Setka, QH 98; 5. Khwin-Khnum, QH 102; 6. Tjetji, QH 103; 7. Khui, QH 34e; 8. Khunes, QH 34h and Ankhes, QH34g; 9. Harkhuf, QH 34n; 10. Pepynakht Heqaib1, QH 35; 11. Pepynakht Heqaib2, QH 35d, and 12. Sabni2, QH35e. When isolated examples from other tombs are occasionally considered, they will be identified.

Style Groups

The concept of style used in this analysis synthesizes archaeological and art historical concerns and presumes the central role of embodied agents as producers and consumers of their visual culture, in order to address the formal qualities of the architecture, space, landscape, and the painted relief images in concert; this will be addressed in greater depth in Chapter 3. In this initial engagement with the style of the images, the focus is on clarifying how relief and painted styles have been identified and distinguished.

Defining the style of an image or object is ultimately a subjective process, but it is one that can be reasonably quantified. Egyptian art requires a meticulous approach, as the intentional essential consistency of form in two-dimensional imagery, especially during the Old Kingdom, heightens the significance of even minor formal variations. In order to provide a solid foundation for the subsequent analysis of style and its use in this cemetery, I provide here the criteria used in analyzing and categorizing the images.

1. **Type of medium**: In this cemetery there are a few examples of purely painted scenes, but the majority of texts and images are carved in

relief, most of which was likely painted, as well.[9] There are two types of relief: raised, in which the area surrounding the image is carved away so the image projects from the surface; and sunk, in which the image is recessed into the surrounding surface of the wall. In this analysis, I use the type of medium as an automatic dividing line between styles, in part because it is a formal element of the image, and in part because, in Egyptian art, the medium used is often meaningful. In particular, relief type can have functional and economic meaning. Sunk relief is often used outside of tombs or temples, as it is more suited to bright, direct sunlight, whereas raised relief is used in interior spaces with less light. Raised relief, particularly in the Old Kingdom, is often perceived by modern viewers as being of higher quality than sunk relief, in part because sunk relief requires less work to execute. The way in which relief type was used in the cemetery at Qubbet el-Hawa suggests there was some sense of meaningful differentiation between the two types, beyond location in the monument.

Even this seemingly definitive criterion is problematic. Some raised relief images share many stylistic qualities with examples of sunk relief. There is a type of raised relief used in several tombs that is so low it is nearly flat and thus closely linked to several painted figures, as well. This type of overlap and interweaving of images and styles is typical of the visual material at Qubbet el-Hawa.

2. **Proportions of Figures**: The proportions of the human figure are fundamental in defining styles in Egyptian art. They were a primary tool for the development and execution of images throughout most of Egyptian history, and they strongly affect the appearance of the figure. Although the squared grid was not yet in use during the Old Kingdom, there is evidence for the use of guidelines at the hairline, neck, armpits, elbows, upper thigh, and knees. Gay Robins identifies the proportions used in the later Old Kingdom as the "classic" proportions of Egyptian art, yet during the Old Kingdom they appear to be only loosely followed. Therefore, only visually obvious differences in proportions are used to divide styles. Proportions are assessed in comparison to the classic proportions as defined by Robins, and are presented most often in descriptive terms (longer torsos, larger heads) rather than mathematical ones.[10]
3. **Scale and Shape of Facial Features**: The eyes, eyebrows, noses, mouths, and ears of the figures in the art of this cemetery take many

distinctive shapes and sizes. Also variable and hence important is their scale relative to each other and to the head and face of the figure, and their spatial relationships in the image.

4. **Iconography**. Overall, the iconography of posture, dress, and accoutrements among these figures is consistent with the majority of figures in Old Kingdom elite art, and thus does not offer an avenue of differentiation (i.e., short pointed kilts, some longer kilts with older figures, halter dresses for women, broad collar necklaces, both short and long hair for men and women, almost all standing, holding objects, or hands to their sides, or hand to the chest, and so forth). However, there are object types depicted as offerings that appear repeatedly with certain styles and never with others, and thus do indicate relationships among scenes.
5. **Character of the Figure**: This criterion is more subjectively determined, and the language used to describe it is less precise; nonetheless, it is an essential aspect of the style and useful in the process of differentiation. Character of the figure includes, for example, if the outlines are modulated or smooth; if the parts comprising the figure form irregular shapes or are instead based on geometric shapes; if these elements are angular or rounded; and if the figure incorporates small details and elements of naturalism or if it is more simplified into abstract forms. These descriptive concepts will be more fully explained and illustrated in the individual style discussions.
6. **Paleography and Panel Design**: These two separate issues are categorized together because although they are not integral to differentiating style groups, both are formal aspects of the panels that are vital to an analysis of the visual material as a whole. In particular, both elements help to isolate sets of more closely interrelated images within a style group, as well as to identify groups of images from separate style groups that are nonetheless formally related.
   a. ***Paleography***: Nearly every panel and figure in the cemetery is accompanied by an inscription. Hieroglyphs within a single panel or associated with a solo figure are almost always stylistically consistent; yet between the panels, the styles of the hieroglyphs differ in much the same way as the figures. Labels for paleographic styles are included in the style group descriptions.
   b. ***Panel Design***: This refers to the layout of a panel, primarily the placement of the figures and the accompanying inscriptions,

but can also include color palette. Not all panels have a clearly definable design pattern.

The existence of clear formal relationships, based upon these criteria, among many scenes and figures in the tombs at Qubbet el-Hawa allows for a rough demarcation of related images into style groups. Certain of these groups, as I have outlined them, include a greater degree of internal variation than others. Furthermore, there are clear connections between some examples of separate style groups, which are likely the result of different artists working in a single community, sharing and trading influences. Isolated examples remain uncategorized, and a few styles that appear limited to a single tomb or instance of use remain unlabeled, but their presence and their style are significant to the study of the image programs and the cemetery in general. These issues will be discussed more fully in Chapter 3.

Here is a delineation of the style groups (with an example of the style):

1. **Raised A1** (Figure 44): This style group incorporates most of the large-scale figures of the tomb owners. The images are cut in a low raised relief, and the mainly flat surfaces of their bodies show only select areas of modeling, usually on the face, in details of clothing or jewelry, or of an arm that crosses the body. The figures have standard Old Kingdom proportions, and they were carved with attention to subtle detail, especially in the outline of the body; for example, indications of the knees and elbows and the swelling of arm and leg muscles. The facial features have a similar degree of fine detail and usually include almond-shaped eyes, full lips, and relatively large, somewhat bulbous noses. Individualistic detail appears in the shape of the ear, the depiction of the inner nostril, and elaboration of the area around the mouth. This category includes both muscular, youthful adults and the more mature, heavier figures, both of which are typical to Old Kingdom elite tomb art. Most of the figures stand holding a staff and either a scepter or a piece of cloth, but several seated figures and one figure leaning on his staff appear, as well.

   The hieroglyphs that accompany images in this style tend to be large, very clear sunk relief signs. Although many of the signs have lost any trace of painting, the paint that does survive reveals a greater degree of variation in the detailing of these large signs than in their relief-carved outlines.

Note that not all of the tomb owner images fit into this category; some fit into one of the styles associated with subsidiary figures, and some use rarer styles, discussed next.

The other style groups refer primarily to offering and other subsidiary figures.

2. **Raised A2** (Figure 13): This style group incorporates mainly offering and other subsidiary figures carved in a low raised relief similar to the Raised A1 style; however, a handful of tomb owner figures are also best categorized in the A2 style. The main, though not only, division between these two groups is scale. Most of the figures also have standard Old Kingdom proportions, although in several examples the legs are longer than normal. Perhaps due in part to their smaller scale, these figures show less subtlety in their outline, and their facial features, usually indicated only with paint, are less finely detailed than the larger figures of Raised A1. The few scenes that depict figures engaged in activities other than offering (MS7: Figure 12 and Kh8: Khunes south wall) use this style of relief. Some examples of this style have formal links to Sunken A, as well.

   The accompanying hieroglyphs are similar to those with Raised A1 figures; however, because they are smaller, they lack the detail of the larger glyphs. These glyphs are also stylistically related to signs in the Sunken A panels.
3. **Raised B** (Figure 23): This raised relief style is closely related to the Sunken B relief style, and like Raised A1 and A2, Raised B figures are carved in low raised relief, but otherwise they are clearly different. The figures have disproportionately large heads and upper bodies. Their outlines tend to be cursory with smooth, unmodulated lines that show few details, giving the figures a stiff appearance. For the women a long, smooth line beginning at the front armpit curves outward to indicate the breast, in to the waist, and out again for the upper thigh. The heads and faces of men and women are the same, with a point for the nose and chin in profile. Incised lines indicate the thin, wide eye and simple, curved ear, both of which are set low on the face, exaggerating the high crown of the head.

   The figures in this style offer to the tomb owners a wide variety of goods, including many that are similar to objects offered by figures in the Sunken B and Sunken C styles, such as vessels, live birds, and triangular breads or cakes held by the women. Objects associated only with this style include a covered basket/vessel and different forms of altars and vessel stands.

Only one example in this rare style has an associated inscription; the glyphs are small and less regular than those of Raised A1 and A2. They are formally linked to signs used in the Sunken B, C, and E styles.

4. **Sunken A** (Figure 30): Figures in this style can be easily recognized throughout the cemetery. They are carved in sunken relief and the body surfaces are slightly rounded up from the sunken outlines. In a minor variation, the bodies are more angular in form, and the interior edges of the body are beveled rather than rounded. Overall, the figures are elongated, with long necks, long legs, and thin limbs, though often the first, primary figure in a row done in this style is less elongated and the limbs are more substantial. Within the group proportions do vary, with some figures being more elongated than others, but overall the visual effect is very similar.

   The heads are generally oval; sometimes they are circular with a flat top, other examples are more egg-shaped and elongated at the crown. Few figures have detailed facial features, but they do have small, pointed noses below which a straight line extends to the chin, which is squared and connected to the neck by a slightly curving line.

   Men's kilts angle down from the small of the back to the front, and the tie at the front angles up and is usually rounded, though examples of a squared tie exist. The female figures appear more diverse; the main area of difference amongst them is the amount and type of incised inner detail, which ranges from being entirely absent to indicating the broad collar necklace, halter straps, and hem of the dress, and dividing line between the legs. The use of incised inner detailing among the male figures, being generally limited to the hairline and ear, kilt sash, and belt, also varies. The presence and type of incised detailing on the figures provides the main formal difference among panels in this style.

   In almost all panels of this style, the first figure is male and burns incense in a bowl-shaped censer; the remaining figures can include both men and women. The majority of female figures carry shallow bowls holding triangle-shaped breads or cakes; a few carry birds by their wings. Some male figures carry vessels, a leg of meat, or large geese.

Although there is some stylistic variation among the hieroglyphs accompanying these panels, in general the signs are very similar. They are all carved in sunk relief, they are compact, simple, and very clear. Often the signs are painted and are multicolored, though the coloring pattern is not always consistent.

The remaining styles of sunken relief, B–E, are more closely related to each other than to Sunken A. The hieroglyphs from panels in these styles appear to be interrelated stylistically, as well, although there is a much greater degree of variation among the signs in these panels than those in the Raised A1, Raised A2, or Sunken A styles.

5. **Sunken B** (Plate XVII)**:** As noted previously, this sunken relief style is very similar to the Raised B style. The figures have the same stocky proportions dominated by large heads, and generally simple outlines; although here, the outlines of the legs indicate knees and calves, unlike in the Raised B style. The ear and necklace are raised against the sunken surface of the body, as is the hand when it is held against the torso. The women have the same outline with a curving front profile, and there is a line dividing the legs that runs straight up from the feet and curves back at the hip, touching the back profile line. Most female figures in this style appear to be nude; there is no indication of a dress, and the bodies with surviving paint are fully covered with the same red-brown color used for the skin of the men.

   This style is also closely related to another sunken relief style, Sunken C.

6. **Sunken C** (Plate XV)**:** These figures are generally elongated with long, tapering torsos and long thighs. Their heads and upper bodies are also disproportionately large, though not to the same extent as the figures in Sunken B. Within this style proportions do vary somewhat, with some figures having slightly broader shoulders and torsos, and others with shorter thighs. The outline of the body is angular with very few curves, as typified by the sharp armpits. There are select areas of surface modeling on the legs, parts of the face, and individual fingers. A raised relief ear, a raised, narrow collar necklace, and usually a raised kilt belt stand out against the flatter surface of the bodies, also similar to Sunken B. Figures in this style have especially distinctive faces dominated by long, thin, tube-like noses carved in relief, which run from the area of the eyes to almost the tip of the chin. The wide,

oval eyes are set high on the faces. There are figures that fit into this style category in every respect except for the tube-like nose.

Most of the figures in this style are male. The few long wigs on male figures do not touch the shoulders; instead, they stick out to a point behind the head. As in Sunken B, the few female figures in this style appear to be nude, based upon the lack of indication of the long dress, and also upon the surviving paint signifying the skin, which for all figures is a reddish-orange and clearly covers the entire bodies.

In other styles, figures hold one or two offerings, but panels in this style often depict a set of offerings that includes not only items held by the offering figure, but also additional objects laid out in the surrounding area. In some cases, depending upon available space, individual pieces do appear alone. The visually distinctive group incorporates several pieces of meat, including a long, narrow leg that is usually carried, a set of ribs, and a joint, as well as two somewhat vague forms that likely represent bread, or perhaps other pieces of meat. There is often a tall *hes* vase, a type used for ritual liquid offerings and often seen in mortuary art, and another oval vase held by a strap. The birds being offered are particularly unusual, with long necks, fish-like tails, small rounded wings, and rather awkward legs. The final piece common to this group is somewhat obscure, a circle containing three small oval objects above a horizontal line with many small lines beneath it. It is perhaps an offering table holding other food items.

7. **Sunken D (Figure 48, bottom)**: The characteristic aspect of this style is the deep sunk relief and the consistently flat, non-modeled surface of the bodies. The head is not as oversized as in Sunken B and C, though the head and neck are elongated, similar to Sunken A. The torso is long in comparison to the legs, and the figure overall is geometric in shape, with a triangular upper body meeting a triangular kilt. The outline of the figure is composed of simple, unmodulated line segments. Like Sunken B and C, the ear, necklace, and kilt belt are raised against the flat surface of the body. Few facial features are indicated, just the almond-shaped outline of the eye and a small point for the nose. The offerings include birds similar to those from the B and C groups, incense burners with a bowl and lid, and ambiguous round objects (similar to those offered in Sunken B.)

8. **Sunken E (Figures 46, 47**, Plate XIII): This style is defined by two figures of the tomb owner Pepynakht Heqaib2 on the bottom of the entrance thicknesses to his tomb, both carved in the same finely detailed, highly original sunk relief style. (I will discuss these two images more fully in the tomb overview.) Most other members of this category are offering figures carved in the area around these two images of Pepynakht Heqaib2, which appear to result from the artists' efforts to copy or in some way evoke these larger, distinctive images. These offering figures all differ in their attempt to recreate the style, but they share certain qualities. The relief is relatively shallow, and the bodies are slightly modeled, in particular the back arm that crosses the body and is raised against it. The outlines are softer than those of B, C, and D, less angular, and created with longer, more modulated lines. The proportions vary, although they all have large heads and long torsos, and in general they are elongated with thin legs and arms. They have distinctive feet that are very thin and slightly curved. Their heads are round or oval, and the forehead line slopes down to the tip of the nose, where the nostril is rounded. Their eyes are large and set high on the face, while the nose is set low, just above the narrow lips, which sit just above the thin chin. The ear is carved in raised relief and at a back-leaning angle, and they all have small, circular, incised navels. Many of these figures are shown censing, with a mushroom-shaped censer.

Although this last group primarily includes figures from one tomb only, I include them in the section because they are intimately related to other Sunken styles, in particular B, C, and D, examples of which do appear in several other tombs in the cemetery.

Three other style groups seem to be limited to only one or two tombs, although they share some formal aspects with styles from other tombs. These groups appear in the tombs of Harkhuf and Pepynakht Heqaib1, Mekhu and Sabni1, Ii-Shemai Setka, and Sabni2. First, the large-scale figures in the small tomb of Harkhuf and on the façade only of the tomb of Pepynakht Heqaib1 are carved in sunk relief, which is rare for images of tomb owners at Qubbet el-Hawa, and the figures have proportions similar to the Raised A1 figures, although they have the longer torsos and shorter upper legs familiar from earlier Old Kingdom art. This "Harkhuf" style also shares with Raised A1 figures the shape of the body and some of the details, such as the shape of the long wigs and the staffs and scepters. The surface of the body is softly rounded, similar to Sunken A, but Sunken A figures are more elongated and show less fine detail. The collar necklaces, kilt belts and sashes, and arms that cross the body are all raised against the body's surface, and incised details indicate kilt folds and wig curls (Figures 33, 34, 37).

The second narrowly limited style of "Painted" panels occurs only in the double tomb of Mekhu and Sabni1 and the small chapel of IiShemai. While the fishing and fowling scene of Sabni1 and the two panels belonging to the subsidiary owners within the chapel space of Mekhu share a modified painted style that also incorporates engraved lines to form the exterior shape of the main figures, the two panels in IiShemai's chapel appear more purely painted. Nonetheless, in both cases the bulk of the images including all the interior details are executed only in paint. The figures share their proportions and overall form with Raised A1, and their facial features are generally similar (Plate VII). Along with these surviving panels, two false doors retain evidence of painted decoration – a subsidiary false door in the tomb of Mekhu, and the primary false door of Pepynakht Heqaib2 – yet, beyond medium, a close stylistic parallel cannot be established.

The third group of spatially focused styles occurs in the tomb of Sabni2. Although the images of this tomb owner on the façade are carved in Raised A1 (Sb1: lintel) and Raised A2 (Sb2, Sb5, Sb7: east jamb and west wall) styles, the raised relief images of Sabni2 inside his tomb are carved in a style with different proportions, body shapes, facial features, and details of clothing and musculature, called here "Sabni2 Raised" (Figures 58, 60). Furthermore, the sunken relief offering figures on his entrance thicknesses do not fully relate to any other styles in the cemetery, yet they share some qualities with the Sunken A style, and evoke aspects of the Sunken E style, as well; this style is labeled the "Sabni2 Sunken" (Figure 58, behind Sabni2).

Beyond these style groups, both the cemetery-wide and single-tomb types, there remain figures resistant to categorization, and certain panels and figures that are categorized retain non-conforming elements. This situation is a reminder that such processes of categorization are subjective and imposed upon the material, with the potential to obscure possibly significant visual details, but any unique or atypical details of individual figures and scenes can be more easily observed within the context provided by these broad categories.

Individual Tomb Overviews

The following discussion begins with the double tomb of Mekhu and Sabni1 at the southern end of the cemetery and proceeds northward, moving back and forth between the upper and lower tiers. Because the tombs have been published fully by Edel, Seyfried, and Vieler, what follows is a general description to provide a visual sense of the cemetery and each tomb. Pillars are designated by row, "E" for east, "W" for west, and "M" for middle if there is a third row; they are then numbered from south to north. Table 2 provides a complete list of scenes, with location and style identified, as well as correlation to the relevant references in the Qubbet el-Hawa volumes. Texts are provided in Appendix B organized by tomb, scene, and figure.

MEKHU AND SABNI1: QH 25, 26 (MS)

From the town site at Elephantine, the most visible marker of the elite cemetery is the double tomb of Mekhu and his son Sabni1 (Plate I). It marks the southern edge of the cemetery nearest to Elephantine, and is cut into the cliff that curves toward the south, its façade angled toward the island. The high doorways cutting through the pale, horizontal striations of the uniquely broad rock-cut façade and the parallel ramps running across the otherwise undisturbed pale surface of the slope create a visually dramatic statement that is easily visible from the town site and especially from the river. The sandy slope dropping steeply in front of the tomb makes it difficult to access directly, and today visitors to the site use a stairway more centrally situated along the cemetery's length, backtracking through the southern half to reach this monumental tomb. While ancient visitors may well have taken a similar roundabout way to the tomb, its visual dominance in the region is undiminished.

Originally begun as single monument for Mekhu, the tomb was expanded over a series of building phases to incorporate a separate chapel space for his son Sabni1. The chapels share a continuous façade, and a continuous forecourt enclosed by a rock cut wall, creating the image of a single monument, yet the dual ownership is also carefully indicated (Figure 6). Two parallel ramps, used to facilitate the transport of the sarcophagi from the river to the tomb, lead from just above the river's edge to the forecourt, and two doorways are cut into the façade opposite the ends of the ramps. Only the south entrance, leading into Mekhu's chapel,

6. View of the courtyard of the tomb of Mekhu and Sabni1.

is open its full 4-meter height. The workers encountered a number of complications in the northern expansion of the chapel, thus the northern entrance required greater structural support, so the builders incorporated a secondary, interior rock-cut wall that fills just over half the height of the doorway. Above the rock-cut wall, they left an open "window," which allowed light into Sabni1's chapel space. This structural resolution allowed the outer side of the entrance to mimic very closely the entrance to Mekhu's tomb, providing an element of ordered symmetry to the façade and thus visual parity between the two tomb owners. The locally popular obelisk-shaped stele flank both sides of both entrances, set up against the recessed jambs and secured into place with mortar. These highly unusual stele appear throughout the cemetery, and in all cases lack any text or images.

The evidence of dual ownership in the interior chapel space is more subtle (Figure 7). The chapel is essentially a single space, as the west wall runs directly from the south to north ends of the chapel. In addition, the interior columns that fill the space run along the same north-south axis, with relatively consistent spacing throughout. Thick, numerous columns dominate the space, lending the tomb a hypostyle-hall like quality that is quite different from other tombs here, such as those of Khunes

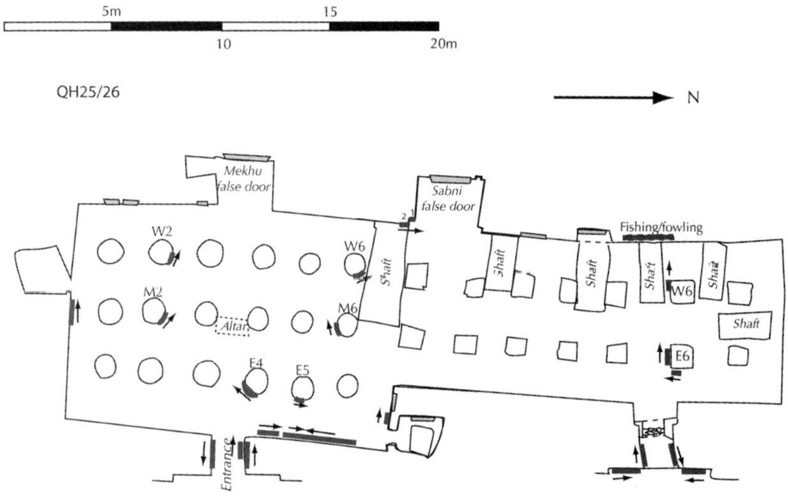

7. Plan of QH25/26, tomb of Mekhu and Sabni1.

and Harkhuf, where the columns do not overwhelm the chapel space. Although a visitor to the tomb perceives it as a coherent chapel, architectural features do in fact distinguish two separate spaces, divided roughly at the midpoint of the north-south axis. The later, northern expansion is narrower, so Sabni1's chapel has only two rows of supports, rather than the three rows present in Mekhu's section. Furthermore, the supports in Sabni1's chapel are rectangular pillars rather than the much rarer true columns of Mekhu's space. The result is a design that effectively unites two distinct spaces into a single form.

Another unusual aspect of this tomb is the presence of small chambers accessed from Mekhu's chapel, used for subsidiary burials. Although subsidiary burials occur in every other tomb in the cemetery, both within the chapels and more often in the forecourts, no other such burials included a separate, enclosed cult space. One subsidiary chamber extends off the south wall, the other off the northeastern corner. Both chambers include false doors, images of the buried officials, and a shaft and underground burial chamber.

The program of images and texts begins in the brightly lit forecourt and on the façade, and continues along the door thicknesses and into the interior chapel spaces. Within the chapel, the panels occupy areas illuminated by the sunlight streaming in through the doorway and Sabni1's window (Figure 8). Only the two panels associated with the interior subsidiary burials are not positioned to receive light. The composition and

8. View of interior columns in the tomb of Mekhu and Sabni1.

distribution of the panels reflects the conception and development of the double tomb's architecture; two separate programs, one for each tomb owner, can be identified, yet they are not fully divided by space. Elements of Sabni1's program appear in areas more directly linked to Mekhu; most likely these elements were executed prior to the final expansion of Sabni1's chapel area. Elements of composition and style link the two programs, but overall each program has distinct elements that set them apart.

Both Mekhu and Sabni1 are depicted in Raised A1 relief with family members and *ka*-priests on the thicknesses of their entrance doorways, which is common in elite tombs; however, the images here are unusual in the orientation of the tomb owner figures. Typically the tomb owner is depicted facing *out* of the tomb, meeting the priests and visitors who enter it, and representing his spirit's ability to exit the tomb after death; the images on the north thicknesses of Mekhu and Sabni1's doorways show the tomb owners in this position. On the south thicknesses, in contrast, the tomb owners face *into* the tomb. Edel et al. see symbolic intent in this orientation, suggesting the tomb owner was perceived to enter the tomb after death, depicted on the south, and then achieve resurrection within the sacred space of the tomb, to allow him to reemerge, as shown on the north.[11]

Mekhu and Sabni1 each have a stela set at opposite sides of the upper end of the southern ramp showing them facing a *ka*-priest, carved in a version of Raised A1 that is higher than typical, used perhaps for greater visibility in the bright sunlight. Mekhu's façade lacks embellishment, while Sabni1's façade had a full program of images and texts. The natural striations in the rock of the exposed façade have deepened over time, creating wide furrows and leaving only faint traces of the images and texts once inscribed here. Based on the relief type, shape of the bodies, and shape of the faces, it appears the images were carved in the Sunken A style. The texts carved above these images comprise Sabni1's autobiography, a long and well-known text in which Sabni1 details his journey into Nubia to retrieve the body of his father Mekhu. Above the figure of Sabni1's son Mekhu(2), just south of the entrance, a badly damaged text conveys Mekhu2's role in burying his father and serving his *ka*-cult, just as Sabni1 did for his own father.[12]

The builders attempted to compensate the structural instability of the northern entrance by further filling in the lower door with broken rock. As a result, only the southern entrance allows access to the chapel. As is true with the majority of tombs at Qubbet el-Hawa, the false door of Mekhu is set directly opposite the entrance, cut into the back of a deeply recessed niche in the west wall, which is partially enclosed by a short, rock-cut wall with a passageway in the center. Today, the axis from doorway to false door allows a view of the latter, but physical access is impeded by an offering table set up between the middle pair of columns. Furthermore, the excavators of this tomb found evidence of original mud-brick walls blocking off the area in front of the niche, which would not only control physical access to the niche, but prevent visual access, as well. The spiritual value of this central "cult axis" from entrance to false door, as it is described by Edel et al., seems to have conflicted with the Elephantine builders' perception of the false door area as a sacred space in need of protection and hiding. The consistency with which false doors are located directly across from tomb entrances throughout the cemetery strongly implies the local community's understanding of this architectural arrangement as functionally and spiritually essential. The presence of mud-brick blocking walls, in this case, equally indicates a concern with controlling levels of visibility, which may suggest that a mixed audience had access to the tomb chapel space.

The presence of visitors to the tomb chapel is also implied by the way the image and text panels are distributed throughout the space. Today a visitor to the tomb can see the false door, but even in the Old Kingdom when the cult niche was hidden, a person standing at the main doorway would have been able to see every other image in Mekhu's half of the chapel space, as they were located near eye level, facing toward the doorway, and in areas where sunlight entering through the doorway would illuminate them. Even part of Sabni I's false door is visible from Mekhu's entrance.

Interior walls adjacent to the entrance are typically illuminated by ambient light from the doorway, as is the case in Mekhu's tomb. The artists at work in this space exploited this visibility by attempting a somewhat unusual and ambitious panel on the northern section of this east wall (Plate IV). After preparing a long, narrow area centered between the edge of the door and the northeast corner of the chapel, the artists filled this surface with a set of loosely connected images, including agricultural subjects nearly absent from the rest of this cemetery. The artists arranged the figures in registers, but the organization is inconsistent, moving from two registers to three and back to two. These areas are carved in Raised A2 relief, but the upper south quadrant of the panel is carved in Sunken A, showing a scene of offerers led by Mekhu's inspector of *ka*-priests, Iienkhenit, seemingly disconnected from the rest of the composition. The height of the scene does not match up with the registers behind, and the figures face in the opposite direction, toward a figure of Mekhu in the Raised A1 style leaning forward on his staff with his front foot pulled back in a "watching" posture. It seems probable that either the upper scene of offerers was carved over earlier raised relief images, or that in the process of carving the full panel the decision was made to incorporate this panel of Iienkhenit and his family. In either case, interest in the image of identified offering figures wins out over the inclusion of a fully executed daily-life scene.

The remainder of Mekhu's program is comprised primarily of panels carved in Sunken A depicting *ka*-priests and their families. Also, a single figure with no accompanying inscription appears on column E5, on the east face nearest the extensively carved east wall. Though the figure is damaged, the broad, shorter proportions and raised relief ear and eye suggest a relationship to the Sunken D group. This figure faces to the north rather than toward Mekhu's false door. It may be directed toward SabniI's chapel, or alternately toward the subsidiary burial in the small chamber in the northeast corner. The last panel of Mekhu's program consists of a large-scale figure of SabniI that was drawn, but never carved, on column W2.

The choice to place images on columns M2 and W2 surely relates to the original presence of the mud-brick walls protecting the cult niche, as these columns were closest to the access point into the enclosed space. The fact that such images exist only outside this enclosed space, however, suggests again a concern for visibility by an audience. The specific placement of the relief panel on the northeast side of column M2 clearly reveals the effect of light on the location of the panels, as the west edge of this panel aligns with the edge of the band of sunlight that passes through the intervening columns. The same can be seen with the placement of two other relief panels on columns, M6 and W6, set along the path of light from the entrance that leads back to SabniI's false door (reference Figure 8). This location implies these figures were conceived as offering to SabniI rather than Mekhu, and were most likely carved here prior to the final expansion of SabniI's chapel to the north.

The remaining two image panels in Mekhu's chapel space belong to the two aforementioned subsidiary chapels. The panel next to the northeast corner chapel shows the presumed burial owner, Khwti, being censed by a *ka*-priest. Damage to this panel inhibits a clear assessment of its style, but it correlates with a larger group in this tomb best described as "engraved Painted." The figures are only slightly raised relief that in most places amounts to little more than an incised outline. Paint provides the majority of details, and the distinctive blue-gray background also appears in panels from other tombs. The panel associated with the southern chapel depicts the official Metjenw, who may be a brother of Mekhu,[13] along with his family and a *ka*-priest. This panel is similarly engraved painted, but is more directly linked stylistically to the large, painted fishing and fowling scene in SabniI's chapel.

The false doors of both Mekhu and SabniI are set into deep niches, and both are nearly 2.5 meters high. Both were covered in whitewash, and carved and painted with images and texts, though SabniI's false door was unfinished. Unlike Mekhu's, SabniI's niche does not have an enclosing rock-cut wall. Because the niche is not on axis with the entrance, the builders may have felt less of a need to protect it from access and view. They did build similar mud-brick walls to enclose the area in front of his false door; however, these walls enclosed only the east and north sides, leaving the southern side open. Both niches were reused in the past for habitation, resulting in extensive damage, blackening the paint and obscuring much of the original color and detail of the figures and hieroglyphs. The images do not fit securely into a style group, nor do they compare well to figures in other tombs. I noted before that several tombs contained images in a style that did not reach outside of the tomb; this may be an example of that phenomenon.

Along with the panels on columns M6 and W6 noted previously that are oriented toward Sabni1's false door, two more Sunken A panels are carved into the recess framing his false door niche. Both are badly damaged, though they retain some original paint. On the outer panel, the front figure is painted a light color that looks yellowish, while the rear figure has very dark skin that looks brown. Perhaps this color differentiation is due to environmental factors rather than original paint, but this remains unclear, and Edel et al. state the figure shows no remains of paint, which is odd[14] (Figure 9).

9. View of the false door of Sabni1 showing offering panels along the niche (MS28, MS29).

The remaining images in Sabni1's program are arranged along the axis from his entrance to the opposite wall, between pillars 5 and 6, the area that is illuminated by light entering from the window above Sabni1's doorway, and the area that is the ideal cult axis of his tomb. The smoothed north face of pillar W5 was never carved, while the opposite pillar holds only a single, small male priest carved in Raised A2. A large-scale figure of Sabni1 is carved on the south face of pillar E6 in the Raised A1 style and with a distinctive pointed earlobe, which the small figure on W6 echoes. The east face of E6 has a small panel of priests carved in Raised A2.

These images cluster around the axis to the focal point of Sabni1's program on the west wall, where light from the window creates a rectangular, illuminated surface filled with a fishing and fowling scene (Plate V). Above the panel there is a vertical niche (perhaps for a statue). The fishing and fowling scene with figures of the tomb owner placed in heraldic opposition and iconic postures is well known from Memphite and other provincial tombs and is one of the few scene types, other than offering figures, to be employed in this cemetery. This scene is clearly related to the larger, relief version on the east wall of Khunes's tomb, based upon the nearly identical shape and proportions of the tomb owner and compositional elements including the location of family members. A highly unusual detail more directly links these two scenes: the presence of the headrest leaning on its side. In Sabni1's version, the headrest sits atop two other objects (perhaps boxes of some kind) resting on the stern of the fowler's raft. Khunes's composition more awkwardly shows the headrest set well above the surface of the raft of the right-side fisher instead, but because the detail is so unusual, its incorporation into both scenes likely reflects local influence.[15]

This image fits best into the Painted style, yet it has a few lines outlining parts of the main figure that are more like grooves, given their width and shallow depth, than the incised outlines employed in the subsidiary panels in Mekhu's tomb. The bluish background and the strong black outlines around the painted figures link the style of this panel to the southern panel in Mekhu's chapel. While an exact version of this painted style does not appear in other tombs, some of the stylistic elements are used elsewhere, and the facial features of the fisher and fowler fit in well with those typical to the Raised A1 style.

The distribution of the discussed panels throughout the chapel reflects Mekhu and Sabni1's ownership of the space. Also within the space of their chapels, five additional, smaller false doors carved into the west wall, three south of Mekhu's cult niche and two north of SabniI's, stand as visual evidence of subsidiary burials. The numerous offering tables and basins recovered from the tomb also reveal the original use of the chapel space for the cult of several figures beyond the elite owners, presumably lower-ranked officials with connections to the family.

SOBEKHETEP QH 90 (SH)

Leaving the forecourt of Mekhu and SabniI's tomb and heading north, a path along the cliff's edge leads along the upper tier of tombs, coming first across the small tomb, QH26a. Along the northern edge of this tomb's forecourt, the slope of the cliff is cut away to facilitate the formation of a second, lower tier of tombs. The tomb of Sobekhetep sits on this lower tier, the largest tomb among a series cut side by side into a projecting section of the cliff's face (Figure 5). A visitor today accesses this lower tier from above by climbing down a sloping surface composed of packed debris from excavations in the cemetery. Originally, a stairway or more secure path may have been present; however, in the Middle Kingdom two additional small tombs were built into the sloping area at the southern end of the tier, obscuring any earlier architecture.

The tomb of Sobekhetep is located about 30 meters northwest of Mekhu and SabniI's forecourt, and shares with that tomb a close visual relationship to Elephantine and the surrounding environs. As tombs on the lower tier tend to be smaller than those on the upper tier, Sobekhetep's tomb is more difficult to distinguish from a distance. The neighboring tombs have façades of a similar height, and their respective forecourts are divided by partially built stone walls, conveying a kind of visual unity of this group, rather than distinguishing them individually (Figure 10). Evidence remains, however, of a ramp leading from the bottom edge of the escarpment directly into the forecourt of Sobekhetep's tomb, which may have enhanced the visual impact of his monument on the local community.

The ramp led directly into the forecourt that was at least partially paved, and the excavators found a number of unusual features within it, including small niches, possible model burials, and an unusual mud-plastered built feature in the floor, which they suggest was related to ritual activity that took place in the forecourt.[16] The façade of Sobekhetep's tomb is approximately 14 meters wide, roughly a third as wide as the façade of Mekhu and SabniI's tomb. The shorter doorway on the lower

10. View to the north from tomb of Sobekhetep.

façade is proportionately similar to the high doorways of Mekhu and Sabni1, and it is cut near the north side of the façade, set within a narrow rectangular recess. Two obelisk-shaped stele flanked both sides of the doorway, but no evidence of text or images inscribed on the façade survives, nor are there any reliefs on the thicknesses of the entrance leading into the tomb.

The roughly rectangular yet irregularly shaped tomb is significantly smaller than the double tomb of Mekhu and Sabni1, but at roughly 90 meters square, it is among the larger Old Kingdom tombs in the cemetery, especially those on the second tier (Figure 11). Sobekhetep's tomb was also expanded over a series of building phases, beginning only with the area around the doorway, and then extending southward. Like all tombs on the second tier, the ceiling is much lower than the ceiling in Mekhu and Sabni1's tombs, reaching just over half that height (2.55 m). The space is filled with roughly rectangular pillars arranged in three rows that follow the angled line of the east wall. The size of the pillars varies, and several pillars do not maintain consistent surfaces from floor to ceiling. The irregular angles of the chapel and the high number of pillars arranged in bent rows create a crowded and somewhat disorienting space, but this effect is countered by the primary cult axis from entrance to main false door.

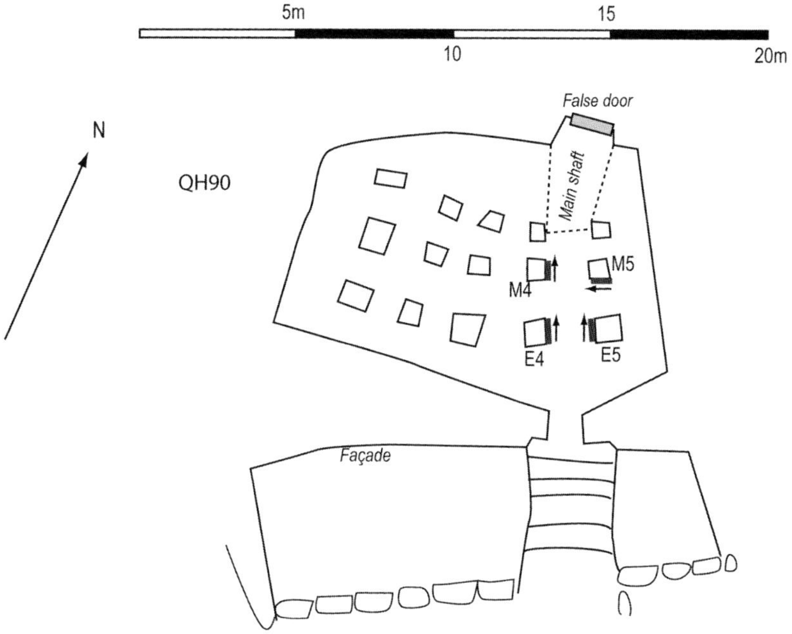

11. Plan of QH90, tomb of Sobekhetep.

As in the tomb of Mekhu, Sobekhetep's false door is cut into a niche recessed into the west wall directly across from the entrance (Figure 12). It retains a thick layer of bright whitewash, but no texts or images survive. The whitewash similarly survives throughout the northern area of the tomb, on the pillars and wall surfaces. By focusing this visual tool in the area between the entrance and false door, the combination of sunlight streaming in through the entrance and whitewashed surfaces produce a brightly illuminated area devoted to the cult of Sobekhetep. The four painted relief panels comprising the tomb's program are located on pillars E4, E5, and M4 on the side facing the entrance axis, and on the east face of pillar M5. All of the panels receive direct light through the doorway, are set near or slightly above eye level, and are easily visible from the entrance of the tomb. Similarly to Mekhu's tomb chapel, evidence remains of a partial wall blocking easy view of the false door, but not of the four panels. This evidence suggests, as it did in Mekhu's tomb, a concern with the visibility of the images, as well as visually protecting the false door, indicating a possibly mixed audience in the tomb.

Although Sobekhetep's tomb is relatively large, it employs a small, concise text and image program that focuses on the tomb owner and two of his high-ranking *ka*-priests, Sobekhetep and Mekwt. Each *ka*-priest is

12. View from entrance to false door in tomb of Sobekhetep.

shown once with the tomb owner and once with his own family. The two tomb owner panels are carved in Raised A1/A2, and both retain some paint. The panel on pillar M5 has the blue-gray background seen in other tombs, but no evidence of that survives on the other. An unusual detail of the M5 panel is the bolt of cloth Sobekhetep grasps with his back hand, which the artist apparently envisioned as attached to, or part of, his long kilt (Plate VI).

The higher-ranking "overseer of *ka*-priests" Sobekhetep appears on pillar E5 with his family, carved in Raised A2, which is uncommon for full panels of offering figures; it is used more often for single figures associated with images of the tomb owner (Figure 13). The postures and offerings are similar to those in Sunken A style panels, a reminder of the links between different styles and the likely existence of shared or overlapping artistic influences. Diagonally across the axis on pillar M4, a panel carved in Sunken A depicts the lower-ranking "inspector of *ka*-priests," Mekwt, with his family (Plate VIII). The relatively lengthy text written across the top of the panel refers to the payment of *ka*-priests in the form of food via a reversion of offerings.[17] It is one among several such texts throughout the cemetery that provide insight into the role of *ka*-cults in the local economy. This theme will be discussed further in Chapter 4.

13. Relief of a *ka*-priest and his family in the tomb of Sobekhetep (SH2).

Whether a larger program or additional cult places had been planned is unclear; as it exists, the distribution of the image and text program concentrates the visitors' attention in the area of the cult axis of Sobekhetep. Three styles are represented: Raised A1 and A2 and Sunken A, but all the figures here have individualistic character and extensive attention to detail.

II-SHEMAI SETKA: QH 98 (IS)

A mild flattening of the cliff slope and the recessed position of the tombs allows for relatively easy passage along the lower tier, moving north from the tomb of Sobekhetep. One passes a number of small tombs, some no more than short tunnels, following the curving line of the cliff face, until approximately 50 meters north, where the southwest to northeast line returns. Another series of primarily small tombs is cut into this area, extending up to the edge of a ramp leading to the upper tier tomb QH34a; this group includes the tombs of Ii-Shemai Setka, Khwin-Khnum, and Tjetji (Figure 5).

Although still in the southern section of the cemetery, this group is significantly less visible from the town site and environs than either Mekhu and Sabni1 or Sobekhetep. The tombs here are set slightly lower than those further south on the same tier, and the ground in front of them slopes up from their forecourts, leaving their relatively small façades less visible from a distance. Large sections of the cliff above these tombs remain hanging over their façades. The tomb of Ii-Shemai Setka is the southernmost in this section, with views that encompass a wide scope of the surrounding area. The island and the west and east banks flanking it all remain fully visible, and to the north one can see the initial bend of the river before it disappears around the mountain.

The ramp leading up to this tomb is entirely buried, if indeed any significant portion remains, but is evident in the stairs leading up into the forecourt, as in the forecourt of Sobekhetep's tomb. The unstable rock at this location required the façade to be both relatively small, approximately 5 meters wide, and built up with broken stone on the north. A section of the cliff face projecting over the entrance to Ii-Shemai's tomb was incorporated into the rectangular area of the façade like an exaggerated, albeit irregularly shaped, lintel. The doorway, set within the recessed portal niche, rises just under 2 meters, less than half the height of the façade (Figure 14).

The tomb of Ii-Shemai Setka is the smallest of the tombs discussed here. The plan is an irregular rectangle running nearly 8 meters long

14. Façade of tomb of IiShemai.

north to south with a single row of three pillars and a low ceiling, about 2 meters high, similar to the tombs of Pepynakht Heqaib1 and Harkhuf (Figure 15). The entrance to the tomb is slightly south of center, and the false door stele is carved into the west wall slightly north of center, between the two northern pillars. This bent axis from entrance to false door is also similar to the arrangement in the tombs of Pepynakht Heqaib1 and Harkhuf. Several brick walls were built within the tomb, dividing the interior space into smaller cult areas, but only one, extending northward off the south wall, remains. Three low doorways lead out of the main chapel space, one on each of the south, west, and north walls, all to separate burial chambers. Despite the clear indications that the space was utilized for several separate cults, the images and texts all refer to the primary tomb owner, IiShemai Setka.

The program consists of four panels: one on the east face of both the south and north pillars; one above the passageway cut through the south wall; and one on the east wall, north of the entrance. The panel on the south pillar shows Ii-Shemai facing south, wearing a leopard skin robe and set against a blue-gray background that is bordered on the top and left sides with bands of colored hieroglyphs set against a white background, the same design used in the tomb of Sobekhetep, and which also appears in the tomb of Khwin-Khnum. The panel on the north pillar (Plate VII) uses the same composition, but here two small priest figures face him. Both panels employ grooves around the edges of the figures,

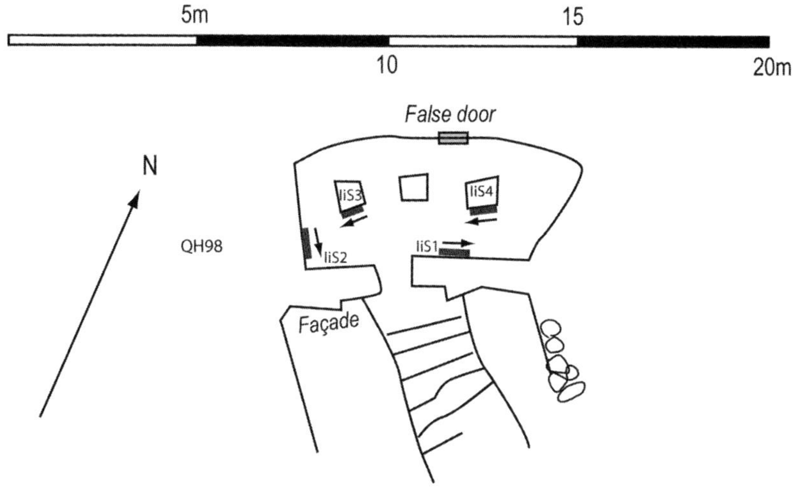

15. Plan of QH98, tomb of IiShemai Setka.

but the panel on the north pillar more fully qualifies as relief through deeper and wider grooves, while the panel on the south pillar is much flatter and closer to pure painting. The use of grooves in a largely painted image recalls the fishing and fowling scene in the chapel of Sabni1.

The two other panels are slightly more complex, both pieced together from separate panel parts, and both showing IiShemai with *ka*-priests and offering figures leading animals. The south panel is painted, with no outline grooves, and with black outlines and a blue-gray background. At the back, three lines of hieroglyphs set against a white background inscribe a text referencing the payment of the *ka*-priests. The east panel is carved in the Raised A2 style, except above the area of offering figures there is a narrow band of painted birds. Differing ground lines and media here indicate that different parts of the image were composed and executed separately, which in turn emphasizes the scene of tomb owner faced by a *ka*-priest as the conceptual heart of the image. Although images of offering bearers accompanying animals are quite common in elite tomb programs of the Sixth Dynasty, only a handful of such scenes exist at Qubbet el-Hawa. The content and style of relief and painting closely link this panel to the large east wall panel in the tomb of Mekhu, which corresponds to the chronological links between these tomb owners evident in offering vessels from several tombs.

KHWIN-KHNUM: QH 102 (KK)

Just north of IiShemai's tomb, past a soft curve of the cliff face, the slope of the cliff alters, and as a result the tombs here are cut 4–5 meters lower than those to the south. This area is occupied by three tombs: QH102-102a-102b, a main chapel with two associated chambers of Khwin-Khnum; QH102c, belonging to a man named Imbi; and QH103 of Tjetji.

The tomb of Khwin-Khnum is located just 30 meters north of Ii-Shemai's tomb, but because of its lower level the tomb forecourt and entrance are easily encroached by blown sand and debris. Modern efforts to keep this process at bay allow continued access to the tomb, though much of the forecourt is covered with sand. The views from the tomb entrance itself are rather limited, but views from the higher area in front of the tomb encompass both the island of Elephantine and its surroundings, as well as to the north the initial bend of the river and green trees of the fertile area north of the cliff. Though one can presume the tomb in its original state was more clearly visible, the tomb's lower setting and connection to surrounding tombs would have made it less distinctive than other, especially larger, tombs in the cemetery.

By working at a lower level, the original builders were able to isolate a sufficient area of solid stone for the creation of the tomb, including a 10.5-meter-wide and 6-meter-high façade. The 2.5-meter-high doorway is cut through the center of the recessed portal niche, following the model for Qubbet el-Hawa tomb façades. Two obelisk stele flank the doorway, and within the doorway itself two stone slabs are set along both door thicknesses, and a third slab functions as a threshold. Passing through the doorway, one steps down to enter the chapel space.

Khwin-Khnum's tomb chapel is about two-thirds the size of Sobekhetep's, with a rectangular plan measuring roughly 9.5 meters by 6.5 meters (Figure 16). The uneven ceiling is overall rather low, just more than 2 meters high. The two rows of irregularly shaped, squared pillars dominate the small space. Overall, the small area, inconsistently sized and shaped pillars and uneven floor, create a confined space of difficult access (Figure 17). A low opening in the north wall leads into the neighboring tomb, 102a, that likely belonged to Khwin-Khnum's wife. A similar architectural arrangement exists in the tomb of Khunes and his wife Ankhes.

The primary cult niche is situated directly opposite the entrance, creating a cult axis that divides the space. A wall built from broken stone between pillars W2 and W3 survives approximately 1 meter up from the ground, though the excavators estimate it originally rose around 1.6 meters, blocking the false door from view but allowing light through a space between the wall and ceiling. An offering table stood in front of this wall, centered between the two pillars. The cult niche is a bit deeper than Sobekhetep's, and along the front edge of the niche a small rock-cut ledge with a rounded top and small gap at the center encloses the space. The form is similar to that of the large cult niche in the tomb of Mekhu, though here on a much smaller scale. The false door is carved out of the back wall of the niche, though no texts or images survive.

As in Sobekhetep's tomb, the image and text program occupies four pillars along the cult axis. The two pillars closest to the entrance, E2 and E3, each have two faces with carved and painted images – the east faces visible from the entrance and their north and south faces, respectively, lining the entrance axis. Pillars W2 and W3 have panels only on their east

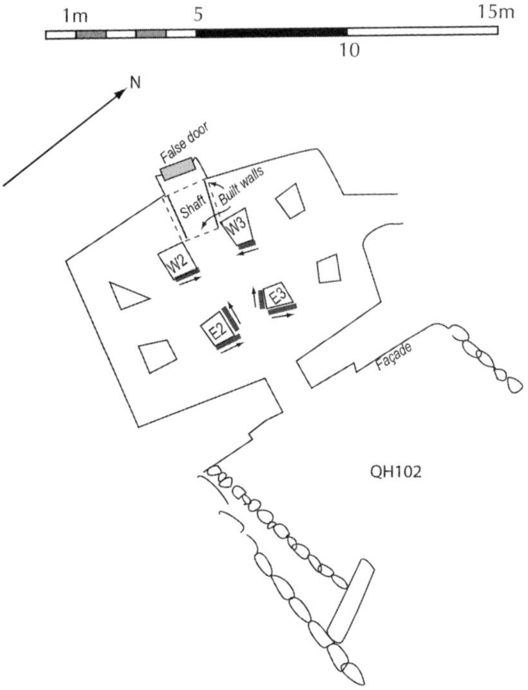

16. Plan of QH102, tomb of Khwin-Khnum.

17. Interior view of the tomb of Khwin-Khnum.

faces. Four of the six panels in this tomb include an image of the tomb owner, and the variations in detail displayed among these images well illustrates the visual range encompassed by the Raised A1 style, as well as the ways in which different styles may overlap.

On the east face of pillar E2 Khwin-Khnum is depicted seated, holding a staff in front of him and a scepter angled up from his lap; Khui, Pepynakht Heqaib2, and Sabni2 are shown in the same posture in their respective programs. A small chest, a headrest, and a scribal palette are stacked underneath his chair, reminiscent of the stack of offerings at the back of the fowler's raft in Sabni1's fishing and fowling scene. A handful of subsidiary figures in other tombs at Qubbet el-Hawa are shown with scribal palettes, but this is the only example of one belonging to an elite tomb owner.

This panel shares the same basic design with the other three depicting Khwin-Khnum of the tomb owner faced by his wife and/or a *ka*-priest, with framing inscriptions. On pillars E2 and W2, the blue-gray background survives, but on E3 the surviving inscriptions are painted in blue-gray, suggesting the background here was not painted. The pillar on W3 not only has a different color palette, consisting of red, yellow, black, and white, as well as a light gray on the background, it is also carved in a shallow version of Sunken A, rather than Raised A1 as the other three (Plate IX).

The other two panels show cult officials, both including the *ka*-priest Kari. On the north face of E2, two registers of priests carved in the Sunken A style bring offerings and animals, though the ox and oryx here are carved in raised relief (Plate XIa). The ox is nearly identical to the oxen in the tombs of Mekhu and IiShemai. Another small panel in the tomb of Sabni2 combines a sunk relief human figure and a raised relief animal. On the south face of pillar E3, a group with Kari following his two daughters is carved in the Raised A2 style (Plate XIb). A light blue-gray fills the background behind the inscription and the figures.

All four figures of the tomb owner are stylistically linked, yet they show distinctive formal variations. One figure is carved in a more standard low raised relief, two are carved in a much lower raised relief using deep grooves around the outline, and the fourth is carved in sunk relief. In addition, there are variations in the style of facial features, shape of the body, and color palette. The small figures show a similar range of variations, and the composition on pillar E2 unusually combines sunk and raised relief. The subtle yet unmistakable visual diversity in this small constellation of images speaks to underlying aspects of the local conception of style in their tomb programs. An apparent sense of visual decorum diverges from ideal standards, and does not seem to limit flexibility and experimentation.

TJETJI: QH 103 (TJ)

The path northward along this row of tombs continues along the mound of excavated debris and blown sand, above the level of the tomb entrances. Approximately 20 meters north of Khwin-Khnum's tomb, the slope of this mound begins to descend as one reaches the bend of the cliff. The last tomb along this southern stretch is the tomb of Tjetji. The view from Tjetji's tomb encompasses Elephantine and the breadth of the Nile surrounding it, though the tomb itself faces the east bank. From Tjetji's forecourt it is possible to see the initial westward bend of the Nile, but like the views from Khwin-Khnum and Ii-Shemai, the river quickly disappears behind the cliff. Just north of Tjetji's tomb, the escarpment begins its gradual curve back toward the west, and this eastern-most projection is home to a number of tombs cut at different levels and with higher entrances (Plate II, center). These tombs are significantly more prominent, especially as a group, than Tjetji's tomb, yet the geographical juxtaposition in fact makes Tjetji's tomb more easily identifiable from a distance. The wide façade aids its visibility, as does the ramp leading to the upper tier of tombs that frames its northern edge.

The floor of Tjetji's forecourt is today layered with blown sand, fallen stones, and debris, covering the end of the ramp that leads up into his forecourt, as well as the steps from the ramp to the entrance. The façade is more than 10 meters wide, framed on the south and north by partially rock-cut walls. The doorway sits off-center to the south, and the deep, vertical faults in the façade suggest the structural concerns that made this asymmetry necessary. The top of an obelisk stele is visible on the south side of the entrance.

Despite the wide façade, Tjetji's tomb is relatively small, just over half the size of Khwin-Khnum's tomb. The plan is roughly rectangular along a north-south axis, but is skewed to the north (Figure 18). The slant of the walls disturbs the typically orienting role of the axis from entrance to false door that in this case is both off-center and interrupted by a column. There are also two niches in the west wall, one at the southern

Plate I. View of southern end of Qubbet el-Hawa.

Plate II. View of northern end of Qubbet el-Hawa.

Plate IIIa. View south from Qubbet el-Hawa.

Plate IIIb. View north from Qubbet el-Hawa.

Plate IV. East wall in the tomb of Mekhu (MS7, 7a).

Plate V. Fishing and fowling scene in the tomb of Sabni1 (MS27).

Plate VI. Sobekhetep with *ka*-priest (SH3).

Plate VII. IiShemai with two *ka*-priests (IiS4).

Plate VIII. *Ka*-priest and family in the tomb of Sobekhetep (SH4).

Plate IX. Khwin-Khnum with *ka*-priest (KK6).

Plate X. Offering figures in the tomb of Tjetji (Tj4).

(a)

(b)

Plate XI. (a) Offering figures with animals in the tomb of Khwin-Khnum (KK2); (b) *Ka*-priest and family in the tomb of Khwin-Khnum (KK4).

Plate XII. Interior view of the tomb of Harkhuf (H9–12 visible).

Plate XIII. Lower portion of the north entrance thickness in the tomb of Pepynakht Heqaib2 (PnH7).

Plate XIV. North section of the east wall in the tomb of Pepynakht Heqaib2 (PnH15–21).

Plate XV. Panel F in the tomb of Pepynakht Heqaib2 (PnH13).

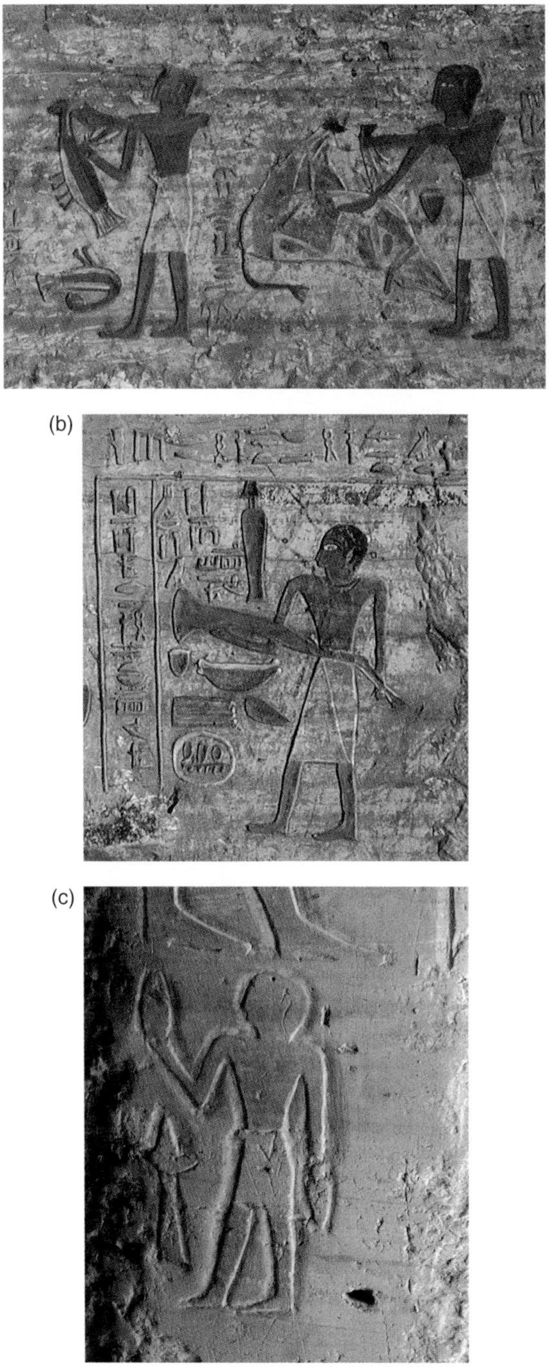

Plate XVI. (a) Detail of Panel C in the tomb of Pepynakht Heqaib2 (PnH10); (b) Detail of Panel E in the tomb of Pepynakht Heqaib2 (PnH12); (c) Detail of offering figure in the tomb of Tjetji (Tj3a).

Plate XVII. Panel I in the tomb of Pepynakht Heqaib2 (PnH15).

Plate XVIII. Panel T in the tomb of Pepynakht Heqaib2 (PnH28).

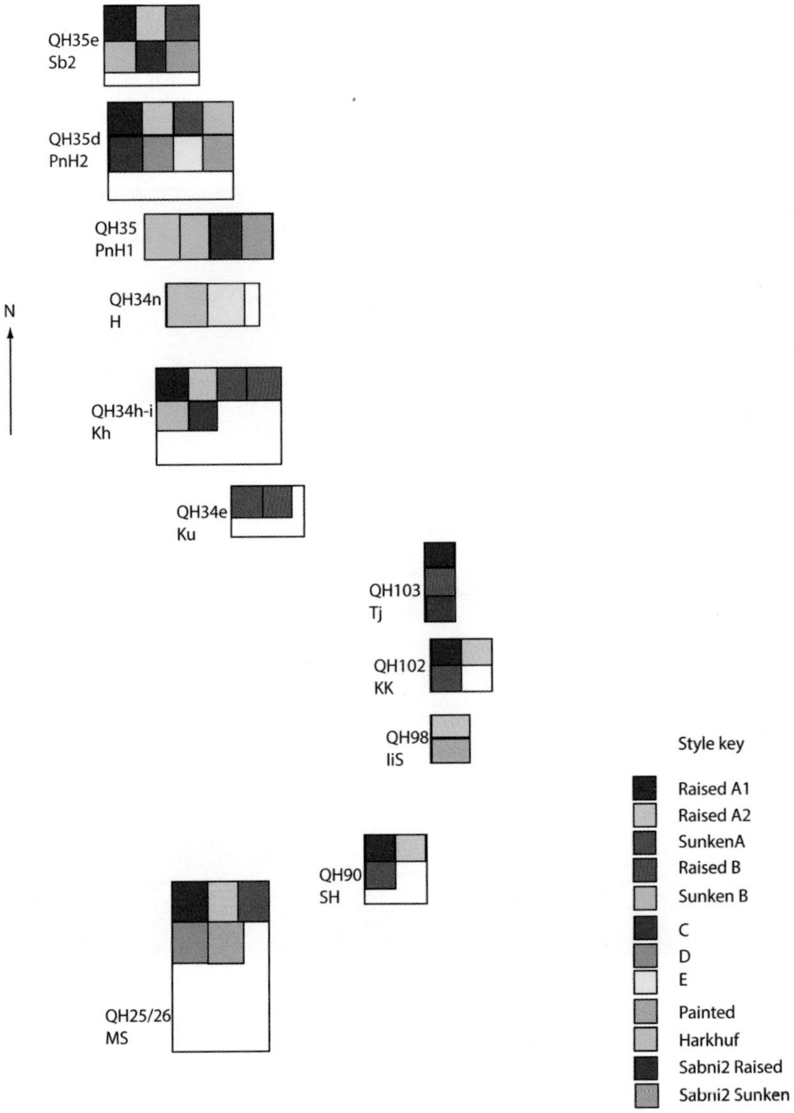

Plate XIX. Schematic plan of the distribution of styles among the Old Kingdom tombs at Qubbet el-Hawa.

end that appears to have been covered by a false door stele, and a second directly opposite the entrance that seems likely to have housed a statue of the tomb owner. Columns are very unusual in rock-cut tombs in Egypt, and they appear in this cemetery only a handful of times, most notably in the tomb of Mekhu. In Tjetji's chapel, the two rows of three columns align more strictly than the walls to the local north-south axis. The disjuncture in angles and axes between columns and walls contributes to an overall effect of an unorganized space.

Evidence remains of a somewhat complicated building history that appears to have included structural adaptations during the initial phases of cutting and decorating the tomb. Two walls built from broken pieces of stone filled the spaces between columns W1, W2, and E2, creating barriers between the entrance and access to the main false door. Enough of the north-south wall survives to show the original passageway left in the wall, as well as one obelisk stela in place on the north side of this passage, an arrangement that mimics the entrance to the tomb chapel itself. Evidence for additional mud-brick walls survives in several other places, creating barriers between a central cult area and the secondary shafts and cults.

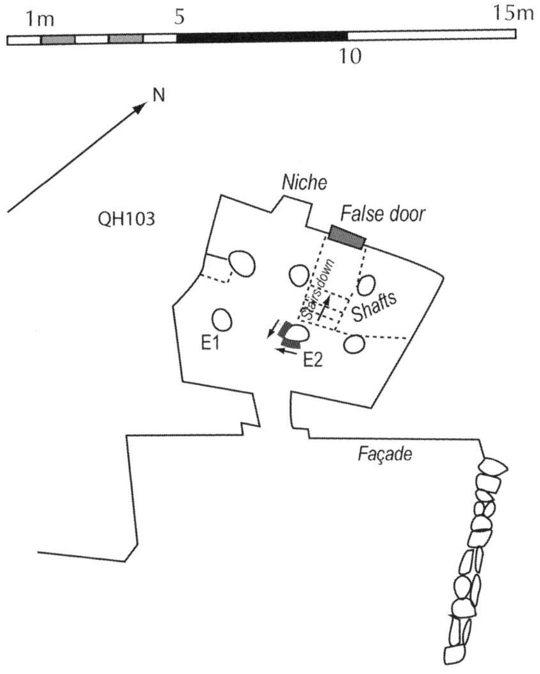

18. Plan of QH103, tomb of Tjetji.

The excavators also discovered that the north side of column E1 initially had been prepared for an inscription prior to being covered by stone slabs and integrated into a wall connecting the column to the east wall of the chapel. The east side of the column was also initially prepared for an image, and a surviving hieratic inscription indicates the intended content of the image, which was apparently carved on the neighboring column E2 instead. Other than these elements, the program occupies only one column – E2, centered in the tomb and set between the entrance and the primary false door. The prepared surfaces flatten the curve of the column, rather than following it as in Mekhu's tomb. The south face of column E2 originally mirrored the design of E1; remnants of the painted black hieroglyphs are visible near the top of the column. A second inscription that began with a title of higher rank was inscribed on top of the painted signs. Below the inscription there is an image of the tomb owner facing toward the tomb entrance carved in the Raised A1 style (Figure 19). Below, a small offering figure facing the opposite direction is carved in the distinctive Raised B style (Plate XVIc). A panel of offering figures carved in the Sunken C style fills the upper part of the east side of column E2 (Plate X). The panel has two registers of cult officials. The two figures on the top are both named Khnumhetep, and the female figure below is identified as Hrwemkawes, who we know from an inscription in the tomb of Khui to be Khnumhetep's daughter.

The program in Tjetji's tomb chapel is unusually concise, but it nonetheless incorporates three different styles. Evidence indicates that initial plans for the program were changed in response to architectural concerns and adaptation, as well as to an elevation of Tjetji's titulary, suggesting the passing of an uncertain amount of time over the course of the tomb's initial construction and ultimate completion for use.

KHUI: QH 34E (KU)

North of Ttjetji's tomb, the remains of a ramp running to a tomb on the upper tier mark the edge of the southern section of the cemetery, where the cliff begins to curve back toward the west. On the upper section of the cliff's curve, the rocky face was cut and dressed to create a high, 45-meter-long continuous span, slightly curved to follow the shape of the cliff, and divided only by one low, rock-cut wall. Four tombs are cut into this area; three on the north are linked together in a family group; the southern tomb belongs to Khui. The entire area was reused

19. Column in the tomb of Tjetji (Tj3, 3a).

by the ancient local Coptic community, and each of these four tombs was adapted for use as spaces for living and ritual. Significant remains of this reuse survive, including in Khui's tomb mud-brick walls in both the forecourt and interior, and extensive plastering of the interior surfaces of the chapel. On the top of the cliff above Khui's façade, several mud-brick walls of monastery buildings survive nearly their full height. These walls exaggerate the visual impact of the vertical reach of Khui's façade, as they mimic in color, flatness, and orientation the façade of Khui's tomb. Although this visual impact is anachronistic, the Coptic community's selection of this location speaks to its appeal within the cemetery, as it is both visually conspicuous in the area and one providing both cool breezes and encompassing views.

The tomb of Khui marks the approximate midpoint of the cemetery's upper tier, cut into the first part of the cliff that faces northeast, rather than southeast toward the island. The tomb thus cannot be seen from the settlement site or the area around the island, but as you sail downstream and pull alongside the bend of the cliff, the tomb is easily recognized given its wide façade and prominent location on the easternmost projection of the cliff. From the forecourt of Khui's tomb only the north half

20. View south from the courtyard of tomb of Khui.

of Elephantine Island is visible, but the east bank and the river stretching northward can be fully viewed (Figure 20).

The high façade of Khui's tomb is enclosed only on the northern end by a low, rock-cut wall. The southern side of the façade extends continuously to the edge of the cliff's curve. The expansiveness of the façade was matched initially by a large forecourt, which is now mostly covered by the remains of Coptic buildings and the debris from their decay. Damage to the façade does not hide the original recessed portal niche, into which the entrance to the tomb chapel was cut.

Upon entering the tomb chapel of Khui, it appears both more open and more orderly than many of the other Qubbet el-Hawa tombs. The plan is nearly square, only slightly wider than deep, and the axis from entrance to false door divides the space almost equally (Figure 21). Four large pillars arranged in two rows align the central axis and enhance the sense of careful organization in the chapel plan. The strength of the rock in this area likely contributed to the consistent alignment of the four walls as well as the smooth surfaces and regular angles of the pillars. The size of the door in relation to the size of the space, as well as its regular layout, allows the full chapel space to be relatively well lit, unlike other tombs thus far visited.

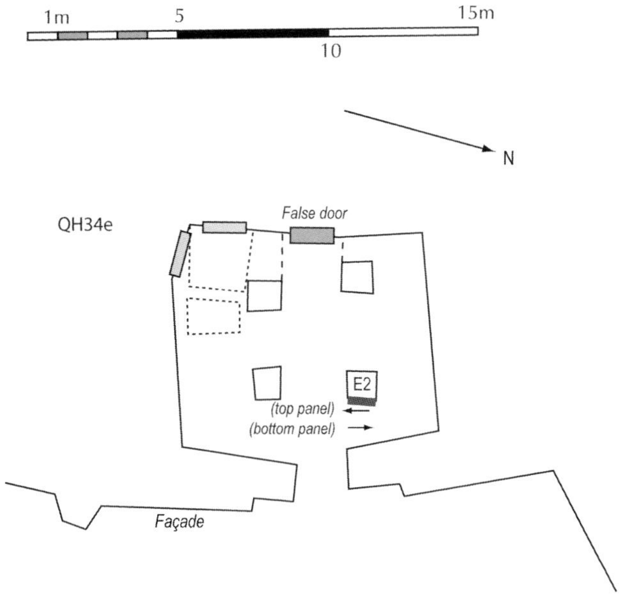

21. Plan of QH34e, tomb of Khui.

Especially distinctive to this tomb is the visual and physical accessibility of the primary false door (Figure 22). It is situated on the west wall directly opposite the entrance, as is traditional in the cemetery, but in this case it is not set into a recessed niche. Remains of two built stone walls between the western pillars and the west wall originally enclosed the cult area around the false door, but there remains no evidence of internal walls along the east side blocking the cult axis, such as those that survive in the tombs of Tjetji and Khwin-Khnum, or that once existed in the tombs of Mekhu and Sabni1, Sobekhetep, and IiShemai. Given the reuse of this chapel by the Copts and the extensive modifications to the space, it is difficult to be certain of the tomb chapel's original status; however, the excavators are fairly convinced that the other surviving interior walls were Coptic, and that no other original walls have been lost. The possibility of such openness between the exterior of the tomb and the large and visible false door veers from the local tradition.

The primary false door extends 2 meters up on the west wall and is nearly 1.5 meters wide, visually filling the space between the rows of pillars. Whitewash covers the surface of the false door that is now quite damaged, though faint remains of sunken relief texts and images survive, including a standard offering formula along the lintel, two standing figures of Khui along the jambs, and Khui seated at an offering table on the

22. View of the interior of the tomb of Khui.

stela. The damage to the door hinders certain identification of the style, though the images appear to be related to Sunken A.

Two smaller false doors are carved into the walls forming the southwest corner. No images or texts survive on the southern false door, but enough survived on the west wall door at the time of excavation for Edel to identify its owner as one Khnumhetep. This Khnumhetep also appears in one of only two scenes in the tomb's image program, in an unusual composition with an even more unusual text, providing support for the idea that Khui would grant him the favor of sharing his tomb, despite his apparently not meeting sufficient elite status to earn his own.

Khui's tomb chapel, with its smooth surfaced walls and pillars and far-reaching light provides numerous areas for images and texts. Nonetheless, it appears that only the east face of pillar E2 was carved with relief images, although the damage caused by reuse may have obscured scenes on the other eastern pillar. A large area on pillar E2 was smoothed, and there are two scenes carved here. At the top, a relatively small figure of Khui is depicted seated facing south, holding a staff and a scepter angled up from his lap. In front of him are two columns of hieroglyphs, and south of the inscription, two small male offering figures. All the figures are carved in the Sunken A style.

Below this image of the tomb owner, a larger scene consisting of three registers of offering figures all carved in the Raised B style fills the width of the pillar (Figure 23). In total there are eighteen figures, which is high for a single group in this cemetery. Most of the figures carry offerings, but one figure on the top register butchers a cow, and the back three on the bottom register are engaged in production activities including grinding grain and stirring beer. Other than in the Memphite-like sections of Khunes's tomb, these activities are depicted in only one other panel in the cemetery, in the tomb of Pepynakht Heqaib2. Twelve of the eighteen figures are identified via inscriptions accompanying their figures; all four figures on the top register bear the name Khnumhetep, and may represent the same individual. His wife and children, including his daughter Hrwmkawes, appear in the middle register, and additional cult officials appear in the third.

A lengthy inscription written in very small, uneven hieroglyphs runs across the top of the top register in irregular rows. It is written as if spoken by Khnumhetep, and it describes his work on expeditions under the leadership of both Khui and Tjetji, the owner of tomb 103. The entire panel is carved in the relatively rare Raised B style that also appeared in

23. Detail of relief of Khnumhetep in the tomb of Khui (Ku2).

the tomb of Tjetji. The dominant image of Khui atop the pillar forms the focal point of the offering activities of these figures, who all apparently functioned in his *ka*-cult. Yet the unusually lengthy inscription of Khnumhetep, the presence of his burial and false door in this chapel, and the large group of figures in this scene suggests some of the figures may have been perceived as supporting his personal *ka*-cult, as well.

KHUNES: QH 34H (KH) AND ANKHES: QH 34G (AN)

Moving northward from Khui's crowded forecourt, one follows the face of the cliff as it bends back toward the west and comes upon a wide-open forecourt fronting an extended, though now damaged, façade. This high and very wide façade encloses three tomb chapels, linked together through interior passages. The largest of these chapels is the northernmost, belonging to the elite official Khunes. Set at the top end of the longest surviving staircase in the cemetery, the tomb presents the most dramatic space in the cemetery. Possibly under the impact of an earthquake, the north side of the high façade collapsed, exposing the extremely high interior space of the chapel and leaving massive chunks of sandstone along its eastern edge (Figure 24). The later adaptation of the space by the early Coptic community survives in fragmentary remains both within the chapel and to the north of it, in the form of ruined brick walls and a painted apse. The damaged façade south of Khunes's was recarved into a staircase, allowing access to a church built atop the eastern projection of the cliff. The intense interest in this location is easily understood under the sway of the sweeping views to the north and south, and cool breezes along the exposed edge of the site, but the natural damage and centuries of human activity also render this space extremely complex and overwhelming at first sight.

A modern visitor first encounters Khunes's tomb from more than 100 meters away, at the base of the longest ramp in the cemetery, which leads from the low desert surface directly to his chapel. While the surviving ramps of Mekhu and Sabni1 are flanked by steps, Khunes's ramp is in fact entirely steps. At the upper end of the staircase, just before the stairs reach the tomb, they are divided by a horizontal passage leading westward, ending at a vertical surface on line with Khunes's façade. Into this surface, three shaft entrances for subsidiary burials are cut side by side, and a small false door is carved to their south. Smaller staircases lead from both sides of this horizontal passage up to the ground level

24. View of the façade of the tomb of Khunes.

of Khunes's chapel. This unusually structured upper part of the ramp hinders access into the chapel, as well as passage from the southern to northern parts of the cemetery. Most likely it was filled at some point to facilitate movement through the space.

Edel et al. argue that this unusual formation represents one of many adaptations made by the builders to the traumatic effects of an earthquake.[18] The massive sandstone chunks of façade debris that equally impede passage into the chapel provide the most apparent support for this theory, yet determining the timing of the event presents more uncertainty. Edel et al. argue that the earthquake occurred during the construction of Khunes's chapel, and they knit together several unusual architectural features as responses to the disaster, including not only the upper area of the ramp, but also the presence of a supporting column in the burial chamber (for added stability), and the arrangement of the interior program, concentrated as it is in the southern half of the tomb, the only area suitable following the destruction of the northern façade. Their ingenious analysis provides a persuasive argument for the complex architectural situation of the tomb; however, the Jaén team led by Alejandro Jimenez Serrano currently working at the site identified the fragile nature of the rock in this location, suggesting the destruction could have resulted simply from the process of excavating the tomb.[19] Either scenario implies the damage occurred during the creation of the tomb, and thus provides a useful framework for examining the tomb as it stands.

Despite the extensive damage and reuse, enough remains of the chapel to hint at its original (or only intended) appearance. The façade reaches more than 6 meters high on the standing southern half, where the outer edges of the recessed portal niche and the southern side of the tomb entrance also remain. The niche was a bit more than 5.5 meters high, while probably only 3.8 meters wide, and the entrance reached more than 5 meters, as well, on par with the monumental entrances of Mekhu and Sabni1. This elaborate façade and entrance dominates the tomb group; the other chapels were accessed through much smaller and simpler doorways cut through their continuous façade.

Khunes's tomb chapel is relatively large with a rectangular ground plan (Figure 25). Although the floor area is slightly smaller than the tomb of Sobekhetep, the ceiling is nearly twice as high, approximately 5 meters, one of the highest spaces in the cemetery. In addition, this tomb has only two rows of four pillars each, in contrast to Sobekhetep's three rows of five pillars. In proportion to the large interior space, the pillars are very thin. The use of fewer pillars combined with such a high ceiling created a soaring space that emphasizes openness, in contrast to the subdued, enveloping space in Mekhu and Sabni1's tomb, or the close, disordered feel of Sobekhetep's and Tjetji's tombs.

Stepping out of the bright sunlight and into the chapel space proper, the extent of the Coptic community's work here unfolds. The fallen north façade was transformed into a platform between the northern pillars, and a small staircase leads from the platform's surface down to the chapel floor. Distinct pinkish-white plaster remains on most of the interior surfaces, where it has not been chipped away in efforts to access the ancient carvings beneath. The curved outline of an apse remains visible on the south wall, and two rectangular cuts through the east wall allow sunlight to enter and illuminate the apse area (Figure 26). Although the extensive renovations to the tomb render it difficult to be certain about the entirety of the original text and image program, it is possible to deduce aspects of its organization based upon the remaining visible elements.

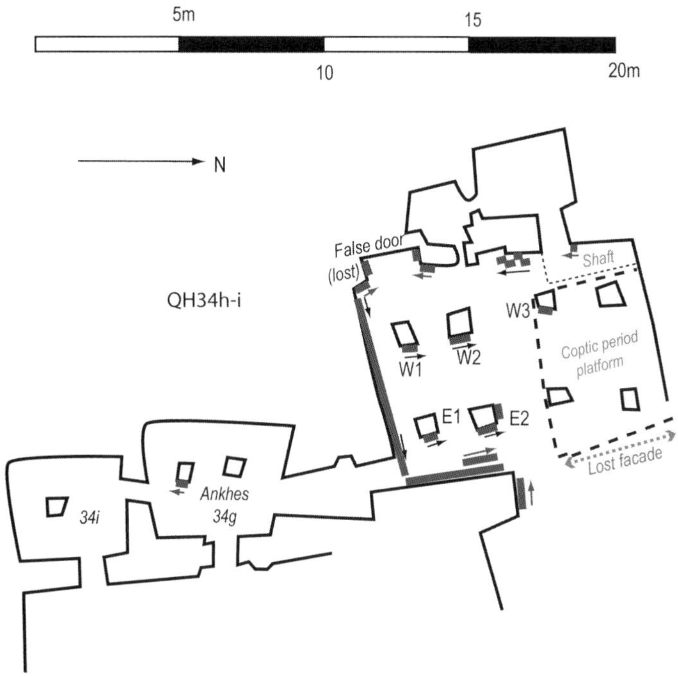

25. Plan of tombs QH34h–i, of Khunes and Ankhes.

26. View of the interior of the tomb of Khunes.

Khunes's chapel program is, among all the Old Kingdom tombs in the cemetery, the one most similar to a typical Memphite tomb program, as the east and south walls are covered with relief images rather than smaller, isolated panels. Pillars E1, E2, W1, W2, and W3 have reliefs on their east faces, and pillar E2 also has relief on its north face, along the entrance axis. Although the north wall is covered with a thick layer of plaster that could possibly obscure images or texts, the fact that the northern pillars have only sparse relief carving suggests this is unlikely. Several surviving offering panels are distributed over the west wall, in a way that would make any extensive relief program, such as that of the east and south walls, impossible. A number of these panels are carved around a rectangular section of the wall that has been cut away, directly opposite the entrance. It is possible there was a large, single scene in this area, similar in mode to the large fishing and fowling scene in Sabni1's tomb, and the offering figures were place around it. Unfortunately, this cannot be ascertained, and it seems much more likely this large cut dates to the period of Coptic reuse.

The false door niche is located at the south end of the west wall, anchoring cult activity in the southwest corner of the chapel space. Although it is reasonable to suggest, as Edel et al. do, that the damage to the northern half of the tomb necessitated this placement of the false door, it is not uncommon in other areas during this time period for false doors to be located off-axis, and perhaps the location here reflects an initial tomb design that associated the tomb owner with outside, rather than local, traditions. The large niche is 2 meters wide, 3 meters high, and 80 centimeters deep, and set a 0.5 meter up from the floor. Extensive damage to the niche has fully erased the false door itself, leaving no indication of the original design, images, and texts.

In the northwest corner of the chapel, the floor is cut away in an L-shape, facilitating access to two tomb shafts that extend to the north and west. The western shaft entrance cuts partly through the lower section of the west wall, and leads back to the primary burial chamber. Above this shaft entrance, a large doorway, approximately 1.5 meters high and 1 meter wide, cuts through the west wall, leading back to two small chambers that are separate from the main chapel space. Edel et al. hypothesize this space was used for offering gifts; alternately, it could have been a kind of serdab, though the large doorway leading into the space would be unusual.[20] Modifications to these small chambers, including the creation of a window connecting the smaller chamber back to the primary chapel space, are rather mysterious and may have been the work of the later Coptic community, but Edel et al. feel the chambers themselves were almost certainly original, as such extensive rock cutting was rarely done by the Coptic monks. Despite the complex architectural situation of the tomb, the elements necessary for a properly functioning cult are all in place. The complexity of the architecture is in many ways paralleled by a rather complex program of images and texts, as well.

Remains of a large-scale figure carved in Raised A1 survive on the southern thickness, facing into the tomb as appears in other Qubbet el-Hawa programs. Within the chapel space, the south section of the east wall and the full south wall are covered with relief of large figures in the Raised A1 style and smaller figures in Raised A2. The east wall shows Khunes's son Shemai at an offering table, next to a fishing and fowling scene with Khunes and his family. Shemai appears behind the fishing figure on the south, and beneath him (but not on the raft) is a somewhat incongruous headrest turned on its side, which forms a strong link between this scene and the fishing and fowling scene in the tomb of Sabni1. The shared scale of the primary figures, the continuous upper and lower boundaries of the scenes, and the consistent style of the carving strongly suggests the two scenes on the east wall were designed and carved together.

Turning to the south wall, the relief images are even more difficult to discern, due to the remains of Coptic-era plaster as well as damage and debris accrued over the millennia. In addition, a low doorway cut through the east end of the south wall, leading into the neighboring tomb of Khunes's wife Ankhes, weakened the rock and caused areas to shear away. The overall design of the south wall is conceptually and stylistically similar to the east wall; above a blank dado, the wall is fully covered with relief scenes carved in the Raised A1 and Raised A2 styles (Figure 27). Khunes, Ankhes, and their son Shemai appear in large scale, while the remainder of the wall program depicts subsidiary figures engaged in various activities including craft-making, brewing beer, leading in oxen, sailing ships, and bird catching, all known from Memphite tomb chapels, as well. Although this wall is not decorated in the panel system common to this cemetery, the composition retains some quality of this divided-scene type system. Each thematic scene is composed with a width and height of its own, and then these scenes are fit into the

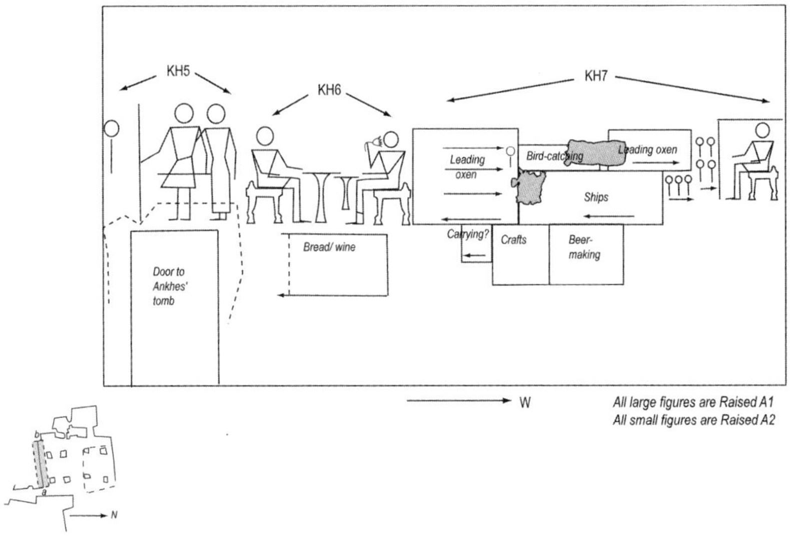

27. Diagram of the south wall in the tomb of Khunes (Kh5–7).

overall design like pieces in a puzzle. Such piecemeal design occasionally occurs in Memphite tombs, but in those cases the scale of the registers and the figures remains consistent throughout, which is not the case on this wall.

The relatively Memphite-like design of the program continues around the false door niche, adjacent on the west wall. The niche is framed by four registers of offering figures in pairs on the south jamb, and one pair on the north. The top three southern pairs are carved in Raised A2, but the lower and northern pair are carved in Sunken A, a Qubbet el-Hawa rather than Memphite contrast of style. Fragments of relief showing a seated figure of Khunes carved in the Raised A1 style survive on both inner thicknesses of the niche.

The last element of the program that appears more traditional are the three large-scale figures of Khunes on the east faces of pillars E1, E2, and W1 (Figure 28). All three are carved in Raised A1, linking them to the east and south walls, but figures of a tomb owner on a pillar are not uncommon at Qubbet el-Hawa. Only the seated figure of Khunes on pillar E2 is accompanied by his highest-ranking title, implying that the east and south walls as well as pillars E1 and W1 were executed earlier in the construction of the tomb.

This Memphite-like foundation is accompanied by a number of Qubbet el-Hawa style panels of offering figures carved in a variety of

28. Relief of Khunes (Kh19).

styles. Two registers of C-style figures are carved into the lower section of the east wall, beneath the seated Shemai, and a combination of C- and D-style priests and offering figures cover the north face of pillar E2 (Figure 29). Above these priests stands a solo figure whose style is closest to Sunken A, but with unusual facial details that distinguish it from other Sunken A figures in the program, including on panels set beneath Khunes on both pillars E1 and E2 (Figure 30). It is more closely related to the Sunken A figure that partially survives along the edge of the serdab doorway. A Raised A2 panel of offerers on pillar W2 is accompanied below by a rather unusual solo offering figure in a style best identified as a combination of Raised B and a raised version of C. The west wall is even more complex, as four separate panels are distributed in the area between the false door and the serdab door, around the section that has since been cut away (Figure 31). Legs of two C-style figures survive next to each other, though not on a shared smoothed surface, and traces of a solo figure in a Sunken B- or C-related style stands beneath them. To the right of these there are two more panels with two figures each, but in both cases the figures differ stylistically, which is highly unusual. The four separate figures are all carved in sunken relief, including B and C

29. Relief of offerers in the tomb of Khunes (Kh25, 26).

30. Relief of offerers in the tomb of Khunes (Kh20).

styles and an unusual figure in a style that cannot be categorized. All four figures are stylistically related, but even the two C-style figures show formal variation.

The last two panels of this program are equally unusual. On the lower part of the east face of pillar E2, beneath the seated image of Khunes and

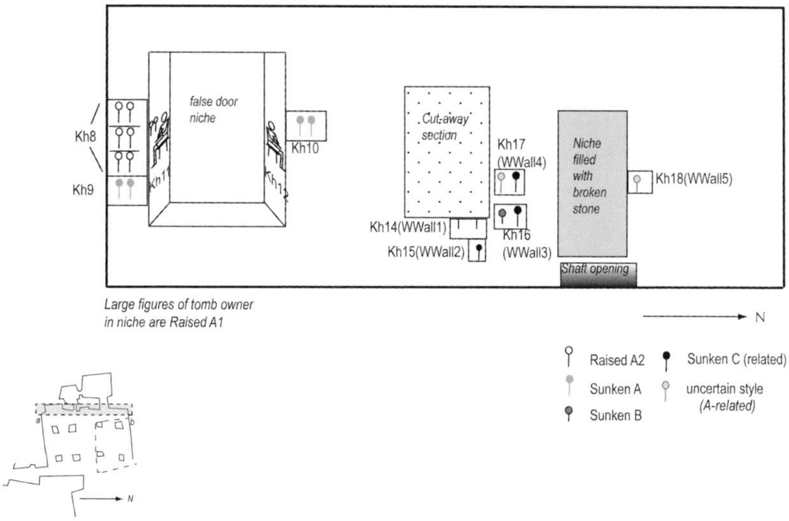

31. Diagram of the west wall in the tomb of Khunes (Kh8–18).

the Sunken A style offerers, is another panel depicting two bulls head to head with an attending male figure standing on a lower groundline but with his head turned up as if facing the bulls. This scene is one of three surviving bullfighting scenes in the Old Kingdom tombs in the cemetery, including one on the south wall of this tomb in a section of men leading oxen for offering, and one that is part of a larger composition in the tomb of Sabni2. Bullfighting scenes are very common in the provinces, though they do not appear in Memphite tombs.[21] This composition is intriguing, not only in the symmetrical arrangement of confronting bulls, but also in the presence of a figure that is conceptually linked with the action of the bulls but physically separated on the pillar. The man raises both hands in front of him, grasping a long pole directed at the bulls. He is most closely linked to the Sunken B style, although the long lower legs and long, detailed wig are uncommon in that style. The two sunk relief bulls, characterized by the fluid, sweeping lines of their backs and the delicate quality of their horns and faces, are distinctly different from the raised relief animals in the tombs of Mekhu and Khwin-Khnum, but similar to animals in the tomb of Pepynakht Heqaib2, and to another group on pillar W3 in this tomb.

The relief images on pillar W3 can just be seen above the Coptic platform it abuts. Two male figures facing north and a third facing south form the top register, all carved in the Sunken C style. They bear a group of offerings typical to this style, as well as two small oryx and an ox, similar in their fluid outlines to the bulls on pillar E2. More animals carved in a similar style appear below this register, dispersed in a nonlinear arrangement. A single male offering figure also carved in the Sunken C style stands along the south edge and holds a very large crane. The long, thin beak of the crane comes down on a fish, which appears to be floating against the surface with no further indication of context. Beneath the fish there is a large figure of a cow in the same style, turning her head back to look down at a nursing calf. In front of the nursing cow there is another oryx, and beneath the nursing cow is another of the same, though her head turns toward the ground while her calf nurses beneath her legs. None of these animals share groundlines with each other or the offering figure.

The last image in this tomb is carved low on the south face of pillar E3. It is a male figure standing in a short raft and holding a spear directed into two fish, carved at the level of the raft's raised prow. The style of this image stands apart from the other styles present throughout the tomb program, combining a deep and flat sunken relief with relatively standard proportions and curved outlines to the torso and feet. The distinctive style and the location and content of the image separate it from the other elements of the program, suggesting it was a later, perhaps graffiti-like, addition.

Khunes's tomb chapel delivers an overwhelming visual impact. The complicated building history is already apparent from the long ramp leading up to its façade, and the high-ceilinged, open interior space filled with light and breezes create an environment unlike any other in the cemetery. The program of images and texts is equally complex, combining diverse styles distributed in some instances in a quite standard manner and in others with some irregularity. In all, the program gives the impression of having been executed in at least two separate phases, with the more traditional east and south walls done together with the Raised A1 figures of Khunes on pillars E1 and W1. Integrated into this set program are the numerous images of offering figures in various styles, distributed on both the pillars and the west and east walls. The possible implications of this two-phased approach will be investigated in further depth in the following chapters.

Ankhes QH34g The doorway cut into the east end of the south wall of Khunes's tomb leads down a narrow corridor to the small tomb of his wife, Ankhes (Figure 27). Ankhes's tomb is also accessible via an entrance through its façade, which is a continuation of the façade of Khunes's tomb, and her doorway is much smaller. Two pillars flank the axis from entrance to the burial chamber opening, and the false door is just south of this opening on the west wall.

Only the east face of the north pillar was carved with relief, and it depicts Ankhes standing, facing south and holding a lotus to her nose; in front of her are two female offering figures arranged in registers. They are carved in low raised relief that fits into the Raised A1 and Raised A2 styles, respectively. Large-scale female figures are scarce in this cemetery, appearing only on the entrance thickness of Mekhu's tomb and on the southern pillar in the tomb of Harkhuf, other than the three images of Ankhes here and in her husband's tomb. While the sunken relief figure in Harkhuf's tomb is a clearly different style, the images of Ankhes here are very similar to the image of Mekhu's wife on his north entrance thickness.

Leaving Khunes's chapel and moving northward is most easily accomplished by climbing the short staircase from the entrance axis up to the interior platform and following this new ground surface out of the chapel. It leads immediately into an area filled with remains of a Coptic structure, mainly mud-brick walls covered with plaster, until at the northern end of these remains one comes across a still-standing apse, painted with images of Christian saints. Edel et al. determined that these remains likely blocked additional ancient tombs in the area, but given the limits of the space, the changing slope of the cliff, and the enthusiastic reuse of the chapels of Khunes and Ankhes, they were most likely much smaller chapels.

Just north of these remains, around the edge of a stone-built wall, the cliff slope was divided into two tiers, rather than the single tier, as in the southern section. The first group of tombs arranged in these two tiers includes tombs 34i and 34p on the lower section, and the small tombs 34k, 34l, and 34m in the upper southern quadrant. The final tomb of this group is tomb 34n, occupying the upper northern section, set back to allow for a wide forecourt enclosed by rock-cut and built stone walls. This last tomb belongs to the elite official Harkhuf (Figure 32).

HARKHUF QH34N (H)

Harkhuf is the most famous elite tomb owner at Qubbet el-Hawa, due to the extensive texts inscribed into the façade of his relatively small tomb. A lengthy autobiography detailing his expeditions into Nubia represents an

32. View of tomb group including tomb of Harkhuf.

important historical document of the period, and it is overshadowed only by a copy of a letter he received from the young Pepy II, carved prominently north of the tomb's entrance (Figure 33). This tomb remains today the oldest surviving with images and texts. Cut into the cliff well north of the bend, it is not visible from the settlement at Elephantine, nor is the island visible from it; rather, it faces northward toward the river flowing downstream and eventually out of sight. Within the extended cemetery as it survives today, Harkhuf's tomb blends into the overall environment, difficult to isolate due to its low façade and doorway and similar neighboring tombs.

The entrance to the tomb is centered on the façade and set within a rectangular recess that creates flanking jambs and a lintel. Both jambs and the lintel are filled with inscribed texts providing offering formulae, Harkhuf's titulary, a catalog of virtues that also includes warnings to passersby not to enter his tomb "unclean," and the aforementioned autobiography. In addition to the surfaces of the wide jambs, the workmen smoothed an additional broad section of the façade, north of the entrance, to receive the copy of the letter from Pepy II. This smoothed and inscribed section aligns at its top edge with the bottom of the entrance lintel and is wider than both jambs, allowing the letter visual weight equal to that of the autobiography. The profusion of texts on the façade of this tomb exceeds that of any other tomb at Qubbet el-Hawa, a pattern continued in the interior program, as well.

33. View of the façade of the tomb of Harkhuf.

Along with the extensive use of texts, the façade program incorporates large-scale images of the tomb owner and his eldest son, Djemi, carved in an uncommon style of sunken relief that appears only in this tomb and on the façade of the neighboring tomb of Pepynakht Heqaib1 (Harkhuf style) (Figure 34). Two much smaller offering figures are carved into the south façade beneath Djemi's feet. Positioned back to back, the two sunken relief figures appear in distinctly different styles. The overseer of linen, Imetjy, stands on the left, and in style and content seems to evoke the figure of Djemi above him. On the right, the "overseer of the *Khent*-box," Khonsu-hetep, appears to be carved in the rare Sunken E style, with a large head, large eye, long torso, and smoothly curved back profile.

This chapel is one of the smallest in the group, with a floor area of just more than 33 meters square, and a ceiling height of approximately 2 meters (Figure 35). The plan is a long north-south rectangle that curves slightly west at the southern end, and four pillars line the central north-south axis. Standing at the doorway, one confronts, directly across the chapel, the square opening of the tomb shaft cut into the west wall and sunk into the floor, leading to the main burial chamber. Harkhuf's false door is carved into the west wall just north of the shaft opening. This situation within the confines of the chapel space allows the third pillar to

34. Detail of the façade of the tomb of Harkhuf (H2).

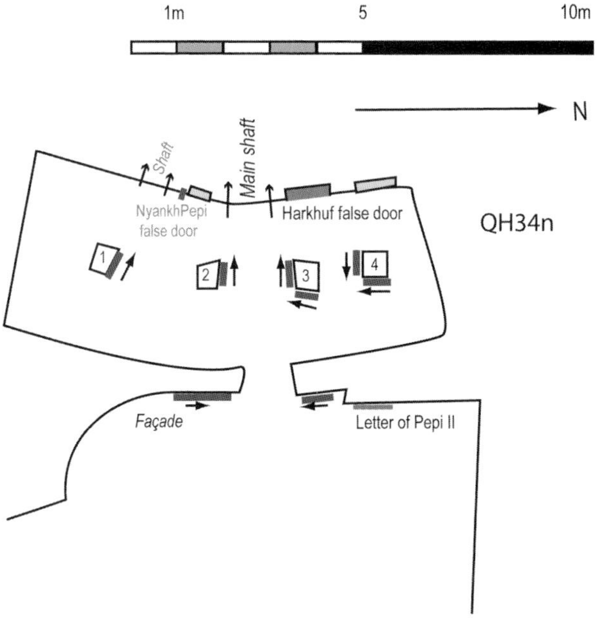

35. Plan of QH34n, tomb of Harkhuf.

block the false door from view from the entrance, facilitating the visual protection of the primary cult place achieved in other tombs through the construction of interior walls. Another false door the same size as Harkhuf's but left uninscribed fills the north end of the west wall. A third, much smaller false door is carved into the west wall just south of the shaft opening. It sits above a small ledge left in the wall, and it is inscribed for a man named Sabni Nyankh-Pepy, who is also pictured on the south face of the third pillar (Plate XII).

The program within Harkhuf's tomb chapel is largely confined to the pillars, with the exception of the false doors and a single, small offering figure carved next to Sabni's small false door. The emphasis on text that characterizes the design of the façade program continues inside the tomb, where each pillar is carved with a single figure standing under several columns of text listing titles and epithets. The two southern pillars have figures carved only on the north face, while the two northern pillars have figures carved on the south and east faces. Only three of the six figures depict Harkhuf; the other three represent family members and Sabni, whose relationship to Harkhuf is unclear. The standing female figure on the southern pillar is likely Harkhuf's wife, though this relationship is not specified in her titles. His son Djemi appears on pillar 2. Across from this image, on the south face of pillar 3, is Sabni Nyankh-Pepy. The three images of Harkhuf are gathered in the northern section of the tomb, on the east faces of pillars 3 and 4 and the south face of pillar 4 (Plate XII). The northern half of the chapel forms the heart of the cult space; the two northern pillars are closer together than the southern pillars, the two large false doors fill the north section of the west wall, and there are twice as many images on the north pillars as on the south. The unified style of the interior figures is consistent with the style of the façade figures.

There are three small offering figures placed around the tomb. Meryt is a small female figure holding a mirror, standing behind the tall figure of Tepemnefret on pillar 1. The figure is carved in sunken relief, and although it survives now as little more than an outline, it was likely carved in the same style as the large figure here. The second figure, named Ipy, stands just below the feet of Sabni on the south face of pillar 3. The style is similar to the left offering figure on the façade, a small version of the Harkhuf style, and he also wears a puffy wig and broad collar echoing the large figure of Sabni on the same pillar. The third offering figure is Ipy again, carved in the same style into the west wall facing the false door of Sabni.

As the earliest surviving inscribed tomb in the cemetery, it is unsurprising that Harkhuf's tomb stands out from the other Old Kingdom examples discussed here, in its use of a rare sunken relief style, an emphasis on lengthy texts even inside the tomb, and the presence of fewer than a handful of offering figures carved in different styles. This program represents the first step in the new cemetery, and likely provided conceptual options to the elite owners who followed.

Architectural Situation of I: Pepynakht Heqaib1 QH 35, J. Pepynakht Heqaib2 QH 35d, and K. Sabni2 QH 35e Leaving Harkhuf's tomb, one descends from the forecourt to rejoin the main pathway running along the east edge of the rock-cut and stone-built wall enclosing the forecourts of Harkhuf and QH34p. Just beyond this wall, immediately north of the tombs of Harkhuf and his neighbors, one of the most distinctive areas of the cemetery emerges fully into view (Figure 36). At first glance, two distinctive architectural features, each unique to the cemetery, grab the visitor's attention. The first is a rock-cut staircase leading from the courtyard surface up to the doorway of tomb 35, almost 4 meters above the ground. The second feature is just north of this staircase, the remains of two rock-cut columns standing before the high façade of the neighboring tomb, 35d. Although columns appear within several tomb chambers in the cemetery, no other tomb complexes show this kind of exterior structure. One's eye then travels around the area to comprehend the full complex: numerous smaller tomb chambers and ground shafts distributed around the main monuments and contained within two nested enclosing walls that demarcate an important subspace within the landscape of the cemetery as a whole. Three main tombs anchor this complex: tomb 35 of Pepynakht Heqaib1, tomb 35d of Pepynakht Heqaib2, and tomb 35e of Sabni2.

As discussed in the Introduction, Labib Habachi conducted the first scientific excavation of this area. When he examined the two tombs, 35 and 35d, both owned by elite officials named Pepynakht Heqaib, Habachi decided that these two Heqaibs were in fact one and the same man – the man later deified as a local saint. Edel and the Bonn mission picked up Habachi's work, and their combined efforts have now been synthesized by the editors of the Qubbet el-Hawa volumes; all accepted Habachi's initial view that one, great man earned these two tombs in the cemetery. In Appendix A, I argue instead that these two tombs were owned by two different men, both named Pepynakht Heqaib. This perspective underlies the following description of their tombs, in that each

36. View of the tomb group QH35, QH35d, and QH35e.

is considered a separate monument dedicated to separate, though most likely related, individuals.

Habachi's interpretation of the identity of the tomb owners was due in part to the nature of the tombs' architectural setting. A stone-built wall creates a broad, albeit irregularly shaped exterior courtyard almost 22 meters long from north to south. The western edge of this courtyard is defined by a second enclosing wall, formed of two rock-cut spans running parallel to the cliff face. This inner wall creates a smaller, more intimate courtyard that links tombs 35, 35d, and 35e, leaving remaining space for a handful of additional single chamber tombs. Tomb 35d dominates the inner courtyard, which is organized around this tomb's façade, and the entrance through the enclosing wall lines up, slightly off, to the entrance to the tomb. Though the courtyard may be best viewed as belonging to 35d, the other tombs necessarily share the space; 35e is in fact connected to 35d, and its separate entrance opens onto 35d's forecourt. Also, once the workers cut away the cliff face around tomb 35 to create tomb 35d, the staircase they left provided the only means of access to the earlier tomb; this staircase can only be reached via this internal courtyard. Thus, these three major tombs are linked visually by the architectural elements that bind them, as well as via means of access and directed movement of visitors.

Edel et al. present a highly detailed overview of this complex's building history; the following descriptions incorporate only a brief summary with primary attention on the three main monuments. Tomb 35 is the earliest of the three. The double tomb of the other Pepynakht Heqaib2 (35d) and Sabni2 (35e) was cut into the cliff just north of tomb 35; however, for this tomb the workmen extended the façade down vertically, using the full layer of sandstone that had been divided into two separate tiers of tombs in the area around Harkhuf. To create such a high façade, the workmen lowered the ground level in front of these tombs, cutting the staircase for access to 35 and low forecourt wall in the process. The second enclosing wall eventually extended the forecourt to the east.

This group of tombs is located near the northern end of the cemetery and cannot be seen from the settlement at Elephantine; however, the high façades and strong shadows created by the many architectural elements render the complex plainly visible from the river. The view south toward Elephantine is blocked by the eastern projection of the cliff, while the view down the river is limited by another natural projection of the cliff just to the north.

PEPYNAKHT HEQAIB1: QH35 (PN)

The southernmost major tomb in the complex belongs to Pepynakht Heqaib1. Today, access to the tomb requires a relatively lengthy passage, starting with entering the exterior forecourt through its eastern sides, crossing to the narrower entrance to the interior forecourt, and climbing the seventeen steps to the entrance. The transformation of the cliff face during the construction of 35d resulted in a high, continuous vertical surface around the entrance to tomb 35, creating a visual impression of the door, and the tomb it accesses, floating high above the ground and the other monuments that surround it. Originally, however, the façade was low and wide, mimicking very closely that of its southern neighbor, Harkhuf.

Although the later architectural evolution of the area around tomb 35 conjoined it quite closely with its neighbors to the north, initially the tomb would have had a strong affiliation with Harkhuf's tomb. It is cut into the cliff next to the tomb of Harkhuf, slightly higher on the cliff face, with a shared rock-cut wall dividing their respective forecourts. Like both walls of Harkhuf's forecourt, the remaining south wall of

Pepynakht Heqaib1's forecourt connects to the façade on its upper part at a ninety-degree angle and on the lower part via a smooth curve. The horizontal emphasis of the two façades is very similar, although the façade of Pepynakht Heqaib1's tomb is proportionately wider, and the central entrance recess occupies less of the façade's width. Two rectangular cuts through the façade survive in its southern half; both most likely remnants of earlier tunnel tombs. Edel et al. argue that Pepynakht1's initial tomb plan was smaller, thus the expansion to the north and south are what ultimately involved these earlier tunnels. Nonetheless, the willingness of Pepynakht Heqaib1 to deal with such complications and "imperfections" in his monument suggest that he found the location particularly desirable.

The design of Pepynakht Heqaib1's façade, including the recessed portal niche and the use of texts and images, also closely follows that of Harkhuf's. Both jambs of the portal niche as well as the lintel are fully inscribed with texts providing an autobiographical text much like Harkhuf's, detailing Pepynakht1's activities in Nubia. On the south jamb, the text is inscribed above an image of the tomb owner leaning on a staff (Figure 37), and on the north jamb, another image of him standing holding a staff and scepter. The only significant difference from Harkhuf's façade is the lack of a second figure on the south jamb. As well as design, the façades of Harkhuf and Pepynakht1 share the style of relief images, which survives only in these two tombs. The related autobiographical texts of the respective tomb owners are carved in the same sunk relief-style hieroglyphs.

The plan of Pepynakht1's tomb also evokes Harkhuf's model, a long north-south rectangle that is slightly concave with a single row of pillars and with the opening of the descending tomb shaft cut into the floor and wall directly across from the entrance (Figure 38). Like that of his neighbor, the false door of Pepynakht1 is carved into the west wall just north of the shaft entrance, although it is slightly smaller and remains uninscribed; perhaps it was originally painted. Pepynakht1's tomb is a bit less broad, and has only two rock-cut pillars to Harkhuf's four.

Unlike the location, plan, and façade of Pepynakht1's tomb, the internal text and image program does not mimic Harkhuf's. No additional figures of the elite owner appear inside the tomb, nor are there any large-scale subsidiary figures such as a wife or son. Instead, four panels of offering figures and two panels with only a single offering figure

37. Detail of the façade of Pepynakht Heqaib1 (Pn2).

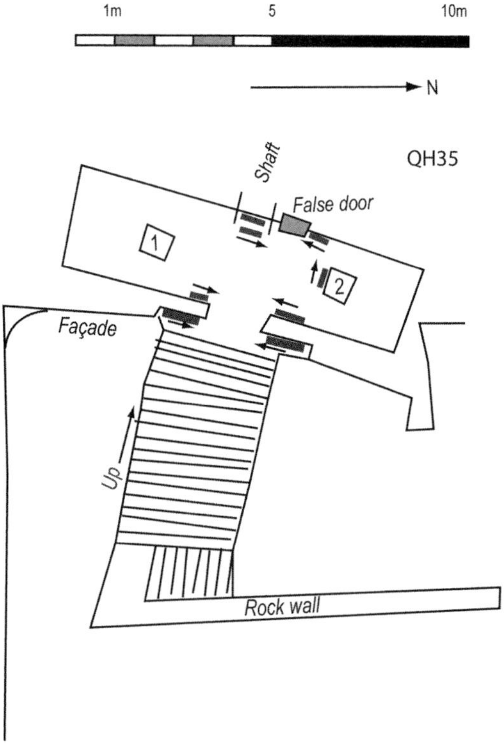

38. Plan of QH35, tomb of Pepynakht Heqaib1.

are distributed around the central area of the chamber. The tomb has suffered extensive damage due in part to later habitation, and an area of the wall above the shaft that may have held additional figures has been cut away. The surviving images appear around the doorway, the shaft opening, and the false door.

The panels are carved in varying yet closely interrelated styles of sunk relief that are distinctly different from the style of the façade figures. Interestingly, several of the panels are carved in styles that tend to blend characteristic features of both Sunken B and Sunken C. While these styles clearly relate in all cases, the somewhat idiosyncratic blends produced here evince the fluid artistic world the local artists worked within. The two panels on the east wall, on either side of the entrance, show offering figures, including on the south a single, female *ka*-priest, the only one known in the cemetery. Both are carved in Sunken C style, though the female figure has aspects of Sunken B, as well.

Three panels embellish the west wall; two above the shaft opening and one north of the false door. The two panels above the shaft opening share similarities in style, but they clearly were carved separately. The top group of cult officials are carved in Sunken C, though they differ slightly from the east wall figures. The bottom panel is also related to Sunken C, but has aspects of Sunken B style, as well, including a distinctive offering vessel, making this closer to a true blend of the two styles. The panel north of the false door shows a male cult official with his wife and daughters. This panel fits more securely into the Sunken B style (Figure 39). The final panel is carved on the south face of the north pillar, with only a single small figure. The figure is not technically relief, as it was only outlined with incised lines and never fully carved, and it appears closely linked to the rows of offering figures on the entrance thicknesses of the tomb of Sabni2, downstairs from this tomb.

PEPYNAKHT HEQAIB2: QH 35D (PNH)

The small forecourt at the bottom of the stairs is enclosed at the north by a 6-meter-high rock-cut wall. Within this space, the two rock-cut columns rising upward on the left dominate the visual field. Today, the columns survive just less than (south) and more than (north) 5 meters high, tapering from roughly a meter in diameter to just over 0.5 a meter where they are now broken off. Originally, the columns supported a ceiling that covered a portico that was shared, like the

39. Relief of offerers in the tomb of Pepynakht Heqaib1 (Pn8).

40. View of the shared façade of tombs QH35d and QH35e.

continuous façade, by tombs 35d of Pepynakht Heqaib2 and 35e of Sabni2 (Figure 40).

Each column stands on a low, circular base, and a stone-built wall fills the space between the southern column and the southern wall of this small forecourt, no doubt to provide stability. The columns flank the axis to the high doorway of tomb 35d, across the slightly raised floor of the small inner forecourt and shallow stairs to the door opening. The recessed portal niche occupies the full height of the almost 6-meter-high façade and nearly two-thirds of its width. This niche has a more elaborated cornice at the top edge, underneath the modern rough edge of the cliff and originally underneath the portico ceiling. In addition, a secondary, narrow band above the doorway – projecting slightly beyond the jambs but slightly less than the lintel above – accentuates the natural horizontal grain of the stone and adds further visual interest to an already rich entrance complex.

The entrance to the tomb runs more than 4 meters high, similar to the grand doorways to the tombs of Mekhu, Sabni1, and Khunes, and is flanked by an obelisk-shaped stela to each side. Numerous relief images fill the northern end of Pepynakht Heqaib 2's façade, but these belong clearly to the program of Sabni2, establishing the northern end of the façade and the forecourt as part of his monument. This area and the relief images will be discussed in the next section.

Unlike the much smaller and simpler tomb 35, tomb 35d does not boast a lengthy autobiography on its façade, nor anywhere else within the tomb. Instead, this tomb is remarkable for the extensive and diverse collection of images carved and painted throughout. The program begins simply on the exterior with two panels carved into the northern jamb of the portal niche, including a very degraded raised relief image of the tomb owner, and below a group of offering figures carved in Sunken A. Inside the chapel, starting on the wide entrance thicknesses, the image program is much more complex.

The somewhat skewed design of the floor plan and the other irregularities in its execution resulted most likely from obstacles confronted during the construction process. The floor plan is roughly rectangular, but leans overall to the west (Figure 41). Within the space of the chapel, the doorway does not mark the midpoint, instead set in the northern half of the tomb. Two pillars support the ceiling, which rises to more than 4 meters, though it varies slightly from east to west. The pillars sit closer to the west wall than the east, leaving the most open area in the northeast corner of the chapel. In this corner a passageway cuts northward to join the interior space of tomb 35e, belonging to Sabni2 (Figure 42).

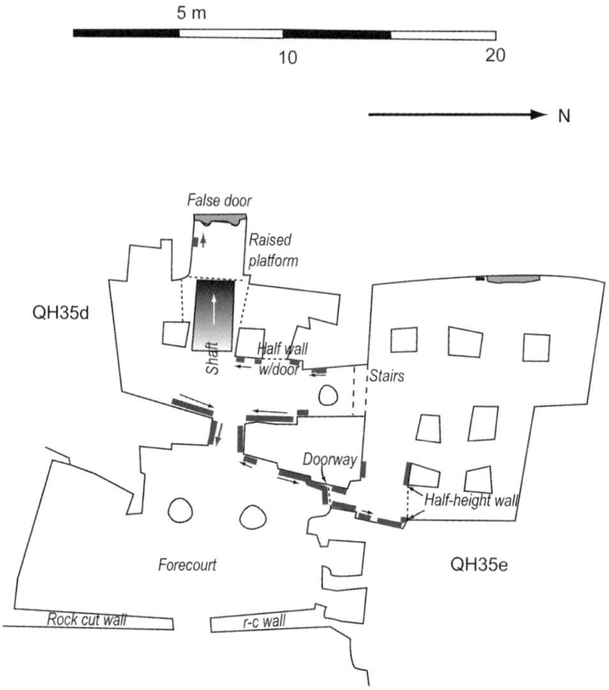

41. Plans of the tombs QH35d of Pepynakht Heqaib2 and QH35e Sabni2.

42. Interior view of the tomb of Pepynakht Heqaib2.

In contrast to the continuous, rectangular room of Mekhu and Sabni1, the tomb of Pepynakht Heqaib2 and Sabni2 is composed of two clearly separate areas connected by this much narrower internal passageway, as well as by the shared forecourt and façade. The passageway marks the architectural transition from the higher floor and much higher ceiling of Pepynakht Heqaib2's tomb to the lower floor and lower ceiling of Sabni2's tomb. A supporting column centered in the passageway and steps leading down to Sabni2's chapel further mark the division of space.

The main cult space consists of a deep niche cut into the west wall with a false door carved into its rear west wall. The floor of this niche rises 60 centimeters over the floor of the chapel space itself, while the ceiling reaches roughly the same height as the chapel's. The niche is slightly off-axis from the entrance. Two stone-built and plastered walls just more than a meter high enclose the front of the niche, which mimics very closely the cult niche in the tomb of Mekhu. The primary shaft opening fills the area in front of the niche and between the two pillars. A series of steps leads from the chapel floor down into the shaft, which cuts underneath the false door niche as a vaulted tunnel leading back to the main burial chamber.[22] A secondary cult space fills the southwestern corner of the tomb, a smaller niche similarly constructed with a higher floor and a front enclosing wall. The rough outline of a false door is carved into the west wall of the niche, but it was never fully shaped.

As they do in numerous other tombs in this cemetery, interior walls survive around the central cult area of the tomb. Two-meter-high walls flank the cult axis, and a smaller wall with a doorway cut through it runs from pillar 2 to the north wall underneath a band of rock left in place during construction, likely due to structural concerns. Edel believed these walls were built during the Coptic era, due to reuse of the chapel space.[23] While the cemetery does show intense reuse by the Coptic community, most often such interior walls are described by the excavators as part of the original tomb complex. These interior walls, like many other examples, clearly frame and protect the central cult area, which strongly suggests their affiliation with the original intent of the space. Further, little evidence survives in this tomb, or the larger area, to argue for the kind of Coptic interest so obvious in the tomb of Khunes. Still, there is evidence that the implementation of images and texts began before the walls were built. On the north face of the north pillar, a panel with four offering figures drawn in black paint is partially covered by the built wall running to the north chapel wall. Given the Egyptian practice of working on multiple aspects of a monument simultaneously, it is reasonable to consider that artists cut and painted images while other craftsmen worked to complete the architectural elements of the tomb, resulting in this overlap of image and architecture. Yet the long history of activity at the cemetery remains a complicating factor, and Edel's presumption that the walls represent Coptic reuse remains equally viable.

The combination of the high doorway, high ceiling, and relatively compact floor plan of Pepynakht Heqaib2's tomb allows the sunlight to illuminate much of the chapel. Nonetheless, the text and image program is concentrated mainly in the northeast section of the tomb. In number of images, array of styles, and quality of execution, the interior program comprises a rich body of art that represents a large and diverse community standing in support of the tomb owner. Beginning on the high entrance thicknesses, the program continues on both the north and south sections of the east wall, as well as on the east face of the north pillar. A few additional scenes are carved into the west wall leading into the passageway, providing additional links between the two tombs 35d and 35e.

High and wide entrance thicknesses provide ideal surfaces for images and texts here at Qubbet el-Hawa, as already evident in the tombs of Mekhu and Sabni1 and Khunes. Here, large images of the tomb owner anchor the program, surrounded by numerous single offering figures, as well as a few grouped figures (Figure 43). These thicknesses show right away the tomb owner's interest in vividly diverse styles brought together in concentrated areas. The south thickness is divided into two registers, the north into three. The upper registers of both thicknesses have large-scale images of the tomb owner with smaller *ka*-priests and, on the north upper section, a large-scale figure of his son. The large figures are carved in Raised A1 style relief, but the southern, larger figure is much more detailed, with indicated pleats and necklace beads and subtly modeled facial features (Figure 44). Another Raised A1 figure of Pepynakht Heqaib2 stands in the central register on the north, facing into the tomb like the figure above. Here he is paired with two Sunken A style priests standing in front of him, one much larger than the other and than typical subsidiary figures (Figure 45).

The bottom registers of the two thicknesses have mirroring compositions, anchored with large-scale (though smaller than the figures above)

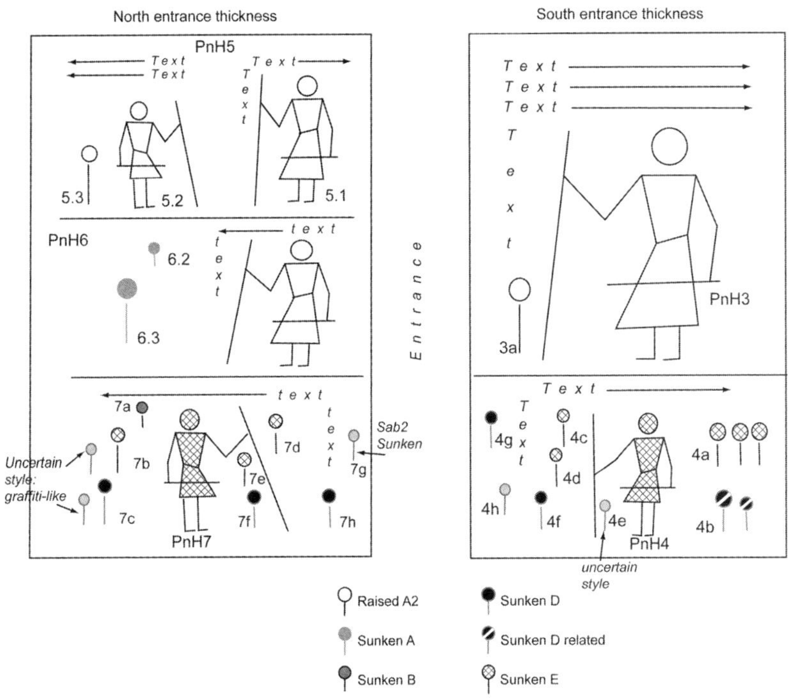

43. Diagram of the entrance thicknesses in the tomb of Pepynakht Heqaib2 (PnH3–7).

images of Pepynakht Heqaib2 carved in the highly original Sunken E style (Figure 46, Plate XIII). These two figures are the most fully realized examples of the style. Sunken E shares with the sunken relief of Harkhuf the deeply cut edges and nearly standard proportions of the figure, although the upper legs of the Sunken E figures are slightly longer. Unlike in the Harkhuf style, however, in Sunken E surface modeling is used to convey more extensive information about the body. The surfaces of each arm and leg are treated differently to indicate that different parts of each limb are visible, based on a single perspective. This technique reveals the artist's attention to anatomy that is also seen in the meticulously carved kneecaps and soft ankle bones. This naturalistic strain is also vividly illustrated in the hand holding the scepter, where individually rounded fingers press against a subtly carved palm, and in the raised relief ear set against the non-detailed hair (Figure 47). In contrast to the naturalistic modeling and details of the body, the striking head and facial features are highly abstracted. The crown of the head is rounded, and the forehead rises high above the low set features. The eye, nose, and mouth are simplified into almost geometric shapes, with the eye and

44. Relief of Pepynakht Heqaib2 on the upper section of the south entrance thickness (PnH3).

wide mouth disproportionately large, compared to the small, rounded tip of the nose. A similar example of the play between naturalism and abstraction is found in the torso, where the relatively large, deep, circular navel contrasts with the soft modeling of the stomach and chest.

On both thicknesses, smaller offering figures flank the tomb owner on both sides; however, the number and arrangement of figures differs. On the south, two registers of figures stand behind him, and six others are distributed over the space in front of him, all facing toward him. These offering figures show a rich diversity of style and individualistic detail. The two male offering figures "floating" in front of the tomb owner are

45. Middle section of the north entrance thickness in the tomb of Pepynakht Heqaib2 (PnH6).

both carved in the Sunken E style, showing clear formal relationships to the adjacent figure of Pepynakht Heqaib2. While the two offering figures are clearly related, they are not exactly alike. Three more male offering figures stand in front of Pepynakht Heqaib2 along the same groundline. The smallest figure stands nearest Pepynakht Heqaib2 and is carved in a style that cannot be categorized. The proportions are related to Sunken D, but the relief of the body is not, and the face is especially idiosyncratic.

Behind him, the next figure, holding an unusual object, perhaps a lidded vessel, is carved in the Sunken D style, characterized by a deep, flat sunken relief and the schematic portrayal of the body. The fifth offering figure in this area is carved along the outer, east edge of the thickness, and is much more abridged than the others on the wall; overall, difficult to categorize stylistically. The final figure in front of the tomb owner is also carved along the edge of the entrance, but higher up. While it is most closely related to the Sunken D style, it is a less carefully shaped and carved version.

46. Lower section of the south entrance thickness in the tomb of Pepynakht Heqaib2 (PnH4).

47. Detail of relief of Pepynakht Heqaib2 on the north entrance thickness (PnH7).

Behind the figure of Pepynakht Heqaib2 two groups of offering figures arranged in registers face toward the back of the tomb owner. The upper register shows a man and two women, carved in the Sunken E style (Figure 46). These female figures are the only two that can be certainly attributed to this style, based upon their formal relationship to this male figure, but there are other female figures that appear formally linked to these two while not fully conforming to the style. The lower register shows a father and son bearing offerings. Their style is difficult to categorize as it combines the flat relief of the Sunken D style with unusual proportions that fall between the elongated figures in Sunken C and E and the shorter, squat figures of Sunken B.

On the north thickness, single figures rather than groups stand behind Pepynakht Heqaib2 as well as before him. Directly behind him and level with his upper body, an offering figure two-fifths his size is carved in the Sunken E style, in a version formally closest to the two large figures that define the style, with the assured modeling of the legs and of the arm crossing the body and facial features nearly identical to those of the tomb owner. Like other subsidiary figures in this style, the figure has long upper thighs, but the torso is less triangular, and the back profile is formed with a distinctive curving line from shoulder to ankle (Plate XIII, left middle). Below him is another male offering figure carved in the Sunken D style, and squeezed into the space above him is a male offering figure carved in the Sunken B style holding an acorn-shaped vessel typical of this style.

Five additional offering figures are arranged in front of the tomb owner, with evidence suggesting a sixth figure may have been cut away, just in front of Pepynakht Heqaib2's face. As on the south, the two figures in front of the tomb owner are both carved in versions of Sunken E style; the upper figure closely matches his counterpart on the south wall, while the lower is slightly more geometric (Figure 48, top). Two figures titled "director of the hall" stand in front of Pepynakht Heqaib2 on the same groundline. The figure nearest Pepynakht Heqaib2 is carved in the Sunken D style (Figure 48, bottom), similar to the figure on the other side of the tomb owner. The other director of the hall is carved along the east edge of the wall, also in the Sunken D style, but in a version more similar to figure 4f on the south thickness than the others here. The final figure higher up along the outer edge of the thickness appears to be most closely related to the Sabni2Sunken figures common to the neighboring tomb.

48. Detail of relief of offerers on the north entrance thickness (PnH7e–f).

Stepping into the chapel space proper, the well-illuminated east wall grabs the viewer's attention with extensive imagery both north and south of the entrance (Figure 49). As the ambient light is brightest near the doorway, the images on both sides align closely with the interior edges of the entrance, which are recessed on both sides. On the southern part of the east wall, the program ends approximately half-way across its breadth, comprising a total of seven panels of figures (Figure 50). At the lower north corner of the main wall, a horizontal ledge juts out from the wall, apparently having been left during the construction of the tomb, and a single scene (Panel G) fills a rectangular area beneath this ledge. The remaining four panels (Panels C–F) are arranged closely together in three registers that are roughly the same width. Although the painted relief images are closely grouped, the rough, untreated strips of wall visible between the panels indicate they were separately conceived. With the exception of the scene carved below the horizontal ledge, the panels on this wall all are carved in the Sunken C style with only small variations among them. Paint survives on all panels except the one beneath the horizontal ledge. The limited palette is comprised of a bright red-orange, white, and black (Plate XV). The red-orange color is used for the skin of all figures, including the two women, whose full bodies are covered with this color, implying they are portrayed nude. Many of the scenes incorporate all or some of the group of offerings distinct to this style, and one includes birds and an ox that are painted with patches of color and patterns to create visually striking objects (Plate XVIa and b). These panels, in particular Panel F low on the wall showing a man and woman, well illustrate the often confounding formal aspects of these different styles. Panel F combines the seemingly awkward design of the female figure, which is depicted with exceedingly thin legs separated by space rather than the typical incised line, with the apparently skilled carving evident in the details of hands and subtly modeled jaw lines of both figures (Plate XV).

Underneath the horizontal rock ledge a more complex composition is carved in a somewhat looser version of the Sunken E style, which in this context appears related to the Sunken C style, as well. Extensive texts surround a large figure of the *ka*-priest Semenimy facing a much smaller figure of his son, and behind them are his wife and children. Along the bottom, a small male figure grasps the ends of ropes attached to an ox, an oryx, and a saluki carved in the space before him. The head and horns of the ox are unnaturally large, but the animals are carved with fluid lines that contrast sharply the stiffer outlines of the surrounding human

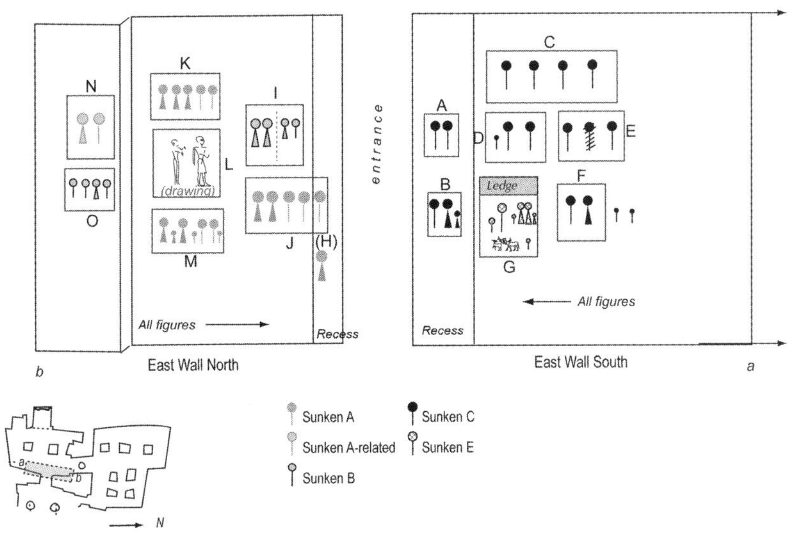

49. Diagram of the east wall in the tomb of Pepynakht Heqaib2 (PnH8–21).

50. East wall, south of the entrance in the tomb of Pepynakht Heqaib2 (PnH8–14).

figures. These animals recall those in the tomb of Khunes, on pillars E2 and W3.

The painted reliefs on the north section of the east wall cover approximately the same area as the group on the south section; however, the north wall is narrower than the south, thus the scenes fill this wall from the edge of the entrance to its northern limit (Plate XIV). A lower ceiling marks the beginning of the passage into Sabni2's chapel, and two of the panels are carved along the north edge of the passage (Panel N, Panel O). As on the south part of the wall, the scenes are grouped closely together and in an orderly arrangement, although here the dominant organizing principle is columns rather than the more traditional horizontal registers. All of the panels show *ka*-priests and other officials in family pairs or larger groups.

Unlike the south part of the wall where the Sunken C style and the palette visually link together the separate panels, here they show a diversity of styles and color patterns. Panel I at the upper south edge appears to have been recarved, as the front two figures are at a smaller scale than the rear two, but all are carved in Sunken B. Some paint survives on this panel, the palette of red-orange, black, and white familiar from the south section of the wall, and like the women there, all three women here are fully painted with the red-orange skin color (Plate XVII).

Panel J below is carved in Sunken A, as is panel K at the upper part of the central column and panel M at the bottom; however, none of the three match exactly (Figure 51). Panel L between K and M was drawn but never carved, and only fragments of black paint survive, making stylistic determination difficult; it seems closest to Sunken B. Atop the final column, panel N seems to be a very shallow version of Sunken A, with highly unusual oversized hieroglyphs, and panel O below shows two men and two women carved in the Sunken B style (Figure 52). The first figure, Heqaib, beautiful name Neferi, is a "chancellor of the palace", an uncommon and relatively high-ranking title among subsidiary figures in this cemetery. Heqaib Neferi and his family appear again, across the way on the north side of pillar 2, in the panel that was only drawn and subsequently partially covered by the built wall.

Because of the slightly skewed ground plan, the north pillar stands directly opposite the entrance, and a band of rock still connects the north pillar to the north wall, about mid-height, to maintain stability in an area weakened by earlier tomb shafts. Underneath this band, between the northern pillar and the north wall, the space was filled with a stone-built wall with a passage through it. The result of this architectural arrangement is the creation of a kind of "west wall" in this northeastern corner of the chapel. There are two panels high on the east face of pillar 2, two

51. Relief Panel K in the tomb of Pepynakht Heqaib2 (PnH17).

52. Relief Panel O in the tomb of Pepynakht Heqaib2 (PnH21).

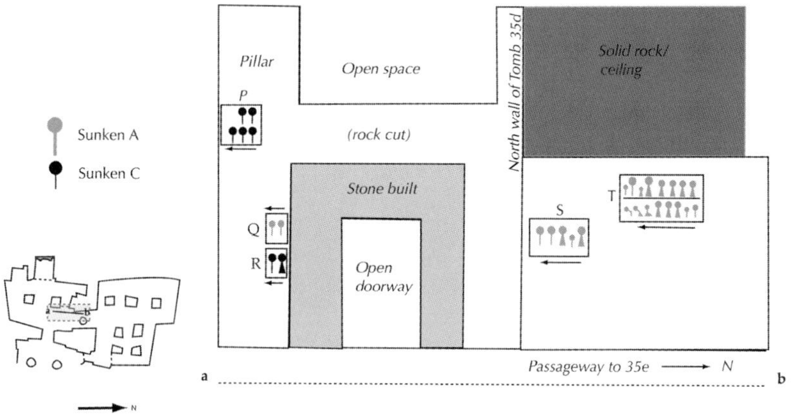

53. Diagram of the internal "west wall" in the tomb of Pepynakht Heqaib2 (PnH24–28).

more lower on the same pillar along its northern edge, and two more on the west wall of the passage underneath the low ceiling (Figure 53).

The highest panel on the east face of pillar 2 was only drawn and is now almost entirely lost, but based upon the drawing done by the Bonn epigraphers, the scene appears to have been planned in the Sunken A style. The panel carved and painted beneath this drawing consists of two registers of figures that seem to have been separately composed and executed, but in relationship to each other. Both registers of figures are carved in Sunken C style, and they bring small animals and other offerings, including a rare chest containing a libation vessel.

Both panels carved lower down on the pillar, along the north edge, are badly damaged (Panels Q, R). The upper panel shows two men carved in what appears to be the Sunken A style; the second panel shows two figures carved in the Sunken C style. The two panels carved into the west wall of the passage survived in a much better state. Panel S, carved along the south edge of this section, shows five figures facing south carrying birds, bread, and other food offerings in the Sunken A style. The second panel is placed slightly higher on the wall just behind Panel S, where it can still be illuminated by light coming from Pepynakht Heqaib2's entrance; only the back edge of the panel is shadowed. This large panel is divided into two registers of offering and other figures, all facing south, carved in the Sunken A style (Plate XVIII). The unusual composition includes several individual figures engaged in isolated agricultural and production activities, of the type more often seen in large scenes devoted to these themes.

The final figure completing Pepynakht Heqaib2's program appears on the southern wall of the main false door niche. Here a single male figure carved in Sunken C style bows slightly forward and holds with both hands a very large vessel, perhaps a beer jar used for libations in the tomb. The inscription identifies this man as Shemai, a "director of the food hall ... who brings food for Heqaib every day." The false door filling the west wall of the main niche is elegantly carved, with a cavetto cornice and thick torus molding. The images and text were painted rather than carved, but bits survive including yellow on the cornice, black on the torus molding, and red-orange on the skin of the tomb owner seated on the offering stela.

For a modern visitor to the tomb of Pepynakht Heqaib2, the view is somewhat chaotic – faults in the rock threatening the structure, a narrow metal pole trying to support the ceiling in the northeast corner, slabs and pieces of broken stone leaning against walls and lying on the floor, various baskets and buckets from modern workers. Yet through this all, it is possible to grasp a fleeting vision of the chapel as it originally was. With the doorway open, sunlight illuminates much of the oddly shaped space, and within this space the images convey an exceptionally large community standing in support of Pepynakht Heqaib2.

SABNI2 QH 35E

From Pepynakht Heqaib2's chapel it is easiest to move south into the chapel of Sabni2 via the internal passageway. The passage lines up with the widest axis in the tomb, between the western and central rows of pillars (Figure 41). To the left, the larger section of the tomb is shrouded in darkness, and often home to a large population of bats. To the right, sunlight let in through the entrance from the forecourt fills the southeastern corner of the tomb, bouncing off the south faces of two pillars and illuminating relief carved images on the east wall. The additional two pillars in this smaller area of the chapel are hidden from view. Given the very limited area in the chapel space reachable by sunlight, the concentration of the interior program in the southeast section is unsurprising.

Rather than the internal passage, the ideal entry into Sabni2's chapel is via his own doorway from the forecourt shared with tomb 35d. Here, too, however, access into Sabni2's chapel requires first engaging the monument of Pepynakht Heqaib2, passing between the rock-cut columns before turning right and moving to the north end of the forecourt. The doorway to Sabni2's chapel takes up nearly the full width of the north wall, leaving only minimal flanking surfaces to function as a façade. The architecture nonetheless adapts to the differently sized space to create an elaborate and distinctive entrance. The door is cut into a very narrow but deep recess that reaches the same height as Pepynakht Heqaib2's. Unlike that doorway, Sabni2's is not cut the full height of the recess; instead there is a double-tiered lintel in the upper half, with the upper lintel recessed about 30 centimeters less than the lintel below, creating extra wall surfaces for more light and shadow interplay. Narrow jambs flank the doorway, and at the extended east side it is framed by a rock-cut pilaster. The pilaster roughly lines up with the rock-cut columns, linking the façade back to the overall architecture of the forecourt.

A significant proportion of the images and texts comprising Sabni2's program are located on the exterior of his tomb. The surfaces framing the doorway have texts and images, and the program continues onto the adjacent surface of the façade technically belonging to Pepynakht Heqaib2, which, via this series of panels devoted to Sabni2, is visually claimed for his monument (Figure 54). The scene carved into the lintel immediately above the entrance recalls the large scenes typically on entrance thicknesses, with two large-scale figures of Sabni2 carved in Raised A1 relief attended by smaller priests carved in Sunken A and two small female figures also carved in Sunken A.

Four other images of Sabni2 appear on the façade, two flanking the doorway underneath the texts, and two on the west wall. The figure on the west jamb is carved in Sunken A style, perhaps to act as a kind of

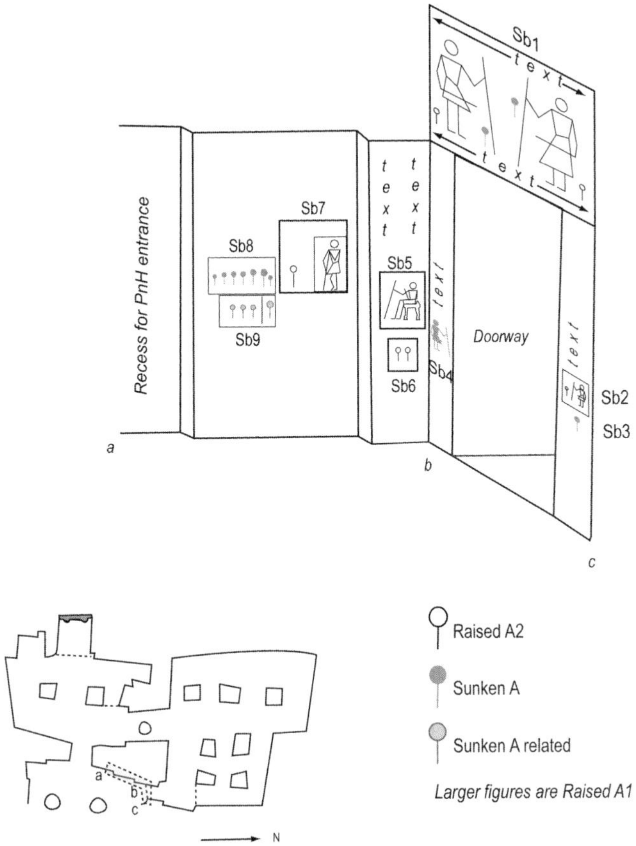

54. Diagram of the façade of the tomb of Sabni2 (Sb1–9).

determinative for the texts above. The other three are carved in a style of relief that falls between Raised A1 and Raised A2. The small scale, high relief, and modeling of the surfaces of the figures are atypical for the Raised A1 style, yet the unusual amount of carved detail is greater than normal for Raised A2 figures (Figure 55). On the east jamb Sabni2 faces the *ka*-priest Seni, who appears again directly below in Sunken A. On the west wall Sabni2 sits in a chair holding a staff and a scepter angled up from his lap, and a small dog named Sabni-is-his-lord sits loyally below his owner's chair. The third image is adjacent to the south, with Sabni2 leaning on his staff in a "viewing" posture and paired with a priest, Hehu.

Below the seated image of Sabni2, an unusual panel of offering figures was seriously damaged in an apparent attempt to remove a piece of it (Figure 56). The scene consists of two figures, the overseer of *ka*-priests,

55. Relief of Sabni2 on the façade of his tomb (Sb7).

Seni, and his wife, Wadjewkawes, and four much smaller figures of their children. While the husband and all four children are carved in sunken relief, the wife is carved in raised relief, which is a highly unusual combination in Old Kingdom art. In spite of this difference, the figures of husband and wife share the same proportions, general shape, and nearly identical forms of hands and ears; the only visible difference is the type of relief. They are both stylistically related to the figures of Sabni2 above them and on the east jamb. Immediately south of the panel with Hehu, another panel extends behind him, with images of his family carved in Sunken A style. His wife is named Nefer-wawet, and this same husband and wife pair appears on a panel on the north section of the east wall in Pepynakht Heqaib2's chapel. Below this family panel another small panel of offering figures was carved in an apparent attempt to imitate the composition above, and in a similar Sunken A style.

The large collection of images on the exterior of the tomb helps to redirect a visitor's focus from Pepynakht Heqaib2's entrance to the northern end of the forecourt and the smaller entrance to Sabni2's own chapel. Stepping through the doorway, the passage into the chapel proper is slightly longer and narrower than the entrance to Pepynakht Heqaib2's,

56. Relief of offerers on the façade of the tomb of Sabni2 (Sb6).

and the lower ceiling limits the upward expanse of the door thicknesses, both of which are covered with relief-carved images. The two sides of the corridor have mirroring compositions, with a large figure of Sabni2 at the front, holding a staff and scepter, facing out of the tomb and three registers of offering figures behind him, as well as other single offering figures in the space in front of him (Figure 57). On each side, lines of text frame this main composition, and on the western thickness a longer text provides an autobiography detailing Sabni2's work in building barges in Wawat to transport obelisks on behalf of the king.

Although several figures on these thicknesses and throughout Sabni2's tomb are carved in styles used in other tombs, a number of figures are carved in styles that appear to be limited to this tomb. These include all five large figures of the tomb owner, including the two on these entrance thicknesses, two in a fishing and fowling scene, and another on the north wall. Their style, which I term Sabni2 Raised, is similar to Raised A1 in the low raised relief and the usually smooth surfaces of the body (Figures 58, 60, 61). The straight line of the shoulders, interrupted only by small bumps indicating the collar bones, gives the figure a stilted quality. The facial features of the different figures are all clearly related, and

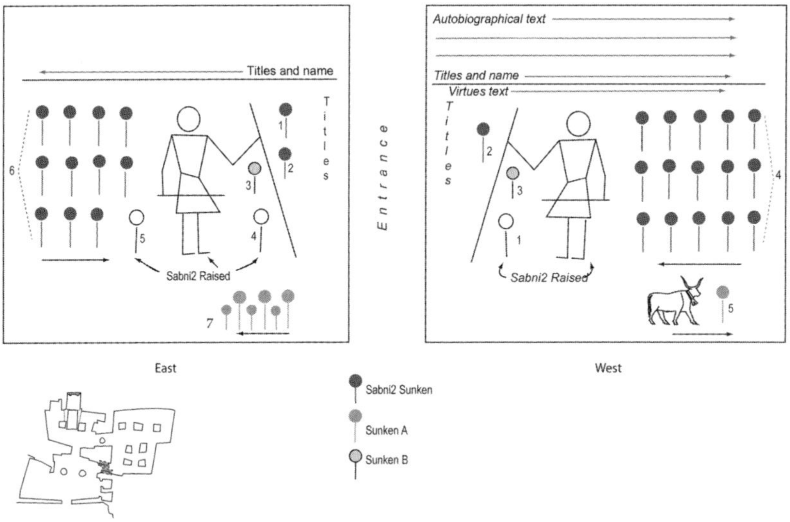

57. Diagram of the entrance thicknesses in the tomb of Sabni2 (Sb10–13).

most distinctive are the hairline and the ear; a band of raised relief begins at the forehead and outlines the hair down to the sideburn, where it then becomes the outer ridge of the ear.

Several small figures share this relief style, including an official at the feet of Sabni2 on the west thickness, and two women flanking him on the east, one of whom is identified as his daughter Merti. Other offering figures stand in front of both images of Sabni2. A figure named Dwa-Sobek is carved in the same place on each thickness, near Sabni2's hand, and both are Sunken B style. The other officials, one on the west and two on the east, are carved in Sabni2 Sunken style, the other style primarily limited to this tomb, with the exception of single figures in both 35 and 35d. This style combines the large head and slightly long torso of the Sunken B style with the delicately modulated outline and softly rounded surface of the Sunken A style (reference Figure 58, left side). The figures all have a short, angled line from under the front armpit to the main part of the torso, usually quite narrow waists, and overall thin but carefully nuanced limbs. The faces have small, rounded noses and square jaws, and the hairline and eye are almost always incised. Interestingly, the middle figure on the east thickness holds a vessel that is carved in raised, rather than sunk, relief. The tip of the vessel nearly touches the staff held by Sabni2, which is also carved in raised relief; perhaps in carving the image of Sabni2, the artist began carving the offering figure, as well, before realizing it was meant to be in sunk relief.

58. East entrance thickness in the tomb of Sabni2 (Sb10–11).

The remainder of these mirrored compositions is more uncommon. Behind each large figure of Sabni2 are three registers of offering figures, all carved in the Sabni2 Sunken style. Texts providing the names and titles of the figures are carved in narrow registers above them, or in some cases around them. Although all the figures are male and carved in the same style, small variations in iconography serve to break up the scene, and more importantly to differentiate individuals. Each thickness also has one additional panel carved into the low dado beneath the primary composition. On the west, a male offering figure carved in the Sunken A style leads a bull carved in raised relief. The juxtaposition of a sunken relief figure and a raised relief animal is familiar from the tomb of Khwin-Khnum, and the male figure and the bull are very similar to those from his tomb. On the east thickness, a *wab*-priest and his family are carved in Sunken A.

The rest of the program is concentrated in the area around the entrance. A large fishing and fowling scene occupies the main part of the east wall (Figures 59, 60). The composition, style, and many of the details of this fishing and fowling scene differentiate it from those in the tombs of Khunes and Sabni1 (Plate V), which are much more similar. Each image of Sabni2 is flanked by two small figures, a seated woman on

59. View of the interior northeast area in the tomb of Sabni2 (Sb14, 15 visible).

60. Fishing and fowling scene in the tomb of Sabni2 (Sb15).

the outside and a standing man on the inside. The figures of Sabni2 and of the two women are carved in the Sabni2 Raised style, the small male figure to the south is carved in Sabni2 Sunken style, and the priest figure in front of the fowler is carved in the Raised A2 style. This large scene is accompanied by a small panel of offering figures to its south carved in Sunken A style, and another panel on the adjacent north wall. This panel shows two men and a woman carved in the Sabni2 Sunken style. This female figure is the only one carved in this style, and she also stands out for her unusual dark-colored dress.

When Habachi excavated this tomb, he found in place a small offering table, created with three stone slabs, set up beneath this large fishing and fowling image. Given the location of the false door, normally the primary cult place of a tomb, in the far reaches of the very dark western side of the tomb, it is perhaps unsurprising that a secondary ritual area might be established in this image-centric area of the tomb. The presence of panels of offering figures on either side of the image reinforces the sense of the image and the location being a focus of cultic activity. A half-height stone wall is built between the pillar and the east wall of the chapel, perhaps to further enclose and define the cult space around the fishing and fowling panel.

On the south face of pillar E1, a more complex scene than is typical of Qubbet el-Hawa shows the tomb owner watching three registers of bulls (Figure 61). The figure of Sabni2 is clearly in the Sabni2 Raised style, and the bulls are carved in raised relief as well, but the male figure on the middle register with his hand to his chest is carved in Sabni2 Sunken style. Two registers of larger sunken glyphs run across the top of the scene, providing the titles of Sabni2 and identifying his activity as "watching the great ones."[24] One more panel of offering figures was drawn across from this scene, apparently intended to be carved in the Sunken A style.

Despite the shared forecourt and linked interior space, the tombs of Pepynakht Heqaib2 and Sabni2 are conceptually independent. Both tomb programs are large and complex, incorporating a high number of different figures and a wide range of styles, including two unique large figure styles: the Sunken E figures on the entrance thicknesses of Pepynakht Heqaib2, and the Sabni2 Raised style of all five figures of Sabni2 inside his tomb.

The cemetery continues northward from the large group of 35–35d-35e, first to an interesting grouping of three tombs (QH35g, h, i) cut into an enclosing curve of the cliff. These tombs sit at a higher level than Pepynakht Heqaib2 and Sabni2, and in their arrangement along the curve of the cliff all open onto a kind of shared forecourt. Most

61. Bull-fighting scene in the tomb of Sabni2 (Sb17).

likely, these tombs were constructed during a similar time period, at the end of the Sixth Dynasty.[25] Beyond this grouping, more tombs continue apace, coming to a close with the large and elaborate tomb of Sirenput I, QH36 from the Twelfth Dynasty. In the intervening space, one or more of the chapels may have originally been constructed during the late Old Kingdom, but of the surviving texts and images, the earliest date to the Middle Kingdom. Most likely, the tombs around the curve of the cliff just north of the Pepynakht Heqaib-Sabni2 complex marked the end of the Old Kingdom cemetery.

3

Figure, Panel, Program: Form and Meaning

The image and text programs in the Old Kingdom tombs at Qubbet el-Hawa exhibit a visual complexity due to the systematic use of their three defining elements: the organization in panels, the thematic focus on identified offering figures, and the diversity of style among the images. The resulting programs represent a unique visual expression among Old Kingdom elite tombs in Egypt.

Although each aspect of the program system clearly fulfills a different function, all three are engaged in a symbiotic relationship: the use of one can be seen to facilitate the use of the others, and they all evolve concurrently through the growth of the cemetery as the community, including the tomb owners and artisans, establishes this new tradition of elite tomb building in their local cemetery. An analysis of each of the three defining elements individually highlights both the consistencies and the variations in their use throughout the programs in the cemetery, and this information provides a basis for hypotheses about possible origins of each element and reasons for its adaptation and development.

The programs in the elite tombs at Qubbet el-Hawa must be viewed as the result of the purposeful actions of the people who invested significant time and effort into their design and execution. These tomb owners and artisans acted with evident knowledge, as will be discussed below, and made clear choices in their use of these unusual program elements. As products of material culture, these programs not only reveal aspects of the particular environment in which they were created, but, once produced, they themselves became part of that environment and influenced the process and results of the programs subsequently created.

The tombs analyzed here were all created during a relatively narrow time span (second half of the Sixth dynasty), and establishing a clear chronological sequence among them remains problematic. Despite the difficulty in establishing which programs could have influenced others (by being earlier), the fact of the transformation and development of the system among these twelve programs is essential to examining how the programs functioned on behalf of these tomb owners. The discussion here begins with an analysis of the panel system and then thematic content, followed by a longer assessment of the diversity of style. Included in this section is a statistical analysis of each style's presence within the cemetery, followed by discussions of the intent and meaning of this particularly unusual element of the programs.

"Panel" System

The consistency with which the Qubbet el-Hawa tomb programs utilize the small, discrete panels of images and texts strongly indicates that this method found favor among the tomb owners, but it does not imply that this panel mode emerged fully formed from the minds of the artisans and patrons. It appears that they developed this system, along with the other unique aspects of their programs, in response to an array of influences and changing circumstances.

Because the standard model of an elite tomb program included fully decorated chapel walls, some scholars have mistakenly viewed the Qubbet el-Hawa tombs as "unfinished."[1] Construction of a tomb often began late in the tomb owner's life, thus chapel programs often remained unfinished, but none of the Memphite programs described as unfinished appear anything like the Qubbet el-Hawa tombs. An unfinished tomb may have several blank walls, or sections of scenes may not be fully carved or painted, but in all cases the underlying design principle based upon registers of images fully covering the walls is clear. In the Qubbet el-Hawa tombs, the artist prepared only a small section of a wall for relief and the carved scene fully fills this smoothed area of the wall. Even on walls with several adjacent scenes, the area between them remains rough, indicating that each panel was conceived separately as a complete and finished image (Figures 17, 50, 59, Plate XIV).

Despite the clear intent to use small panels as program components, the use of programs leaving extensive blank wall surface provides such a stark contrast to the vast majority of Old Kingdom tomb programs that it could suggest the patrons had few options. In particular, the blank walls could be interpreted as the consequence of the tomb owners' access to only a small group of artisans who were not capable of fully decorating all of the tombs, but evidence does not support this view.

By the Sixth dynasty, the lack of an artisan community in any Egyptian town of the size and importance of Elephantine seems highly unlikely, and indeed there is evidence from the settlement site of local artisans. The few surviving artifacts (other than pottery) from the Old Kingdom include many stone vessels, a number of wood fragments with relief carving, and a granite naos dedicated to Satet.[2] Furthermore, the site excavators discovered evidence of workshops associated with a public building in the Old Kingdom town, including unfinished small statues and fragments of stone indicative of sculpture carving, as well as evidence of working ivory and wood, and even faience.[3]

The size of the artisan community is less certain than the fact of its existence, and it could well have changed over time. When the first tombs were cut at Qubbet el-Hawa, perhaps the size of the local artisan group was small enough to be a factor in the design of tomb programs. Before the founding of the cemetery the opportunity for relief carving work would have been smaller, but following the establishment and subsequent growth of the cemetery, the available work may have encouraged a concurrent growth of the artisan community. Alternately, the early tombs may have been less of a focus of artistic concern among the established artisan community, and thus larger, more elaborate chapel programs were not initially feasible. Unfortunately, the complexity of establishing a certain chronology among the tombs makes it difficult to ascertain a path of change over the course of the cemetery's history, but a hypothesis can be presented based upon the available evidence.

The program in the tomb of Harkhuf does not use panels in the same manner as all of the other Old Kingdom tombs in the cemetery. His program consists primarily of large-scale figures carved on the façade and on the interior pillars, which was a common practice in elite tombs during this time (Plate XII). The interior walls of Harkhuf's chapel remain empty and somewhat roughly finished, however, indicating they were never intended to be carved. Thus, although the large relief figures accompanied by lengthy texts on the pillars cannot truly be designated as panels (as they cover a large percentage of the pillar face surface and have no clearly defined edges), the program of Harkhuf's tomb *is* limited to select areas of the chapel and much of the interior surface is left blank, creating the same effect as the use of panels in other tombs.

Harkhuf's tomb was one of, if not the, earliest decorated tombs in the cemetery.[4] As such, it was constructed during a time when the practice of decorating elite tombs in Elephantine was relatively new and thus possibly during a period in which the local artisan community was relatively small. The limited image program in his tomb could have been designed for a small group of artisans with limited time, but the chapel is small, and fully decorating it would seem manageable even for a very small group of artists. The likely presence of local artists and relative manageability of the project implies a choice to not fully decorate the interior walls; perhaps at this early stage elite tombs were not yet considered an artistic priority. Harkhuf's tomb program is dominated by lengthy texts both on his façade and on the interior pillars. This unusual emphasis on textual inscriptions must also have been a purposeful choice by the tomb owner and artists, given both the lack of comparable programs and the fact that typically the same artisans who carved images carved hieroglyphic inscriptions, as well. The desire to emphasize text may have been part of the reason for the limited image program. Regardless of the balance between specific desires of the patron and limitations on his options in the shaping of his program, once the program was executed it set a standard for all the tombs decorated after it. Although no other tomb program relies on texts to the same extent, the lack of fully decorated walls in Harkhuf's tomb and the use of individual figures may have influenced later tomb owners and artisans, in their sense of what was acceptable for an elite tomb program.

In all of the tombs it is appropriate to assume a similar mix of influences on the program; for example, in the tomb of Mekhu and Sabni1, while the choice of a panel-based program distributed over largely undecorated walls may have been encouraged in part by Harkhuf's model, the extreme size of the tomb may have also rendered any hope of covering the walls impractical. Yet the tomb of Khunes is relatively large, as well, and two of the very high, long walls of his tomb are fully covered with relief. This tomb provides the only example of such Memphite-like wall design in the cemetery. Furthermore, although the south wall, the false door niche, and the figures on pillars W1 and E1 compose the initial core of Khunes's tomb program, numerous smaller panels of offering figures are also carved throughout the tomb. These panels integrate the anomalous program of Khunes's tomb into the cemetery's system, which implies the predominance of the panel system as well as the importance of participating in it. The program in the tomb of Pepynakht Heqaib2, likely one of the latest among the Old Kingdom tombs in the cemetery, further proves the predominance of the panel system; large areas of two walls are covered with relief, but in both cases the relief is executed in discrete panels rather than registers (Figures 49, 50, Plate XIV). Thus, it is clear that while a limited artisan pool, limited artistic concern, or other practical reasons and personal preferences may have been factors in the early stages of tomb decoration and thus in the original development of the panel system, ultimately this system fulfilled particular needs of these tomb owners in a more satisfactory manner than the fully covered walls typical of Memphite and most other provincial tombs. There are some exceptions in the provinces, most often in larger tombs, which implies that the practical difficulty of decorating a very large space came into play, although this cannot be assumed to be the determining factor. An example is the tomb of Hem-Min at Hawawish, which is an exceptionally large tomb in a cemetery of mostly smaller tombs. The smaller tombs are fully decorated; only the west wall of Hem-Min's tomb is decorated. This wall is, however, fully covered with a large scene of the tomb owner and registers of smaller figures, as in the other fully decorated tombs. This pattern links Hem-Min's tomb more closely to Memphite style tombs than to the Qubbet el-Hawa pattern of panels.[5]

The use of panels gave the artists greater flexibility in locating scenes within the tomb chapel space. In most elite tomb chapels, an array of factors including the perceived needs of the deceased tomb owner, the needs of the mortuary ritual, connections to temple programs, and other religious concepts potentially determined the location of scenes in the program. The relative importance and degree of influence of any factor no doubt fluctuated from tomb to tomb. In the fully decorated chapels typical to the majority of elite tombs, an internal hierarchy of needs thus determined the layout of the program; priorities, such as the false door stele, were located first, and the remaining scenes were distributed over the available wall space according to the perceived importance of the different scenes and an overall concept of the chapel space. A similar array of factors was surely present in determining the layout of the Qubbet el-Hawa tomb programs, yet the more adaptable system of panels meant less need for a hierarchy of priorities.

Among the Qubbet el-Hawa tombs, light and visibility are clearly the main determining factor in the layout of the programs. Excepting a handful of examples, the artists stringently avoided carving panels or figures in unlit spaces of chapels. The exceptions in the tomb of Mekhu are painted panels associated with subsidiary burials, and the offering figure in the tomb of Sabni2 in the rear of the tomb is carved next to the false door. This layout emphasis on lighted areas suggests the tomb owners and artisans prioritized the needs of a living audience rather than those of the deceased tomb owner. Further evidence for this priority is found in the placement of the panels on the parts of columns and pillars that are oriented toward the tomb entrance, even when the figures in the scene are oriented toward the false door. West faces of pillars are never decorated, nor are the north or south faces when they are directed away from the entrance.

A perceived living audience is not unique to Qubbet el-Hawa; all tomb owners assumed, at a minimum, the presence of priests in charge of their mortuary cult. The religious function of these priests more greatly influenced the program than did the perceived needs of any individual priest himself. For example, Egyptian funerary ideology dictates that the false door be located on the west wall of a tomb. Very often, especially in the larger, multi-roomed chapels of Sixth dynasty tombs, this meant the false door was in the furthest reaches of the chapel, more difficult to access and far from any natural light.[6] The inscription of ritual prayers and offering lists near the false door could be interpreted as a convenience for the mortuary priests; however, the primary determinant is clearly the false door itself. The location of other scenes may be influenced by the activities of mortuary priests, but this currently remains unclear.

At Qubbet el-Hawa panels are often placed along an axis leading to the false door, which would presumably be the path of the mortuary priests. In almost all of the Old Kingdom tombs here, the false door is directly opposite the entrance into the tomb, thus the axis *to* the false door leads *from* the entrance, and this axis is one of the most well-lit areas of the tomb. This coincidence of ritual path and lighted areas may be purposeful; perhaps the tomb plans were designed in part to facilitate the ritual activities of the priests. In many tombs there exists evidence of original mud-brick internal walls set up between columns in order to enclose a more sacred ritual space, and the placement of the panels in these tombs can also be linked to the location of the internal walls (usually not full height), and thus the path of the priests to the false door. Seyfried emphasizes the significance of this relationship, but also implicates the living audience of priests, describing the role of the panels essentially as "path indicators" for these priests, signs visible to them upon their entrance into the tomb.[7]

Other aspects of the programs suggest, however, that ritual was not the determining factor. Images are rarely clustered around the false door, being much more often placed closer to the entrance. In Mekhu's chapel, the panels on columns M6 and W6 are placed along the path of light that squeezes through the array of columns to reach Sabni1's false door, a path unlikely to be primarily ritual (reference Figures 6, 8). And although the lighting was temporary, every panel was placed to receive as much sunlight as possible to be fully illuminated at some point during the day. An illustrative example is the large part of Sabni2's tomb program carved into the façade of his tomb and the rest in the small southeast corner, all far from the false door in the rear of the tomb (Figures 41, 54, 59). This unusual program distribution can only be explained as an adaptive response to the very limited lighted area available inside his chapel. It seems unlikely this program layout was intended to assist the priests in their ritual activities.

The priests were not the only members of the audience for an elite tomb program; family members and others visited tomb chapels, as well. The essential structure of the Egyptian tomb, comprising a burial chamber and the tomb chapel, divided the monument into one part sealed off from the living (burial chamber) and the other part open to the living visitors (tomb chapel). A significant purpose of the tomb chapel was to keep the tomb owner in the collective memory of Egyptian society, and this required the active participation of living members of the community.[8] Family members visited tomb chapels to honor their deceased brethren and to celebrate with them on festivals and holidays.[9] The proximity of the Memphite cemeteries to the local settlements and the ease of access to the tombs facilitated these visits. Although in certain provinces access to the cemeteries was difficult, for example, the cemetery at Hawawish near Akhmim, the proximity of Qubbet el-Hawa to the settlement at Elephantine and the ease of access to the tombs likely encouraged visits by members of the local community in a manner similar to the Memphite cemeteries. The inscription on Harkhuf's façade explicitly addresses such visitors.[10]

Despite the assumed presence of an audience in most elite tombs, the extent to which this audience influenced the layout of the program is less certain and less consistent. While in New Kingdom Theban tombs a section of the program was composed with the visitors in mind,[11] in the Old Kingdom it seems only small vignettes within overall programs were specifically designed to entice passersby.[12] This suggests that the program layout was primarily determined by other factors (be they ritual needs, needs of the tomb owner, or other factors), and the needs of the living audience were secondary, thus the previously organized scenes were shaped to fulfill these needs. Among the Qubbet el-Hawa programs the need for visibility takes precedence, and so the needs of the living audience appear to be a much greater priority. Ritual and other religious needs as well as those of the deceased tomb owner were surely considered; these needs may have been satisfied through this living audience.

The use of the panel system also affects the organization and expression of the tomb programs' content. In a register system, strings of synonymous offering figures form correlative parts of larger scenes devoted to offering or other themes (i.e., bird catching, fishing, and so forth). In contrast, the use of panels parses the program content into coherent components of small groups of figures, usually families. In panels incorporating images of the tomb owner, the component still consists of a small group of figures, in these cases more often unrelated, grouped around the dominant figure of the tomb owner. This communicative effect of the panel system may have contributed to its appeal to the Qubbet el-Hawa tomb owners.

Thematic Focus

The panel system is clearly symbiotic with the thematic focus on offering figures, the second characteristic aspect of the programs. Only seven panels in the cemetery have content other than a group of offering figures (or the tomb owner), including the three fishing and fowling scenes, two scenes with bullfights, the agricultural panel on Mekhu's east wall, and the series of active scenes on the south wall of Khunes's tomb. A handful of working figures are integrated into three of the larger panels (Kh4, Ku2, and PnH28: Plate XVIII), which consist mainly of offering figures. Of the fifty-six panels with tomb owner figures (excepting the false doors and lintels), only thirteen lack an offering figure on the same surface, and nearly half of these are in the tomb program of Harkhuf.

This thematic focus raises questions similar to those raised by the use of the panel system, regarding the tomb owners' and artisans' familiarity with the standard tomb program model and the possibility that a small artisan pool limited their options. As discussed previously, the tomb owners and artisans at Elephantine were familiar with more typical elite tomb programs, in part via contact with the capital and other provincial sites. In addition, the presence of other scene types, no matter how few, is proof of their knowledge of the *possibility* of additional scene types. The south wall of Khunes's tomb alone contains images of craft production, brewing beer, making wine and bread, leading rows of cattle, bird catching, and sailing ships. The agricultural scene in Mekhu's tomb, although fragmentary, includes the key elements of sowing, harvesting, and storing grain (Plate IV). The same scene includes a vignette of two figures butchering a cow. Among the small working figures incorporated into the offering scenes noted are additional beer and bread makers.

The tomb owners and artisans thus made an informed choice when they emphasized scenes of offering figures. As in the use of the panel system, external factors such as a small artisan pool or limited artistic interest in the programs could have influenced this choice, but the result remains the same. Offering figures appear in the earliest tomb programs and remained an essential part of the elite tomb program throughout the Old Kingdom, thus this choice by the Qubbet el-Hawa tomb owners is not surprising. Yet the near total absence of other scene types clearly suggests an intentional focus. If the tomb owners felt other scene types were necessary, surely they would have been incorporated on a more frequent basis. Again, as with the panel system, it is possible that an early choice to leave out these scene types set a standard of acceptability that eventually became a tradition, and, like the panel system, the thematic focus must have fulfilled the particular needs of these tomb owners. In addition, the symbiotic relationship between the two elements of panels and offering figures indicates that as one developed into tradition it would have encouraged the other to develop, as well.

The presence of identifying inscriptions on nearly every panel significantly refines the theme from generic "offering" to one of specific individuals supporting the tomb owners (for example, Figures 13, 30, 39, 51, 52). Five of the seven panels with content other than offering still incorporate identified subsidiary figures; the two with primarily anonymous figures are both part of the east/south wall program in the tomb of Khunes. Most elite tomb programs incorporated identified figures into their programs, most often family members but also in some cases high-ranking figures (based on their titles) without a specified relationship to the tomb owner. Almost all elite tombs incorporate subsidiary figures, both family and non-related, into their programs, but typically these figures are integrated into scenes depicting different activities and with numerous anonymous figures, as well. At Qubbet el-Hawa, the separation of identified figures from active or other scene contexts, their organization into groups, and the lack of anonymous figures and other scene types that the majority of even provincial programs have all emphasize the thematic focus.

The panel system and the thematic focus together create a tomb program built from small groups of identified offering figures organized around significantly fewer, yet larger, tomb owner figures. The identity of these figures and their relationships will be discussed in Chapter 4.

Diversity of Style: Data

The diversity of style among the images at Qubbet el-Hawa is one of the most striking aspects of the programs. Careful attention to the form of the images reveals variations within styles, as well as relationships among the styles and among images in different tombs, which provides a possible window into the realm of artistic process in the cemetery. In addition, an analysis of the distribution of the styles among panels, figures, and location within the cemetery affords a useful tool for inquiring how style may have been conceived and employed by the tomb owners and their artists. This section discusses these issues for each individual style, while the following section explores the intent and meaning behind the overall stylistic diversity in these programs. Table 1 shows the distribution of styles through the tombs.

Raised A1

Raised A1 is the low raised relief used primarily for large-scale figures, and thus mainly tomb owners (for example, Figures 28, 44, Plate IV). Among the twelve tomb programs, fifty-four figures distributed over twenty-seven separate panels are categorized as Raised A1 style. Of the fifty-four, half are primary tomb owners including Mekhu, Sabni1, Khwin-Khnum, Tjetji, Khunes and his wife Ankhes, Pepynakht Heqaib2, and Sabni2. Of the other twenty-seven Raised A1 figures, twenty-one are family members of these tomb owners, and with one exception they share panels with Raised A1 figures of the tomb owners. The final six figures are *ka*-priests, all of whom share panels with a Raised A1 figure of an elite tomb owner.

The Raised A1 figures appear throughout the cemetery, and both the southernmost programs of Mekhu and Sabni1 and one of the northernmost tombs, of Pepynakht Heqaib2, have a large number of them: six, nine, and five, respectively. Overall, the Raised A1 figures are concentrated in the southern half of the cemetery, with twenty-one figures in the south group of tombs from Mekhu and Sabni1, Khwin-Khnum, and Tjetji, and twenty-eight in the centrally located tomb of Khunes (including the image of his wife in her chapel), and only seven in the northern four tombs of Harkhuf, Pepynakht Heqaib1, Pepynakht Heqaib2, and Sabni2.

Although male figures usually account for 70 percent to 75 percent of the figures in individual styles, in individual tombs, and in the cemetery overall, in the Raised A1 style male figures make up just more than 80 percent of the total, as the style is reserved primarily for images of the tomb owner, and only one chapel belongs to a female owner (Ankhes, connected to her husband Khunes's tomb chapel). The figures comprising the Raised A1 category show little variation, generally limited to small details. Overall, they have unusually uniform facial features, though several have pointed earlobes (MS24, PnH5, PnH6) rather than the more common rounded ones, a feature they share with several tomb owner images carved in Raised A2.

Painted

A small group of images among the tombs are either entirely, or nearly entirely, executed in paint alone rather than relief carving. This Painted group includes both tomb owner and subsidiary figures; however, in all cases the subsidiary figures appear with at least one image of a tomb owner. In the double chapel of Mekhu and Sabni1, the fishing and fowling scene (MS27: Plate V) and the two panels depicting the subsidiary tomb owners within the chapel of Mekhu (MS8, MS9) all fit into this category, as well as forming a subset distinct from the panels in the tomb of IiShemai. On the Mekhu and Sabni1 panels, visible incised lines outline the figures, and the inscriptions are incised, as well. Yet the images cannot correctly be called relief, as the interior and exterior surfaces around these lines run together as a single surface. Paint is used for the majority of the details, including the facial features. In contrast, the two painted panels in the tomb of IiShemai have no incised lines. In total, four tomb owner images and nineteen subsidiary figures populate these panels; however, as the two panels in Mekhu's chapel depict subsidiary tomb owners, the two main figures there may be considered tomb owner images as well.

All figures in these panels have the same standard proportions, overall body shape, facial features, and scale as most of the A1 figures; the primary difference is medium. The paint surviving on a number of the A1- and A2-style figures, including three of Khwin-Khnum (KK1, KK3, KK5), two of Sobekhetep (SH1, SH3), and the other images of IiShemai (IiS1, IiS4: Plate VII) further show the close links between the Painted and A styles. The two painted relief panels depicting Sobekhetep (SH1, SH3: Plate VI), two of the painted relief panels in Khwin-Khnum's program (KK1, KK5), the two Painted IiShemai panels (IiS2, IiS3), and the two subsidiary tomb owners' panels in Mekhu's chapel all have the same design. The figure of the tomb owner stands within a rectangular frame against a blue-gray background. Above the frame, a band of hieroglyphs is painted or carved inside its own frame against a lighter background. The fishing and fowling panel in Sabni1's chapel utilizes a related design with the main figures set against a blue background, although here the glyphs share this background. Shared details such as the leopard skins worn by the two figures of IiShemai and the figure of Khwin-Khnum on pillar W2 (KK5), as well as the hieroglyphs on these two panels and on the east face of pillar E2 in Khwin-Khnum's program (KK1), provide further formal correlations among the Painted and A1-A2 styles.

Unlike in raised relief, in which scale can impact the execution of details in any given style, the large- and small-scale Painted figures more closely correlate, especially within the same composition. Unsurprisingly, the small-scale Painted figures also share formal aspects with both the Raised A2 and Sunken A styles, with proportions similar to the A2 figures and finer details such as musculature in the outline of the body and facial features similar to Sunken A.

Raised A2

The primary distinction between the Raised A1 and Raised A2 styles is scale; secondary aspects such as the height of the relief and the nuance of details also differentiate them. The two styles are formally closely related, and the use and distribution of the two styles further illustrates the close connection between them.

There are sixty-six Raised A2 figures, not including the anonymous figures on the south wall of Khunes's tomb (Kh7, roughly eighty-plus figures) and on the agricultural panel on the east wall of Mekhu's tomb (MS7, eighteen figures), although the identified figures from each scene are counted, two from Khunes and two from Mekhu (Table 1).[13] Of these sixty-six figures, ten depict primary tomb owners.

Twenty-three of the remaining fifty-six figures share panels with a Raised A1 figure; typically, a small A2 figure of a priest or offering figure faces a large A1 figure of a tomb owner. Further, fifteen A2 subsidiary figures occupy panels physically linked to an A1 image of the tomb owner; for example, the A2 figures from Mekhu's east wall (MS7: Plate IV) and on Khunes's south wall (Kh7) are part of larger scenes filled with A2 figures and juxtaposed with a Raised A1 figure. Also linked, though not as directly, are the four figures leading oxen on the south entrance thickness of Sabni1's tomb (MS22), below a large scene of Sabni1 and his son, and six figures carved along the south jamb of Khunes's false door (Kh8) that essentially extend the south wall program, filling the space between the continuous east/south wall designs and the false door niche, in which two seated A1 style figures of Khunes are carved. The last A2 figure in this group is the female offering figure on the west façade of Sabni2's tomb, who is part of the panel of figures (Sb6: Figure 56) set beneath the seated figure of the tomb owner. As the only raised relief figure in the group, her style is indistinguishable from the distinct A2 version of the figures of Sabni2 on his façade (cf. Figure 55).

Only seventeen Raised A2 figures distributed over five panels are fully independent of a Raised A1 figure, yet in most cases an A1 style figure is nearby. Four of these panels depict a group of raised A2 offering figures: one in Sabni1 (MS25), one in Sobekhetep (SH2: Figure 13), one in

Khwin-Khnum (KK4: Plate XIb), and one in Khunes (Kh29). The fifth panel, on pillar W6 in Sabni1's tomb (MS26), has only a single offering figure. The last Raised A2 figure is part of the fishing and fowling panel in the tomb of Sabni2 (Sb15: Figure 60).

The Raised A2 figures closely follow the Raised A1 pattern of distribution, and are largely concentrated in the middle and southern parts of the cemetery, with thirty-one figures in the southern group, twenty-six figures in the tomb of Khunes, and only six in the northern tombs. In addition, the two large panels with anonymous A2 figures are in the tombs of Khunes and Mekhu, and all five independent panels with A2 figures are in the southern group and Khunes. Taking into account the anonymous A2 figures, the percentage of female figures is less than 20 percent; however, among the identified offering figures, the gender divide follows the typical pattern of approximately one-third women and two-thirds men.

The stylistic consistency among Raised A2 figures follows the same pattern as among Raised A1 figures; most fit easily into the category. The less uniform figures are usually associated with similarly discordant A1 figures. For example, both the standing A2 figure of Mekhu and the accompanying *ka*-servant on his ramp stele have elongated legs unusual for the style (MS1: Figure 14). The female offering figure on Sabni2's façade previously noted shares with the Sabni2 façade A2 figures their higher relief and intricate surface detail, which is less common in typical A2 figures.

Raised B

Raised B style panels are much less common than the A1 and A2 styles. Only nineteen figures on two panels are carved in Raised B, while a twentieth figure from a separate panel links to this style yet does not fully conform to it. One unusually large offering panel in the tomb of Khui comprises eighteen of the Raised B figures (Ku2: Figure 23). Another clearly Raised B figure stands alone on a column in the tomb of Tjetji (Tj3a: Plate XVIc) directly beneath a Raised A1 figure of the tomb owner. The twentieth figure appears on the bottom of pillar W2 in Khunes's chapel (Kh30). Eight of the twenty figures are female, all on Khui's pillar. On the bottom register of the Khui panel there are three figures engaged in activities related to beer making, in postures similar to several figures on another multi-register offering panel in the tomb of Pepynakht Heqaib2 (PnH28).

The figures on Khui's panel and the figure on the column of Tjetji are fairly consistent in terms of style, and both panels incorporate an image of an altar often also seen in Sunken B panels. The figure in the tomb of Khunes appears more similar to Raised B than either A1 or A2, but it differs enough from the standard that it cannot truly fit into this category. The long, sloped nose, incised ear and eye, and offering vessels are typical, however, of both Raised B and Sunken B, and are distinct from the A styles. Because the Qubbet el-Hawa artists never used the Raised B style for a tomb owner figure or other large-scale image and reserved it only for images of offering figures, it is not surprising that there are only nineteen Raised B figures in the cemetery and that the sunken version of the style is more common.

Sabni2 Raised

The final raised relief style in the cemetery is the Sabni2 Raised style, present only in the interior tomb program of Sabni2. Five images of the tomb owner appear in the chapel, and all are carved in the Sabni2 Raised style (Sb10: Figure 58, Sb12, Sb15: Figure 60, Sb17: Figure 61). Out of sixty subsidiary figures in the interior program, six are raised relief, and five of these are Sabni2 Raised; the sixth figure is Raised A2. The five Sabni2 Raised figures all share compositions with figures of the tomb owner.

The bulls being watched by Sabni2 on the panel on the inner "north wall" (Sb17) are also carved in the Sabni2 Raised style. Many of the relatively few animals in the Qubbet el-Hawa programs are carved in raised relief, including two panels that have subsidiary figures carved in sunken relief (KK2: Plate XIa, Sb13). The bulls on this bull-watching panel are integral to the meaning of the composition in the same way the fish are integral to the fishing and fowling scenes; thus, it is not surprising they are carved in the same raised relief style as the watching tomb owner. A very small, nonidentified subsidiary figure included in this raised relief composition assists the cow in the middle register giving birth. The single identified offering figure in this scene was carved in sunken relief.

Among the Raised A1, Raised A2, Raised B, and Sabni2 Raised styles, 113 of 150 figures depict either the tomb owner, someone sharing a panel with the tomb owner, or individuals on a panel juxtaposed with an image of the tomb owner (i.e., MS7 and Kh7). Thus, more than 75 percent of the raised relief in the cemetery is directly connected to the tomb owners. Of the remaining thirty-seven figures, nineteen are carved in Raised B on panels that share the same pillar surface (although in separate panels) with an image of the tomb owner, meaning 88 percent of the raised relief is closely associated with images of tomb owners.

Overall, the use of raised relief in the tomb programs is reserved primarily for tomb owners and figures closely associated with them, while the majority of offering figures are carved in sunk relief. This obvious distinction via medium suggests an intention on the part of the artists and tomb owners to express status through the form of the image. The relationship between style and status will be more fully examined next.

Sunken A

Sunken A relief is the most prevalent style in the cemetery, accounting for 15 tomb owner figures and 154 subsidiary figures. Thirteen of the fifteen tomb owners appear on the façade of a tomb, twelve of these on the façade of Sabni1, including on both portal jambs large-scale figures of Sabni attended by smaller-scale figures of priests and a son (MS18, MS19), and a now almost entirely lost series of ten figures across the upper lintel of his entrance (MS20). The location of these reliefs rationalizes the choice of medium despite the high status of the individual, as sunken relief is common for exterior images in Egyptian monuments, including Memphite and provincial Old Kingdom tombs. In addition, the programs of Harkhuf and Pepynakht Heqaib1 provide models in this cemetery for using sunken relief (Harkhuf style) for tomb owner images on the façade. That the two other pieces of exterior relief in Mekhu and Sabni1's tomb, the two stele set along the sides of the ramp, are carved in raised relief might suggest a developing preference to use relief style to convey status or meaning at the possible expense of visibility or tradition.

The other exterior tomb owner image carved in Sunken A is located on the west jamb of the façade of Sabni2 (Sb4). This small figure of Sabni2 stands at the bottom of a column of large, sunken relief hieroglyphs. Although again the exterior location would seem to explain the choice of Sunken A, the bulk of the façade program here, which includes five other images of the tomb owner, is carved in raised relief, perhaps because such a large percentage of the program appears on the façade of the tomb. The one Sunken A figure may have been intended as a determinative for the column of text above it and was thus carved in the same medium as the hieroglyphs.

A seated figure of Khui at the top of pillar E2 is carved in Sunken A on a panel with two smaller Sunken A offerers (Ku1). The relatively small image of Khui is about twice the size of typical offering figures but much smaller than most images of tomb owners. The rationale for carving this tomb owner image in sunken relief is unclear. The final tomb owner image carved in Sunken A is a figure of Khwin-Khnum on pillar W3 of his tomb (KK6: Plate IX). The sunken relief of this large-scale figure is rather shallow, as is that of the associated small *ka*-servant. The design of this panel complements the panel on pillar W2 across the entrance-to-false door axis. The figures on W2 are, however, carved in raised relief, and the choice of sunken relief for this pillar is intriguing.

Among the 154 Sunken A subsidiary figures, 7 share panels with Sunken A tomb owners. Six more share panels with figures carved in different styles. These include the four offering figures accompanying the two large Raised A1 images of Sabni2 on the panel above his lintel (Sb1), and the two independent offering figures sharing the middle register of Pepynakht Heqaib2's north thickness with a Raised A1 figure of the tomb owner (PnH6).

The remaining 141 figures fill 31 panels distributed throughout the cemetery; although nearly 65 percent of Sunken A figures are located in the northern tombs, the proportion of Sunken A to other styles is actually slightly higher in the southern tombs, where more than 33 percent of the offering figures are Sunken A, compared to Sunken A as 29 percent of the figures in the northern tombs. The gender division among Sunken A is slightly skewed, with just more than 35 percent female.

The distinctive Sunken A style figures comfortably incorporate small variations including proportions and detailing, the design of the panels, and the shape of the accompanying hieroglyphs. The proportions vary only slightly and some figures, especially male, are wider than others (cf. Figure 51 versus Figure 30). The use of incised lines to indicate internal details also differs. The selection of details follows no clear pattern, but typically any detailing includes the hairline of the male figures, and no panels use incised details on the female figures unless the male figures have them, as well. Otherwise, there are a variety of combinations, ranging from extensive detail on both figures (Figure 30) to only bits of detail on single figures (MS12). The paint remaining on many of the figures is a reminder that even those figures with no incised lines at all would have had painted details (Figure 51, Plate VIII).

With two exceptions, all Sunken A panels depict a single register of offering figures sharing a ground line. Differences of panel design occur in the arrangement of the accompanying inscriptions: either individual, in which the inscriptions fill an area in close proximity to the figure identified (PnH17); or a grid design, in which the texts are laid out with respect to the shape of the panel. The grid designs differ slightly; most have a line of text across the top and smaller inscriptions in vertical or shorter horizontal lines over the figures (MS5). In some cases, an additional vertical line of text at the front creates a frame (Kh22), and in a few examples there is no horizontal line of text, but the vertical inscriptions over each figure align across the top (Sb8). The hieroglyphs used in Sunken A panels are also generally consistent in style and form.

The use and combination of these formal variables of the Sunken A style follow no apparent pattern, nor is there any pattern or clear association of formal variation based on location in the cemetery. The Sunken A style also shares several formal aspects with the Raised A2 style, including the type and form of offerings, which are fairly consistent among both types of panels, and the shape of the hieroglyphs. Although in general the Sunken A figures are more elongated and have subtler outlines and finer details than Raised A2 figures, a comparison between two panels in the tomb of Khunes (Kh22 and Kh29) suggests these formal differences are due in some degree to the type of relief used. The small-scale Painted figures on Sabni1's fishing and fowling scene (MS27: Plate V) and IiShemai Setka's two panels (IiS2 and IiS3) also provide a formal link between Sunken A and Raised A2. As noted, the large Painted figures are very similar to Raised A1 figures, and in a similar way the small Painted figures are linked to Raised A2 figures, in part by their close formal connections to the large Painted figures they accompany. Although in the shapes of their bodies and their proportions these Painted figures are closer to A2 style, they have obvious visual similarities to examples of Sunken A figures, as well.

The sunken styles B–E are visually distinct from the A group styles, and they display interrelated formal aspects. All but two of the panels in these styles are carved in the northern group of tombs including Khunes. The formal relationships among the styles will be considered following a brief summary of each style.

Sunken B

Twenty-five figures carved in the Sunken B style are distributed over ten panels. The drawing on the north face of pillar N2 in the tomb of Pepynakht Heqaib2 (PnH22) also appears to be in the Sunken B style, bringing the total number of figures to twenty-nine. No Sunken B style panels exist in tombs south of Khunes, although the tombs of Khui and Tjetji both have Raised B panels. There are ten women out of twenty-nine total figures, eight women out of the twenty-five carved figures.

Only small details of the generally consistent Sunken B style figures differ. In most examples, the torso and upper legs of the body form a rectangular core, but in some cases the slightly broader shoulders and more widely pointed kilt alter this core, rendering it more similar to the two-triangle form of Sunken C (Figure 29). The elongated proportions of a few Sunken B figures are also similar to Sunken C style figures (Pn7). In one case, the distinctive heads and faces of the figures recall the Sunken A style (PnH4b: Figure 46, lower right), which is an unusual combination. Other Sunken B figures that blend different formal characteristics seem to be influenced by surrounding images. For example, although the female figure at the back of the bottom row of the panel low on the east wall in the chapel of Khunes (Kh4) fits well into the Sunken B style based on her distinctive curving profile, her male pair has the elongated proportions and broader shoulders with pointed armpits of the numerous C style figures on the row above. A similar influence can be seen on the front figure of Pn7, whose elongated proportions and wide, pointed kilt may have been inspired by the C style figures in the panel above (Pn6) or in the panel on the opposite wall (Pn5). Despite these types of variations among the male figures, the female figures always maintain the distinctive curved profile and curved leg-dividing line.

The Sunken B panels use a number of different designs; a couple use a frame type with a vertical and horizontal line of text outlining the front figure (PnH15: Plate XVII and PnH4b), others have several vertical lines of text (PnH21: Figure 52, Pn7, Pn8: Figure 39), and in many others small inscriptions fit above or around the figures. The hieroglyphs on these panels vary rather widely. A few panels share specific signs; for example, on the east wall in the chapel of Pepynakht Heqaib2, panel O (PnH21) and panel I (PnH15: Plate XVII, right) use the same distinctive *tp* (profile head) sign, and a west wall panel in the tomb of Pepynakht1 (Pn8: Figure 39) and panel I use the same oddly shaped *z3* (pintail duck) sign. Despite these isolated links, the full inscriptions in these two pairs of panels are not the same. The hieroglyphs inscribed on another Sunken B panel (PnH4b) have no clear parallel anywhere, while a Sunken B figure in Khunes is accompanied by signs similar to some from Sunken C panels. In terms of texts, the Sunken B panels show greater variation than the Sunken A panels, but overall both styles incorporate a relatively similar range of difference in the figures.

Sunken C

Sunken C style is the second most popular in the cemetery, with seventy figures distributed on twenty-two panels. Like the related Sunken B style, the panels appear primarily in the northern part of the cemetery; the tomb of Tjetji is the furthest south C appears. The majority of the Sunken C figures, fifty-six, are split between the two large tombs of Khunes and Pepynakht Heqaib2. The gender divide in the Sunken C style leans heavily toward male figures, which account for nearly 85 percent of the figures.

The heads, faces, and upper bodies of Sunken C style figures are visually uniform. In some cases the long, tube-shaped nose is shorter than in others, but the unusual facial features are always recognizable (Plate XV). The lower bodies do have different forms. While the standard form of this style has very elongated and tapered upper legs, some figures have more typically proportioned upper legs. Kilts that are tight to the legs of these figures emphasize their smaller overall proportions (Kh26). In another variation the kilts are wider and the legs are set further apart, so the figures appear less elongated and more geometric (Kh25) (cf. Figure 29, top and bottom). Although both variations appear in at least two tombs, they are most common in the tomb of Khunes.

The design of the panels divides them roughly into two categories. In approximately half the panels with text, the inscription fills the open area around the figures either above or in front of them. In the other half, the inscription is organized in lines; a vertical line at the front of the panel, in some cases two framing lines set between boundary lines (Figure 50). Examples of the latter half are found mainly in the tombs of Pepynakht1 and Pepynakht Heqaib2, while the first type is found mainly in the tomb of Khunes.

As in Sunken B, the hieroglyphs on Sunken C panels take a wide variety of form, and in many cases hieratic signs are mixed in with hieroglyphs. Some consistency in paleography can be seen in panels in the same tomb. Among the C style panels in Pepynakht Heqaib2, two general paleographic groups can be identified, and these two groups appear to be connected, as well. Not all of the inscriptions fit into these groups. The first group is defined by panels A, C, and D on the south part of the east wall (PnH8, 10, 11). These glyphs generally lack detail and many are similar in size and shape. The C style panel in the tomb of Tjetji has hieroglyphs in this style, as does a panel in the tomb of Pepynakht1 (Pn6). The glyphs in the second group, as seen in panels B, E, and F on the east wall of Pepynakht Heqaib2's tomb (PnH9, 12, 13), tend to be larger, with wider interior surfaces and more distinct forms.

Sunken D

Only six figures, all but one on the thicknesses in the tomb of Pepynakht Heqaib2, comprise the Sunken D style. Despite clear formal connections to other sunken styles, their shared, unique details separate them as a group. On the thicknesses of Pepynakht Heqaib2 there are essentially two pairs of figures, and the fifth figure may represent an effort to copy the others. The figures set underneath the column of text on the bottom panel of both thicknesses are the more distinctive pair (PnH4f: Figure 46, lower left and PnH7h, ref. Figure 43), and they seem to clarify the basic concept of this style. The triangles underlying the form of the Sunken C figures are here distilled into two simpler shapes, and the semicircular necklaces, deeper relief, and very flat internal surfaces emphasize the geometric nature of the figures. The other pair, flanking the tomb owner on the bottom panel of the north thickness (PnH7c and PnH7f: Plate XIII, Figure 48, bottom) have the curved necklace and kilt details similar to B and C figures, which counter the strongly geometric basis of the style. The fifth figure (PnH4g) with its semicircular necklace and pointed kilt seems to be an abbreviated version of PnH4f below it. Each pair shares hieroglyphs of the same style.

The sixth figure is a single, apparently unfinished figure on a column in the chapel of Mekhu (MS11). The proportions, shape of the figure, raised eye and ear all link this figure most closely with Sunken D, despite its seemingly unusual location.

Sunken E

The Sunken E style comprises a small group of only twenty figures, almost exclusively restricted to the tomb of Pepynakht Heqaib2, with nineteen of twenty figures found there. The last figure in this category varies somewhat from the Pepynakht Heqaib2 models, and rather surprisingly appears on the façade of the tomb of Harkhuf. Five of the twenty figures are women, and nine of the twenty are solo offering figures.

Two of the twenty Sunken E style figures are large-scale images of Pepynakht Heqaib2, carved on the bottom of the north and south thicknesses of his tomb (Plate XIII, Figures 46, 47). The commonality of the smaller offering figures derives from the unique style of these larger figures. The large, solo offering figure on the north thickness (PnH7b.1: Figure 46, middle left) behind the tomb owner provides a model for adapting this unique style to smaller figures. This finely carved image stands out within the Sunken E group, and clearly replicates several specific details of the larger figure of Pepynakht Heqaib2; perhaps the same artist carved both. The artist pays careful attention to the knees of this offering figure, using soft surface modeling that provides naturalistic detail similar to that in the tomb owner. The same pattern of modeling differentiates the two knees with a clear, angled band under the front knee and a rounder swelling around the back one. The face of the offering figure is also very similar to the tomb owner. Although the head of the smaller does not have the same exaggerated crown as the larger, it shares the large, almond-shaped eye with a raised band around it, the small nose slightly pointed at the tip and rounded at the nostril, and the wide, relief-carved lips. Even the small relief ear has a central incised line, a detail possibly inspired by the finely detailed ears of the large figures.

The main differences between this offering figure and the large figure of Pepynakht Heqaib2 are in the shape of the body and the proportions. The head of the smaller man is larger in proportion to the body, which may be due to the artist's desire to ensure the visibility of the unique facial features. The torso is close to standard, but the upper legs are elongated.

The kilt almost appears to be the long type worn by "mature" figures, yet the clearly indicated knees just below the hem make that impossible. Equally distinctive is the long, curving line forming the back profile from the shoulder to the heel. These two aspects, the elongated upper legs and the curved back profile, are not found in the large figure, and it is unclear what inspired them; apparently it was an artistic choice.

This unique offering figure forms the bridge between the large Sunken E images of Pepynakht Heqaib2 and the remaining offering figures in this style. They all share the same distinctive facial features and ear, and they also share the elongated upper legs of PnH7b.1. Many of these figures have longer, more tapered torsos, a further development away from the model of the large figures that could have been an effort to balance the longer, narrow upper legs.

There are differences among these figures. For example, the middle offering figure in front of the south image of the tomb owner (PnH4d: Figure 46) has a very large, oddly shaped head, but the facial features and the elongated upper legs clearly link it to Sunken E. The similarly placed figure on the north thickness (PnH7e: Figure 48, top) has a larger torso and slightly shorter legs; this could have been an effort to more closely approximate the proportions of the large figure or might have been due to space limitations or could have simply been an artistic choice. The heads of the three figures standing behind the tomb owner on the south side (PnH4a: Figure 46, top right) are slightly different shapes, and the face of the first figure has a more angled nose. Nonetheless the eye, wide lips, long proportions, and subtly carved knees clearly link this figure to the Sunken E style. The female figures are harder to connect, as there is no model for them, but because they accompany the Sunken E male figure and because they clearly share his style, they should also be categorized as Sunken E. The final group of Sunken E figures on panel G, set beneath the rock ledge on the south part of the east wall (PnH14), are most closely linked to the three members of group PnH4a.

The hieroglyphs writing the accompanying inscriptions also connect the figures in this style. In spite of differences among the signs – some signs are thinner and less deep (PnH4c), others are blockier and more deeply incised (PnH7d) – many of the signs are similar, and in particular the viper-"f" has the same unusual form in every inscription, with a vertically angled head separately written from the body.

The final figure carved in Sunken E shows up on the lower façade of the tomb of Harkhuf (H6). This image is the only one in the entire program not carved in the more traditional Harkhuf style; in addition, the presumed time-span between the creation of Harkhuf's program and that of Pepynakht Heqaib2, the apparent "home" for the Sunken E style, is equally unusual. Yet the distinctive facial features and the curving back line of the figure clearly link it to the formal characteristics of Sunken E. It may be that this small figure was added later to Harkhuf's program, a kind of distant offering to an exalted ancestor and attempt to bring his long-standing program into the Qubbet el-Hawa family.

A formal interplay similar to that among the Sunken E figures can be seen to a lesser extent between figures in different styles. For example, despite strong visual differences between the finely carved Sunken E offering figure on the bottom north thickness (PnH7b.1) and the figure beneath him (PnH7c:), the latter could also be seen as an alternative interpretation of the large Sunken E figure (Plate XIII, left). The form of the figure is simplified, and the facial features are more abstracted and less detailed, so the small nose is simply a point, the eye is less symmetrical and lacks the outer ridge, and the lips are reduced to incised lines. The ear is smaller, but it maintains the central incised detail line. The body has become more geometric, and the proportions are closer to the standard ones of the large figure, but the smooth curve of the back profile and raised belt and sash of the kilt echo the form of PnH7b.1 above. In another example, the slightly stiff form of the E style figure in front of the tomb owner (PnH7e) visually evokes the geometric form of the D style figures, such as the one below him (PnH7f), in which the eye is narrower and the ear is a simple shape (Figure 48). A similar narrow, outlined eye and raised ear are used in the B style figures (PnH7a), which could indicate a relationship between the two styles or a shared method of conceiving the figure or no specific relationship at all.

Some aspects of C and B style figures suggest formal interplay with E style figures, as well. For example, the narrow, elongated bodies of the E figures PnH7d (Plate XIII, upper right) and PnH4c (Figure 46, upper left) resemble the elongated bodies of the C style figures on the south part of the east wall. Pushing this possible relationship further, the unusual long tube noses of the C style figures (Plate XV, Plate XVIa, b, Figure 50) could be another version of the high raised eye and low nose combination of the E figures. The unusual versions of the faces of the

E style female figures in PnH4a (Figure 46, right) and even the face of PnH4d could provide the formal middle ground for this connection.

The women depicted in PnH4a may provide common ground for the differently derived shapes of female figures in the B and C styles. The curved outline and curved leg line of the first figure, PnH4a.2, can be connected to the more exaggerated curves of the women in the B style panels (i.e., PnH15: Plate XVII, left), while the narrower, straighter body of the second figure, PnH4a.3, more closely correlates to several of the C style women (i.e., PnH13: Plate XV). Both figures have only a narrow necklace indicated in relief, which is true for all female figures in both the B and C styles.

Additional formal links between figures in the B and C styles were noted; for example, in the tomb of Pepynakht1, Pn7 fits best into the B style, but the elongated proportions of the first figure render it similar to C style figures, and several elements of the C style offering group are present at the center of the panel. Similarity in offerings is another way these different styles can be cautiously linked. For example, the birds held by the D style figure PnH7c (Plate XIII, left bottom), though smaller, have the same fish-like tails and large angled legs and feet of the C style birds (Plate XVIa).

Determining direct influences between figures in separate styles is complicated, especially given the lack of more contextual information such as other objects or monuments in which images such as these are used. Artistic development no doubt extended beyond individual tombs in the cemetery; however, these tombs provided an important arena in which the work and processes of the artists took shape. My intent in addressing these possible formal connections is not to establish certain relationships among them, but rather to emphasize the evidence in the images of the processes of the artists who individually interpreted various aspects of the figure.

Sabni2 Sunken

All but two of the figures carved in the Sabni2 Sunken style belong to the tomb program of Sabni2. The two other figures are close by; one is carved on a pillar in the tomb of Pepynakht Heqaib1, though without any inscription, and the other appears along the outer edge of the lower north entrance thickness of Pepynakht Heqaib2 (PnH7h). In the program of Sabni2, Sabni2 Sunken figures occur only inside the tomb chapel. Out of the eighty-four offering figures populating Sabni's program, sixty of which are inside the chapel, the Sabni2 Sunken style incorporates thirty-five figures; all but one are male. Most of these figures (twenty-six) stand in registers behind the large figures of the tomb owner on the entrance thicknesses (Sb10, Sb12: Figures 57, 58).

The style of these figures is highly consistent. Small variations of proportion, slight differences in the shape of the head, and some different iconographic details do not disturb the overall uniform, and rather distinctive, visual effect of the figures.

Harkhuf Style

The Harkhuf style, as the name implies, is defined by the relief used throughout the tomb of Harkhuf, and then again only on the façade of the neighboring tomb of Pepynakht Heqaib1, twenty-one figures in total (Plate XII, Figures 33, 34, 37). Five of the nine large-scale figures in Harkhuf's program depict the tomb owner, and the remaining figures include two images of his son and one of his wife. The ninth large-scale figure depicts another man who also must have been buried in the tomb since the small false door on the west wall is inscribed with his name. The two figures carved in this style on the façade of Pepynakht1's tomb depict the tomb owner, standing alone on each jamb. Six more figures depict these two tomb owners; the small seated figure of each tomb owner situated at the south end of their respective façade lintels and four additional images of Harkhuf at the bottom of each jamb of his false door all fit into the style category, but in these significantly smaller images the style is evoked with far less nuance, reliant mainly on the medium, proportions, and overall quality of the carving.

Four of the five small offering figures in Harkhuf's program stand at a similarly small scale to the false door images of the tomb owner himself; however, these images follow the large-scale style more fully, with greater attention to facial features, wigs, and jewelry (H5, H9.2). One offering figure (Kh17a) among the diverse group in the tomb of Khunes has details, particularly the facial features, which may be linked to these small Harkhuf-style figures, but due to the damage in Khunes's tomb and the mix of style characteristics it is difficult to be sure of a connection.

Tomb Program Summary

In all, there are 85 tomb owner figures and 463 subsidiary figures in the 12 programs discussed. Due to the unusual lintel design, Sabni1 has the highest total number of tomb owner figures (twenty), while only one survives in the program of Khui. The tomb owner images are evenly distributed in the south and north sections of the cemetery, with forty in the south and forty-three in the north. Due to the large and complex programs in the tombs of Khunes, Pepynakht Heqaib2, and Sabni2, more than 70 percent of the subsidiary figures (326) are concentrated in the northern group of tombs. Among the subsidiary figures, approximately 70 percent (327) are male. If the large scenes on the south wall of Khunes's program (presuming these are largely if not all male), the east wall panel in Mekhu's chapel (where it is clear they are all male), and all of the tomb owner images are counted, the male proportion is closer to 80 percent.

The Sunken A style is by far the most prevalent style, accounting for 169 total figures, almost 31 percent (Table 1). The next two most common styles are Sunken C and Raised A2, used for seventy and sixty-six figures or roughly 13 percent and 12 percent, respectively. Raised A1 is naturally less common as it is primarily reserved for images of tomb owners, but it is the next most common style, used for fifty-four figures or almost 10 percent. The Sabni2 Sunken style, even though primarily confined to one tomb program, accounts for 7 percent of the figures, while Sunken B figures make up just more than 5 percent. The less common styles of Raised B, Sunken D and E, Harkhuf style, Sabni2 Raised, and the Painted figures account for almost 20 percent of the figures. The remaining figures have been left uncategorized.

Diversity of Style: Intent

During the Old Kingdom, elite tomb programs typically had a uniform style of relief carving throughout. Furthermore, the style used in all elite tomb programs was fundamentally the same; visible stylistic variations occurred globally rather than in small sets of tombs. The use of a carefully consistent style in Egyptian visual culture in the Old Kingdom, and indeed throughout Egypt's history, has often been explained via the style's communicative function and its vital role in maintaining the delicate stability and order so fundamental to Egyptian socio-religious ideology:

> Style is vital to a civilization's definition and to its demarcation against what lies outside. High culture has specific carriers and a particular status as a tradition, and it is integrated in particular ways into a civilizational, cultural, and stylistic context.... The style ... is sustained by an elite that commissions and consumes the works that transmit the stylistic tradition, and incorporates fundamental values.... This value-laden stylistic complex is crucial to the transmission of the civilization's essence through time.[14]

Within this paradigm, the meaning of style is sought mainly in its consistency, and pronounced stylistic variations become difficult for us to assess as an intentional product of knowledgeable participants, especially elite participants who are particularly invested in the transmission of tradition and stable values. Discussions of artists' and patrons' intentional use of different styles to communicate are therefore rather rare, and more often reasons for the differences of style are sought in external factors that determine what the artisans produce.

The difference of style in the tomb programs at Qubbet el-Hawa in fact includes two separate but interrelated aspects: the use of diverse styles together within a chapel and the use of non-Memphite styles for individual scenes. Because both aspects are *other* than standard, their interpretation can become entangled. An illustrative example is found in Habachi's response to the tomb program of Pepynakht Heqaib2 (35d) when he writes, "Seeing most of the representation on the walls inside ... it can be observed that the standard of art is varying, showing that such representations seem to have been carved over a relatively long period."[15] He clarifies his opinion of the artistic standard when addressing the large Sunken E figures on the thicknesses and the smaller figures surrounding them as "of much inferior standard of art."[16] Although he does not elaborate, one assumes he based his qualitative assessment on the distinct design of the large figures, visibly different from Memphite styles.

In analyses of Old Kingdom art, chronological determinations are often interwoven with assessments of artistic quality (in nontraditional images) in part because of the character of material created during the following First Intermediate Period. The non-Memphite style images from places such as the cemetery at Nag'-ed-Der are neatly explained via historical circumstance, as the decentralization and perceived disorder of the period provide external (i.e., not intentional) reasons for the failure of the monuments to conform to previous standards. These external reasons include a belief that the disorder of the period limited the artists' access to Memphite-style models and also limited their option for training. Less clearly linked to the historical circumstance is a sense of a general lack of skill among the artists during this period. Many scholars argue that the "best" (i.e., most highly skilled) artists would have been based in Memphis in order to work on behalf of the king and his highest officials, and though they may have traveled to the provinces on short-time journeys, they would not have permanently settled there. As a result, this argument goes, the artists in the provinces would necessarily be lesser skilled, and thus during the decentralized First Intermediate Period, only such lesser-skilled artists were available to create art and to train new artists.[17] While it is reasonable to assume many of the more highly skilled artists would have served in Memphis, this view limits the possibility of seeing naturally skilled artists originating in the provinces and possibly choosing to stay there to serve the growing needs of the provincial elite. We have no evidence suggesting that a provincial artist would be recruited to work in the capital based upon his talent or accomplishments. Part of the problem with this overall narrow view is the equating of "skill" with "training." Regardless of the nature of Egyptian art, clearly an innate artistic skill and technical training are two separate things, though the first enhances the second, and vice versa.

These contextual "reasons" for nonstandard images cannot be reconciled with the material at Qubbet el-Hawa, beginning with the assumption that the tombs were decorated over a "long span of time." The evidence throughout the Old Kingdom tombs at Qubbet el-Hawa indicates that a number of diverse styles were in fact in use during the same time period, meaning within the lifetime of a given individual, and thus with the awareness and or intent of the involved tomb owners, artists, and even audiences.

The contemporary use of different styles can be ascertained by determining a sequence in the carving of different reliefs and establishing a set of relative chronological points among different tombs. For example, in the inner chapel of the tomb of Sabni2, on the west wall, a panel of offering figures carved in the Sunken A style (Sb14) is adjacent to and oriented toward the large fishing and fowling scene carved primarily in the Sabni2 Raised style (Sb15). Because the smaller panel (Sb14) depicts offering figures facing toward the larger fishing and fowling scene that includes two images of the tomb owner (i.e., the natural recipient of their offerings), we can reasonably assume the fishing and fowling panel was carved first (reference Figure 60). Thus, either Sunken A was developed after Sabni2 Raised, or Sabni2 Raised was developed after Sunken A, and Sunken A remained in use. Given the widespread use of the Sunken A style throughout the cemetery, and the strong likelihood that Sabni2's tomb was decorated after other tombs with A style panels (in particular the tomb of Mekhu and Sabni1), the latter explanation seems most likely. There is also a small Raised A2 figure within the fishing and fowling scene, in a place of prominence at the feet of the fisher, which strongly implies that both the Raised A2 style and the Sabni2 Raised style were also in use at the same time.

Another example appears in the tomb program of Pepynakht Heqaib2. The upper parts of both entrance thicknesses are carved with figures in the Raised A1 style. These figures are framed with inscriptions listing a series of titles typical of the tomb owners in this cemetery, as well as less common though existent titles related to the pyramids of Pepy I and Merenre. The figures on the bottom of each thickness are the much-discussed Sunken E style figures, and while the bottom figure on the south thickness has the same series of titles inscribed above it, the titulary of the north thickness figure includes a group of three higher-ranking titles: *ỉmy-ỉś; mnỉw Nḫn;* and *ḥry-tp Nḫb,* likely gained by Pepynakht Heqaib2 later in his career.[18] Given the arrangement of the figures and the differences in the titulary, it appears that the higher, Raised A1 figures with lower-ranking titles were carved first, and the lower, Sunken E figures with higher-ranking titles were added later. Yet these later figures must have been added during the life, or very nearly after a possibly unexpected death, of Pepynakht Heqaib2, as a tomb owner would certainly prioritize the inclusion of his highest-ranking titles in his tomb program. Furthermore, the titularies framing these two Sunken E figures do not incorporate the highest ranking *ỉry-pꜥt* (though space seems to have been left just in case), while the Raised A2 image of Pepynakht Heqaib2 on the façade of his tomb does. Therefore, it seems impossible that these bottom figures were added to the program after any significant amount of time had passed. These Sunken E figures are nonetheless strikingly different from the Raised A1 figures they accompany, and the reasonable assumption is that either this was the intention of the tomb owner, or it was at the least acceptable to him to have distinctly different styles in his program.

Because the programs are comprised of small panels, it can be difficult to determine carving sequences in many cases. If we assume a basic rationale to the artists' process in decorating the tombs, we may reasonably determine sequences in some cases. When Habachi assumed the panels in different styles comprising the interior program of Pepynakht Heqaib2's tomb were separated by long periods of time, he implied that related styles were more roughly contemporary. If this were true, the distribution of the different styles in the chapel would have resulted from artists choosing panel locations randomly, leaving suitable and more desirable (well lighted, closer to the entrance, opposite the false door) areas open for panels they could not have known were to be carved (i.e., are in different styles and therefore should be from later time periods). It seems more reasonable to assume the artists (or patrons) chose the most prominent, available place in the chapel, or, if they did not, that these prominent locations were left open intentionally for another panel specifically meant for the space (i.e., contemporary).

A similar example with less disparate styles appears in the tomb of Mekhu and Sabni1. This tomb began as a single chapel for Mekhu, and it was expanded in four phases to also incorporate a chapel for Sabni1. The initial expansion included only Sabni1's false door in the northwest corner of the then-existing chapel; the additional chapel space to the north was added later. The panels on columns M6 and W6 in Mekhu's chapel, both carved in Sunken A and both depicting Sabni1's chief *ka*-servant, are oriented toward Sabni1's false door. While it is not the only explanation, it seems possible to assume those panels were carved before the expansion of Sabni1's chapel, as they would probably have been placed in his chapel space if it were available. Many or even all of the Sunken A panels in Mekhu's chapel thus likely predated the Raised A1 and A2 and Painted figures in Sabni1's chapel.

Because the majority of figures in the offering panels are labeled with names and titles, it is sometimes possible to identify the same figure or group of figures in separate panels, which provides further evidence in support of different styles used during the same general time period. One clear example is the figure of Khnumhetep, who appears in the programs of both Khui and Tjetji; in Khui's program he is depicted in Raised B (Ku2: Figure 23), while in Tjetji's program his panel is carved in Sunken C (Tj4: Plate X).

This argument for the contemporary use of several styles is not meant to suggest that the tombs were all built at once; in a cemetery comprising tombs built over several generations, the passage of time must be acknowledged as an important factor affecting the form of the monuments and their formal relationship to one another. When Habachi saw a long span of time in Pepynakht Heqaib2's program, he implied that an elite tomb owner would not *choose* to use different styles in his tomb program and therefore the images in different styles must have been added when the elite tomb owner had no control (i.e., long after his death). Yet it is clear that at Qubbet el-Hawa the tomb owners consciously incorporated different styles in their programs.

The other circumstances cited to explain nontraditional images are typically limited access to models and training, and a general lack of skilled artisans. Even scholars who find value in the unusual styles found in the provinces, primarily from the First Intermediate Period, characterizing it as "freer" and "lively," nonetheless cite these reasons in their interpretations. Although analyses seeing "freedom" and "originality" in provincial work touch upon the important aspects of distance from the capital and local independence in the creation of art, frequently they see these artistic forms resulting from the artists' and patrons' adaptation to circumstances beyond their control (i.e., lack of models and so forth).[19] The evidence at Qubbet el-Hawa suggests that the use of several non-Memphite styles in these programs cannot be explained via these usual suspects of lack of access to models, lack of training, or lack of artistic skill.

The presence of Memphite-style figures has been discussed at length, and includes many of the tomb owner figures carved in Raised A1 (i.e., MS7, KK1, Kh19, PnH3) as well as the east and south walls of Khunes's tomb, and elements of the east wall panel in Mekhu's tomb. All of these reliefs certainly provided models for artists to use when designing and carving additional figures, and for tomb owners to cite as bases for their own programs.

The question of skill is more subjective; viewers may see skill manifest in different forms and often prioritize the design of the figure over the quality of the carving as evidence of skill (or a lack thereof). For example, the Sunken E figures viewed by Habachi as "much inferior" seem to indisputably reveal a notable skill in carving relief (Plate XIII, Figures 46, 47). More subjective is an appreciation for the unique design of the figure, which was perceived by Habachi to reflect inability rather than creativity. The Sunken C figures present a similar combination, where an unusual design is often carved with subtle modeling and fine detail (Plate XV). Many examples in different styles are beautifully carved with controlled lines, smooth surfaces, and fine details, and nearly all of the panels display at least a basic competence with carving.

A lack of training is also not a viable explanation for the stylistic diversity among the images. Evidence of training (i.e., the transmission from one individual to another of techniques of producing images) is present to some extent in the panels themselves. Even though the specific nature of the training is unclear, the fact that they are carved in relief is proof that the artists were trained to carve relief, and the repetition of figures in the different styles implies a similar transmission of design principles. Acknowledging a likely range of skill and experience among the artists does not explain how even an unskilled and inexperienced artist intending to produce a Raised A2 figure (for example, SH2: Figure 13) would end up producing a Sunken C figure (PnH13: Plate XV).

The presence of numerous Memphite-style figures as models in the arena of a generally competent artistic workforce that apparently included a number of highly skilled members, and the perceptible presence of communication among the artists, as exemplified by repeated styles, reveals a context in which Memphite-style images could have been more consistently produced. Furthermore, artists developed several different non-Memphite styles and they were incorporated into the same programs rather than maintaining stylistic consistency. The different styles and their use in the programs appear to be conscious and even intentional elements and should be approached as meaningful products of the people creating these tombs, including both the elite tomb owners and the different artists working in the different styles.

Diversity of Style: Meaning of Use

As discussed in the Introduction, the analysis of style here focuses on how styles are used throughout the cemetery. The diverse styles make a striking visual impact, and once we acknowledge their intentional implementation by the artists and their patrons, it is possible to consider the value and possible meaning of creating this visual mosaic.

Underlying this investigation into the use of style is the assumption that the different styles represent the work of different groups of artists. The possibility that all the artists working at any given time were trained in all the different styles seems less efficient and much less likely. Ultimately, a conclusive answer cannot be found that consistently explains what the use of each different style in the programs at Qubbet el-Hawa communicated, but an examination of the use of styles in their broader context, including especially the associated inscriptions of names, titles, and family relationships, reveals an awareness of the communicative power of style and an active and developing desire on the part of the artisans and their patrons to manipulate it. One important question, which will be addressed next, is the identity of the patrons; was the use and choice of a given style influenced by the tomb owners or rather by the figures that are depicted in the various panels? This issue of patronage raises questions regarding not only what a style may communicate, such as status, family relationships, or professional affiliation, but also about whom it conveys this information.

The Egyptian system of representation encodes status primarily through the relative size of figures depicted in the same scene. In the Qubbet el-Hawa programs, size is used to differentiate the status between figures. Large-scale figures depict only tomb owners and their family members, while all the remaining figures are much smaller in scale. Although the subsidiary figures are not all exactly the same size, there is no significant hierarchical scale at work; their size appears to be primarily determined by the space of the scene, and they all fall generally into the same range. Many panels showing family groups do use relative size within the panel to indicate status, as the front male figure is taller than the following family members in a pattern very common to Egyptian representation. The difference among the figures is very small, hardly one of scale, and does not compare to the difference between the tomb owner figures and the subsidiary figures. One clearer exception appears in the tomb of Pepynakht Heqaib2 on the north thickness, where two of the subsidiary figures (nonfamily members) are distinctly larger than the remaining figures (PnH6.2, PnH7b.1). These two figures are not carved in the same style, however, being in Sunken A and Sunken E, respectively.

The medium of a two-dimensional scene can indicate status, as well. Although the difference between sunk and raised relief seems more directly linked to function and environment (exterior versus interior surfaces), in some cases they may also represent a status differentiation based upon the fact that raised relief requires more time to execute. However, given that most Egyptian monuments have stylistically uniform programs, this differentiation in status within a scene or a monument rarely comes into play. By composing programs with different styles, the tomb owners and artisans at Qubbet el-Hawa had a greater opportunity to exploit this area of signification, and there are many indications that they did.

Four separate styles are carved in raised relief: Raised A1, Raised A2, Raised B, and Sabni2 Raised. Raised A1 is used almost exclusively for figures of tomb owners and of their family members. Given that scale provides a key characteristic of this style, this is not surprising; each way of expressing status serves to reinforce the other. Raised A2 figures are closely linked to Raised A1 figures both spatially and in terms of content. As discussed previously, the majority of Raised A2 figures are *ka*-servants or other offering figures facing a Raised A1 figure of the tomb owner. To share space, or more specifically a composition, with the tomb owner implies a higher status for the figure through his apparently important role in the tomb owner's cult. The use of related styles for the tomb owner and the subsidiary figure visually expresses this connection.

The way in which Raised A2 is used among figures on independent panels also implies an intent to express status. For example, in the program of Sobekhetep, both his "overseer of *ka*-servants" and his "inspector of *ka*-servants" are depicted twice, once on a panel with the tomb owner and once with their respective families. The independent panel of the higher-ranking overseer is carved in raised relief (A2) (SH2: Figure 13), while the panel of the lower-ranking inspector is carved in sunken relief (A) (SH4: Plate VIII), paralleling the standard interpretation of raised relief as higher status than sunken relief. On the façade of Sabni2's tomb, the *ka*-servant Hehu shares a small panel with Sabni, and they are both carved in raised relief (Sb7: Figure 55), but Hehu's family depicted behind him is carved in sunk relief (Sb8). In the tomb of Khwin-Khnum, the overseer of *ka*-servants, Kari, appears four times, twice with the tomb owner and twice on independent panels, one of which depicts him with his two daughters. Kari has several different titles, but on the panel with his daughters he is accompanied by several relatively high-ranking titles such as "overseer of the estate" and "overseer of builders," and this panel is carved in raised relief (KK4: Plate XIb).

The other two types of raised relief, B and Sabni2 Raised, are far less common. Sabni2 Raised is used primarily for figures of the tomb owner; the exceptions include four female family members and a small figure burning incense at Sabni's feet on the west thickness (Sb12c). Raised B appears in only three places, one group panel and two solo figures, all of whom are offering figures. The solo figure in Tjetji's tomb is carved beneath a raised relief figure of the tomb owner in a spatial relationship similar to most of the Raised A2 figures. The solo figure in the tomb of Khunes does not share space with a tomb owner and unfortunately lacks an inscription to indicate his identity. The panel of offering figures above this figure are carved in raised relief, and Khunes's program incorporates much more extensive raised relief than most; perhaps these aspects influenced the artist, if status was not at issue. The Raised B panel in the tomb of Khui depicts eighteen figures all connected to Khnumhetep. The long text accompanying this panel describes Khnumhetep's work on behalf of Khui as well as Tjetji, which indicates his high status, as well.

In all, 150 figures are carved in raised relief. Forty-two are tomb owners, twenty-four are family members of tomb owners, and thirty more appear on panels with the tomb owner, meaning 65 percent of the figures are intimately connected to the elite tomb owners. Among the raised relief styles, the only clear form of status differentiation is through the scale of the figures, noted previously.

Other relationships between status and different styles are not as clear as the connection between raised relief and higher status. Among the subsidiary figures, information regarding their status relative to one another comes primarily from the accompanying inscriptions that include their titles. The majority of titles in the programs relate to functions in the mortuary cults of the tomb owners such as *ka*-servants and "directors of the food hall." (The meaning, status, and distribution of these titles will be discussed in detail in Chapter 4). There appears to be a relationship between the higher tiers of the *ka*-cult priesthood and the styles that are most like the Memphite styles at this time, Raised A2 and Sunken A. Of the twelve highest ranked "overseer of *ka*-servants," six are carved in Raised A2, one in the closely related engraved Painted style, and five in Sunken A. Of the twenty-one middle-ranked "inspector of *ka*-servants," thirteen are carved in Sunken A, five in Raised A2, one in Raised A1, one in Painted, and one in Sunken D. A greater diversity of style appears among the forty-four figures at the lowest rank of *ka*-servant (though many have at least one additional title): fifteen are carved in Sunken A, twelve in Sunken C, seven in Raised A2, three in Raised A1, three in Painted styles, two in Sunken B, and two in the Harkhuf style.

These numbers suggest a connection between the higher ranks of funerary cult administration and the A, Memphite-like styles, yet alternate factors make a specific cause (status)-effect (style) correlation impossible to ascertain. Many of the overseers of *ka*-servants are carved in Raised A1 or A2 because they appear in a composition with a figure of the tomb owner, facing him and burning incense. Because the meaning of the scene requires both figures, the artist may have used a consistent medium to unify the composition, and because the tomb owner would be depicted in raised relief, so, too, was the overseer figure. The high status of the overseer allowed him a privileged position, sharing a composition with the tomb owner, but the choice of style for his figure is determined not only by his status but also largely by the needs of the tomb owner. Furthermore, it may be that the tomb owner's access as patron to certain artists allowed the subsidiary figure access, as well, which he might not have had under other conditions; for example, in a scene not incorporating a figure of the tomb owner.

The stronger correlation between the lower-ranked inspector of *ka*-servants figures and Sunken A, rather than Raised A2, is suggestive, as is the fact that only one of the inspectors is carved in a non-A type style, but the overall dominance of Sunken A among the panels makes any real status indication nearly impossible to see. As noted previously, five overseers are also carved in Sunken A, as are fifteen of the simple *ka*-servants, as well as numerous other figures of varying ranks such as "overseers of the *per-shena*," "overseers of herds," an "overseer of crews," two "directors of the food hall," and two "sealers." In general, a lack of consistency makes ascertaining the status level of any style impossible: while the Sunken B style is used for only two *ka*-servants, who are neither overseer nor inspector, and for several lower-ranking directors of the food hall, it was also used for the relatively higher ranking "chancellor of the royal palace" figure all three times he appears in the tomb of Pepynakht Heqaib2. Sunken C is also left out of the upper ranks of *ka*-cult priests, although it is used for 12 twelve simple *ka*-priests, but high-ranking figures such as an "overseer of judiciary scribes" and an "overseer of the army/ troops" are carved in this style.

An alternate possibility to seeing status in the use of certain styles is to see socially defined groups patronizing different groups of artists. In her study of New Kingdom Theban tomb painting, Melinda Hartwig illuminates just such a pattern of patronage between two groups separated not by status, but by professional (and thus social) affiliation. Officials connected to the palace employed artists working in one style, while officials connected to the temple employed artists working in a distinctly different style.[20] Again, it is difficult to see any such pattern consistently among the Qubbet el-Hawa figures. Of the eighty-five different *ka*-priests, 22 percent are carved in Raised A2, compared to 12 percent of the figures overall, and 39 percent are carved in Sunken A, compared to 31 percent overall. These numbers suggest a tendency toward A styles, but nothing comfortably certain. In addition, those identified as "overseer of the *per-shena*" and "overseer of linen" also show tendencies toward A styles (54 percent and 50 percent, respectively). While "overseer of linen" indicates responsibilities specific to the *ka*-cult, the "overseers of the *per-shena*" likely had functions outside of the *ka*-cult, as well. This means that A artists were favored not only by *ka*-servants; yet they cannot be linked to overall *ka*-cult officials. Of the seventy-two directors of the food hall, thirty-three have only this title (the others have additional titles, often as *ka*-servants or others). Nine different styles are used among these thirty-three figures, and they are fairly evenly divided: one Raised A2, four Raised B, one Sab2 Raised, three Sunken A, four Sunken B, three Sunken C, four Sunken D, ten Sab2 Sunken, one engraved Painted, and two uncertain. Similar patterns occur with other titles such as "overseer of the estate (two Raised A2, two Sunken B, two Sunken C, one Sunken E, one Sab2 Sunken, one B/C drawing, one uncertain).

In Hartwig's study, she linked the style of the paintings to the identity of the tomb owner who commissioned them, in contrast to this examination of possible links between styles and the figures who are depicted in the programs. Suggesting these styles conveyed information about the identity of the depicted figure implies that the choice of style was made by or because of the figures represented in the programs; it is their status and their identity that is conveyed, and only a small percentage of these figures are tomb owners.

That supporting figures would have such a prominent role in determining the appearance of an elite tomb owner's program is an unusual possibility based on what we understand of these monuments. Typically, we view the final form of an Old Kingdom elite tomb as almost entirely determined by the tomb owner's needs. It is an essential monument for the elite person, and the program is a key element of its perceived ability to function effectively. As discussed previously, the stylistic consistency of the images is interpreted as serving the communicative and functional requirements of the tomb, thus the style is used so that the tomb will fulfill the tomb owner's needs. If the use of the different styles somehow conveys information about the identity of the represented figures, this indicates either a significant shift, or perhaps broadening, of the tomb program's focus from the tomb owner to a wider community of supporters, or that the identity of the represented figures was important to the tomb owners and to the success of their programs. Although the available information does not support a certain connection of styles to aspects of identity, the presence of the accompanying inscriptions of names and titles seems to support a view that the identity of the represented figures was significant to the success of the programs in service to the tomb owners.

By emphasizing the tomb owners as the creators of the programs and users of style, a number of alternate possible meanings can be considered. It is tempting to view the tomb owners as the patrons of different artists/schools, but a number of factors complicate this view. The surviving evidence does little to help clarify if patterns of patronage were based on some aspect of social organization, as they were in the New Kingdom Theban tombs studied by Hartwig. The tomb owners in her study were divided by their professional affiliation, but the tomb owners at Qubbet el-Hawa were connected to each other by their unique professional role in the country. Despite some variations in titulary, they were all involved in the same aspect of the administration, and no temple officials are identified among the tomb owners.

Patronage could have been organized in part along family/extended family lines. Again, the cemetery provides only limited contextual material to investigate this question. The only tomb owners who are certainly related are Mekhu and Sabni1; not only do they share a tomb, but Sabni1 appears in Mekhu's program identified as his son. The group of Pepynakht Heqaib1, Pepynakht Heqaib2, and Sabni2 are most likely related, given the architectural association of their tombs, although none of the three are represented or identified in the others' programs. The small tomb attached to Khunes's chapel belongs to his wife Ankhes, and she is identified in his program. No other evidence exists to suggest any family relationships among the remaining tomb owners. Based on these examples it may be hypothesized, however, that family members or otherwise closely connected tomb owners built their tombs near each other in the cemetery.

An examination of the distribution of the styles throughout the cemetery does indicate that several styles are concentrated in certain areas. For example, the Painted style appears mainly in the southern tombs; the main Painted panels are in the chapels of Mekhu and Sabni1 and of IiShemai Setka, and panels related to the Painted style (although carved in relief) appear in the tombs of Sobekhetep and Khwin-Khnum. Several other styles are confined to the northern group of tombs including the Harkhuf style, used only in the tombs of Harkhuf and Pepynakht Heqaib1, both Sabni2 styles, confined almost exclusively to his tomb, and the Sunken E style. The related styles Sunken B, Sunken C, and Sunken D, are primarily associated with the northern half of the cemetery.

Perhaps these distribution patterns reflect the patronage of certain groups of artists by certain groups of tomb owners, but the data is suggestive at best. The significance of the patronage is impossible to discern, especially given that the surviving evidence does not reveal specific relationships among the southern or northern tomb owners. The distribution of styles in the northern group further illustrates the subjective nature and potentially distorting effect of grouping the tombs by location in the cemetery. For example, the Sabni2 Raised and Sunken styles used in the chapel of Sabni2 extend only via two single figures to two neighboring northern tombs; even the attached chapel of Pepynakht Heqaib2 has only a single Sabni2 Sunken figure. The distinctive Sunken C, D, and E styles used heavily in Pepynakht Heqaib2's program do not appear at all in Sabni2's program, and Sabni2's program includes only two figures in the Sunken B style. Thus, two tomb owners who are among the most likely to be related do not in fact use many of the same styles.

Ultimately, it seems most productive to consider each whole program individually. As stated, the programs share the *use* of several different styles; what mainly differentiates them is the number of different styles in use. At one end of the spectrum are the programs of Harkhuf and IiShemai Setka that use only one and two styles, respectively (with the exception of one figure in Harkhuf's tomb; also the two styles in the tomb of IiShemai are closely related), and at the other end is the program of Pepynakht Heqaib2 that uses eight different styles. The fact that Pepynakht Heqaib2 is the highest ranking tomb owner among this group and IiShemai is one of the lowest, being one of only two lacking the "count" title, suggests the influence of status, but Harkhuf is a high-ranking tomb owner, as well. Most of these twelve tomb owners are of fairly equivalent rank, which complicates further analysis of a relationship between status and number of styles.

An alternate interpretation of the use of style posits a progressive development of the programs. Previously I argued against the tendency to explain non-Memphite-looking styles and especially the use of different styles together as the result of the passage of long periods of time, showing how diverse styles were certainly in use simultaneously in creating the programs at Qubbet el-Hawa. The goal of this argument was to prioritize the agency of the tomb owners and artists, not to remove the essential element of time from the creation of their monuments. The cemetery at Qubbet el-Hawa evinces the passage of time, with several identifiable generations of families memorialized. The architecture of the double tomb of Mekhu and Sabni reveals four successive phases of construction, and the staircase in front of Pepynakht Heqaib1 marks the passage from the construction of his tomb and that of Pepynakht Heqaib2 and Sabni2. Several tomb programs betray a passage of time between separate elements; for example, in the tomb of Khwin-Khnum the western panels belatedly received the higher-ranking title "count" that the eastern panels incorporated in their original form, and in the tomb of Tjetji, the painted texts are covered over by carved hieroglyphs and a relief figure of the tomb owner. Furthermore, we are reminded of the span of time encompassed by the lives of the tomb owners in the autobiographies of Harkhuf, Pepynakht Heqaib1, and Sabni1.

As discussed in the Introduction, objects of material culture not only represent a creative process, they contribute to the process, as well. Once an object has been created, the context in which all future objects are made has been affected. With regard to the tombs at Qubbet el-Hawa, this view encompasses the many different formal aspects of the tombs and the programs. For example, once a new style has been used, in later panels it is no longer new and eventually may become even traditional. Once a program uses two styles together it becomes acceptable, and eventually may in fact become a goal. Although it may not be possible to pinpoint the initial reasons for the development of a certain style or for the use of multiple styles together, the distribution of the styles in the different programs can be interpreted to show an evolution in the tomb owners' use of style.

This analysis is necessarily hypothetical, as it is not possible to ascertain a sequence of construction among the tombs. Even when we can establish the date of a moment in the life of a tomb owner, we cannot know how long he lived or at what point in his life he began constructing his tomb. For that matter, we cannot be sure over how long a period of time the tomb was constructed or decorated.

The initial phase in the development of the system is represented by the anomalous program in the tomb of Harkhuf, which Edel determined to be the earliest in the cemetery, and the program on the façade of the neighboring tomb of Pepynakht Heqaib1. The close formal relationship between these two tombs, including the size and plan, the design of the façade, and the style of the figures and of the hieroglyphs, indicates that the tomb of Pepynakht Heqaib1 was designed to either self-consciously recall the tomb of Harkhuf, or it was constructed around the same time, by artists trained in the same style. Because the relief style of both the figures and the glyphs are so similar, and because this distinctive style of sunken relief is entirely absent from the remaining tomb programs, the latter seems most likely to be the case. Based upon their titles and their autobiographies, we can assume that Pepynakht Heqaib1's tomb followed Harkhuf's. Also, unlike Harkhuf's interior program, Pepynakht Heqaib1's chapel does not include Harkhuf style figures, but rather smaller panels of subsidiary figures in different styles, more typical of the remaining tombs. Thus, although the initial construction and decoration of the façade of Pepynakht Heqaib1's tomb may have been close in time to the construction of Harkhuf's tomb, the completion of the interior program could have occurred later, after the development of the Qubbet el-Hawa system.

A group of tombs connected by Edel through his analysis of the pottery forms the second chronological anchor. We know that the tombs of Mekhu and Sabni1, Sobekhetep, Khwin-Khnum, and IiShemai Setka all overlapped to some degree, with Mekhu and IiShemai on the earlier side, Sobekhetep in the middle, and Sabni1 and Khwin-Khnum more likely later.[21] It is not possible to determine how long after Harkhuf's tomb these tombs were decorated, although the autobiography of Sabni1 and the titles of Khwin-Khnum clearly set them in the reign of Pepy II.

The tomb of IiShemai Setka is the most similar to the tombs of Harkhuf and Pepynakht Heqaib1 in size and layout. Like Harkhuf's program, the interior of Iishemai's chapel has panels executed in a consistent style and focusing on the tomb owner, but Iishemai's panels are painted rather than carved. And unlike the programs of Harkhuf and Pepynakht Heqaib1, Iishemai's tomb façade is blank and the program incorporates very little text. Also unlike Harkhuf's program, Iishemai's has no subsidiary figures depicted in large scale, instead incorporating the subsidiary figures in panels with an image of himself.

Among the remaining programs in this group, only Sabni1 uses a lengthy text and extensive imagery on the façade. All of the programs use large-scale figures of the tomb owner, but most are carved in raised relief rather than sunken, and none of the figures are carved in the same Harkhuf style. Yet they all have panels that are stylistically connected to the panels in Iishemai's tomb, in the Painted style. As discussed in Chapter 2, painted figures in the programs of Mekhu, Sabni1, and IiShemai show formal similarity that suggests they were executed by the same artists or artists trained in the same style. Painted relief panels in the tombs of Khwin-Khnum and Sobekhetep and a subsidiary panel in Mekhu's tomb share a similar design with Iishemai's panels, with a figure of the tomb owner set against a framed, blue-gray background with rows of hieroglyphs across the top. Figures of Khwin-Khnum, IiShemai, and of Sabni1 in his fishing and fowling scene share stylistic details, as well.

Unlike Harkhuf and Iishemai's programs, the rest of the tombs in this group all include panels of subsidiary figures, and all of them use more than one style. Changes in the method of decorating tombs seem to have occurred between the decoration of the tomb of Harkhuf and the decoration of the tombs in this second group. Iishemai's tomb may represent a transitional phase. The programs of Mekhu, Sabni1, Sobekhetep, and Khwin-Khnum all incorporate Raised A1, Raised A2, and Sunken A figures, which also means these styles were developed prior to the execution of their programs. Also among these programs, the majority of figures of the tomb owner are in raised rather than sunken relief, which is true for the rest of the programs, as well.

The tombs of Khui, Tjetji, and Khunes are the most difficult to locate in time. Although Khui and Tjetji are connected by the presence of the same Khnumhetep in both of their programs, they could be separated by as much as a generation. Both programs incorporate a panel of subsidiary figures and both juxtapose different styles. Both also have figures carved in the rare Raised B style, which appears only one other time in a modified version. The use of a raised relief style for subsidiary figures, and in

Khui's tomb the use of sunken relief for an interior figure of the tomb owner, could suggest these programs were also part of a transitional phase sometime after Harkhuf and perhaps contemporary with Mekhu's group to some degree. The evident change of the original program in Tjetji's chapel is a reminder that parts of different programs may be contemporary with only parts of other programs.

The tomb of Khunes presents an even more complicated problem in terms of dating. Khunes's partial Memphite-like program design distinguishes it from the remaining tombs, and his lack of expedition-related or site-specific titles also sets him apart from the group. The program does also include small panels, however, in styles that appear in many other tombs, as well. One additional formal connection appears in the fishing and fowling scene on the east wall, which appears to be very similar to the fishing and fowling scene in the tomb of Sabni1. Yet which was the model for the other, or whether both were modeled on something else, remains unclear.

Although the program of Khunes is difficult to locate in the sequence of the programs, viewed alone it hints at the developmental process in the cemetery overall. The combination of an underlying Memphite-like program design with many smaller panels in diverse styles testifies to the appeal of the panel method of tomb decoration even when the more "standard" version was a real option. Two distinct phases of the program utilize the more Memphite style, with the long south wall program, the false door niche, and the two southern pillars forming the first part, and the east wall and at least pillar E2 forming the second, after Khunes received the higher-ranking "count" title. Although the timing of the smaller panels cannot be pinpointed, the evidence indicates that at different phases Khunes chose to use large-scale, low raised relief Memphite scenes along with smaller panels in varied styles.

The final group comprises the programs of Pepynakht Heqaib2 and Sabni2, although their place in the sequence remains speculative. Clearly they were both constructed later than the tomb of Pepynakht Heqaib1 based upon the architecture. Sabni2 has a title connected to the pyramid of Pepy II, as well. One reason these two tombs may be placed later than the rest of the tombs in the group is found in the titulary of Sabni2. Edel suggested that in the earlier phases of the cemetery there was a divide among the tomb owners' rank and place in the administration, with the expedition leaders and "overseer of Upper Egypt" on one side, and the "great overlord of the king" on the other. Sabni2 is the only tomb owner known thus far to hold both titles, and Edel reasoned that perhaps later in the evolution of the town and the cemetery those two responsibilities were more closely linked.[22] Further support may be found in the presence of the title "overseer of Upper Egypt." Although the significance and use of this title remains debated, it is possible that at Qubbet el-Hawa (and at other individual sites) only one person could hold this title at any given time. Here at Qubbet el-Hawa Harkhuf, Sabni1, and Sabni2 hold this title (and fragments from Mekhu's sarcophagus indicate he held it, as well, although it is not included in his tomb program). Harkhuf could well have died before Mekhu, and we know Mekhu died before Sabni, who would have inherited his father's title. Following this pattern, Sabni2 must have followed Sabni1, and therefore these programs were created around the same time or after those of Mekhu, Sabni1, Sobekhetep, Khwin-Khnum, and IiShemai.

Like those programs, those of Pepynakht Heqaib2 and Sabni2 use both large-scale figures of the tomb owner and panels of smaller subsidiary figures carved in different styles. The Raised A1, Raised A2, and Sunken A styles common to the rest of the cemetery show up in both programs. Although Raised B is not used, several figures in the sunken version of B appear, and the painted false door of Pepynakht Heqaib2 suggests a link to the Painted style from the earlier tombs. Overall, these programs show much greater stylistic diversity than the others, and in addition, each of these tomb programs includes unique styles that do not appear in other programs, including two visually distinctive styles (Sunken E and Sabni2 Raised) used for figures of the tomb owners.

In summary, this interpretation of the use of style in the cemetery emphasizes the development of the system from uncertain origins. The early emphasis on text and the use of the sunken Harkhuf style is abandoned, perhaps in favor of raised relief styles for the status they convey. The Painted style used in Iishemai's program and adapted to panels of raised relief may have been a practical response to poor quality stone or limited resources; in any case it was not widely used, as the status and durability of carved relief proved more appealing. In a cemetery with elite programs using both raised and sunk relief as well as painting, the tomb owners apparently felt some flexibility in their use of style, as shown in the chapels of Mekhu, Sabni1, Khwin-Khnum, Sobekhetep, Khui, Tjetji, and Khunes. By the later phases of the cemetery it appears that diversity of style in a program may well have been a desire of the tomb owner. The creation of unique styles for figures of the tomb owners also implies that the tomb owners saw value in visually distinct styles, perhaps especially if the style was associated with a certain tomb owner. This relationship between identifiable style and powerful person is not out of step with much Egyptian art.

The way in which style is used in the tombs at Qubbet el-Hawa indicates that, at a minimum, stylistic diversity and styles that were non-Memphite in appearance were acceptable to the tomb owners. This suggests that these tomb owners did not perceive a stylistically homogenous program to be essential to a successfully functioning tomb. If the tomb owners held little interest in the specific form of the images and were primarily concerned with the content of their programs, this would suggest an unusually high degree of freedom allowed to the artists that they then exploited with particular creativity and originality. In contrast, if the tomb owners actively encouraged the development of new and different styles, this implies that they valued style as a mode of communication and felt this unique use of style was an option available to them. In either case, the artists and their creative processes held an essential role in the development of this program system. Based upon the thematic content of the programs, it appears that other members of the community, especially those involved in the *ka*-cults, had an integral and visible role in the creation of these programs, as well, in that depictions of themselves as identified individuals constitute the majority of the programs. The formal aspects of the programs reveal the combined effort and support of a broad community of people including artists and others, led by the desires of the elite tomb owners.

4

Individuals, Community, Identity: Summation and Interpretation of Program Content

The thematic focus of the programs' content on subsidiary/offering figures that are identified by accompanying inscriptions equally distinguishes them from standard Old Kingdom models.[1] Only a handful of scenes in these twelve programs have content other than such figures. These include the south wall program of Khunes 34h (Kh7); the three fishing and fowling scenes in the tombs of Sabni1 (MS27), Khunes (Kh3), and Sabni2 (Sb15); the disjointed panel of agricultural activities in the tomb of Mekhu (MS7); and the scenes related to bulls in Khunes (Kh23) and Sabni2 (Sb17). Images of offerings appear from the earliest elite funerary monuments, the carved stele from the Second Dynasty, and figures bearing these offerings become part of tomb programs from the late Third to early Fourth Dynasties, as the programs begin to expand beyond just the offering niche. They remain integral to tomb programs over the Old Kingdom, but they normally constituted only one part of a larger program that included scenes such as bird catching, fishing, fowling, and craft production, among others.

Memphite and provincial tomb programs customarily include identified subsidiary figures, both family members of the tomb owners and other non-related people. Many of the officials depicted in the Qubbet el-Hawa programs hold titles similar to those in elite tombs at other sites, including three tiers of the priests of the *ka*-cult (overseer, inspector, and *ka*-priest) and other cult officials such as the "directors of the food hall." In most elite tomb programs throughout Egypt, family members and other identified figures represent only a small percentage of the program's population in total; however, in the Qubbet el-Hawa programs the reverse is true. Only 79 subsidiary figures (17 percent) out of 463 (including family members of the tomb owners) have no visible text with them. Many of these were badly damaged, and at least fifteen almost certainly originally had associated inscriptions: for example, two offering figures on the west wall in Khunes's tomb survive only via their legs (Kh14), while identifying inscriptions would have appeared near their faces or above their heads, as they do on all other panels in this area. Thirty-five of these seventy-nine figures can be at least partially identified via connection to other identified figures, which will be discussed in more detail later in this chapter. This accounting leaves only twelve figures, or just more than 2 percent of the entire population of subsidiary figures, with no clear means of identification. Such a dramatic statistic clearly differentiates these programs from the standard Memphite and provincial models. Often larger, more complex tombs have higher numbers of identified figures, but these programs incorporate a higher number of anonymous figures, as well. An interesting variation on the typical model is found in another provincial tomb, of Pepyankh the Middle at Meir. Pepyankh's program includes 50 figures identified as family and another 110 identified dependents. It still incorporates a large number of anonymous figures, but the balance is very different in this particular program.[2] It may be significant the Pepyankh supposedly lived to be 100 years old.

Along with the identification of the vast majority of offering figures, the limited subject matter of the scenes also sets Qubbet el-Hawa programs apart from most elite programs, and both elements imply active and intentional choices by the tomb owners. Following an overview of the figures in each tomb program, these choices regarding the programs' content will be more fully examined, and the identity of the people depicted will be considered.

Tomb Program Figures

MEKHU (QH25)

Although the initial description of the tombs addressed the programs of the double tomb of Mekhu and Sabni1 as one, it is more appropriate to consider them separately in this discussion. The primary division between the two programs arises from the architecture of the tomb; however, two panels technically in Mekhu's chapel space belong properly to Sabni1's program, based upon the orientation and identities of the figures. In addition, the north stela along the southern ramp depicts Sabni1 and his *ka*-priest Khui, and thus belongs to Sabni1's program, as well.

Mekhu's program includes nine images of the tomb owner, a relatively high number among these Old Kingdom tombs, because five survive on his false door, which is one of only three false doors in this group to retain any of the original texts and images (MS17). Most likely, other false doors originally had figures of the tomb owners, as well. The other four are concentrated around the entrance into his chapel, with one on the stela along the ramp to the forecourt (MS1), two on the thicknesses of the doorway (MS3, MS4), and the fourth on the east wall just inside the entrance (MS7).

The remainder of Mekhu's program includes fifty-six subsidiary figures. Eighteen of these are the anonymous, active figures engaged in agricultural activities on the east wall panel, which is the only panel outside of the tomb of Khunes to incorporate such actions (MS7). As they lack specific, personal identification, these figures differ from the majority included in the tomb programs. The artists' reconfiguration of the panel to incorporate the offering scene in the upper right corner, as well as the addition of the small, identifying inscriptions to the butchery scene below, suggests their awareness of a meaningful difference between the anonymous, active figures and the identified figures presenting offerings (MS7a). This action could be interpreted as an effort to adapt the more anomalous scene into the Qubbet el-Hawa system.

Of the remaining thirty-eight figures, thirty-seven have inscriptions. Of these thirty-seven, eight are from the two panels associated with the subsidiary burials off the south and northeast walls of Mekhu's chapel (MS8, MS9), and two are on a subsidiary false door south of Mekhu's main cult niche. These figures, too, occupy a somewhat different position in Mekhu's program than the others, as three of them are receivers rather than offerers of cult support, and the remaining figures are depicted either offering to or in support of these officials rather than of Mekhu. Khwti, buried in the north chapel, faces his *ka*-priest Shemai, while Metjnw, in the south chapel, is surrounded by a *ka*-priest, his wife, two daughters, and son. The final two figures, another Sabni and his wife Sabt, appear on the subsidiary false door. The relatively high ranks of these three officials could explain their independent chapels and panels and the false door, but no identified familial connection between any of the three subsidiary officials and Mekhu explains their presence within his chapel.[3] Their cult places can be accessed only by first entering Mekhu's chapel, implying a type of dependent relationship between the officials and Mekhu that may have been based upon professional or social bonds other than family. The two panels showing the officials and their subordinates are carved into the walls of Mekhu's chapel rather than in the attached spaces, probably in part for visibility, but this choice makes the officials and their subsidiary figures part of Mekhu's program, as well. In this way, they are part of Mekhu's community, implying their support for Mekhu's cult.

Three images depict members of Mekhu's family, including the image of his wife Ity on the north entrance thickness (MS4), and two figures of Sabni1 as his son on the south entrance thickness (MS3) and on column W2 (MS14). The remaining twenty-four identified figures are all linked to Mekhu's *ka*-cult. One individual, Iienkhenit, called both the "inspector of *ka*-priests" and the "overseer of *ka*-priests," appears in three different places; on a panel alone with Mekhu (MS1), on a panel with his own wife and children (MS5), and on a panel with his son and two additional figures both named Iienkhenit, as well (MS7a).[4] He is the only figure with the top-level "overseer of *ka*-priests" title, making him the highest ranking member of Mekhu's cult, and he accounts for twelve figures in this program, including his family members. A second "inspector of *ka*-priests," Khwwi, appears one time, with his family, on the east wall (MS6). The *ka*-priest Shasef appears on column E4 with his wife and son (MS10). The final group of identified figures shows another *ka*-priest with his wife and daughters (MS12). He has an additional title that apparently refers to his membership in a phyle, a group of part-time workers in a mortuary cult (priest) of the *ta-wr* phyle.[5] The unidentified figure appears alone on column E5, and there is no indication of an inscription (MS11).

SABNI1 (QH26)

Sabni1's program includes twenty figures of the tomb owner, an exceptionally high number among programs in the cemetery, and a result of the unusual façade lintel decoration that incorporates ten images of Sabni1. The full program includes thirty-six subsidiary figures, closely matching Mekhu's program (minus the east wall panel with eighteen anonymous figures). The composition of Sabni1's program is somewhat different; however, as at least eleven of the subsidiary figures depict six (or more) separate members of his family. Likely, one of the four very damaged images on the façade is a son. The majority of these eleven figures appear in the fishing and fowling scene, a type that traditionally incorporates members of the tomb owner's family (MS27). They include his wife Setka, one son named Ini-itef, and a second son whose name is lost, probably his eldest son Mekhu, and four daughters, though two are named Itety and called "sole ornamented one of the king" and thus may represent the same daughter. The other four family members are Sabni1's sons Mekhu and Ini-itef, who appear on the entrance thicknesses (MS21, MS23).[6]

All the remaining figures with clear inscriptions are connected to Sabni1's *ka*-cult. Three figures bear *ka*-priest titles; these include the top-ranking overseer, Ima-Sobek, who appears once with his son Sabni (MS15) and once alone (MS26); the second-tier inspector Khui, who appears on the ramp stele with Sabni1 (MS2), on the north entrance thickness (MS23), and on an internal pillar (in raised relief) with his son (MS25); and Srwdj-nefri, who appears four times identified as only a *ka*-priest, on column M6 with his son (MS13), on the south thickness (MS21), in the fishing and fowling scene (MS27), and along the south edge of Sabni1's false door niche (MS28). A fifth image of Srwdj-nfri with his son appears on column W6 behind Ima-Sobek and his son, and in this case the title "inspector" appears to have been added later (MS15: Figure 26). The first of two figures along the south edge of Sabni1's false door niche could be any of the three *ka*-priests, as the second figure is called "his eldest son Sabni," and all three are depicted in the program with a son named Sabni (MS29). In addition, one or more of the façade figures probably depicted *ka*-priests. Including only the clearly identified figures, the overseer accounts for three figures, the inspector for five, and the simple *ka*-priests for seven. This pattern reverses the one in Mekhu's chapel in which the top-level cult official Iienkhenit appears the most.

The four figures completing Sabni1's program appear on the lower part of the south entrance thickness, leading oxen into the tomb. Original inscriptions, if any, have not survived.

SOBEKHETEP (QH90)

The program in the tomb of Sobekhetep is small and carefully balanced, with four panels holding a total of twelve subsidiary figures and two images of the tomb owner. No family members are included; instead, the program focuses on the top two members of Sobekhetep's *ka*-cult, the overseer Sobekhetep and the inspector Mekwt. Each man is depicted once with a figure of the tomb owner and once on a panel with his family. The overseer, also named Sobekhetep, stands censing the tomb owner on pillar M5, though here he lacks the "overseer" in his *ka*-priest title (SH3). On neighboring pillar E5, he is "overseer of *ka*-priests" and "director of the food hall." The panel is carved in raised relief and includes his wife, who is titled "priestess of Hathor," three sons, only one of whom is identified as a *ka*-priest, and his daughter (SH2). The inspector Mekwt offers geese to the tomb owner on Pillar E4 (SH1), while his own panel is carved on Pillar M4 in sunken relief and shows him accompanied by his wife, with the lesser title of "sealer," and two daughters (SH4). This panel includes a longer text across the top, describing the payment due to *ka*-priests of the cult, a type of text found also in the tombs of IiShemai and Pepynakht Heqaib2.

IISHEMAI-SETKA (QH98)

The similarly small program in the tomb of IiShemai-Setka also comprises four panels, but incorporates greater diversity in the form of animal offerings. On the east wall, the composite panel includes the tomb owner at the right side, facing a man also named IiShemai, here identified as the "director of the food hall" and the "inspector of *ka*-priests" (IiS1). The additional small male figures leading in cattle and gazelles have no identification, and the damage to the female figure on the rear of the top register has removed any possible identification. The south wall panel, also composed of two seemingly separate panels, again shows the tomb owner at the right side, facing another "inspector of *ka*-priests" named Nekhtw (IiS2). In the area behind Nekhtw, two small male figures flank a single inscription identifying "his son, the *ka*-priest, IiShemai." A longer text above the two refers to the payment due priests who service the cult, of the type seen in the tomb of Sobekhetep and Pepynakht Heqaib2, but does not identify the offerers.

The tomb owner also appears on each panel; on the south pillar he stands alone (IiS3), while on the north pillar two priests attend him, one identified as a *ka*-priest and one as both a *ka*-priest and a director of the food hall (IiS4). Both figures have the name IiShemai included in their inscriptions, and based upon the image on the south wall, it seems likely these two figures represent either two sons, or one son shown twice, of the higher-ranked inspector of *ka*-priests, Nekhtw.

KHWIN-KHNUM (QH102)

Khwin-Khnum's tomb program, like Sobekhetep's, includes twelve subsidiary figures, though here they are distributed on six panels, and the program includes four figures of the tomb owner rather than two (KK1, KK3, KK5, KK6). Khwin-Khnum's wife Senet, who is a priestess of Hathor, accompanies him twice (KK3.2, KK5.2). The remaining ten figures service his *ka*-cult, led by two priests: Kari, the overseer, and Seni, identified as only a *ka*-priest. Kari appears four times, twice with Khwin-Khnum (KK1.2, KK5.3), once with two of his own daughters (KK3), and once with Seni (KK2), while Seni appears only twice and never with his family (KK6). Both figures have additional titles including several unusual ones that do not appear elsewhere. Seni is "director of grain measures" and "elder of the domain" (KK2.1), while Kari is identified as "overseer of the estate; overseer of the gateway; overseer of workers" (KK4), as well as "libationer in the tomb" (KK2.2)

TJETJI (QH103)

In Tjetji's incomplete program there are textual references to seven subsidiary figures, though only five images were carved in relief. The southeast column retains inscriptions on both the east and north faces. On the north face, the inscription painted in large hieroglyphs refers to the tomb owner; however, this surface was later covered by an internal wall (Tj2). The smoothed area on the upper part of the east face of the column holds hieratic references to two individuals who no doubt were meant to be represented here: "overseer of the estate" Khnumhetep and "director of the food hall" Mentjet (Tj1).

Khnumhetep appears again, now in both image and text, on the east face of the north column, on a panel with two registers with two figures each (Tj3). Both figures on the top row are identified as Khnumhetep, and they may both represent the same man, identified in the first image as a *ka*-priest and in the second as a director of the food hall and an overseer of either troops (*mšꜥ*) or people (*rmṯw*). The male figure on the bottom appears to be a "carrier of valuables," a rather unusual title, and is named Nysw-Heqa. A woman named Hrwemkawes who follows him is an "overseer of the estate." The relationship of these figures to the tomb owner is not certain; however, a large group of figures in the tomb of Khui is headed by a man named Khnumhetep, who has a daughter named Hrwemkawes. A long inscription accompanies the figures, detailing Khnumhetep's service to both Khui and

Tjetji on expeditions to several different places, indicating at the least a professional relationship.

The sole image of the tomb owner Tjetji is carved into the south side of the north column, accompanied by an inscription carved over part of the painted texts (Tj4). Beneath Tjetji stands one small offering figure, but no accompanying inscription survives, if indeed one was ever there.

KHUI (QH34E)

The extensive damage to Khui's tomb makes it probable that the surviving relief on one pillar face does not represent the entire program. The face of this pillar holds two panels that include twenty subsidiary figures. In the top panel, two figures face a seated Khui; they are his "overseer of *ka*-priests, Khenty," and Khenty's son Khwti, who is an "inspector of *ka*-priests" (Ku1). Below this scene, a second panel divided into three registers has eighteen figures, although possibly several figures represent the same individual (Ku2). On the top register, each of the four figures is identified as Khnumhetep, and three of them are called directors of the food hall, while the fourth is called an "overseer of the *per-shena*" (storehouse). As noted previously, a text running across the top of this register recounts Khnumhetep's service on behalf of both Khui and Tjetji. It is very likely this Tjetji and the owner of tomb 103 are the same man, and thus this Khnumhetep is the same person depicted on Tjetji's column.[7]

The second register is led by a figure of Khnumhetep's wife, Senti, followed by two daughters and two sons; the final two figures in this register lack inscriptions. The first of the daughters is Hrwemkawes, and the second son is named Tjetji, which increases the likelihood these figures represent the same family depicted in Tjetji's tomb. The bottom register is led by another director of the food hall named Khnumhetep, perhaps the same Khnumhetep from the top register. Next are three figures identified as "his assistant," two of whom are also directors of the food hall and the third a "keeper of beer." The final three figures on this register are engaged in beer-making activities; they do not have accompanying inscriptions.

None of the figures on the lower panel have *ka*-priest titles; they all appear to be connected to food production and preparation for the cult, with six directors of the food hall, a figure butchering a cow, and others preparing beer behind. Khnumhetep's relatively high status may account for the absence of *ka*-cult titles, as well as allowing his rather prominent burial within Khui's chapel. The large, rock-cut false door south of Khui's centrally placed door belonged to Khnumhetep, whose name is inscribed on both jambs. His ownership of a secondary, though prominent, cult space within the chapel of Khui parallels the presence of subsidiary chapels in the tomb of Mekhu.

KHUNES (QH34H)

The difference of Khunes's program extends as well to the subsidiary figures that populate it. Eleven figures of the tomb owner survive, none of which are from the eroded false door, although two are from the thick sides of the false door niche. Only one entrance thickness still stands, and although the accompanying inscription does not survive, the large standing figure facing into the tomb is clearly Khunes. Two figures of the tomb owner appear in the fishing and fowling scene, three on the long south wall and three on separate pillars, being thus evenly distributed throughout the decorated south section of the tomb.

As discussed before, the south wall of Khunes's tomb holds numerous scenes of activity that incorporate at least eighty separate, anonymous figures. As in Mekhu's program, these anonymous figures should be considered as metaphorical support for Khunes's cult, but they are not equivalent to the identified offering figures. The rest of Khunes's program includes eighty subsidiary figures, though again, more were quite possibly lost to damage. Thirteen of the subsidiary figures are members of Khunes's family. Like Sabni1's program, this high number is due in part to the presence of a fishing and fowling scene, which here incorporates eight smaller figures, six women and two men (Kh3). Only the figure of his son Shemai along the north edge of the scene retains an inscription; it is difficult to say if the other figures were originally identified, as in Sabni1's fishing and fowling scene, or whether their identity was implied, as in more typical Memphite versions of this scene type. Shemai is featured prominently in Khunes's program, depicted seated at an offering table in a typical tomb owner posture on the east wall along the high doorway into the tomb (Kh2). The top male figure facing the standing couple of Khunes and his wife Ankhes on the south wall is likely Shemai as well, though the inscription is too damaged to read (Kh5). Despite the presence of an adjacent tomb specifically for his wife Ankhes, she appears, identified, two times in Khunes's program, in both cases at his same scale (Kh5, Kh6). She is also likely the figure pulling on a papyrus stalk in the fishing and fowling scene.

Of the eighty subsidiary figures, thirty-nine lack individual inscriptions. This high number is due in large part to the extensive damage to the tomb. Of these thirty-nine, only fourteen seem likely to have never had inscriptions; these include the seven family members noted from the fishing and fowling scene, whose identity is implied by context. Six of the remaining seven are the offering figures just south of the false door niche, which are conceptually part of the south wall program comprised primarily of anonymous, active figures. Only one individual offering figure, on pillar W2 (Kh30), of those that fully survive lacks an inscription; the reason for the anonymity is not clear.

Twenty-nine of these thirty-nine figures are part of scenes that include inscriptions, usually associated with other figures. Anonymous figures occur on panels with identified figures in other tombs as well, and most likely represent family members or other dependents of the identified figures or, in some cases, perhaps the identified figure himself. For example, the panel of offering figures on the east wall includes a damaged inscription down and across the top of the front part (Kh4). The inscription may have continued, but most likely it identifies the front one or two figures, and the string of anonymous figures following represented this figure's family or household.

As in most programs, many of the titled subsidiary figures here are connected to the *ka*-cult of the owner. No clearly identified overseer of *ka*-priests is present; the eldest son Shemai may have fulfilled this role in his father's cult. Possibly the lost front figure of the top panel on pillar W2 was the overseer, as this panel was carved in raised relief, which seems generally reserved for higher-status figures, though the widespread use of raised relief in this program makes this correlation uncertain here. Two inspectors of *ka*-priests are present. One, Nebem-iterw, appears only once with three other figures in a composition that suggests they are his children, though they are not labeled as such (Kh22). The other inspector, Menew-hetep Kari, appears three times; twice with his son on panels flanking the false door niche (Kh9, Kh10), and once with an anonymous male figure and a woman, likely his wife, who is a priestess of Hathor (Kh20).

Ten *ka*-priests are identified; six have only this title. One named Nebem-imehu appears on the east end of the south wall, standing beneath the tomb owner's son (Kh5) and again on the south thickness of the false door niche (Kh11). The second figure on the south thickness was likely a *ka*-priest as well, though his inscription is lost. Nebem-imehu shows up a third time, again on the south wall, standing at the edge of the numerous anonymous groups populating the scenes here; in this case he also holds the title "director of the food hall." A *ka*-priest named Khunes follows the inspector Nebem-iterw on the middle panel on pillar E2, east face (Kh22), and another Khunes – perhaps the same figure – appears on the west wall (Kh16a). The two others are both on the north face of pillar E2, one named Ini-senef, the other with no name (Kh26.3, Kh26.4). Along with these six, four more figures have *ka*-priest titles along with at least one other, including the previously mentioned figure of Nebem-imehu. The other three share the north face of pillar E2 with the two already noted; two stand in the middle section and have phyle-related titles as well – "controller of a phyle" and "inspector of a phyle," respectively (Kh25). The third appears at the bottom of the panel and holds the title "libationer" (Kh26.1). The other common cult-related title, "director of the food hall," occurs in the program only five times, and three of the occurrences refer to the inspector of *ka*-priests Mnw-hetep. One figure on the west wall whose name is illegible holds only this title.

On the south wall among the numerous anonymous figures, a second inscription can be discerned. It identifies a man leading a register of oxen as an "overseer of herds." This title occurs again, next to the single figure associated with the fighting bulls on the bottom of the east face of pillar E2 (Kh23). On the top of this pillar, a scribe named Nfr-tjebaw stands facing an image of Khunes seated before a table (Kh21).[8]

The handful of remaining titles includes two possible "overseer of linen," one on the north face of pillar E2 (Kh22.3), the other on the west wall (Kh15). One figure on the west wall is called "sealer" (Kh17b), and one of the figures on pillar W3 holds the title "overseer of crews," familiar from this cemetery. The much less common title "elder of the workshop" is held by another figure on the same panel.

HARKHUF (QH34N)

Harkhuf's simple tomb program does not conform fully to the Qubbet el-Hawa system, although there are hints of its development. Six figures of the tomb owner are distributed on the façade and the interior north section of the tomb, and four more small figures of him are carved at the bottom of each of the four jambs of the false door. Of the nine subsidiary figures, four are depicted in the same style and at the same scale as Harkhuf. Harkhuf's wife Tepemnefret, who would also have been buried in this tomb, is shown once (H7), and his son Djemi appears on the façade (H2) and on an interior pillar (H8). The third figure depicted at large scale is a man named Sabni Nyankh-Pepy, who has no specified relationship to the tomb owner (H9). Despite his uncertain connection to Harkhuf, he holds many of the same titles, and he appears also to have been buried in this tomb since his name and titles are inscribed on the small false door on the west wall between the shaft openings.

Five small offering figures complete the program. Two represent Ipy, a priest of Sabni Nyankh-Pepy's cult, which further supports the likelihood that this tomb was the location of his burial and cult (H9.2, H14.4). Tepemnefret is also accompanied on her pillar by a small female figure named Mererit with the title "sealer" (H7.2). The final two subsidiary figures appear on the south façade beneath the main scene of Harkhuf and Djemi, positioned back to back under Djemi's rear foot. One is an "overseer of linen," and the other is a "*ka*-priest who is head of the *khent*," an unusual title that appears to be limited to Qubbet el-Hawa and also held by several figures in the tomb of Pepynakht Heqaib2 (H5, H6). Seyfried identifies the "khent" in this title as a special type of box that held valuable objects used in the cult.[9]

PEPYNAKHT HEQAIB1 (QH35)

The façade program of Pepynakht1's tomb follows the pattern of Harkhuf's, except the tomb owner stands alone on both jambs. Inside the tomb, however, the program conforms more closely to the Qubbet el-Hawa model with several panels of offering figures. Because the interior program includes no figures of the tomb owner, his presence is limited to the three façade figures, one on each jamb and one on the lintel.

Nineteen figures constitute the internal program, and in contrast to Harkhuf's program but like those of Sobekhetep, Khui, and Tjetji, none of them are Pepynakht's family members. The west wall holds three panels with four figures each, while a panel on the east wall north of the entrance holds five figures. The final two figures stand alone, one south of the entrance on the east wall and one on pillar 2. Of these nineteen figures, eight have no surviving inscriptions, but seven of these eight appear on panels with other identified inscriptions, and the panel on the east wall may show the same figure five times, as a name and titles run across the top. Only the solo figure on pillar 2 lacks any potential means of identification; the panel may have been unfinished (Pn9).

No surviving inscriptions identify an overseer or inspector of the *ka*-priests, but the front figure in panel 1 on the west wall, Meheshes, has an unreadable title that begins "overseer" and may well have been "overseer of *ka*-priests" originally (Pn6). Three inscriptions identify *ka*-priests, including the man Mery who follows Meheshes on panel one. Most interestingly, and uniquely at Qubbet el-Hawa, one of the *ka*-priests is a woman (Pn4). The last *ka*-priest title appears on the panel north of the entrance; if all five figures represent the same man, then the number of *ka*-priest figures in the program rises from three to eight.

The front figure on each of the four group panels holds the title "director of the food hall," but the composition of the following three figures differs in each. The east wall panel already discussed includes four more men offering, with no separate titles. On the west wall panel one, the group includes one of the *ka*-priests and a female "overseer of the *per-shena*," as well as an untitled fourth figure. On panel two only the front figure is identified, followed by three anonymous male figures (Pn7). Only panel three clearly depicts a family, as the front figure is followed by a woman, presumably his wife, and her two daughters, all three without titles (Pn8).

PEPYNAKHT HEQAIB2 (QH35D)

Pepynakht Heqaib2's program has the highest total number of figures among these tomb programs: 7 figures of the tomb owner and 132 subsidiary figures. Of the seven images of Pepynakht Heqaib2, five survive in excellent condition, while the other two left only traces. Only the barest outline of the head and shoulders of the seated figure on the façade remain, and the inscription accompanying this figure, readable when Edel recorded the tombs, is now almost entirely gone (PnH1). Areas of paint remain on the false door, indicating it was originally painted and not carved in relief. Faint traces of color indicate the seated figure of the tomb owner, but the rest of the text and images are lost (PnH29). The other five figures of the tomb owner are all carved on the two high entrance thicknesses (PnH3, PnH4, PnH5, PnH6, PnH7).

Several of the 132 subsidiary figures appear to be more peripheral than others. These include the rear three figures of panel F on the south part of the east wall (PnH13), and a small figure on the lower part of the north thickness (PnH4g), though these figures have identifying inscriptions. An additional four figures beneath the main scene on the bottom section of the south entrance thickness are even less integrated, being primarily indicated with incised outlines and lacking inscriptions. They have the quality of graffiti and so are not included in the count of Pepynakht Heqaib2's community, while the previously mentioned four are, though it remains possible they were later additions to the program.[10] Three more panels (panel L, PnH18; PnH22 on the north face of pillar 2, and PnH23, east face of pillar 2 at the top) with eleven total figures were only drawn and never carved. All three are in positions of relative prominence (though one is now partially covered by a secondary, built wall) and depict specifically identified people with official titles. It is unclear why they were not carved.

Out of 132 figures, only 1 depicts a family member of Pepynakht Heqaib2; his son, Nynwbt, on the upper part of the north entrance thickness (PnH5.2). Habachi, among others, argued that Sabni2 was a son of Pepynakht Heqaib2, based on the architecture of the tombs and on evidence from a Middle Kingdom shrine, but there is no indication of Sabni2 in Pepynakht Heqaib2's program.[11] Pepynakht Heqaib2's wife is neither depicted nor mentioned.

An exceptionally high percentage of the figures are identified with inscriptions. Of 132 figures, only 10 lack texts; an 11th figure was hacked out, though the surrounding inscriptions were left intact. Of the ten, five appear on panels with other identified figures, which links them to specific groups. For example, the front figure of panel C on the east wall has no inscription but the following three figures do, and because all three share the same, relatively uncommon name Ny-Khnum/Ny-ba, the four figures may represent the same person (PnH10).[12] Two of the smallest figures in the façade panel of subsidiary figures have no inscriptions, but identified family members surround them (PnH2.1, PnH2.3). Another of these figures is part of the possible peripheral group, added at the back of panel C on the east wall (PnH10.5), and the last is the figure executed only in paint, following behind an identified figure on panel Pa (PnH24a.2). Only the three figures below, on panel P, and the two figures on panel R have no means of identification (PnH24, PnH26); in both cases later damage to the tomb could have erased any initial texts.

Because of the high number of figures comprising this program, a greater array of titles occurs. Several individuals seem to be represented in more than one panel, although this can be difficult to determine. Some names are very common and cannot alone be a basis for assuming a single individual. Even when figures with the same name share a title, a single identity can only be hypothesized, as some of the lower-ranking titles are common. The overseer of Pepynakht Heqaib2's *ka*-cult, Seni, appears only once, standing alone opposite the largest and most detailed carving of the tomb owner, on the upper part of the south thickness (PnH3.2: Figure 44). The raised relief style of the figure of Seni is closely related to that of the tomb owner here, and he also holds the titles "overseer of linen," "djet priest," and "sealer." Two figures hold the "inspector of *ka*-priests" title: one named Shemai stands alone on the north thickness behind the bottom figure of Pepynakht Heqaib2 (PnH7c.1),[13] while the other, Hehu, stands with his wife on a panel far back on the east wall north of the entrance (PnH20.1). Although this figure appears only once in Pepynakht Heqaib2's program, a man named Hehu – perhaps the same man – appears again, with his family, on the façade of Sabni2's tomb, burning incense before Sabni; he may have held positions in both *ka*-cults.

Ten figures have the title "*ka*-priest." Anu, standing behind the figure of Pepynakht Heqaib2's son Nynwbt on the north thickness, may be the same Anu depicted with his family on panel M on the east wall (cf. PnH5.3 to PnH19.3). A relatively large figure of a *ka*-priest named Shemai, on the middle of the north thickness (PnH6.3), could be the same Shemai on panel A (PnH8.1), though this is a relatively common name. Half of the ten *ka*-priests are on the south section of the east wall (Figure 50), on panels with groups of figures that do not comprise families, and no *ka*-priests appear on the south entrance thickness.

Another type of *ka*-priest, the "*ka*-priest who is head of the *khent*," occurs five times in this tomb. The only other example in the cemetery appears on the façade of Harkhuf's tomb. In Pepynakht Heqaib's tomb, two appear on the south entrance thickness, one with his son (PnH4b.1) and the other alone (PnH4c.1). Two more stand alone on the bottom section of the north thickness, in front of the tomb owner (PnH7e.1, PnH7h.1), and the fifth is represented in the prominent spot on the east wall beneath the rock ledge, in a relatively elaborate panel that includes his family and several animals along the bottom (PnH14.1). Although it is not certain how this title fits into the *ka*-cult or its hierarchy, the possibility that these priests were responsible for especially valuable objects suggests they were ranked above regular *ka*-priests. This possibility is supported by the balance of figures for the ka-cult: one overseer, two inspectors, five heads of the khent, ten *ka*-priests.

The other common cult title, "director of the food hall," appears twenty times in Pepynakht Heqaib's program. Ten of these twenty hold only this title, but the other ten have additional titles including "inspector of *ka*-priests," "*ka*-priest who is before the khent," "*ka*-priest," and "overseer of the *per-shena*," as well as titles related to phyle organization. Six figures in all have titles related to phyle organization (PnH4c.1, PnH9.1, PnH10.2, PnH11.2, PnH11.3, PnH12.1), which could be the organization of the priests for Pepynakht Heqaib2's cult, or of other groups of workers related to the cult or of work unrelated to the *ka*-cult.[14] There are five "overseers of the *per-shena*" (PnH1.2, PnH2.2, PnH7a.1, PnH16.7, PnH17.1), one of whom is a woman (PnH16.7), and there are four "overseers of linen" (PnH3.2, PnH6.2, PnH15a.1, PnH23.1), which is a relatively common title of a rank generally similar to "director of the food hall."[15]

Six times the title "overseer of the estate" appears, but three refer to the same individual, Heqaib Seni (PnH7d.1, PnH21.1, PnH22.1). He is also a "royal chamberlain of the great house," a higher-ranking title than most here and one which may indicate a close connection with the administration in Memphis. The other three overseers of the estate all have scribal titles as well; two are scribes (PnH13.3, PnH18.1) and the third is an "overseer of scribes of the judiciary" (PnH13.1). Three other figures are also called scribe, making a total of six figures in the program with scribal titles (PnH13.4, PnH21.3, PnH23.2).

Rarer titles include two examples of "overseer of crews," one who is alone (PnH4d.1) and one with his family (PnH17.2), one "stone mason" depicted with his wife and daughter and holding his tools (PnH4a.1), and one "inspector of embalmers" who is one of the more carefully carved and detailed figures in the program (PnH7b.1) The sign designating the title of the first figure on panel Pa may be a whetstone, indicating a butcher, or perhaps an axe, indicating a carpenter (PnH24a.1). The front figure on panel S may be a "keeper of emmer" (PnH27.1), and the active figure at the front bottom of panel T may be called "brewer," or the inscription could give his name (PnH28.9). One of the women on panel G is identified as a "wet nurse" (PnH14.4), while another woman may hold the title "mistress of the house," though the signs are obscured (PnH16.2). The more general title "sealer" is much more common for women, as nine hold it.

SABNI2 (QH35E)

Despite the close architectural connection between the tombs of Pepynakht Heqaib2 and Sabni2, their programs are distinctly different and very few of the same individuals appear in both. Eleven figures of Sabni2 are split between the exterior (six) and interior (five). Eighty-four subsidiary figures complete the program, with twenty-four on the façade and the remaining sixty inside. Four subsidiary figures, all female, are family members of Sabni2. Khai-nefri appears in front of Sabni2 on the east entrance thickness (Sb10d.1), and although she is not identified as a daughter there, she is in the fishing and fowling scene (Sb15.3). Merit, standing behind Sabni2 on the east thickness, is identified as his daughter (Sb10e.1).[16] The fourth figure, Senit, mirrors Khai-nefri in the fishing and fowling scene, and she is there called "noblewoman of the king," a high-ranking title that Merit and Khai-nefri also hold, and one that implies a family relationship to the tomb owner (Sb15.4). The two women on the lintel panel might have been family as well, though they are not identified as such. Edel suggests the figure of Heqaib next to the false door was a son, but again he is not called son on this relief.[17]

Sabni2's overseer of *ka*-priests, like Pepynakht Heqaib2's, is named Seni; they could be the same individual, but it is a common name. Three figures of Seni appear on the tomb's façade, and a fourth in the fishing and fowling scene. Two of the three on the façade are called "overseer of *ka*-priests in this tomb" (Sb2.2, Sb3.1), a characterization that seems intended to distinguish his duties from another tomb (i.e., Pepynakht Heqaib2's). The figure of Seni in the fishing and fowling scene shares two of the three additional titles that Pepynakht Heqaib2's Seni holds, providing support for the view of a single individual, or alternately suggesting a possibly close relationship between the two Senis (Sb15.5).

The two inspectors of *ka*-priests of Sabni2's cult, Memi and Dwa-Sobek, appear on the lintel panel (Sb1.4, Sb1.5). Inside the tomb, two additional figures are named Memi, both identified only as directors of the food hall (Sb10f.2, Sb16.1). One appears on a panel with two additional figures. Two figures named Dwa-Sobek are carved on the entrance thicknesses, one on each side in the same position relative to the respective image of Sabni2 (Sb10c.1, Sb12b.1). Both of these figures are also called only director of the food hall, but given the rarity of this name it seems likely they represent the same Dwa-Sobek who appears on the façade.

Only one figure in the entire program holds the title "*ka*-priest." He is named Hehu, and is most likely the Hehu depicted in panel N in Pepynakht Heqaib2's program, based upon both the rarity of the name and that of his wife, Neferwawet, who appears with him in both instances (cf. PnH20 to Sb7, Sb8). That Hehu is carved in raised relief, in a panel alone with a figure of Sabni, implies a higher status than would be typically assumed for a *ka*-priest and director of the food hall. In addition, his family, including his wife and six children, appear behind him on the façade of Sabni2's tomb. Perhaps Hehu's higher status as inspector in Pepynakht Heqaib2's cult earned him a position in Sabni2's cult, although why this position was not accompanied by a higher title as well is unclear.

Although *ka*-priests are rare in Sabni2's program, nineteen directors of the food hall are present. Fifteen have only this title, while the other four include both inspectors of *ka*-priests, the *ka*-priest Hehu, and the "overseer of herds," Mery, on panel W (Sb18.2). Although Mery is joined by five members of his family, the panel was only drawn and never carved. Two of the other three panels with groups of figures are both led by directors of the food hall (Sb14, Sb16).

Additional titles are evenly distributed among the remaining figures. There are five figures identified as "overseer of linen" and five figures with scribal titles. Two of the five are simple scribes (Sb10f.7, Sb12d.5), two are "overseer of scribes of the judiciary" (Sb10f.10, Sb12d.2), and the fifth is a "judicial scribe" (Sb9.3). Several more titles come in pairs: two "overseer of herds" (Sb13.1, Sb18.2), two "overseer of the *per-shena*" (Sb11.4, Sb12d.14), one of whom is a woman, and two "chief of the estate" (Sb10f.6, Sb17.2). Two stonemasons are both named Heqaib, possibly the same person, though the common use of this name makes this uncertain (Sb12d.11, Sb12d.13). There is one "overseer of the estate" (Sb10f.6), and one "physician of the palace" (Sb10f.9), a title that does not appear anywhere else in the cemetery. The specification "of the palace," as in the title of Heqaib Seni in Pepynakht Heqaib2's program, implies a close connection between this subsidiary figure and the capital, and thus suggests a type of personal connection between the king and Sabni2.

Although many figures in Sabni2's program share names with figures in Pepynakht Heqaib2's program, and some people may be represented in both, the common names and shared titles make it difficult to identify specific individuals. Although these two programs are similar in their high number of subsidiary figures, they are composed differently. The wide entrance thicknesses of Sabni2's tomb were carved with compositions that in some ways recall Memphite designs, with a large figure of the tomb owner followed by three registers of smaller figures. These compositions enabled the incorporation of more single figures, meaning figures that are less clearly grouped among themselves, and grouped instead in respect to the tomb owner. While in Pepynakht Heqaib2's program 86 percent (116 out of 135) of the figures are part of groups of subsidiary figures (that is, clearly linked to each other), only 43 percent of the figures in Sabni2's tomb are so arranged.

Cemetery-wide Summary

In total, 548 figures have been incorporated into this analysis; 85 of tomb owners and 463 others including family members of tomb owners, offering figures, and a handful of subsidiary tomb owners. The tomb owners thus represent only 15 percent of the total population of images. Family members of the tomb owners, including wives and children, account for thirty-seven certain figures and likely another three (MS23.3: one of the male figures on Sabni1's entrance thickness, and Sb1.3, Sb1.6: the two women on Sabni2's façade lintel panel), constituting 7 percent of the total population and 9 percent of the non-tomb owner figures. Twenty-six of the forty family members have titles; those who do not include ten family members depicted in fishing and fowling scenes in the tombs of Khunes, Sabni1, and Sabni2, whose daughter in that scene, Khai-nefri, carries a title in another image. Two more figures without titles are sons of Sabni1, whose titles have likely been lost to damage. The final figure is Khunes's son Shemai, who in one image does not have a title, though he has many in other images.

The titles held by the family members are primarily of rank and status. The men have the same titles as the tomb owners, including one "count," six "sealer of the king of lower Egypt," eleven "sole companion," and eight "lector priest." The son of Harkhuf, Djemi, is also an "overseer of Egyptianized Nubians." The women carry the typical titles of high-status women, including one "royal acquaintance," two "noblewoman of the king," six "sole ornamented one of the king," and three "ornamented one of the king." Four are also "priestess of Hathor."[18] Although in the Old Kingdom, sons of elite tomb owners often fulfill roles in their father's *ka*-cults, such roles are not specified among the family members depicted at Qubbet el-Hawa. The lack of *ka*-cult titles with the sons does not necessarily mean they did not function in the cult; it may have been important to separate the sons of the tomb owners from the rest of the *ka*-cult staff, including using entirely separate groups of titles.

Of the remaining 423 figures, primarily offering figures, 234 have titles.[19] Priests of the *ka*-cult constitute the largest group, with a total of eighty-five of various levels. The "overseer of *ka*-priests" title appears twelve times, identifying eight (or possibly nine) different individuals, several of whom also appear without the overseer designation. The twenty examples of the "inspector of *ka*-priests" identify fifteen different people; only one figure, Iienkhenit in the tomb of Mekhu, appears with both the overseer and inspector titles. Six figures have the apparently site-specific "*ka*-priest who is before the *khent*" title.[20] Forty-one different figures are called "*ka*-priest," and for twenty-eight of them this is their only title. Ten *ka*-priests are also "director of the food hall," which is the next most common title in the cemetery, used with seventy-two different figures. This title refers to the preparation of food for the funeral and the mortuary cult, and figures with this title are more often depicted carrying food offerings and only rarely shown burning incense, which is a more common activity of the *ka*-priests. The title "director of the food hall" and *ka*-priest titles are common to all elite tomb programs.

Among the more than fifty additional titles that appear in the cemetery, none is nearly as frequent. The next most common title is "overseer of linen," which is used with sixteen figures. This title also often appears in elite tomb programs and seems to refer to activities specific to the mortuary cult, although it may refer to activities in the household, as well. A handful of other titles held by male figures, such as libationer, butcher, and embalmer, also clearly relate to cultic activities. There are ten "overseer of the *per-shena*," a reference to storage and processing functions typically linked to the state. Although the *per-shenas* referred to in these titles may have been private, linked to the estates of the tomb owners, there is no clear evidence for private *per-shenas* at this time.[21] Twelve figures have scribal titles, including two "overseer of scribes of the judiciary." Other titles such as "overseer of the estate," "elder of the domain," and "keeper of beer" likely designate jobs carried out for the tomb owner during his life, as well as in service to his mortuary cult.[22] The titles "overseer of crews" and "stonemason," which appear in the tombs of Pepynakht Heqaib2 and Sabni2, could also be connected to the construction of the tombs. Of the 113 non-family female figures in the programs, only 32 hold titles. Nineteen of these are "sealer," which is primarily a status title, and there are also three (possibly four) "priestess of Hathor." Among the functional rather than ranking positions, there are four "overseer of the *per-shena*," one "*ka*-priest," and one "wet nurse."

Program Community I: Titles

The tomb owners at Qubbet el-Hawa played a different role in the elite administration than was typical for provincial officials; distinctively, they lacked the nomarch title and related titles. Nonetheless, they held typical ranking titles, placing them in the upper ranks of the elite.[23]

The family members of the tomb owners also held high-ranking titles, generally the same as those of the tomb owners, though usually without the higher designation of count. In addition to the family members depicted in the chapel programs and to the tomb owners themselves, six more figures hold similar, high-ranking titles. One is a "sole companion, lector priest, overseer of Egyptianized Nubians" named Heqaib, depicted at small scale as the only figure on a panel next to the false door of Sabni2. Edel suggests it is likely this Heqaib is a son of Sabni2, though that epithet does not appear on the panel. Whether this Heqaib received a burial place within Sabni2's tomb is not clear; possibly, he had his own tomb elsewhere in the cemetery.

The other five figures holding these elite titles all had cult places of some kind, and thus presumably burials, within other tombs. Each of the elite tombs in this group held at least one subsidiary burial within the chapel space, manifest in the additional shaft openings cut into the floor and secondary false doors; many of the tombs had multiple subsidiary burials. The presence of such burials, and of subsidiary false doors as secondary cult foci, is not surprising, as the burial of family members in the same tomb was an Egyptian tradition. Yet these five figures hold no epithets indicating any familial relationship to the elite officials in whose tombs they are buried.

The "sealer of the king of Lower Egypt, sole companion, expedition leader " Khnumhetep, who appears as an offering figure in the programs of both Tjetji and Khui, also has his own prominent false door within the chapel of Khui, just to the left of the main cult space. Similarly, the "sole companion, lector priest, overseer of Egyptianized Nubians, overseer of foreign lands" Sabni NyankhPepy has a small inscribed false door carved into the west wall of the tomb of Harkhuf between the two shaft entrances. In addition, a large-scale figure of NyankhPepy occupies the south surface of the nearby pillar 3 (i.e., facing his false door), and he has his own *ka*-priest depicted twice, once on his pillar and once next to his false door. The three other officials in this group are all buried in the chapel space of Mekhu. The "sealer of the king of Lower Egypt and sole companion" Sabni and his wife, the "ornament of the king and priestess of Hathor" Sabt, share a false door carved into the west wall, just south of Mekhu's main cult niche. The two final officials, the "sealer of the king of Lower Egypt" Khwti and the "sole companion" Metjnw have separate chapel spaces extended off of Mekhu's own chapel. They each had at least one false door, as well as a painted panel accompanying their chapel depicting themselves with a *ka*-priest, and in Metjnw's case also his wife and children.

The diversity of these five burials presents some difficulties in determining any set rules or patterns in how such subsidiary burials might work. For example, Sabni NyankhPepy is depicted equivalent to the true tomb owner Harkhuf, in a large-scale standing image carved in the same style and in the posture of elite status rather than in honor of the tomb owner; yet his false door is significantly smaller than that of Harkhuf. In contrast, Khnumhetep has a very large false door in the tomb of Khui, and is allowed to incorporate a brief autobiography of sorts, which is nearly unheard of for subsidiary figures, yet he is depicted quite clearly in a posture of offering on behalf of Khui, and has no image of himself as the focus of cult. In the chapel of Mekhu, the separate chapels awarded both Khwti and Metjnw, as well as the images of each as receivers of cult, would seem higher status than having only a secondary false door on the west wall, yet the owner of the small false door, Sabni, holds higher-ranking titles than the sub-chapel owner Metjnw.

While it may not be possible to determine how these five elite officials gained their respective cult places, or how the differences among the cult places emerged, overall their material components reinforce the higher status of their owners relative to the other subsidiary individuals depicted in the tomb programs, also evident via their high-ranking titles. Yet the location of their burials, images, and false doors within the tomb of another person indicates a lesser status than the tomb owners as well as a dependent relationship. In the case of Mekhu, it may be significant that the panels accompanying two subsidiary burials account for eight figures in his program, which is the difference in the number of family members depicted in Sabni's program and his own.

Thus, there is a clear divide between the status of the tomb owners, their families, and these five subsidiary burial owners (and the sixth anomalous figure of Heqaib in the tomb of Sabni2) and the remaining individuals depicted in the programs. Significantly, Edel discovered a similar division in his analysis of the inscribed pottery from the tombs. He notes that the seventy (or so) different people he identified from the pottery inscriptions includes none of the *ka*-cult personnel depicted in the programs. Many of the tomb owners are named, as are members of their families, and most of the additional figures have similar high-ranking titles; they may have had tombs at Qubbet el-Hawa that have not yet been identified.[24] Edel concluded that only the high-ranking members of the community offered inscribed pottery to each other in a sort of closed circle of support, where both the offerer and recipient occupied the highest tier of elite in the community, while the lower-ranking *ka*-cult officials did not engage in this activity. The offering of pottery inscribed with the offerers' name does not occur in the rest of Egypt during this time. The people depicted in the programs, whether or not identified as cult officiants, occupy a different social rank than the tomb owners and their families.

Information about the burials of these *ka*-cult officials is significantly less complete; however, the Bonn team recovered evidence from many of the shafts sunk into the forecourts of the tombs that suggested they held burials of *ka*-cult officials.[25] Almost all of the elite tombs here had at least one additional burial in the forecourt; several tombs had numerous burials, with the expanded and heavily populated forecourt encompassing the three tombs of Pepynakht Heqaib1, Pepynakht Heqaib2, and Sabni2 standing as the epitome of the practice. These forecourt shafts could be either quite similar to interior shafts, in dimensions and depth, or in other cases much simpler, yet their presence outside the sacred space of the chapel differentiates them from the interior subsidiary burials. Thus, the material evidence of burials also supports a view of the people depicted in the tomb programs – other than the elite tomb owners, their families, and the handful of officials just discussed – as being of a lower status than the tomb owners and their families, at least at the time the programs were carved.[26]

This impression of the social status of these tomb program figures may be further refined by a comparison of the cemetery at Qubbet el-Hawa with that on the island of Elephantine.[27] Although the earliest cemetery at Elephantine closely surrounded the ancient settlement site, the main Old Kingdom cemetery was located on the western half of the southern part of the island, in the area around the Third Dynasty step pyramid. Seidlmayer states that these mastaba tombs clearly belonged to the lower status members of Elephantine society, placing the cemetery in specific contrast to the burials at Qubbet el-Hawa by noting that the richest tombs on the island were approximately equal to some of the forecourt tombs of functionaries at Qubbet el-Hawa.[28] While this evidence does not erase the possibility that some people depicted in the Qubbet el-Hawa programs could have been buried on Elephantine, Seidlmayer's thesis regarding the lack of images and texts in the mastaba field highlights an important division. Although the location of burial was significant, the existence of images and texts of certain people, particularly within the context of the tomb of an elite official, clearly separates them from others who lack such material. It seems reasonable to suppose that this division would be replicated in the location of burial.

This picture of the social status of the *ka*-cult officials and others depicted in the elite tomb programs is not surprising. Although information regarding the structure of private mortuary cults is less extensive than that about royal mortuary cults, they seem to have functioned, in many cases, in a similar manner.[29] High-ranking officials were typically given priesthoods in royal cults, which conferred status as well as financial rewards, due mainly to the reversion of offerings. These priesthoods were part time, usually a month out of every ten, so that the cult was continuously fully staffed by a rotating group of officiants.[30] In this manner, the priests were able to maintain their official jobs in the administration. Ann Roth notes that another benefit of this system for the king was his ability to patronize ten times the number of people, which expanded his circle of loyal supporters and dependents. The same principle applied to service in a private *ka*-cult, as these *ka*-priests (and other officiants) received payment in the form of some percentage of the offerings in return for their service, and so were dependent upon and loyal to the tomb owner as their patron. Several texts among the Qubbet el-Hawa programs make this arrangement explicit, mentioning the rights of *ka*-priests to claim some of the food offerings.[31] And like in the royal cults, the combination of service to the tomb owner and concomitant financial rewards placed the *ka*-cult officials at a higher status than others not invited to serve.

Among the people depicted in the Qubbet el-Hawa programs, few titles identify official positions outside of the cult, which inhibits a more specific picture of the officiants within the context of the larger community; however, a few titles and one longer inscription hint at the types of people included. The official Khnumhetep, one of the "mid-elite" burials, appears as an offerer in the tomb of Khui, possibly (if the top four images represent him) bearing lower-ranking titles such as "director of the food hall" and "overseer of the *per-shena*." Despite the titles he holds in this image, the inscription above describes how Khnumhetep accompanied both Khui and Tjetji on their journeys to Byblos, Punt, and possibly Retjenw.[32] Such journeys were often the responsibility of the elite officials of Elephantine, and it is not surprising that those who aided them in this work would form a key part of the mid- or lower-elite community.

A number of other titles held by subsidiary figures begin with overseer, which clearly identifies this person as higher status than the many others he oversees, such as crews, phyles, and builders. During the Old Kingdom the *per-shena* was a state institution that was responsible for storing and processing agricultural and other surplus products.[33] Perhaps the overseers of the *per-shena* had responsibilities linked to private mortuary cults as well, or perhaps their status in this position earned them positions in the tomb owner's program. And as noted previously, other titles such as "overseer of the estate," "keeper of beer," and "elder of the domain" indicate jobs connected to the running of a large, elite household and as such suggest responsibilities both in the tomb owner's life as well as in his cult, and further designate officials who worked for the tomb owner while they managed other workers beneath them.

Seyfried emphasizes the connection between the titles held by the subsidiary figures in the programs and positions in the household of the elite tomb owner.[34] He argues that all of the figures depicted in a particular program worked in the household of the elite owner of that tomb. In general, this is a reasonable assessment and no doubt many of these figures were household workers for the elite; however, Khnumhetep's text, discussed previously, and several other titles such as "overseer of scribes of the judiciary" indicate jobs outside of the household. Furthermore, a simple *ka*-priest title does not reveal a specific function in a household staff, and many of the titles that can be connected to both the mortuary cult and the household were not *necessarily* held by the figures outside of the cult context. Ultimately, the personal connection between the tomb owner and the subsidiary figure, achieved through work or other social bonds, underlies his presence in the cult.

Titles such as overseers of workers, estates, keeper of beer, and similar also indicate an association between subsidiary figures and local work, on behalf of the locally based tomb owners at their estates and in their households. Although these titles are limited, and the other titles such as overseers of crews and builders do not necessarily specify a locale of work, most likely figures identified as members of the cult of the tomb owners were local (i.e., residents of the settlement on Elephantine). In practical terms, carrying out cult activities would require proximity to the cult space. The evidence of cult-officials' burials at Qubbet el-Hawa also implies these figures were local residents. Another likely group of locally based workers would be the priests of the cult of Satet, whose temple was located at the center of the Old Kingdom town on Elephantine; however, none of the subsidiary figures have titles relating to Satet's cult. This absence of god's cult titles among the figures is unusual, as the priests presumably would have occupied an elevated status among the population similar to these many overseers and other officials, and in Egyptian tradition such important titles would have great value in the mortuary context.[35]

In sum, the titles held by the subsidiary figures in the programs describe a group of local officials who occupied an intermediary rank between the elite tomb owners and the rest of the population. The titles also indicate a patron/dependent relationship between the subsidiary figures and the owner of the tomb in which they appear, based both upon the cult-specific titles and on other, non-cult-related titles.

Program Community II: Names and Relationships

The titles held by the figures in the programs are not the only source of information regarding the identity of this depicted community. As noted in the previous section, just more than half of the subsidiary figures have titles, yet 379 figures, 82 percent, have names.[36] All but 8 of the 260 figures with titles have names. Four of these figures appear in the chapel of Sabni1, and in all cases the names are lost due to damage, but the figures may be otherwise identified via titles, epithets, and context. Three of the other four appear in the panel of Khnumhetep in the tomb of Khui, among the large group including several images of Khnumhetep himself. The final figure appears in the group on the north face of pillar E2 in the tomb of Khunes. The title "*ka*-priest" is incised next to the small offerer, but no name is attached. Thus, in addition to the titled figures, who are those with official jobs in the cult and presumably in the administration of the government or temple as well, there are 121 specifically named figures forming part of these decorative programs. Fourteen of these figures are identified as family members of the tomb owners, but the remaining 107 named figures have no evident familial relationship to a tomb owner.

This aspect of the program deviates from programs in Memphite and most other provincial sites. Offering figures are ubiquitous in tomb programs, named subsidiary figures are also typical, and often a number of subsidiary figures have titles but not names. It is much less common in other elite programs for a nonfamily member of the tomb owner to appear with a name but not the title that indicates the figure's status and/or function within the cult of the tomb owner. At Qubbet el-Hawa, the rationale for including these named yet non-titled figures may be found in the context of their representation. All but three[36] of them appear as part of panels with other figures, at least one of whom does have a title. The three figures that are not part of a clear panel are nonetheless part of a larger group; all three number among the offering figures lined up behind the image of Sabni2 on the west thickness of his tomb. Two are at the back of the middle register and the third is the last figure on the bottom register; possibly, space limitations kept their titles from being included. The figure in front of Hepi and Atju in the middle register is called a "director of the food hall"; perhaps this inscription was meant to apply to these last two figures, as well. Similarly, the figure in front of Hwy on the bottom register is called an "overseer of the *per-shena*," which may have applied to Hwy as well, though that seems less likely. The figure underneath Hepi on the middle register is the "overseer of the *per-shena*" and he is also named Hepi, so they may represent the same person. Thus, essentially all of the non-titled yet named figures are incorporated into the programs as part of group panels headed by a titled figure. The same is true of thirty-five out of the seventy-nine figures with no associated inscriptions mentioned in the introduction to this chapter.

As previously discussed, most of the groups of offering figures divided among the panels consist of families. More specifically, twenty-six panels depict groups of figures that are inscriptionally identified as families, with use of the terms "his wife," "his son," and "her daughter." A twenty-seventh group identified as family share a panel with an image of Pepynakht Heqaib2, and the composite panel on the south wall of IiShemai's tomb incorporates two sons of the *ka*-priest Nakhw, who stands facing the tomb owner. These 28 panels contain 164 figures. In addition, the painted panel associated with the southern subsidiary burial in Mekhu's chapel depicts the burial owner Mekwt with his family, a total of six figures. Nine panels have pairs of figures that are similarly identified, either as father and son or husband and wife.[37] One panel in Mekhu and Sabni1's tomb depicts two pairs of figures of *ka*-priests with their sons, and although on this panel the smaller figures are not specifically identified as sons, they are elsewhere in the program. Another panel in Mekhu's chapel includes his overseer of *ka*-priests Iienkhenit and his son Mekhu as well as two more figures named Iienkhenit, who could be additional sons of the overseer, although they are not identified as such, or perhaps they are meant to represent the overseer himself. The same names Iienkhenit and Mekhu are inscribed next to two butchers in the long panel on the east wall. Two additional family pairs share panels with images of a tomb owner. Thus, a total of 202 figures are clearly identified as part of family groups. An additional seven panels show groups of figures that, based on the composition of the panel with both male and female figures of different sizes, most likely depict families as well, and two panels depict pairs that imply family relationships (one male and female, one large male and smaller male). The lack of epithets may be due to damage in some cases, but not all. These nine panels include 35 more figures, bringing the total of certain and likely family group members to 237.

Other panels with groups of figures seem unlikely to depict families; most are groups of male figures only. Fifteen group panels and one pair panel hold a total of sixty-eight figures, although one of these, in Khunes's tomb with fifteen figures (Kh4), does include female figures and may be a family. Six additional male figures on the west wall of Khunes's tomb are only loosely arranged in three pairs (Kh14, Kh16, Kh17). The first pair is badly damaged, and although they do not appear to share a consistent smoothed surface, the style is nearly identical. The other two pairs share a surface yet are carved in differing styles. In all three pairs it seems possible to consider the figures solo, but the fact that they were placed side by side, given the open expanse of the west wall, suggests an intended grouping. All of the titles on these nonfamily group panels indicate roles in the *ka*-cults, mainly *ka*-priests and directors of the food hall.

One hundred thirteen figures share panels with large figures of the tomb owner. Ten of these figures form groups among themselves; the two registers behind the lower figure of Pepynakht Heqaib2 on his south entrance thickness (PnH4a, 4b), and the family pair facing Khui on the top of his pillar E2 (Ku1) represent a total of seven figures. While IiShemai's *ka*-priest Nekhtw technically shares a panel alone with the tomb owner, the appended panel brings his two sons (IS2). The last figure similarly shares a panel alone with a tomb owner: the *ka*-priest Hehu with Sabni2; however, a second adjacent panel presents Hehu's family (Sb7, 8).

Sixteen of these 113 figures are related to the tomb owners, either wives or children, and another 3 are likely family, as well. Twenty-six of the remaining ninety-four figures are in the tomb of Sabni2, standing in rows behind images of the tomb owner on his entrance thicknesses. Although visually these figures are less clearly solo due to the use of registers, they are not linked to each other by expressed family relationships or other means.

An analysis of the figures based upon groupings and relationships illustrates general trends in the cemetery. Figures are mostly part of group panels, and three-quarters of the group panels depict families rather than figures linked by profession or other social bond. In Memphite and other provincial tombs, identified subsidiary figures are not visually isolated into discernible groups. Often, identified figures appear with other, non-identified figures, sometimes in offering scenes and sometimes attached to other types of scenes such as bird catching or agriculture. Even when several identified figures appear together, they are still part of larger scenes that are composed of registers and usually include a proximate image of the tomb owner. They are not grouped among themselves; rather, they are fit into the design of the scene. Perhaps most significantly, it is exceptionally rare for subsidiary figures in other tombs to appear with their families, in contrast to the Qubbet el-Hawa programs where this mode is the norm.

Significance

IDENTITY AND ELITE TOMB PROGRAMS

A common thread running through many different interpretations of elite tombs and their programs is an understanding of the essential relationship between the tomb and the identity of the tomb owner. The identity of the individual lies at the center of Egyptian beliefs about death and the afterlife, as they are rooted in "the firm belief in a post-mortem existence, not as an anonymous shadow, but in complete preservation of personal identity as it has developed during the lifetime of an individual."[38] The elite tomb played a central role in the successful achievement of this postmortem existence by crafting the appropriate environment for the rituals of the mortuary cult that evolved in service to these beliefs. The tomb chapel was the primary point of contact between the individual deceased tomb owner and the surviving members of his community, and it formed the tomb owner's foremost effort to achieve what Assmann describes as a "focal point" of Egyptian mortuary beliefs: his endurance in social memory.[39] Acknowledging this desire of the tomb owner and the role of the tomb's program in helping to achieve it, Egyptologists have investigated the many ways in which the tomb owner's identity influenced the elite tomb program.[40]

Although the programs at Qubbet el-Hawa are unusual, the tombs have the same primary function as a place for the burial and mortuary cult of the owner of the tomb, thus the connection between the tomb monument and the identity of the owner remains intact. This functional continuity is paralleled by aspects of material continuity as well, through the use of traditional architectural forms and the maintenance of key elements such as false doors and offering tables. To an extent, the programs maintain continuity, as well. The difference of the programs, especially in their content, does not result from the creation of new, never-before-seen elements; rather, the Qubbet el-Hawa tomb owners drew upon familiar types of images and scenes that were present in most elite tombs. The uniqueness of the programs is largely a result of the emphasis on certain aspects (identified offering figures) and de-emphasis or omission of others (daily-life scenes). In essence, the tomb owners and artists drew upon what was traditional and reshaped it. Given the fundamental role played by the identity of the individual in the existence and form of any elite tomb, it is plausible to see in this reshaping the influence of the identity of these tomb owners, as well. Indeed, the very nature of the thematic focus is based upon the practice of identifying individuals.

IDENTITY IN CONTEXT

Because the term "identity" is unwieldy, it is necessary to clarify it briefly here. A recurrent theme in the theorizing of identity concerns a distinction between an identity within a larger context – that is, as defined in relationship to other things and people – versus a more interior, personal identity founded upon subjective experience.[41] Both forms of identity emerge from the core source of a single person. A comparable multilayered concept of personhood/identity existed among the ancient Egyptians, as well.[42] While elements of the interior identity of these tomb owners, including their thoughts, feelings, and desires, are necessarily implicated in this analysis, this discussion focuses upon identity in relationship to other people and elements of social structure. This focus is due in part to the historical context in which the tombs were created. Texts emphasizing a more interior form of identity – for example, those that consider in greater detail the private individual's contemplation of death or personal experiences in the journey through the underworld – are unknown from the Old Kingdom, and as Te Velde notes, during the Old Kingdom identity is "strongly founded upon the social relation with king, family, and fellow man."[43]

Identity as a relationally defined status is a prominent theme in archaeological scholarship of the past few decades, with a range of socially defined aspects under consideration (gender, age, wealth, status, and so forth). These discussions are closely connected to agency methodologies. As expressed by Margarita Díaz-Andreu and Sam Lucy: "Identities are constructed through interaction between people, and the process by which we acquire and maintain our identities requires choice and agency ... They are also socially mediated, linked to the broader cultural discourse and are performed through embodiment and action."[44] This analysis shares these perspectives, emphasizing the interaction among people in the community, considering especially status, family, and other social bonds, though less engaged with questions of gender and age. The actions of the tomb owners, artists, and others both reflect and construct shared identities, with points of difference within larger groups, as well.

Examining identity in relationship to other people also parallels the examination of the formal qualities of the Qubbet el-Hawa programs, which were observed and defined in comparison to each other and to elite tomb programs from other sites. The unusual thematic focus of the Qubbet el-Hawa programs is shared among the tombs in this cemetery, and it differentiates this group within the larger context of all elite tombs in Egypt. Furthermore, within the programs themselves each image is part of a larger context, whether a scene within a tomb chapel or an individual figure sharing a panel with other figures. The relationship of one image to another, and of these programs to each other and to programs from other sites, corresponds to the relationships among the depicted figures and tomb owners, and to the rest of Egypt (i.e., the degree of visual closeness of the images mimics the degree of lived closeness among those depicted – panel, chapel, cemetery, country.)

IDENTITY AT QUBBET EL-HAWA

The thematic focus of the programs in the Qubbet el-Hawa tombs relates to the identity of the local tomb owners. The emphasis on individual identified figures clarifies each tomb owner's membership and specific role in the local elite community to a much greater extent than the content of other elite tomb programs. The Qubbet el-Hawa tomb owners highlighted this role by depicting their local elite community together with images of themselves and their families and omitting other scene types not directly relevant to the representation of this community. The images and the texts together construct and communicate the identity of the local community.

As part of his analysis of cultural memory and political identity, Jan Assmann deconstructs the constitution of individual identity as well as that of a community identity. Stressing a consciousness behind the recognition of an identity, Assmann examines the reflexive relationship between these two forms: "Individual identity is the image, constructed and maintained in the actor's consciousness, of the specific traits distinguishing him from all ("significant") others.... By collective or we-identity I understand the image that a group constructs of itself and with which its members identify."[45] To paraphrase, the individual recognizes himself as *himself* only with reference to other people (i.e., other members of his community), while a community identity in turn is formed through the conscious recognition of similarity among a number of individuals.

The content of the Qubbet el-Hawa programs illustrates this thesis because it constructs an aspect of the identity of the elite tomb owner upon a foundation of the identities of the subsidiary figures. This process begins with the images. The programs consist primarily of panels with groups of offering figures and larger images of the tomb owner and his family members. Using individual human figures and the fixed space defined by each chapel, the artists and tomb owners construct programs that depict a group of people. The individual images/figures create the program/group, and the group/program consists of visually distinct, individual figures. Each individual figure is a member of the group, including the tomb owner and his family.

Observing only the images (not the texts), the unique status of the tomb owner and his family members is clear by the larger scale of his figures. Scale conveys his status within the group, which in turn forms an important part of his identity. The nature of the tomb owner's high-status role becomes clearer as the identity of the group as a whole is clarified, by the identification of each individual member beginning with their names. As noted previously, the majority of figures in the programs were identified with a name, which provides the basis for recognizing an individual identity within a group.[46] Te Velde states that "the Egyptians themselves seem to have considered the name as an aspect of the person," a view confirmed vividly through the practice of *damnatio memoriae*.[47] Naming the individual figures specifies who they represent, transforming the program from *a* group of people to *this* group of people.

The practice of attaching a name to an image was highly significant in Egyptian culture, especially in the context of mortuary beliefs and cult activities, as the inscribed name linked the image or statue to a specific person in the world. Given the potential that an image identified by a name possessed to receive and benefit from mortuary cult activities, its presence in a tomb program expresses both religious and social significance, implying an elevated status for the identified person. Most elite tomb programs incorporate subsidiary figures that are identified, often including family members, members of the tomb owner's cult, and occasionally other officials. Within such a program, the named figures stand apart from the much more numerous anonymous figures that populate the rest of the program, sharing as a group a higher status that stands in contrast to the nonidentified group.

For the identified subsidiary figures in the Qubbet el-Hawa tombs, the benefits and status indication of naming are the same. The primary difference is the lack of the nonidentified figures from which they stand apart. By depicting only the elite, identified group and making no reference to the nonelite community embodied by the anonymous figures, the programs focus on only the elite section of their community: those who are connected closely with the high-status tomb owners. Possibly, the anonymous figures in other programs not only refer to lower classes but also stand for the more general Egyptian community. By omitting this reference, the Qubbet el-Hawa programs focus not only on the elite, but also primarily on the local community.

Names are not the only form of identification among the subsidiary figures in the Qubbet el-Hawa programs. More than half of the figures hold titles as well, and many more are depicted in group panels that indicate their relationships to other people. Most of the titles indicate responsibilities in the cult of the tomb owner, and most of the figures are depicted carrying out activities related to the cult, either burning incense or carrying an offering of food or drink. Membership in the *ka*-cult of an elite tomb owner conveyed not only status and ritual benefits, but also material rewards as payment for service. The identification of specific individuals in elite programs can be seen as a type of will, indicating the rightful heirs of the tomb owner and beneficiaries of his cult.[48] Typically, members of the cult staff participated in the reversion of offerings, taking the food and drink offerings for their own use after they have been used in the rituals. This benefit of cult service is mentioned specifically in several texts associated with images of priests at Qubbet el-Hawa.[49]

Most of the cult officiants appear on panels with their families, which is highly unusual in other elite tomb programs. With regard to the implications of *ka*-cult service, the presence of an officiant's family members has a two-fold effect. First, based on the economic structure of the community, a cult official would have been responsible for supporting his own family. Thus, when an official is shown in other elite tombs, his family is implied as also benefiting from and being supported by the tomb owner's cult, as it supports the cult official they depend on. In the Qubbet el-Hawa programs, this relationship between not only the officials and the tomb owners but also the families of cult officials and the tomb owners is made explicit, rather than implied. In this way, the programs more accurately replicate visually the number and range of people dependent on the elite tomb owner, contributing to a more accurate and specific depiction of the tomb owner's role in his community.

The second effect of the practice of including family members of the cult officiants follows the first, as it more accurately replicates visually the group of people who provide *support* for the tomb owner's cult. While the *ka*-priests themselves are more directly involved in providing this support through their responsibilities in the cult, the family members can be understood as extended support, or in the case of their children, continued support over a longer time period.[50] That the family members of the cult officiants are most often shown carrying offerings implies their supporting role for the cult, as well.

The great majority of titles in the Qubbet el-Hawa programs indicate responsibilities in the *ka*-cult, and many of the additional identified figures are family members of these cult officiants. In his analysis of these identified officiants, Seyfried argues that most of these individuals worked for the tomb owner's household during his lifetime.[51] Many jobs, for instance those connected to food production, would have existed in his household during his life, and Seyfried notes furthermore that the intimate nature of the relationship between household workers and the elite individual were similar to the relationships among family members, and thus these workers were naturally integrated into the *ka*-cult staff. Despite obvious differences in status, these household staff formed part of the tomb owner's community: his family and the people with whom he worked or who worked for him.

While many of the subsidiary figures depicted were likely household staff of the tomb owner during his life, other individuals, non-household workers, would have held positions in the cult, as well. These additional officials would have been of lower status than the elite tomb owners and most likely would have worked for them, but in an administrative rather than household capacity. One example of such a figure is Khnumhetep, who appears in the tombs of both Khui and Tjetji. Although he holds the cult-related titles of *ka*-priest and director of the food hall, he states that he worked on expeditions under the direction of these two elite tomb owners. Several scribes connected to the judiciary appear, as do a number of stonemasons and overseers of crews, who may or may not have been directly linked to the construction of the tombs. In any case, they were not likely to be household workers. Despite the limited evidence, it seems possible that other officials of the administration who were of lower status than the tomb owners but higher than much of the community would have been integrated into the cults of the local elite, as well.[52]

The Qubbet el-Hawa tomb programs are populated with figures that worked for and were otherwise personally connected to the elite tomb owners during their lives. Visually, these subsidiary figures share a similar status, being depicted all at roughly the same scale, and the tomb owners and their family members form a visually distinct group depicted at a larger scale. This visual impression mirrors the structure of a province; thus, the tomb programs essentially reproduce the elite community of which the tomb owners were a part and in which they held a leadership role during their lifetimes and also after their deaths. While all provincial elite presumably functioned in a similar role in their local communities, no other elite tomb owners emphasized this role to the same extent in their tomb programs. This emphasis on this particular aspect of their identities is unique to the tomb owners at Qubbet el-Hawa.

What is the impetus for this unique local emphasis? One reason may be sought in the unique situation of the community at Elephantine, based upon its location and role within the Egyptian state. As discussed in Chapter 1, the elite of Elephantine, and likely many other members of the community as well, fulfilled a special role in the Egyptian state during the Old Kingdom, and this obvious difference is unsurprisingly made manifest in their tomb monuments. That the difference is based on an emphasis on the identity of the local community may be based in the location of the town, far from the center of Egyptian culture and on the border with Nubia, a clearly different culture.

A collective identity is defined and expressed in response to an awareness of difference in another group, the presence of an *Other*: "As part of an ongoing dialectic of collective identification, community may be more explicitly stressed and practices of communal symbolisation and differentiation increasingly called into play in the solidary affirmation of similarity and the defence of perceived collective interests."[53]

For the elite and citizens of Elephantine, the Other was the Nubians, on whose border they lived, into whose territory they traveled. Nubian settlements may well have existed in the immediate vicinity, as well. This extensive engagement with Nubia was unique to this region, and it may have caused the citizens of Elephantine to develop a heightened sense of their similarities to each other, of their identity as a group.

In his discussion of the development of political identity and cultural memory, Jan Assmann analyzes the twin process of integration and distinction in the formation of a conscious unity: "Conversely, heightened distinctions with the outside inevitably lead to a heightened unity within. Nothing forces greater closeness than isolation against a hostile environment."[54] Recognizing their unique status in the Egyptian state and constantly aware of the nearby Nubians, the citizens of Elephantine may have bonded more closely to each other than did citizens of most Egyptian towns, developing a heightened sense of their shared unique identity. The tomb owners at Qubbet el-Hawa recognized the significance of their role as leaders of this special community, and in response they shaped their tomb programs to emphasize this community and their role within it, as an essential part of their own individual identities.

Conclusion: Monuments of a Community

> In short, a dialectical concept of visual culture cannot rest content with a definition of its objects as the "social construction of the visual field," but must insist on exploring the chiastic reversal of this proposition, *the visual construction of the social field*. It is not just that we see the way we do because we are social animals but also that our social arrangements take the forms they do because we are seeing animals. W. J. T. Mitchell[1]

The dominant narratives of ancient Egypt are, in response to what survives to us, descriptive of a narrow sociocultural view: a centralized, wealthy, powerful, literate, largely male experience. Numerous works over recent years have sought to reach beyond these narratives, considering the experiences of women, of lesser elites, and of middle and lower classes.[2] These studies expand our understanding of the many intersecting group connections informing the identity of individuals in ancient Egypt. Thus far, the experiences of groups of people bound not by wealth, status, or gender but by *place* have been of less extensive concern. This analysis of the Old Kingdom tombs at Qubbet el-Hawa has sought to elicit evidence in the material and visual culture of local community bonds and shared identity in ancient Egypt. This brief conclusion will look at the tombs as whole monuments and consider the dynamic relationships that knit the people of Elephantine together with their monuments of material culture and with the landscape they inhabited and transformed.

In the highly centralized society of Old Kingdom Egypt, the authorities who largely controlled the production of monumental art such as elite tombs strove to produce a seemingly homogenous visual language to create an expression of unified experience. Despite this, most Egyptians throughout the Nile Valley and Delta lived in small communities where the vast majority of their life experiences took place. As Knapp notes, "And yet communities undeniably have a strong association with a 'sense of place,' the most fundamental form of identity, contestation, and embodied experience, where self, space, and time become inseparably intertwined."[3] It is essential to acknowledge the influential role of daily life experiences on the development of individual and group identities. While it is less certain to what degree the Egyptians perceived differences among themselves based on their home towns, we do know that connections to place and to communities were strongly valued, evident through a variety of ancient texts from tombs, letters, and other sources.[4] In order to access material expressions of such connections it is necessary to shift focus from the whole of Old Kingdom material culture to a local context, where the monuments were part of daily life experiences.

In addition to this shift of focus, an openness to meaningful variation in material and visual culture can lead down productive paths. In our study of ancient Egyptian culture, the identification of desirable – repeated – forms provides important insight into the central tenets of social and cultural identity. Yet what we determine as within "normal" or, even more limiting, "acceptable" boundaries may not match where the Egyptians perceived those boundaries to be. Rather than bringing the measure to the material, it can be more effective to start with the material, especially material such as these tombs that fulfilled such essential functions on behalf of their patrons, and work outward, considering the possibility that the boundaries of acceptability may have been different for the ancient Egyptians themselves.

In his discussion of regionality in ancient Egypt, David Jeffreys notes that the very limited scholarship on the topic tends to focus on material culture, especially from funerary contexts, and to not particularly fruitful ends. His critique mirrors my own, as laid out previously:

> The term "provincial" as an aesthetic quality judgment is sometimes found applied in assessments of craft proficiency, on the assumption that this describes local variants from the "capital" styles and motifs of Memphis or Thebes. This, however, ignores the fact that even in capital zones, perceived accomplishment may fall short of some modern ideal, and that the mere "provincial" tag hardly gets us much further forward with a proper analysis of regional diversity.[5]

The tombs at Qubbet el-Hawa are just what he speaks of, with their diverse architectural forms and highly unusual mix of styles of relief and painting. Other than the lengthy autobiographies, the cemetery has been largely overlooked, yet analyzing this distinctive body of visual culture within the local context facilitates a push past its "provincial" quality toward a clear expression of regional identity.

In constructing their tombs and filling them with images and texts, the elite individuals from Elephantine took part in a long-standing and widespread tradition, yet the tomb owners and artisans at Qubbet el-Hawa created something distinctly different. The elite owners were buried in these tombs, and there is evidence of the cults conducted on their behalf, so we can be certain that despite the striking difference of the programs, the tomb owners themselves felt the tombs were acceptable and would function effectively. What do the differences of Qubbet el-Hawa suggest?

First, it is apparent these elite tomb owners felt they had some flexibility in shaping the programs used in their tomb chapels, despite the ubiquity of the standard elite tomb program model. Elephantine's physical distance from the capital cemeteries may have contributed to this sense of flexibility, as the Qubbet el-Hawa tombs were not surrounded by examples of standard models that would define them as "wrong"; in fact, following the first elite tomb that was cut into the cliff, each subsequent Qubbet el-Hawa tomb program connected to a tradition, albeit new, rather than existing as disconnected and different. Their sense of flexibility does not necessarily imply, however, that all elite tomb owners throughout the country had this same sense of freedom with regard to their tomb programs. The fact that most other provincial elite used more typical tomb programs in their chapels indicates that simply being *away* from the Memphite cemeteries was not cause enough for transforming the type of program. Yet just because distance (and disconnection) did not result in change in one provincial site does not mean that the same reality of distance could not have effected change in another provincial site; perhaps the extent of Elephantine's distance was a factor.

It is also possible that distance was one factor in a more complex brew that created in this community both the opportunity and the desire to express something different. As previously discussed, the perspective of community employed here incorporates not only the shared locale, but also the shared practice and experiences of the individuals inhabiting the space. As clarified by Mac Sweeney, "While a sense of collective identity does not occur automatically from simple geographic proximity, it can potentially crystallize through the embodied experience of coresidence and shared social practice."[6] At Elephantine, the stage is set for a distinctive identity to emerge, and as discussed in Chapter 1, a number of additional factors could have contributed to a stronger sense of collective experience and a singular kind of relationship between the local elite and the rest of the population. We can perceive that the provincial leadership role held by the Elephantine elite was similar to that held by other provincial elite; yet, at Elephantine the significance of being a local leader seems to have been different. The difference may have emerged in part from the role of the local elite as expedition leaders, probably taking with them into Nubia many members of the Elephantine community. A professional relationship between expedition leader and member of the expedition team may have been more intense than one based in agriculture, being more akin to the military. In contrast to the agricultural work taking place within the stable Egyptian social and political context, the work of the expedition occurred in a less stable, less familiar context not controlled by the Egyptians. As such, they may have relied on each other not only to do their jobs effectively but also to be allies in an environment dominated by foreigners. In a similar vein, at home the potentially destabilizing or even threatening presence of the nearby Nubians could have given the elite of Elephantine not only an economic leadership role but one related to security and safety as well, that certainly would be less essential at provincial sites deeper within the Egyptian interior.

Multiple other kinds of embodied experience would have contributed to the creation of a local community identity. Jeffreys's discussion of regionalism in ancient Egypt highlights the important role of these more ephemeral kinds of differences: "Differences that leave no physical trace in the archaeological record should also be considered. Are local cult affiliations, for example, mirrored in locally shared experience and values?"[7] The unique local temple of Satet at Elephantine provides an excellent venue for considering such distinctive and shared experiences, but it was not the only locale of cult activity in the community: mortuary cults were conducted for the elite people buried at Qubbet el-Hawa. Participation in these cult activities would have varied among the Elephantine community; head priests, lower level priests, and other cult officiants (libationers and so forth) would have had primary access, while other groups would have had secondary or peripheral participation, for example in the preparation of materials and goods for the cult. While many members of the community would have had no direct involvement, their shared townsite implicates them in the cult practice, through awareness of those who were involved, seeing them prepare or head out to conduct cult, and even in the case of this particular townsite, seeing them head up the mountain and into the tombs to conduct their activities. It is hard to know how this kind of close visual connection may have affected those not directly involved, but other evidence from the site suggests widespread engagement with the elite cults.

The famous shrine of the deified Heqaib on the island of Elephantine dates to the Middle Kingdom; however, the excavators of the site discovered evidence for his cult being practiced in the late Old Kingdom in a possibly refashioned section of an official building in the settlement site on the island.[8] Practice of this cult within the boundaries of the town embeds it more directly into the life of the entire community. Additional evidence recovered by the German and Swiss excavators suggests that Heqaib was not the only elite tomb owner deified during the Old Kingdom, which means that multiple elite mortuary cults may have been expanded to incorporate more of the town's resources, and by extension, more of the local population. It is also highly probable that these cults linked the cemetery and the townsite via ritual practice, even processions, and in this way linked the wider community more closely to the cemetery.

The deification of humans was relatively uncommon in ancient Egypt, though it became more popular in the Late Periods. Heqaib of Aswan was, if not *the* first, one of the first ancient Egyptians to be deified (along with Isi of Edfu, whose cult also flourished in the Middle Kingdom.)[9] The deification of a local elite official demonstrates a communal perception of the value of that official, and speaks to the status of elite officials in the community at Elephantine more broadly. The choice to translate high official status into spiritual status, and to establish continuous cult activity in its support and reaffirmation, attests to the community's sense of intimate connectedness within their local realm. Further, it suggests that this community held these local bonds, and their esteem of their local leaders, as such integral parts of their shared identity that they required manifestation in performance and in material culture.

The cemetery at Qubbet el-Hawa was another important arena for the construction and expression of a community identity. As argued by Mark Varien and James Potter, "Material culture is therefore integral to the construction of the self and the creation of social relationships, and it can be strategically employed to define the essence of particular social groups."[10] The differences of the tomb programs can be considered part of the community's construction of its sense of self.

The evident effort by the artisans to make the relief and painted images easily visible indicates that the viewing needs of a living audience formed a driving force of the system's development. So what is the overall visual effect? Within the darkened space of each chapel, rays of light illuminate images of groups of people spread throughout the space and, in their orientation, directing viewers' attention to the larger images of the elite tomb owners and their families. Diverse styles elicit a sense of multiplicity within the image community that populates an open yet bounded space. The inscriptions further draw in the viewers' attention, identifying individuals (readable for the literate audience and a recognizable convention for the others) who are or were members of the same community comprised by the viewers themselves. In this way the inscriptions complete the circle between tomb chapels and viewers, binding them together in shared space, representing their shared membership in this local community.

The architecture of the tombs equally indicates community bonds; chapels of important family members internally connected, such as Mekhu and Sabni, Khunes and Ankhes, and possibly Pepynakht Heqaib2 and Sabni2, speak to the importance of ancestors and heirs among the elite. Such architectural expressions of kin are common in other Egyptian cemeteries; the large mastabas in the East Cemetery at Giza for Khufu's family, the mastabas of the Ptahhotep/Akhethotep family in Saqqara, and the famous mastaba of Niankhkhnum and Khnumhotep also in Saqqara, among many others. Yet at Qubbet el-Hawa, the exterior architecture further reflects the local community structure. Forecourt enclosure walls create exterior spaces filled with subsidiary burials and false doors, expressing close connections beyond family, while maintaining a clear hierarchy. While the family connections among Pepynakht Heqaib1, Pepynakht Heqaib2, and Sabni2 cannot be confirmed via text, the architectural choices (staircase, enclosure wall, interior passageway) illustrate at the least a desire to indicate close connections. Even more distinctively for the local community, the numerous subsidiary tombs surrounding this group indicate many close bonds between lower status individuals and this family. So many individuals sought to express a connection to this family (or perhaps specific members of it) that an additional enclosure wall had to be constructed, clarifying whose sphere they inhabited. This archaeological evidence of extended support coincides with the chapel in the settlement site deifying a Heqaib, no doubt one of this family, whose passionate following was embedded in the local cultural memory and continued for several hundred years.

The evident expansion of this Heqaib complex in the cemetery is an important reminder of the dynamic processes that were at work behind the static material culture that remains. The residents of Elephantine would have borne witness to the transformation of the cliffs of Qubbet el-Hawa with the continuing construction of new elite tombs. The same can be seen in the image and text programs, which show a clear process of development and fine-tuning, culminating in the later programs of Pepynakht Heqaib2 and Sabni2 employing multiple and new styles, expressing creative flexibility and local patronage. In perceiving the dynamic processes at work in the material and visual culture, we can perceive the community's identity as something that was also in a constant process of development and reaffirmation through social practice. As described by Canuto and Yaeger, "It [community] is an ever-emergent social institution that generates and is generated by supra-household interactions that are structured and synchronized by a set of places within a particular span of time."[11]

The cemetery at Qubbet el-Hawa was an important place for this process, along with the townsite itself, where the elite cults took a second home. While their point about a particular span of time is well taken, since daily-life practice formed the backbone of affirming identity, it is important to consider how a community's identity transcends time as well, both here at Elephantine and elsewhere. For all Egyptians, the tombs of ancestors were places for communion between living and deceased members of a family; the same was true of Qubbet el-Hawa. Yet here living visitors saw not only their elite ancestors, but a whole range of identified members of their community, many likely passed on themselves. These tombs, via the specific nature of their image and text programs, memorialized a past community that was kept alive by the engagement of its living members and were as such important actors in the continual generation of the community's identity.

The reflexive relationship between the members of the community and the elite cemetery, as well as all their monuments of material culture, simultaneously involved the landscape they both inhabited. As previously discussed, the ancient name of Elephantine, Abu, referred in ancient texts not only to the townsite, but to the surrounding river and banks, as well as other small islands in the environs. Rock inscriptions found along the west bank indicate the community's claim of this area, and suggests movement through the space. The same is true for Qubbet el-Hawa; clearly the establishment of the elite cemetery claims this high ridge for the residents of Abu, marks off points of movement between itself and the townsite, and also acts as a kind of boundary marker for their region, as the tombs curved around the geographic hinge between Abu and the rest of Egypt. The role of the local landscape in the construction of community identity should not be underestimated. As clarified by Knapp: "Through such patterned and daily activities, values, and beliefs (their habitus), the people who live in communities build, modify, and reshape their physical surroundings in order to preserve memory and experience, to rationalize the meanings bestowed on the landscape, and to provide their community with a meaningful sense of time and space."[12] The inhabitants of Elephantine surely transformed their local landscape and imbued it with meaning; yet, considering Mitchell's insistence on not only the social but the seeing nature of humanity, to what degree might the landscape have contributed to this construction of meaning? The islands, the close west bank escarpment, and the granite outcrops through the river and the land all contributed to a visually distinctive space, with varied colors, shapes, textures, and views to keep the eye engaged. If one presumes, as this analysis does, the important role of embodied, sensory experience in the construction of identity by members of a local community, it may be reasonable to consider that the visually unique world these people inhabited facilitated their construction of visually unique material and visual culture. For the people of Elephantine, the experience of living differently was not just work, it was the space they saw every day, and this may have contributed to a context in which local identity emerged more strongly, and where creating distinctive art made sense. The elite tombs built during the Old Kingdom in the cemetery at Qubbet el-Hawa testify powerfully to the closely intertwined and rather extraordinary lives of the members of this ancient community.

Appendix A

Chronology and the Two Heqaibs

The evidence thus far used for dating the Old Kingdom tombs at Qubbet el-Hawa comes from a number of sources, including titles and inscriptions with royal names and the historical context of the autobiographies. The tombs have also been examined within the broader context of the Old Kingdom, considering historical and architectural trends that may help place them in time. In addition to these sources, Elmar Edel's analysis of the offering pottery from the site provides additional data. Because in the local tradition pottery offerings were inscribed with the name of the offering official, Edel was able to establish relative chronologies among many of the different tomb owners. For example, because both Sabni1 and Khwin-Khnum made offerings to the official Snnw (QH105), we can assume they were contemporaries, while the absence of offerings from Mekhu in the tomb of IiShemai Setka, who is otherwise associated with Khwin-Khnum, suggests Mekhu predeceased him. Through his painstaking analysis of a vast corpus of pottery, Edel was able to reconstruct a relative chronological framework that incorporates many, though not all, of the tomb owners here discussed.

An additional issue that informs the dating of these tombs is the identity of the owner(s) of 35 and 35d, both named Pepynakht Heqaib, who have long been accepted as the same individual. This perspective influences the assumed dates of the two tombs, and runs contrary to the evidence of the tombs themselves. My analysis argues that the visual and material forms of these tombs places them at opposite chronological points on the local spectrum – early and late, respectively. Therefore, before presenting the chronological outline, I will first briefly review how this perspective came to be, and my argument against seeing a single Heqaib as the owner of both 35 and 35d.

The owners of these two tombs were first identified as the same man by Labib Habachi; this view was taken up by Edel, and the editors of the final publication of the cemetery presume the same, though some details of the overall narrative are questioned.[1] In my own opinion, such a view is not supported by the available evidence; it is much more likely these are two separate individuals, though most likely related. Seeing two tomb owners rather than one does not change, however, the likelihood that one of these two is the same Heqaib later deified by the local population, whose memory endured into the Middle Kingdom in the form of an elaborate shrine in the townsite.

Habachi excavated the sanctuary dedicated to a deified elite official named Heqaib in the townsite at Elephantine in the early 1940s, after which, in 1946, he turned to Qubbet el-Hawa. As he states, he was driven by a desire to find the tomb of Heqaib, the namesake of this unusual monument.[2] Habachi at first believed that tomb 35 belonged to the deified Heqaib: the name was correct, many of the titles were similar, it fit the Old Kingdom date he assumed was appropriate, and the impressive autobiography carved into the façade drew a picture of an accomplished man worthy of deification. While working at this tomb, Habachi and his team soon discovered the larger tomb 35d to the north (sanded over until their work) also dedicated to a man named Heqaib. Habachi assessed the larger size and more complex visual program of the monument, based upon which he decided this was a "hall" rather than tomb, a sort of secondary memorial spot to honor the same Heqaib – a proto-sanctuary.

Part of Habachi's assessment relies on the titles held by both tomb owners and those attributed to Heqaib in his sanctuary on the island. The titles on the sanctuary provide what may be considered the "standard" for high officials at Qubbet el-Hawa: *ḥꜣty-ꜥ, ḫtmty bỉty, śmr wꜥty, ẖry-ḥbt, ỉmy-rꜣ ḫꜣśwt, ỉmy-rꜣ ỉꜥꜣw*, or "count, sealer of the king of Lower Egypt, sole companion, lector priest, overseer of the foreign lands, overseer of Egyptianized Nubians." The two less common titles held by Heqaib in the sanctuary are the high-ranking *ỉry-pꜥt*, "prince," that appears only once in the cemetery, on the façade of 35d, and the last title in the string, *ḥry-śštꜣ n tp šmꜥ*, "privy to the secrets of the head of the south," which does not appear in either tomb 35 or 35d, though a version of this title is held by Harkhuf and Khwin-Khnum.

Other than these common titles, the owners of 35 and 35d share the string of honorific titles, *ỉmy-ỉs mnỉw Nḫn, ḥry-tp Nḫb,* or "councillor and guardian of Nekhen, overseer of Nekheb" that no other tomb owner in the cemetery has – although Sabni2 has a different title related to Nekheb (*ỉmy-rꜣ pr-šnˁ m Nḫb*). On the other hand, the titles held by each tomb owner connecting them to royal mortuary cults are different; the owner of 35 is the "overseer of the pyramid city" of Pepy I, "the regulator of the phyles" of the pyramid of Merenre, and the "scribe of the phyles and land tenant" of the pyramid of Pepy II. The owner of 35d is, in contrast, the "inspector of netjer priests" of the pyramids of both Pepy I and Merenre. While the difference between the titles is not definitive, the few similarities seem shaky ground upon which to base a shared identity.

Along with the names and titles, Habachi was swayed by the architecture, images and texts, and subsidiary burials surrounding the tombs. He felt the multiple images of offering figures populating tomb 35d were highly unusual and must have been executed over a long span of time, based in part on their appearance; he also saw the multiple forecourt burials as a unique occurrence in the cemetery. Yet in both cases, 35d is not unusual; as argued in this book, the decorative program of 35d epitomizes the local system used at Qubbet el-Hawa (albeit with a relatively high number of figures), and forecourt burials are quite common. Furthermore, the distinctive appearance of many of the images in 35d is also typical of the cemetery, and represents neither an unusual choice nor a long span of time (see Chapter 3).

Additional evidence for Habachi's identification of the deified Heqaib here comes from the associated tomb of Sabni2 (35e), which shares a forecourt and internal passageway with 35d. On the sanctuary of Heqaib at Elephantine, a figure named Sabni is identified as Heqaib's son, and Habachi assumed that Sabni2 was Pepynakht Heqaib2's son based upon their connected tombs, although neither is depicted nor identified in the other's program. The architectural association of the two tombs does suggest a close, even familial relationship, and it is quite likely that the owner of 35d was in fact the Heqaib who was later deified. Yet this evidence does not support the additional step of seeing the two tombs (35, 35d) as owned by one man.

Habachi's merging of the two tombs appears to have been inspired in part by his search for an individual named Heqaib who was worthy of later deification. The autobiography carved into the façade of tomb 35 describes the accomplishments of a very important man, similar to those described by Harkhuf, but the tomb itself is relatively small and does not have an extensive program. The lower tomb 35d is much larger with a much more extensive visual program, but there is no autobiographical text to clarify the owner's historical accomplishments. It seems that in Habachi's desire to find an individual worthy of the unique and beautiful shrine he excavated, he felt it was necessary to have both textual and visual celebration. There is no reason, however, to assume the ancient Egyptians felt the same way.

The architecture linking the two tombs, especially the rock-cut staircase that leads from the inner courtyard of 35d up to the entrance of 35, clearly communicates a connection between the tomb owners, but the two tombs 35 and 35d are equally clearly whole and separate monuments. Each tomb has an entrance, at least two false doors, a shaft and burial chamber, images of the tomb owner with his titulary, and images of *ka*-servants and other subsidiary figures. Despite Habachi's description of 35d as a hall, it has all the necessary elements of an elite tomb, and the type of hall he suggests has no parallel either in or outside of this cemetery during this period. If Pepynakht Heqaib had lived a long life and decided that his original, relatively small tomb was not sufficient, and therefore chose to cut a new, larger tomb, why would he leave the original tomb intact? And why create the staircase up to the tomb, which suggests that continued access to that tomb was necessary for cult activities? The presence of two active cult places side by side for the same individual would be extremely unusual.

Unfortunately, many finds and information from the excavation of these tombs were lost in the shift of the work from Habachi to Edel, and over the long span of time since. Seyfried and Vieler later gathered much of Habachi's work, in the form of notes, sketch books, and photographs, and incorporated everything available into the final publication of the cemetery, but they point out the many gaps in the data that survived.[3] Regarding the main burial shaft of 35d, they can say only that "surprisingly, no particular comments of Habachi refer to this large burial complex."[4] Habachi himself said only, "Upon examination of such shafts, nothing was found to point to those who were once buried inside."[5] Finds referenced by Habachi in notes and drawings relating to the other burial chambers, including the one associated with the secondary shaft on the south, could not be located by the editors, and Habachi did not indicate the existence of any inscriptions that might be useful. The only finds from the area noted to have inscriptions were several pieces of wood most likely from a coffin (or two), inscribed with the names Pepynakht and Heqaib recovered it seems from 35; unfortunately, it was not clear where exactly they were found, or how they may or may not have fit together. Today, only a photograph of the pieces survives.[6] Overall, the area had been excessively plundered and reused over the years, so such finds might not have been definitive in any case.

Confronting the evidence as it stands, there is no reason not to assume that tomb 35 and tomb 35d are two separate monuments belonging to two separate people. Most likely the two Pepynakht Heqaibs are related, perhaps father and son or maybe grandfather and grandson, and repeated names are common throughout the cemetery. That the later Pepynakht Heqaib(2) would emphasize his connection to his father or grandfather is not surprising. Surely his membership in a family with a history of accomplishments in the local community would only have enhanced his own status.

In the years since Habachi excavated both the sanctuary and the tombs 35–35d-35e the excavators of Elephantine have discovered evidence that at least one other elite tomb owner, Mekhu, was also deified late in the Old Kingdom.[7] This information corresponds to an understanding of tomb 35d as part of a system of expression shared throughout the cemetery. Habachi was not wrong in noting the impressive form of tomb 35d; the way in which 35d stands out in the cemetery (in aspects of its architectural form and the number of subsidiary figures present in the program) may well represent material evidence of the roots that eventually blossomed into a unique cult. But our modern desire to have both textual and visual/material evidence to rationalize the unusual status of an Egyptian official is better replaced with a more nuanced understanding of the local community, and how the process of deifying an individual emerged from the specific context of this place and time. A chronological framework for the Old Kingdom tombs allows an analysis of their form as evidence for some underlying aspects of this process.

Several of the tombs in this study can be dated securely to the reign of Pepy II, due to references in the autobiographies carved into their façades. Titles in the mortuary cults of Pepy I, Merenre, and Pepy II also contribute to dating the tombs, as does Edel's analysis of the pottery.[8] Seyfried and Vieler argue that architectural forms cannot be used with any certainty as chronological indicators at Qubbet el-Hawa, due to both the mix of forms in use and the evidence for numerous tombs having been expanded in a series of phases.[9] In the final publication of the cemetery, the editors posit a date range for each individual tomb when possible, but do not knit together a full relative chronology. While more specific relative dating of the tombs remains problematic, it is possible to divide the tombs roughly into three phases, albeit with some overlapping. Edel identified the tomb of Harkhuf as the earliest tomb in the cemetery, built in the early years of the reign of Pepy II; therefore, it seems reasonable to see all of the tombs in this group as having been built during the reign of Pepy II. It is possible that construction of the tombs extended into the First Intermediate Period; however, an inscription in what appears to be one of the later tombs in the cemetery, of Sabni2, discusses Sabni's trip to Wawat to build barges in order to transport obelisks to Heliopolis on behalf of the king, which seems unlikely to have occurred during the First Intermediate Period. In addition, the tomb of Setka (QH110) dated securely to the First Intermediate Period stands apart formally, in terms of the text and image program, from the group discussed here. Given the likelihood that the tombs under consideration here were all constructed during the reign of Pepy II, the three phases I suggest can be divided over his reign. The length of Pepy II's reign continues to be debated, ranging from sixty to more than ninety years. The specific span is less relevant to this discussion than the relative dating of the tombs in this group, so I use an average of seventy-five years. The divisions are roughly equal, although the middle phase, group two, is probably longer than the other two.

Group 1. Early Pepy II (Years 1–20/25)

Harkhuf (34n), Pepynakht Heqaib1 (35), Khui (34e) and Tjetji (103)

The tomb of Harkhuf can be relatively securely located in time based upon the texts in his tomb, including a letter from a young Pepy II, which is inscribed on the façade. It is clear from Harkhuf's autobiography that he lived and worked under Merenre as well as Pepy II. Based on these texts, there is general agreement that Harkhuf's tomb was built sometime in the early part of the reign of Pepy II.

Construction of tomb 35 of Pepynakht Heqaib1 began, I believe, close on the heels of the tomb of Harkhuf. The location, size, plan, and design of the tomb are nearly identical to Harkhuf's. In particular, the design of the façade, the style of the façade figures, and the layout and style of the façade texts are very similar to Harkhuf's and unlike anything else in the cemetery. It seems highly unlikely that much time would have separated two such similar tombs that are so distinct within the cemetery overall. The interior program of Pepynakht Heqaib1's tomb, however, is very different from Harkhuf's and from its own façade program. Some time likely passed from the initial cutting and decorating of the tomb and the final execution of the interior program.

Baer places (the presumed sole) Pepynakht Heqaib in the very last part of the reign of Pepy II based upon his titles.[10] His titulary follows the same pattern that most others in the cemetery share, with the exception of the string "councillor and guardian of Nekhen, overlord of Nekheb." Baer apparently locates Pepynakht Heqaib in the late part of Pepy II's reign based on the location of the *ḥry-tp Nḫb* title after the title *śmr-wʿty*, as this decrease in status of the title was more common later in the Sixth Dynasty (as well as in the Fifth Dynasty). Oddly, in the certainly later tomb 35d, the *ḥry-tp Nḫb* title appears before *śmr-wʿty*, which according to Baer's charts places the owner in the "middle to late" part of the reign of Pepy II. The ranking of a single title seems uncertain ground upon which to date the whole tomb, especially given the other circumstances.

Edel and colleagues rely on the description of conflict with Nubia found in Pepynakht Heqaib1's autobiography, and argue that this kind of conflict would only have occurred at the very end of the reign of Pepy II.[11] Yet the inscription of Merenre at the Satet temple strongly implies violence (as he took Nubian leaders prisoner).[12] Further, expedition leaders such as Weni dealt with military conflict in the beginning of the Sixth Dynasty, and Harkhuf traveled with an impressive army, indicating violence was not uncommon.

The tombs of Khui and Tjetji are chronologically linked based upon the depiction in both programs of a man named Khnumhetep, who in both instances is accompanied by his daughter, Horemkawes. In a text in the tomb of Khui, Khnumhetep states that he traveled with both Khui and Tjetji, but it is not possible to tell from the tombs or programs which tomb owner preceded the other.

A number of rock inscriptions in the Wadi Hammamat relate to these tomb owners. Eichler catalogs six separate inscriptions naming a Tjetji that he believes identify three separate people, one of whom is the Aswan Tjetji in tomb 103.[13] One of these inscriptions (Nr. 116, 68) shares a rock surface with other inscriptions, dated to the reign of Pepy I, from an expedition on the occasion of his sed-festival in the year after the eighteenth "counting" (i.e., late in his reign). Given that the inscriptions share a rock surface, Eichler and others suggest that the inscription of Tjetji also belongs to the later part of Pepy I's reign. Another inscription connected to this expedition of Pepy I names a Khui, but it cannot be securely linked to the Khui at Qubbet el-Hawa.

Naguib Kanawati suggests that both Khui and Tjetji should be dated earlier than Harkhuf, due to these inscriptions, and based upon a similar conclusion of Newberry.[14] El-Dissouky suggests that Tjetji traveled, worked in Memphis, and came to Elephantine at the end of the reign of Pepy I.[15] Henry Fischer disagreed with this dating (by Kanawati and others) based upon the art in Tjetji's tomb, which he feels is clearly of First Intermediate Period date; however, he refers certainly to the panel on column E2, the east face (Tj5), carved in the Sunken C style that appears in other Qubbet el-Hawa tombs as well and belongs to the Old Kingdom phase of the cemetery (see Chapter 3).[16]

In sum, it is reasonable to see Tjetji and Khui both as contemporaries to some extent of Harkhuf, and thus to see the construction of their tombs around the same time. I suggest that Tjetji began his tomb around the same time Harkhuf was constructing his, but perhaps finished it a while after Harkhuf's had been completed. The initial program seems to have consisted of the two columns of painted text, and a secondary (later) program included carved figures. Khui most likely constructed his tomb in a similar time period, but maybe after Tjetji began his, although some work probably occurred on both at the same time – perhaps the second phase of Tjetji's program was closer in time to Khui's program, although this is entirely hypothetical.

Group 2. Middle Pepy II (Years 20/25–50)

Khunes (34h) and Ankhes (34g), Mekhu (25) and Sabni1 (26), Sobekhetep (90), Khwin-Khnum (102), and IiShemai Setka (98)

This second group is the largest, complicated by uncertain chronological overlaps and building times. Baer dates Khunes to the Sixth Dynasty with no further refinement.[17] Harpur oddly places Khunes in the Seventh or Eighth Dynasty with no clear explanation,[18] while Kanawati places Khunes at the very end of the Sixth Dynasty or immediately after, based primarily on the size of his tomb.[19] Serrano similarly places Khunes at the very end of the reign of Pepy II, again based primarily on the size and design of the tomb.[20]

Eichler lists five rock inscriptions naming a Khunes.[21] Based upon articles by Boris Piotrovski and Edel, he states that four of the five inscriptions refer to the Khunes buried at Qubbet el-Hawa. One of these inscriptions, from Tomas in Lower Nubia, names Pepy I; therefore, Eichler suggests all of Khunes's inscriptions should be dated to Pepy I.[22] The evidence for linking the Tomas inscription to the tomb owner at Qubbet el-Hawa is unclear – the Tomas Khunes holds a title, *śḥḏ ḫnty-š pr ꜥꜣ*, "inspector of the land tenants of the palace," that does not appear in the Qubbet el-Hawa tomb, and he also has the title *imy-rꜣ iꜥꜣw*, "overseer of Egyptianized Nubians," which, while common to the Qubbet el-Hawa elite, also does not appear in the program of the Qubbet el-Hawa Khunes. Serrano, drawing on recent work by Gasse and Rondot, makes a persuasive argument against seeing the Tomas inscription as referring to the owner of tomb 34h.[23] Nonetheless, Edel and colleagues also read the Tomas inscription as referring to the Qubbet el-Hawa Khunes.[24]

Another inscription from Sehel Island is dated by Eichler to Pepy I also, but apparently only based upon the link to Khunes and the inscription in Tomas.[25] Edel does not specifically date the Sehel inscription, and in addition, notes that this inscription appears on the same rock surface as several inscriptions belonging to Khwin-Khnum, owner of QH102 at Qubbet el-Hawa.[26] In his tomb program, Khwin-Khnum has a title referring to the mortuary cult of Pepy II, placing him securely in the reign of Pepy II, and thus possibly, based on the Sehel inscriptions, Khunes could be placed in Pepy II's reign as well, at least to some extent. Khunes may well have worked during the time of Pepy I, and perhaps during his reign Khunes was based in Memphis, which would explain his palace-related title.

El-Dissouky places Khunes much further into the reign of Pepy II. Based on the pottery evidence discussed by Edel, el-Dissouky believes that Khunes was contemporary with Iienkhenit of tomb 92.[27] The lack of pottery offerings from Mekhu or Sabni1 in the tomb of Iienkhenit suggested to el-Dissouky that he lived a generation or so later than them, thus Khunes did, as well. However, the pottery that Edel labels as having been excavated from tomb 34h, Khunes's tomb, in fact came from a burial in its forecourt, as they had not yet fully excavated Khunes's own burial shaft at the time of publication. This fact suggests that the person buried in the forecourt of QH34h, rather than Khunes himself, lived/ died a generation or so after Mekhu and SabniI. Furthermore, Edel places IiShemai Setka (QH 98) into the same general time period as Mekhu and SabniI (i.e., contemporary with one or the other or both), and IiShemai did donate pottery to Iienkhenit.[28] This suggests that Khunes was closer in time to Mekhu and SabniI. The absence of pottery offerings naming Khunes among the corpus studied by Edel is odd.

The evidence from the tomb itself is not clear. Khunes's tomb is one of the largest and the only to have a Memphite-style program, although it appears only on the south and east walls of his tomb. The program was apparently executed over several stages – the earlier images of the tomb owner on the south and east wall and pillars E1 and W1 do not include the title *ḥ3ty-ʿ*, "count," while the images of him on pillar E2E, top, and on the entrance thickness do have this higher-ranking title. The inclusion in Khunes's tomb of numerous panels of offering figures along with the Memphite-style walls suggests that the program was adapted into the Qubbet el-Hawa system after originally being planned as more traditional. While it is reasonable to argue that the program evolved over time, the amount of time is not clear.

Based on the collected evidence, I suggest that Khunes began work on his tomb after the initial phase of Harkhuf, Pepynakht HeqaibI, and perhaps Tjetji and Khui, as well. The larger tombs begun by Khunes and by Mekhu may have marked a second phase of the cemetery. The incomplete agriculture scene in Mekhu's program may be linked to similar daily life scenes in Khunes's program, in terms of the desire of the tomb owner or as inspiration. Similarly, there may have been a close chronological connection between the fishing and fowling scenes in the tombs of Khunes and SabniI (see Chapter 2). Execution of the program may have extended for many more years. One key problem with this theory is the absence of pottery offerings naming Khunes, especially in the tomb of Snnw (QH105) where Mekhu, Sabni, Khwin-Khnum, and others made offerings.

Mekhu was the father of SabniI. From the autobiographical inscription on the façade of SabniI's section of their shared double tomb, we know that Mekhu died unexpectedly in Nubia and that in reward for retrieving his father's body and bringing the expedition products to the king in Memphis, SabniI received land in the domains of the pyramid of Pepy II.[29] Based on the pottery offerings recovered by Edel, he determined that Mekhu was a contemporary of Sobekhetep (QH 90), although Mekhu died before him, and that Sobekhetep died before Sabni1.[30] Khwin-Khnum (QH102) was a contemporary of Sabni1, based on the pottery inscriptions, as well. Edel also indicated that IiShemai-Setka (QH98) was contemporary with Mekhu or Sabni1 or both.

Along with his analysis of the pottery inscriptions, Edel presents a hypothesis regarding the distribution of titles among the Qubbet el-Hawa tomb owners that could provide further dating criteria.[31] He suggests that the title "overseer of Upper Egypt" was passed through one set of local elite, meaning that one person held the title at a time. Mekhu did not have this title in his program as his son Sabni1 did; however, it did appear on his sarcophagus. Harkhuf also held this title, which means that Mekhu must have followed Harkhuf, assuming the title after Harkhuf's death, a view with which Kanawati agrees.[32] Given the uncertainty regarding this title, this remains speculative.

The double tomb of Mekhu and Sabni1 was constructed over at least four building phases, beginning as a single tomb for Mekhu, and then in three subsequent stages expanded to include a comparable chapel space for Sabni1.[33] The first phase was the addition of a false door for Sabni in what was then the northwest corner of Mekhu's chapel. This first expansion stage occurred presumably after Mekhu died and Sabni1 took on the responsibility for finishing his father's tomb. The inscription of texts and images in Mekhu's tomb could have begun during Mekhu's life, but it seems likely the program was completed after he died.

In sum, it seems likely that Mekhu began his tomb and died sometime near the middle of the reign of Pepy II. He likely came after Harkhuf and seems to have been to some degree contemporary with Khunes, and older than Sobekhetep, Khwin-Khnum, and probably IiShemai Setka. Sabni1 died after Sobekhetep and appears to have been closely contemporary with Khwin-Khnum. He likely finished the double tomb around the middle or a bit later in the reign of Pepy II.

Although Sobekhetep (QH90) has no royal names in his tomb or autobiographical inscriptions, and also no securely established rock inscriptions, the inscribed pottery proved especially helpful in situating him within the cemetery group. Edel was able to establish that Sobekhetep died after Mekhu but before Sabni1, placing him toward the middle or into the second half of the reign of Pepy II, as well.[34]

Khwin-Khnum's name also appeared among the pottery offerings, and through this Edel established that he was a contemporary of Sabni1, thus slightly later than Mekhu and Sobekhetep.[35] Along with this relative placement, Khwin-Khnum has a title connecting him to the pyramid cult of Pepy II, in the later section of his tomb program. Eichler lists four rock inscriptions with the name Khwin-Khnum, and he links three of them to this tomb owner. They cannot be independently dated apart from their connection to the royal cult title in his Qubbet el-Hawa tomb.

Based upon pottery offerings, Edel places IiShemai Setka (QH98) as roughly contemporary with Mekhu and Sabni1.[36] El-Dissouky points out that IiShemai offered pottery to Iienkhenit (QH 92), while neither Mekhu nor Sabni1 did. This could indicate that IiShemai Setka was closer in age to Sabni1 than Mekhu, and died after both of them.

Group 3. Later Phase of Pepy II (Year 50 to End)

Pepynakht Heqaib2 (QH35d), Sabni2 (QH35e)

My dating of tomb QH35d begins from the position that this Pepynakht Heqaib is not the same man as the owner of tomb QH35, discussed previously. Based on my hypothesis that this Pepynakht Heqaib2 is either the son or more likely grandson of the owner of QH35 (fairly speculative), then this tomb would be potentially in a time range of 30–60 years after the initial cutting of tomb QH35.

The architecture indicates that both 35d and 35e are clearly later than 35, placing them securely in the reign of Pepy II. Based on the string of titles on the north entrance thickness, bottom section, in which the group *ỉmy-ỉs mnỉw Nḫn, ḥry-tp Nḫb* appears after *ḥ3ty-ʿ* and before *śmr-wʿty*, the tomb would fit into Baer's middle to late in the reign of Pepy II; but as noted previously, Baer's system dates the owner of QH35 to the last part of Pepy II's reign (see previous section), and it is clear the architectural relationship makes it impossible for 35d to predate 35.[37] Harpur's dating would place this tomb well into the First Intermediate Period, as she dates QH35 to the Seventh to Eighth Dynasties, a dating that is no doubt largely contingent on Habachi and Edel's grouping of the two tombs.[38] Unfortunately, as noted previously, no pottery inscriptions survive from tomb 35d, nor are there any rock inscriptions attributed to this elite official.

The architecture of QH35e, with a passage connecting the chapel space to that of QH 35d and their shared façade, suggests that this tomb and program were created soon after that of QH35d. Edel et al. suggest a generation, given the presumption that Sabni2 of 35e is the son of Pepynakht Heqaib2. Sabni2 has two titles connected to the pyramid of Pepy II, placing him securely in the reign of that king. The ranking of the title *ỉmy-r3 šmʿw* in the inscription on the façade of his tomb places him into the last part of the reign of Pepy II, according to Baer. In a discussion about the structure of the local administration, Edel suggests that Sabni2 is one of the later tomb owners of the Old Kingdom. Edel attempts to trace a division in responsibilities, with one group of overseers of Upper Egypt, overseers of foreign land, and overseers of Egyptianized Nubians on one side, and the local nomarch (i.e., *ḥry-tp ʿ3 n nswt*) on the other. Sabni2 holds titles from both groups and is the only one in the cemetery to do so; thus, Edel suggests that at a later point in the history of the site, the various types of responsibilities were joined in the hands of the local elite figures.[39]

Summary

Group 1 (first third of Pepy II) consists of Harkhuf (QH34n), Pepynakht Heqaib1 (QH35), Tjetji (QH103), and Khui (QH34e). It is relatively clear that Harkhuf preceded Pepynakht Heqaib1. Other relationships are unclear.

Group 2 (middle third +/-) consists of Mekhu (QH25), Khunes and Ankhes (QH34h, 34g), Sobekhetep (QH90), Sabni1 (QH26), Khwin-Khnum (QH102), and IiShemai-Setka (QH98).

Based upon direct pottery offerings (i.e., made by these owners) we know that Mekhu died before Sobekhetep, who died before Sabni1, who was contemporary to some degree with Khwin-Khnum. Based upon inscribed offerings to other officials, it appears that Khunes and IiShemai Setka may have overlapped, and that both may have been contemporary to some degree with Mekhu and Sabni1.

Group 3 (last third) consists of Pepynakht Heqaib2 (QH35d) and Sabni2 (QH35e). The architecture indicates that Sabni2 is clearly later than Pepynakht Heqaib2, with the possibility that Sabni2 is in fact his son.

Appendix B

Text Translations

I provide here transliterations and translations of the inscriptions in the tombs. For the titles, references are provided to the volume by Dilwyn Jones, *An Index of Ancient Egyptian Titles, Epithets, and Phrases of the Old Kingdom*, BAR International Series 866 (I), 2000. This appendix is primarily for reference purposes; the publication of the cemetery should be considered the authoritative version (though I have translated a few titles differently): Elmar Edel, Karl-Joachim Seyfried, and Gerd Vieler, *Die Felsgräbernekropole der Qubbet el-Hawa bei Assuan*, I. Abteilung, Band 1–3 (Paderborn: Ferdinand Schöningh, 2008).

The material is organized by tomb, panel, and figure. The order follows the order of the figures, from the front (direction they are facing) to back.

Mekhu and Sabni (25, 26)

1. **Ramp Stele S: (fig. 14)**
    1.1. *ḥ3ty-ʿ ḫtmty-bỉty śmr-wʿty ẖry-ḥbt | ỉmy-r3 ỉʿ3w n(y) śt-ỉb nb.f ỉm3ḫw ḫr 'Inpw tpy-ḏw.f | /'Inỉ-ỉt.f rn.f nfr Mḫw*
    count, sealer of the king of Lower Egypt, sole companion, lector priest | overseer of Egyptianized Nubians, favorite of his lord (he who is in his lord's heart/affection), one honored before Anubis, he who is upon his mountain | Intef, whose beautiful name is Mekhu
    1.2. *śḥḏ ḥm(w)-k3 'Iỉ-(n)-ḫnt*
    inspector of *ka*-priests, Iienkhent
2. **RampStele N: (fig. 14)**
    2.1. *ḥ3ty-ʿ, ḫtmty-bỉty, ỉmy-r3 šmʿw |śmr-wʿty, ẖry-ḥbt ỉm3ḫw | ḫr nṯr ʿ3 Ś3bn(ỉ):* count, sealer of the king of Lower Egypt, overseer

of Upper Egypt | sole companion, lector priest | one honored before the great god, Sabni

2.2. [*śḥḏ*] *ḥm*(*w*)*-kꜣ Ḫwỉ*
[inspector of] *ka*-priest(s) Khui

3. **Mekhu entrance, south thickness, top section (fig. 15)**

3.1. *ḥꜣty-ꜥ* [*?*] *ḫtmty-bỉty śmr-wꜥty, ḫry-ḥbt* | *Mḫw*
count [?], sealer of the king of Lower Egypt, sole companion, lector priest | Mekhu

3.2. *sꜣ.f mry.f ḫtmty-bỉty* | *śmr-wꜥty ỉmy-rꜣ* (*ỉꜥꜣw?*) *śmr-wꜥty* (sic?) *Śꜣbnỉ*(*ꜣ?*)
his son, his beloved, sealer of the king of Lower Egypt | sole companion, overseer of Egyptianized Nubians, sole companion, Sabni

4. **Mekhu entrance, north thickness, top section**

4.1. *ḥꜣty-ꜥ ḫtmty-bỉty śmr-wꜥty ḫry-ḥbt, Mḫw*
count, sealer of the king of Lower Egypt, sole companion, Lector priest, Mekhu

4.2. *ḥmt.f mrt.f ḫkrt-nśwt wꜥtt ḥm-nṯr Ḥwt-Ḥr ꜣItỉ*
his wife, his beloved, sole ornamented one of the king, *netjer*-priestess of Hathor, Iti

5. **Mekhu entrance, north thickness, lower section (fig. 16)**

5.1. *ḫrp-sḥ śḥḏ ḥm*(*w*)*-kꜣ mty n ḥst ỉmꜣḫw ḫr nb.f* | *ꜣIỉ-n-ḫnt*
director of the (food) hall, inspector of the *ka*-priests, regulator of the *ḥst*-phyle, one honored before his lord | Iienkhent

5.2. *sꜣ.f ḥm-kꜣ Mḫw*
his son, *ka*-priest, Mekhu

5.3. *ḥmt.f ꜣImỉ*
his wife, Imi

5.4. *sꜣt.f Ḥst*
his daughter, Heset

5.5. *sꜣt.f R*(*wd?*)*tỉ*
his daughter, Rwd(t)i(?)

6. **Mekhu chapel, east wall, north of entrance, small scene south of main scene (fig. 21)**

6.1. *śḥḏ ḥm*(*w*)*-kꜣ ḫrp-sḥ Ḫwwỉ*
inspector of *ka*-priests, director of the (food) hall, Khwwi (?)
The signs of the name are damaged; it appears to be Khui, but spelled with two "w"s instead of the usual one.

6.2. *ḥm-kꜣ Mḫw/(Ḫm[w?])*
ka-priest Mekhu/(Khemw?)

6.3. *ḫtmt(y) ꞽInt(ỉ)*
sealer, Inti

11.4. *Ḥst*
Heset

11.5. *Nfrt*
Nefret

7. **E Wall main scene (figs. 19–20)**

7.1. *ḥꜣty-ꜥ ḫtmty-bỉty śmr-wꜥty ḫry-ḥbt Mḫw*
count, sealer of the king of Lower Egypt, sole companion, lector priest, Mekhu

7.2. *ḫrp-sḥ ꞽIỉ-n-ḫntỉ*
director of the (food) hall, Iienkhenti

7.3. *Mḫw*
Mekhu

7a. **E Wall, main scene, offering panel in the upper right corner (figs. 19–20)**

One inscription runs across the top of the scene (7a.1); I presume it refers to the largest figure in the panel, the second from the front. The other inscriptions appear next to the smaller figures.

7a.1. *ḫrp-sḥ ỉmy-rꜣ ḥm(w)-kꜣ ꞽIỉ-n-ḫntỉ*
director of the (food) hall, overseer of *ka*-priests, Iienkhenti

7a.2. *sꜣ.f ḥm-kꜣ Mḫw*
his son, *ka*-priest Mekhu

7a.4, 5. *ꞽIỉ-n-ḫnt*
Iienkhent

8. **N Wall, panel associated with subsidiary burial**

8.1. *ḫtmty-bỉty śmr-wꜥty ḫry-ḥbt ỉmꜣḫw Ḫwỉ*
sealer of the king of Lower Egypt, sole companion, lector priest, honored one, Khui

8.2. *ỉmy-rꜣ ḥm(w)-kꜣ ỉry śšr ỉrr ḥsst n.f* | *Šmꜣỉ*
overseer of *ka*-priests, keeper of linen, one who does what is favored for him | Shemai

8.3. (text from above the entrance into the subsidiary chamber):
ḥtp dỉ nśwt ꞽInpw tpy-ḏw.f prt-ḫrw tꜥ ḥnkt n ḫtmty-bỉty śmr-wꜥty ḫry-ḥbt (?) *ỉmy-rꜣ ỉꜥꜣw Ḫwỉ*
an offering that the king gives and (an offering that) Anubis (gives), he who is upon his mountain, an invocation offering

of bread and beer to the sealer of the king of Lower Egypt, the sole companion, lector priest, overseer of Egyptianized Nubians, Khui

9. **S Wall, panel associated with subsidiary burial**
   9.1. *śmr-wꜥty ẖry-ḥbt ỉmy-rꜣ ḫtmty-nṯr* | *ỉmꜣḫw Mṯnw* (?)
   sole companion, lector priest, overseer of expedition leaders (?) | honored one Metjnw
   The sealer of the god/expedition leader title is common in this cemetery (see also Sobekhetep, Harkhuf. Jones, *Index* vol.2, 767, #2791), but the overseer version is unusual. In addition, the overseer appears after the expedition leader, which is equally unusual, but nothing additional follows the overseer group, so it is unclear exactly what this title is.
   9.2. *ḥm-kꜣ ỉrr ḥst nb.f Nḫtw*
   ka-priest whom his lord favors Nekhtw
   Figure standing in front of Metjnw, facing him
   9.3. *ḫrp-sḥ ḥm-kꜣ Sꜣw*
   director of the (food) hall, *kꜣ-śervꜥnt*, Saw
   Figure in front of Metjnw, bottom
   9.4. *ḫtmt* (*Mṯw?*) *ꜥnḫ.*(*ś*)
   sealer/official (unclear word) Ankhes
   She stands behind Metjnw at the top; she is likely his wife
   9.5., 9.6 *sꜣt.ś Nfr*(*-ꜥnḳt?*)
   her daughter, Nefer-(Anket?)
   The inscription is the same for both.
10. **Column E4 (fig. 22)**
   10.1. *ḥm-kꜣ ỉrr ḥsst nb.f Šꜥś.f*
   ka-priest, he who does what his lord favors, Shasef
   10.2. *sꜣ.f ḥm-kꜣ Mḫw*
   his son, *ka*-priest, Mekhu
   10.3. *ḥmt.f Śnt*
   his wife, Senet
11. **Column E5 (fig. 23)**
   no text
12. **Column M2 (fig. 24)**
   12.1. *ỉmy tꜣw* (*or*) *ḥm-kꜣ ỉrr ḥss*(*t*) *nb.f*/ *'Impy*
   he who is in the tA(-wr) phyle (of) *ka*-priests, he who does what his lord favors, Impy

12.2. *ḥmt.f Mṯtỉ*
his wife, Metjety

12.3 *sꜣt.f Rwdỉ*
his daughter, Rwdi

12.4. *sꜣt.f ꞽIbỉb*
his daughter, Ibib

13. **Column M6 (fig. 25)**

13.1 *ḥm-kꜣ ḫrp-sḥ ỉr(r) ḥss(t) nb.f Śrwḏ-nfrỉ*
ka-priest, director of the (food) hall, one who does what his lord favors, Serwdj-nefri

13.2. *sꜣ.f Śꜣbn(ỉ)*
his son, Sabni

14. **Column W2**

14.1. *ḫtmty-bỉty śmr-wʿty Śꜣbnỉ*
sealer of the king of Lower Egypt, sole companion, Sabni

15. **Column W6 (fig. 26)**

Two pairs of figures, each pair has the larger (father) behind the smaller (son)

15.1. *Śꜣbn(ỉ)*
Sabni

15.2. *ỉmy-rꜣ ḥm(w)-kꜣ, ỉmy-[rꜣ] śšr, ỉmy-ỉb nb.f, ꞽImꜣ-Śbk*
overseer of *ka*-priests, overseer of linen, favorite of his lord, Ima-Sobek

15.3. *Śꜣbn(ỉ)*
Sabni

15.4. *śḥḏ ḥm(w)-kꜣ ḫrp-sḥ ỉrr ḥsst nb.f Śrwḏ-nfrỉ*
Inspector of *ka*-priests, director of the (food) hall, one who does what his lord praises, Serwdj-nefri

16. **Subsidiary false door, south of Mekhu's**

16.1 *ḥtp dỉ nśwt ꞽInpw tpy ḏw.f prt-ḫrw n.f*
An offering which the king gives and Anubis, he on his mountain, of bread and beer to him

16.2 *ḫtmty bỉty, śmr wʿty Sꜣbnỉ*
sealer of the king of Lower Egypt, sole companion, Sabni

16.2 *rḫt nśwt ḥm(t)-nṯr Ḥwt-Ḥr šbt rn.ś nfr B//*
friend of the king, priestess of Hathor, Sabt, beautiful name B//

17. **Mekhu's false door (fig. 27)**

17.1. Lintel text

ḥtp di̓ nśwt ʾInpw tpy-ḏw.f i̓my-wt nb tꜣ-ḏśr prt-ḫrw t ḥnḳt n ḥꜣty-ʿ ḫtmty-bi̓ty

ḥtp di̓ nśwt Wśi̓r ḫnty-Ḏdw prt-ḫrw t ḥnḳt n ḥꜣty-ʿ mꜣʿ Mḫw

an offering that the king gives and (an offering that) Anubis (gives), he who is upon his mountain, he who is in the place of embalming, lord of the sacred land (necropolis) an invocation offering of bread and beer to the count, sealer of the king of Lower Egypt–

an offering that the king gives and (an offering that) Osiris (gives), foremost of Busiris, an invocation offering of bread and beer to the true count, Mekhu

17.2. Upper right jamb

ḥꜣty-ʿ ḫtmty-bi̓ty śmr-wʿty ḫry-ḥbt Mḫw

count, sealer of the king of Lower Egypt, sole companion, lector priest, Mekhu

The "*ḫ*" and the "*m*" signs in the writing of "Mekhu" here are reversed

17.3. Upper left jamb

i̓mꜣḫw ḫr Ḥr ḥꜣty-ʿ ḫtmty-bi̓ty Mḫw

Honored before Horus, the count, sealer of the king of Lower Egypt, Mekhu

17.4. Stele

ḫꜣ t ḫꜣ ḥnḳt ḫꜣ kꜣw ḫꜣ ꜣpdw ḫꜣ gḥś ḫꜣ mꜣḥḏ ḫꜣ śšr mnḫt n ḥꜣty-ʿ ḫtmty-bi̓ty śmr-wʿty Mḫw

1,000 bread, 1,000 beer, 1,000 oxen, 1,000 fowl, 1,000 gazelle, 1,000 oryx, 1,000 linen clothing to the count, sealer of the king of Lower Egypt, sole companion, Mekhu

17.5. Lower lintel (below stele)

i̓mꜣḫw ḫr nṯr ʿꜣ nb pt ḥꜣty-ʿ ḫtmty-bi̓ty śmr-wʿty Mḫw

honored before the great god, lord of the sky, count, sealer of king of Lower Egypt, sole companion, Mekhu

17.6, 7 above each inner jamb figure

ḥꜣty-ʿ Mḫw

count, Mekhu

18, 19. **Sabni façade**, both sides of the entrance. The façade holds the long autobiography of Sabni, along with scenes of large figures of the tomb owner addressed by smaller figures on each side. Texts associated with these scenes are lost; the autobiography is also very damaged. For Sabni's autobiography refer to Edel et al., *Felsgräbernekropole*, I. Abteilung, Band 1, 48–58; Strudwick, *Texts from the Pyramid Age*, 335–9; Sethe, *Urkunden I*, 135–40; Breasted, *Ancient Records of Egypt*, 164–9; Edel, "Die Grabungen auf der Qubbet El Hawa 1975," 193–7, Roccati, *La Littérature Historique Sous L'Ancien Empire Égyptien*, 216–20.

21. **Sabni entrance, south thickness, top section (fig. 18)**
This panel and the one on the opposite thickness are similar. The texts on this panel have been damaged, and they are very difficult to see now.
    21.1 *ḥꜣty-ꜥ ẖtmty bỉty ỉmy-rꜣ Šmꜥw śmr-wꜥty Sꜣbnỉ*
    count, sealer of the king of Lower Egypt, overseer of Upper Egypt, sole companion, Sabni
    21.2 *śmśw <Mẖw> ?*
    eldest <Mekhu>? presumably
    21.3 *śꜣ.f mry.f śmr-wꜥty ẖry-ḥbt <ʾInỉ-ỉt.f>*
    his son, his beloved, lector priest
    The name is not visible; Seyfried posits Ini-itef
    21.4 *ḥm-kꜣ ỉrr ḥsst nb.f Srwd-nfr*
    ka-priest, he who does what his lord favors, Srwdj-nefri
22. **Sabni entrance, south thickness, bottom section**. There are no visible texts in this scene of small figures leading oxen into the tomb.
23. **Sabni entrance, north thickness, top section**
    23.1 *ḥꜣty-ꜥ ẖtmty-bỉty ỉmy-rꜣ šmꜣw śmr-wꜥty ẖry-ḥbt | ỉmy-rꜣ ẖꜣśwt mḥ ỉb nśwt m tp-rś(y) Śꜣbnỉ | ỉmꜣẖw ẖr ỉnpw tpy-ḏw.f ḥꜣty-ꜥ ẖtmty-bỉty śmr-wꜥty ẖry-ḥbt Śꜣbn(ỉ)*
    count, sealer of the king of Lower Egypt, overseer of Upper Egypt, sole companion, lector priest | overseer of the foreign lands, confidant of the king at the head of the south, Sabni | one honored before Anubis, he who is upon his mountain, count, sealer of the king of Lower Egypt, sole companion, lector priest, Sabni
    23.2 *śꜣ.f śmśw mry.f n(y) śt-ỉb ẖtmty-bỉty | śmr-wꜥty ẖry-ḥbt ỉmy-rꜣ ỉꜥꜣw M[-]?*
    His eldest son, his beloved, favorite of his lord, sealer of the king of Lower Egypt | sole companion, lector priest, overseer of Egyptianized Nubians M<ekhu>
    23.3 no visible text

23.4 *ỉmy-r3 šśr n(y) śt-ỉb nb.f śḥḏ ḥm(w)-k3, H̱wỉ*
overseer of linen, favorite of his lord, inspector of *ka*-priests, Khui

24. **Sabni chapel, pillar E6, south face (fig. 32)**
ḥ3ty-ʿ ḫtmty-bỉty śmr-wʿty ẖry-ḥbt Ś3bn(ỉ)
count, sealer of the king of Lower Egypt, sole companion, lector priest, Sabni

25. **Sabni chapel, pillar E6, east face (fig. 33)**
25.1 (first part of line across top of panel):
śḥḏ ḥm(w)-k3 ỉm3ḫw ḫr nb.f Mḫw
inspector of *ka*-priests, one honored before his lord, Mekhu
25.2 (second part): *ỉmy-r3 šśr ỉrr ḥsst nb.f* (name below) [*H̱*]*wỉ*
overseer of linen, he who does what his lord praises, [Kh]ui
25.3 inscription lost

26. **Sabni chapel, pillar W6 (fig. 31)**
26.1 *ỉmy-r3 ḥm(w)-k3 ỉmy-r3 šśr | mry.f n(y) śt-ỉb.f 'Im3-Śbk*
overseer of *ka*-priests, overseer of linen, beloved of his lord, favorite of his lord, Ima-Sobek

27. **Sabni chapel fishing and fowling scene (fig. 30)**
27.1. above head of fowler
ḥ3ty-ʿ ḫtmty-bỉty ỉmy-r3 šmʿw śmr-wʿty | Ś3bnỉ
count, sealer of the king of Lower Egypt, overseer of Upper Egypt, sole companion Sabni
27.2. above head of fisherman
śnt mḥt ỉn ḥ3ty-ʿ ḫtmty-bỉty śmr-wʿty ẖry-ḥbt | Ś3bn(ỉ)
traversing the marshes by the count, sealer of the king of Lower Egypt, sole companion, lector priest | Sabni

subsidiary figures, left to right:
27.3 *s3.f* [. . .]
his son (rest is lost)
27.4 *s3.f śmr-wʿty 'Inỉ-ỉt.f*
his son, sole companion, Initef
27.5 *s3t.f ẖkrt-nśwt 'Ittỉ*
his daughter, royal ornamented one, Itety
27.6 *ḥmt.f mrt.f ẖkrt-nśwt wʿtt Śt-k3*
his wife, his beloved, sole ornamented one of the king, Setka
27.7 *ḫrp-sḥ ỉr(r) ḥsst.f | ḥm-k3 Śrwḏ-nfrỉ*
director of the (food) hall, he who does what he (i.e., Sabni) favors, *ka*-priest, Serwdj-nefri

27.8 *s3t.f Šm3(i?)t*
his daughter, Shemait

27.9 *s3t.f ḫkrt-nśwt wˁtt ꜣItti*
his daughter, sole ornamented one of the king, Itety

27.10 *s3t.f Śn*
his daughter, Sen(et)

28. **Sabni false door niche, inner jamb offerer 1 (fig. 29)**
irt ḫt? śnṯr (?)n ḫrp-sḥ ḥm-k3 Śrwḏ-nfri
burning incense? by the director of the (food) hall, *ka*-priest, Serwdj-nefri

29. **Sabni false door niche, outer jamb, offerer 2 (fig. 29)**
29.1. no text/lost to damage or never done?
29.2. *s3.f śmśw Ś3bni*
his eldest son, Sabni

30. **Sabni false door (fig. 28)**
30.1. lintel text
ḥtp di nśwt ꜣInpw tpy-ḏw.f imy-wt nb t3 ḏśr prt ḫrw t ḥnḳt (?) ḥ3ty-ˁ ḫtmty-bity śmr-wˁty ḫry-ḥbt imy-r3 šmˁw imy-r3 ḫ3śwt Ś3bn(i)
an offering that the king gives and Anubis (gives), he who is upon his mountain, who-is-in-the-place-of-embalming, lord of the sacred land/necropolis, an offering (of) a foreleg/oxen?, (?) to the count, sealer of the king of Lower Egypt, sole companion, lector priest, overseer of the Upper Egypt, overseer of foreign lands; Sabni

30.2. Upper right jamb
ḥ3ty-ˁ ḫtmty-bity śmr-wˁty ḫry-ḥbt Ś3bni
count, sealer of the king of Lower Egypt, sole companion, lector priest, Sabni

30.3. Upper left jamb
ḥ3ty-ˁ ḫtmty-bity imy-r3 šmˁw n(y) śt-ib nb[.f Ś3bni]
count, sealer of the king of Lower Egypt, overseer of Upper Egypt, favorite of his lord, Sabni
The lower part of this jamb is damaged.

30.4. Stele
ḫ3 t ḥnḳt ḫ3 k3w 3bdw ḫ3 gḥś m3ḥḏ ḫ3 śšr mnḫt n ḥ3ty-ˁ imy-r3 šmˁw Ś3bni
1,000 bread and beer, 1,000 oxen and fowl, 1,000 gazelle and oryx, 1,000 linen (and) clothing to the count, overseer of Upper Egypt, Sabni

30.5. Inner right jamb
ḥ3ty-ʿ Ś3bnỉ
count, Sabni
30.6. Inner left jamb
ḥ3ty-ʿ Ś3bnỉ
count, Sabni

Sobekhetep (90)

1. **Pillar E4 (fig. 39)**
   1.1 *ḫtmty-bỉty śmr-wʿty ḫtmty-nṯr ỉm3ḫw Śbk-ḥtp*
   sealer of the king of Lower Egypt, sole companion, expedition leader, honored one, Sobekhetep
   1.2 *śḥḏ ḥm(w)-k3 Mkwt*
   inspector of *ka*-priests, Mekwt
2. **Pillar E5 (fig. 38)**
   2.1 *ḫrp-sḥ ỉmy-r3 ḥm(w)-k3 ỉrr ḥsst nb.f Śbk-ḥtp*
   director of the (food) hall, overseer of the *ka*-priests, one who does what his lord favors, Sobekhetep
   2.2 *s3.f Bnfrw*
   his son, Beneferw (?)
   2.3 *s3.f ḥm-k3 Šbḥnỉ*
   his son, *ka*-priest, Shebheni
   2.4 *s3.f Śbk-ḥtp*
   his son Sobekhetep
   2.5 *ḥmt.f ḥm-nṯr Ḥwt-Ḥr | ỉwt-Ḥwt-Ḥr (?)*
   his wife, *netjer*-priestess of Hathor, Iwt-Hathor (Hathor-iwt?)
   2.6 *s3t.f Ḥst*
   his daughter, Heset
3. **Pillar M5 (fig. 37, right)**
   3.1 *śmr-wʿty ḫtmty-nṯr Śbk-ḥtp*
   sole companion, sealer of the god/expedition leader, Sobekhetep
   3.2 *ḫrp-sḥ ḥm-k3 Śbk-ḥtp*
   director of the (food) hall, *ka*-priest, Sobekhetep
4. **Pillar M4 (fig. 40)**
   (long text across the top): *ỉr ḥm(w)-k3 nbw ʿḳ.tỉś ỉs n śmr-wʿty ḫtmty-nṯr Śbk-ḥtp mryw šʿty.śn šdw mw t3.f nt [rʿ] nb ỉw wḥm rṯ(n) nfr*

This concerns all *ka*-priests that will come into the tomb of the sole companion and expedition leader Sobekhetep that wish to receive their two breads/cakes, read out the water and bread entitled to him every day, good things will be returned to you.

FIGURES RIGHT TO LEFT:

4.1 *ḫrp-sḥ śḥḏ ḥm(w)-kꜣ Mkwt*
director of the (food) hall, *ka*-priest, Mekwt

4.2 *ḫtmt Nfr-ʿnḳt*
sealer, Nefer-Anket

4.3 *sꜣt.ś Nfr-ʿnḳt*
her daughter, Nefer-Anket

4.4 *sꜣt.ś Ḥst*
her daughter, Heset

IiShemai Setka (98)

1. **E wall (fig. 44)**

1.1 *ḫtmty bìty śmr wʿty ẖry-ḥbt ḥry-tp ʿꜣ n nśwt 'Iì-šmꜣ*
sealer of the king of Lower Egypt, sole companion, lector priest, great overlord of the king, IiShemai

1.2 *ḫrp sḥ śḥḏ n ḥm(w)-kꜣ ìrr ḥst nb.f 'Iì-šmꜣ*
director of the food hall

2. **S Wall (fig. 45)**

2.1 *ḫtmty bìty śmr wʿty ẖry-ḥbt ḥry-tp ʿꜣ n nśwt 'Iì-šmꜣ Stkꜣ ìmꜣḫw ḥr 'Inpw*
sealer of the king of Lower Egypt, sole companion, lector priest, great overlord of the king, IiShemai Setka, honored before Anubis

2.2 *śḥḏ ḥm(w)-kꜣ ìrr ḥsst nb.f Nḫtw*
inspector of *ka*-priests, he who does what his lord favors, Nekhtw

2.3 text across the top of the smaller panel
ìr ḥm-kꜣ nb ʿḳtyfy ìś pw mry-tyś [. . . ?] *ḥsì(w) ḫtmty bìty 'Iì-šmꜣ šdì n prt-ḫrw n<.f> m rꜣ-pr pn nb ìw* [*wḥm*]*? nfr* [. . . ?]
Each *ka*-priest that enters into this tomb who shall desire that they may reward the sealer of the king of Lower Egypt, IiShemai, may he read the offering in my lord's chapel…

2.4 *ś3.f ḥm-k3 ʾIi-šm3*

his son, the *ka*-priest IiShemai

3. **Pillar 1 (fig. 46)**

ẖtmty-bity śmr-wʿty ẖry-ḥbt ḥry-tp ʿ3 n nśwt ʾIi-Šm3i | im3ḫw ḫr Wśir nṯr ʿ3

sealer of the king of Lower Egypt, sole companion, lector priest, great overlord of the king, IiShemai, one honored before Osiris, the Great God

4. **Pillar 3 (fig. 47)**

4.1 *ẖtmty-bity śmr-wʿty ẖry-ḥbt ḥry-tp ʿ3 Śtk3*

sealer of the king of Lower Egypt, sole companion, lector priest, great overlord, Setka

4.2 *ḥm-k3 irr ḥsst nb[.f?] ʾIi-Šm3i*

ka-priest, he who does what [his?] lord praises, Ii-Shemai (or he who does what [his] lord IiShemai praises?)

4.3 *ḫrp-sḥ ḥm-k3 ʾIi-Šm3i*

director of the (food) hall, *ka*-priest, IiShemai

Khwin-Khnum (102)

1. **Pillar E2, east face (fig. 51)**

1.1 *śḥḏ ḥm(w)-nṯr Mn-ʿnḫ-Nfr-kʿ-rʿ ḥ3ty-ʿ ẖtmty-bity śmr-wʿty ẖry-ḥbt ẖry-tp nśwt | imy-r3 sẖ3(w) ʿprw Ḫwin-Ḫnmw*

Inspector of the *netjer*-priests of the life of Nefer-ka-ra is established (his pyramid), count, sealer of the king of Lower Egypt, sole companion, lector priest, royal chamberlain | overseer of scribes of the crews, Khwin-Khnum

1.2 *imy-r3 ḥm(w)-k3 K3ri*

overseer of *ka*-priests, Kari

2. **Pillar E2, north face (fig. 52)**

2.1 *ḫrp-ḫ3w śmśw pr Śn(n)i*

director of grain measures, elder of the domain, Seni

2.2 *ẖtmty.f ḥry s3ṯ n is K3ri*

(his?) sealer, libationer for the tomb, Kari

2.3 on the bottom register, text over the two animals

iw3 nn (rn?) / m3 ḥḏ

(our? or young?) ox / oryx

3. **Pillar E3, east face (fig. 53)**
   - 3.1 *ḥ3ty-ʿ ḫtmty-bỉty śmr-wʿty ẖry-ḥbt | ỉmy-r3 sẖ3 ʿprw Ḫwỉn-Ḫnmw*
     count, sealer of the king of Lower Egypt, sole companion, lector priest | overseer of the scribes of the crew, Khwin-Khnum
   - 3.2 *ḥmt.f mrt.f ẖkrt-nśwt Śn(t)*
     his wife, his beloved, ornamented one of the king, Sen(et)
4. **Pillar E3, south face (fig. 54)**
   - 4.1 (text at top) *ỉmy-r3 pr ỉmy-r3 rwt ỉmy-r3 ḳdw n(y) śt-ỉb nb.f ḥs.f K3rỉ*
     overseer of the estate, overseer of the gateway, overseer of the workmen, his lord's favorite, one whom he praises, Kari
   - 4.2 (middle woman) *s3t.f*
     his daughter
   - 4.3 (front woman) *s3t.f* (name unclear)
     his daughter, (name?)
5. **Pillar W2 (fig. 55)**
   - 5.1 *ḥ3ty-ʿ | ḫtmty-bỉty śmr-wʿty ẖry-ḥbt ẖry-tp nśwt | ỉmy-r3 ḫ3śwt ḥry śšt3 n mdt (nbt) št3t nt tp-rśy ỉmy-r3 sẖ3 ʿprw Ḫwỉn-Ḫnmw*
     count | sealer of the king of Lower Egypt, sole companion, lector priest, royal chamberlain | overseer of foreign lands, secretary of all the secret matters of the Head of the South, overseer of the scribes of the crews, Khwin-Khnum
   - 5.2 *ḥmt.f mrtf ẖkrt-nśwt ḥm-nṯr Ḥwt-Ḥr Śnt*
     his wife, his beloved, ornamented one of the king, *netjer*-priestess of Hathor, Senet
   - 5.3 *ỉmy-r3 pr ḥm-k3 ỉrr ḥsst nb.f K3rỉ*
     overseer of the estate, *ka*-priest, he who does what his lord favors, Kari
6. **Pillar W3 (fig. 56)**
   - 6.1 *ḥ3ty-ʿ ḫtmty-bỉty śmr-wʿty ẖry-tp nśwt | ỉmy-r3 sẖ3 ʿprw Ḫwỉn-Ḫnmw |*
     ỉmy ḫt wỉ3 ʿ3
     count, sealer of the king of Lower Egypt, sole companion, royal chamberlain | overseer of the scribes of the crews, Khwin-Khnum | attendant of the great bark
   - 6.2 *ḥm-k3 ỉrr ḥsst nb.f Śnỉ*
     ka-priest, he who does what his lord favors, Seni

Tjetji (103)

1. **Column E1, north side**
   śmr-wꜥty ẖry-ḥbt ḫtmty-nṯr ỉnn ḫrt ḫꜣśwt rś(ywt) mḥtwt n nśwt Ṯṯỉ
   sole companion, lector priest, expedition leader, he who brings back the products of the southern [and northern?] foreign lands to the king, Tjetji
2. **Column E1, east side**
   Text painted in red ink appears on the smoothed face of the top of the column, it appears to have been in preparation for a scene to be carved; the Bonn mission saw two different versions surviving on the column.
   - 2.1 (older version)
     mry n nb.f ẖnmw-ḥtp
     beloved of his lord, Khnumhotep
   - 2.2 (later version)
     mry n nb.f ỉmy-rꜣ pr ẖnmw-ḥtpy
     beloved of his lord, overseer of the estate, Khnumhotep
   - 2.3 *ḫrp sḥ <ḥry?> ḫnt Mnṯt/Mṯt (?)*
     director of the food hall, the first? Mentjt or Metjet? name unclear
3. **Column E2, south side (fig. 61)**
   ḥꜣty-ꜥ ḫtmty-bỉty śmr-wꜥty ḫtmty-nṯr Ṯṯỉ
   count, sealer of the king of Lower Egypt, sole companion, expedition leader, Tjetji
4. **Column E2, east side (fig. 62)**
   - 4.1 *ḥm-kꜣ ỉrr ḥsst nb.f H̱nmw-ḥtp(ỉ)*
     ka-priest, he who does what his lord favors, Khnum-hetep
   - 4.2 *ḫrp-sḥ ỉrr ḥsst nb<.f> ỉmy-rꜣ mšꜥ (or ỉmy-rꜣ rmṯw?) H̱nmw-ḥtp*
     director of the (food) hall, he who does what (his) lord favors, overseer of the army (overseer of workers/people?), Khnum-hetep
   - 4.3 [. . . ?] *ẖry? ỉmy ḫt m Ḥḳꜣ.n.ś (?)*
     assistant of? deputy? Heqanes
     very unclear signs
   - 4.4 *ỉmyt-rꜣ pr Ḥr-m-kꜣw.ś*
     overseer of the estate, Horemkawes

Khui (34e)

1. **Column E2, east face, top (fig. 67)**
   1.1 *ḥ3ty-ʿ imy-r3 ẖnw śmr-wʿty ḫtmty-nṯr imy-ḫt wi3(wy) ʿ3 im3ḫw Ḫwwi*
   count, overseer of the Residence, sole companion, expedition leader, attendant of the (two?) great bark(s), honored one, Khui
   1.2 *ḫrp-sḥ imy-r3 ḥm(w)-k3 Ḫnti*
   director of the (food) hall, overseer of *ka*-priests, Khenti
   1.3 *s3.f śḥḏ ḥm(w)-k3 Ḫwti*
   his son, inspector of the *ka*-priests, Khwti
2. **Pillar E2, east face, bottom (fig. 68)**
   Long text across the top register:
   ḫrp-sḥ Ḫnmw-ḥtp ḏd iw pr.k(w)i ḥnʿ nb ḥ3ty-ʿ ḫtmty-nṯr Ṯṯi ḥ3ty-ʿ ḫtmty-nṯr Ḫwi r Kbn, Pwnt, Rṯnw n śp (?). iw in.k(w)i m ḥtp ir.n ḫ3śwt (p?)tn
   the director of the (food) hall, Khnum-hetep says, I went forth together with my lord the count, expedition leader Tjetji (and) my lord the count, expedition leader Khui to Kbn(Byblos), Punt, and Retjnw (in Syria)? times. I was brought back in safety after I had traveled to these foreign lands.
   2.1 *ḫrp-sḥ Ḫnmw-ḥtp śḫpt ḳbḥw*
   director of the (food) hall Khnum-hetep, bringing water/ libations
   2.2 *imy-r3 pr-šnʿ Ḫnmw-ḥtp śḫpt 3pdwy*
   the overseer of the *per-shena*, Khnum-hetep, bringing two ducks
   2.3 *śḫpt śtp n ḥ3ty-ʿ ḫtmty-nṯr Ḫwi, ḫrp-sḥ Ḫnmw-ḥtp*
   bringing the choicest meat to the count, expedition leader Khui. Director of the (food) hall, Khnum-hetep
   2.4 *sfṯ iw3 in ḫrp-sḥ Ḫnmw-ḥtp n ḥ3ty-ʿ ḫtmty-nṯr śmr-wʿty imy-r3 ẖnw Ḫwi*
   slaughtering a bull by the director of the (food) hall Khnum-hetep for the count, expedition leader, sole companion, overseer of the Residence, Khui

Middle register:
   2.5 *ḥmt.f Śnti*
   his wife Senti

2.6 *s3t.ś Ḥr-m-k3w.ś*
her daughter, Horemkawes

2.7 *s3t.ś Nbt-Šm3ỉ-ỉ3m* (?)
her daughter, Nebet-Shemai-iam (?)

2.8 *s3.ś Nfr-m3.f-ỉw* (?)
her son, Nefer-mafiw

2.9 *s3.ś Ṯṯỉ*
her son, Tjetji

Bottom register:

2.10 *ẖrp-sḥ H̱nmw-ḥtp*
director of the (food) hall, Khnum-hetep

2.11 *ỉry ḥnḳt ẖry-ʿ.f*
keeper of beer, his assistant
The "his" here (and in the next two inscriptions) presumably refers to Khnum-hetep.

2.12, 2.13 *ẖrp-sḥ ẖry-ʿ.f*
director of the (food) hall, his assistant
Same for both.

Khunes (34h)

1. **South entrance thickness (fig.71)**
This thickness is damaged and only parts of both a large figure of Khunes and smaller figure of his son remain. Text survives between them, oriented to belong to the son.
ʾItỉ s3.f śmśw ḥ3ty-ʿ[ḫtmty-] bỉty [. . .] *H̱wnś*
Iti, his eldest son, count, [sealer of] the king of Lower Egypt… | Khunes

2. **East wall, main, south of entrance, north half (ref fig. 73)**
2.1 *ḥ3ty-ʿ ḫtmty-bỉty śmr-wʿty ẖry-ḥbt ỉm3ḫw ḫr nṯr* (*ʿ3*) | *H̱nmt-ny rn.f nfr Šm3ỉ*
count, sealer of the king of Lower Egypt, sole companion, lector priest, the one honored by the great god/ Ny-khnemti, good name Shemai
2.2, 2.3 no text

3. **East wall, main, south of entrance, south half (fishing and fowling) (ref fig. 73)**
3.1 text across top
śtt mḥt nbw ỉn [*ḥ3ty-ʿ*] *ḫtmty bỉty śmr wʿty ẖry-ḥbt*

the spearing of all fish by the count, sealer of the king of Lower Egypt, sole companion, lector priest

3.2 (text with male figure on left side) *sꜣ.f śmśw śmr-wʿty ẖry-ḥbt Šmꜣỉ*
his eldest son, sole companion, lector priest, Shemai

4. **East wall, south of entrance, lower panel (fig. 74)**
   4.1 Fragment of text next to second figure, female, on the top register
   ỉmꜣḫwt Šštỉ
   (one) honored, Sheshti
5. **South wall, east end, standing couple with son (fig. 76)**
   5.1 *ḫtmty-bỉty śmr-wʿty ẖry-ḥbt | ỉmꜣḫw ḫr nṯr ʿꜣ () nb pt Ḫwnś*
   sealer of the king of Lower Egypt, sole companion, lector priest | one honored before the great god, lord of the sky, Khunes
   5.2 *ẖkrt-nśwt wʿtt ʿnḫ.ś*
   sole ornamented one of the king, Ankhes
   5.3 text is unclear
   5.4 *ḥm-kꜣ ỉmy ỉb.f Nb-m<ỉỉ-mḥw> ?*
   ka priest, in the heart of his lord, Nebem-y-Mehu
6. **South wall, east end, seated couple (ref fig. 75)**
   6.1 *ḫtmty-bỉty śmr-wʿty Ḫwnś*
   sealer of the king of Lower Egypt, sole companion, Khunes
   6.2 *ẖkrt-nśwt wʿtt ḥm-nṯr Ḥwt-Ḥr, ʿnḫś*
   sole ornament of the king, *netjer*-priestess of Hathor, Ankhes
7. **South wall, main (ref. fig. 75)**
   This section of the wall incorporated a number of active scenes with small figures. The wall is extensively damaged, and almost no text remains, if in fact it existed originally.
   7.1 Figure at the front of a register of oxen: *ỉmy-rꜣ ṯs(w)t n śt-ỉb nb.f ʾInỉn (?)*
   overseer of herds in the heart of his lord, Inin (name unclear)
   7.2 Figure in front of large image of Khunes at west end of the wall
   ḫrp sḥ ḥm-kꜣ [N]b-m-mḥw (?)
   director of the food hall, ka priest, Nebem-mehu (name unclear)
8. **West wall, south of false door niche**
   no text
9. **West wall, south of false door niche, bottom panel (fig. 78)**
   9.1 *ḫrp [-sḥ] [ś]ḥḏ [ḥm(w)-kꜣ] [Śḥtp] Kꜣrỉ*
   director (of the [food] hall) inspector of (*ka*-priests, Sehetep) Kari

9.2 *s3.f Ḫnmw-ḥtp*
his son, Khnum-hetep

10. **West wall, along north edge of false door niche**

10.1 *ḫrp [sḥ śḥḏ] ḥm(w)-k3 Śḥtp K3ri*
director of (the [food] hall inspector) of *ka*-priests, Sehetep Kari

10.2 *s3.f Ḫnmw-ḥtp*
his son, Khnum-hetep

11. **False door niche, south thickness (fig. 79)**

11.1 *ḫtmty-bity śmr-wʿty* (...) | *im3ḫw ḫr nṯr ʿ3* [*Ḫwn*]*ś*
sealer of the king of Lower Egypt, sole companion (lacuna) | honored before the great god, [Khun]es

11.2 (over head of first figure) *ḥtp di nśwt* (...)
an offering that the king gives (rest lost)

11.3 *ḥm-k3 Nb-m-*[*mḥw*]*?*
ka-priest Nebem-mehu?
Name here is unclear.

12. **False door niche, north thickness**
text is lost to damage.

14. **West wall, panel 1 (ref. fig. 77)**
no text

15. **West wall, panel 2 (fig. 80)**
no text

16. **West wall, panel 3**

16.1 (left figure) *ḫrp-sḥ mry nb.f T3...?*
director of the (food) hall, beloved of his lord, Ta...?

16.2 (right figure) *Ḫwnś*
Khunes

17. **West wall, panel 4 (fig. 81)**

17.1 *ḥm-k3 Ḫwnś*
ka-priest, Khunes

17.2 *ḫtmty imy-ib n nb.f im3ḫw ʾIpy*
sealer, he who is in his lord's heart (confidant of his lord), one honored, Ipy

18. **West wall, panel 5, north of secondary niche above shaft**
no text remains

19. **Pillar E1, east face, top (fig. 84)**

19.1 *ḫtmty-bity śmr-wʿty ḫry-ḥbt Ḫwnś*

sealer of the king of Lower Egypt, sole companion, lector priest, Khunes

20. **Pillar E1, east face, bottom panel (fig. 85)**
    - 20.1 no text
    - 20.2 *ḫrp-sḥ śḥd n ḥm(w)-kꜣ n(y) śt-ib nb.f | Śḥtp rn.f nfr | Kꜣri*
      director of the (food) hall, inspector of *ka*-priests, favorite/confidant of his lord, Sehetep, whose beautiful name is Kari
    - 20.3 *imꜣḫwt ḫr nb.ś | mrrt nb.ś Rꜥ | Snty | ḥm-nṯr Ḥwt-Ḥr Śbk(?)-Snty*
      one honored before her lord, beloved of her lord every day, Senty, *netjer*-priestess of Hathor, Sobek-Senty
21. **Pillar E2, east face, top panel (fig. 86)**
    - 21.1 [pyramid name] *śḥḏ ḥm(w)-nṯr ḥꜣty-ꜥ | [ḫtmty-bity śmr-wꜥty] ḫry-ḥbt Ḫwnś*
      inspector of priests of [pyramid], count | [sealer of the king of Lower Egypt, sole companion] lector priest, Khunes
    - 21.2 *sḫꜣ Nfr-Ṯbꜥw*
      scribe, Nefer-Tjbaw
22. **Pillar E2, east face, middle panel (fig. 87, top)**
    - 22.1 *śḥḏ ḥm(w)-kꜣ [. . .fw?] n(y) śt-ib nb.f | imy-[ib?] nb.f [ir]r ḥsst nb.f | Nb-m-ii-mḥw* (?)
      inspector of *ka*-priests, [?], favorite/confidant of his lord, he who is in his lord's heart [?], he who does what his lord praises, Nebem-mehu
    - 22.2 *ḥm-kꜣ Ḫwnś*
      ka-priest, Khunes
    - 22.3 *Nb-m-ii-mḥw*
      Nebem-ii-mehu
    - 22.4 *śnt.f Ḫwit*
      his sister, Khwit
23. **Pillar E2, east face, bottom (fig. 87, bottom)**
    imy-rꜣ ṯs(w)t 'Iii (name?)
    overseer of herds, Iii (?)

All texts from the north face of Pillar E2 are taken from Edel et al., *Felsgräbernekropole*, I. Abteilung, Band 2, 557–61.

24. **Pillar E2, north face, top (fig. 88)**
    - 24.1 *ꜣṯw n(y) ḏt.f Ḫwnś*
      The guard of his funerary estate, Khunes

25. **Pillar E2, north face, middle row of three figures (fig. 88)**

25.1 *[ḥm-]kꜣ śḥḏ n(y) sꜣ [ir]ry ḥss.t nb.f [rꜥw] Ḫw(i)nśi*

ka-priest, inspector of the phyle, he who is beloved of his lord every day, Khunes

25.2 *mty n(y) sꜣ irr(y) ḥss.t nb.f ḥm-kꜣ Ḫw(i)nś(y)*

controller of a phyle, he who does what his lord praises, *ka*-priest, Khunes

25.3 *imy-rꜣ śšr imꜣḫw ḫr nb.f ꞌIpy*

overseer of linen, one honored before his lord, Ipy

26. **Pillar E2, north face, lower section, upper large figure facing east (fig. 88, bottom)**

26.1 right side, behind tall figure

[ḥry-]śꜣṯ ny śt-ib nb.f ḥm-kꜣ ꞌIni-śn.f iri ḥst nb.f m iś pn ḥꜣty-ꜥ śmr-wꜥty ḫry-ḥbt Ḫnmti Ḫwnś imꜣḫw n mrw.t wḥm mrw.t

the libationer, in the heart of his lord, *ka*-priest Ini-senef, he who does what his lord favors in this tomb (of) the count, sole companion, lector priest Khnumty Khunes, one honored, beloved

26.2 Text in front of the figure: *ḥm-kꜣ ꞌIn(i)-śn.f irr ḥsst (nb.f) imy-rꜣ.f* (?)

ka-priest Ini-senef, he who does what (his lord) praises

This text and the one next to it (26.3) are the same, one perhaps a copy of the other.

26.3 Text in front of the figure, next to 26.2:

ḥm-kꜣ ꞌIn(i)-śn.f irr ḥsst nb.f imy-rꜣ.f

ka-priest who comes/carries? to the tomb (of him), he who does what his lord praises

26.4 left side, in front of small figure

ḥm-kꜣ

ka-priest

26.5 bottom with small figure

[ḥry-sꜣṯ] irr(i) ḥsst nbw.f Mry-Ḫwnś | prt-ḫrw n.f

libationer, he who does what his lord loves, Mery-Khunes | offerings for him

27. **Pillar E3, south face. Later image, no texts**

28. **Pillar W1, east face (fig. 83)**

[ḫtmty-bity śmr] wꜥty ḫry-ḥbt Ḫwnś

[sealer of the king of lower Egypt] sole [companion] lector priest, Khunes

29. **Pillar W2, east face, top panel (fig. 89, top)**
    29.1 (small female figure) *Śnty*
    Senty
    29.2 (large female figure) [-] *ʾIwt*
    (?)-Iwt
    29.3 (small male figure) *sꜣ.ś ʾInỉ*
    her son Ini
    29.4 (male figure) *sꜣ.ś Ḥḳꜣỉb*
    her son Heqaib
30. **Pillar W2, east face, bottom (fig. 89, bottom)**
    no text
31. **Pillar W3, east face (fig. 90)**
    31.1 *ỉmy-rꜣ ỉśwt ḫwỉt*
    overseer of crews, Khwit
    31.2 *śmśw wḫrt Ḥꜣkỉỉ?*
    elder of the dock, Haky (name unclear)

Ankhes, 34g

An1. Ankhes pillar (fig. 116)

An1.1 *ḥtp dỉ nśwt ʾInpw tpy-ḏw.f ỉmy-wt | nb tꜣ-ḏśr prt-ḫrw t ḥnḳt n.ś m ỉs.ś*
an offering that the king gives and (an offering that) Anubis (gives), he who is upon his mountain, who is in the place of embalming | lord of the necropolis(sacred land), (consisting of) an invocation offering of bread and beer to her in her tomb

An1.2 *ḫkrt-nśwt wʿtt ỉmꜣḫw ḫr Ḥwt-Ḥr m ś(w)t.ś nb.t | ʿnḫ.n.śn*
sole ornament of the king, honored before Hathor in all her (cult) places, Ankhensen

An1.3 (top figure) *ḫtmt Mrt.ś*
sealer, Meretes

An1.4 (bottom figure) *ḫtmt* [*?*]
sealer, (name unclear)

Harkhuf 34n

Façade: The lintel and both jambs of the façade are largely covered with a lengthy autobiographical text of Harkhuf, and to the right, a copy of a letter from Pepy II. For these texts, see Edel et al., *Felsgräbernekropole,*

I. Abteilung, Band 1, 621–6; Strudwick, *Texts from the Pyramid Age*, 328–33; Lichtheim, *Ancient Egyptian Literature*, vol. 1, 23–7.

1. **South façade (fig. 97)**
   1.1 The final line of the autobiograpy on the south façade gives the following titles:
   ḥꜣty-ʿ ḫtmty-bỉty śmr-wʿty ẖry-ḥbt ḫtmty-nṯr ḥry śštꜣ n wḏ(t)-mdw ỉmꜣḫw Ḥr-ḫw.f
   count, sealer of the king of Lower Egypt, sole companion, lector priest, expedition leader, privy to the secret of the royal/legal decrees, honored one, Harkhuf
   1.2 Text between the faces of Harkhuf and his son Djemi censing him, beneath the autobiography:
   ỉr.t.n kꜣ n ỉt.f śḏt śnṯr śty | ḥꜣb ḥknw [unguent]
   Performing for the *ka* of his father, burning incense, perfume of festival, *hekenew* oil, unguent (?)
   1.3 Text in front of Djemi, below his arms (continuing from 1.2):
   ỉn sꜣ.f śmśw mry.f | śmr-wʿty ẖry-ḥbt | ỉmy-rꜣ ỉʿꜣw | ỉmꜣḫw | ḫr nṯr nb pt | Ḏmỉ rn.f nfr Mśnỉ
   by his eldest son, his beloved, sole companion, lector priest, overseer of Egyptianized Nubians, honored before the god, lord of the sky, Djemi, whose beautiful name is Mesni
2. **North façade (fig. 97)**
   This façade has the second part of Harkhuf's autobiography.
3. **North façade, north part.**
   The inscribed copy of the letter Harkhuf received from the young king Pepy II. See above references.
4. **South façade, offerers below, left (fig. 98)**
   ỉmy-rꜣ śšr ḥs(w).n nb.f Ỉm-ṯy
   overseer of linen, one whom his lord rewarded, Imetjy
5. **South façade, offerers below, right (fig. 98)**
   ḥm-kꜣ ḥry-ḫnt Ḫnsw-ḥtp
   ka-priest who is head of (in charge of) the *khent*-box, Khonsuhetep
6. **Pillar 1 (fig. 101)**
   6.1 *ḥtp dỉ nśwt prt-ḫrw t ḥnḳt n.ś m ẖr(t)-nṯr ỉmnt | n rḫt* (or *ỉryt ḫt*) *nśwt n ḥm-nṯr Ḥwt-Ḥr ỉmꜣḫw ḫr | Wśỉr nb Ḏdw Tp-m-nfrt rn.ś nfr Tpỉ*

an offering that the king gives (consisting of) an invocation offering of bread and beer for her in the necropolis, to the king's acquaintance and *netjer*-priest(ess) of Hathor, one honored before Osiris, lord of Busiris, Tepemnefert, (with) good name Tepi

6.2 *ḫtmt Mrryt*

sealer, Mereryt

7. **Pillar 2 (fig. 102)**

ḥtp di nśwt ḥtp (di) ʾInpw tpy ḏw.f ḫnty sḥ-nṯr imy-wt nb tꜣ-ḏśr | ḳrśt.f nfr m is.f n ẖr(t)-nṯr (imnt) śmśw | wrt nfr iʿ.f n nṯr ʿꜣ nb imntt śmꜣ tꜣ.f ḏꜣ biꜣ prt-ḫrw t ḥnḳt n.f m imntt imꜣḫw ḫr nṯr ʿꜣ | śmr-wʿty ẖry-ḥbt imy-rꜣ iʿꜣw Ḏmi rn.f nfr Mśni

an offering that the king gives and an offering that Anubis (gives), he who is upon his mountain, foremost of the god's booth in the place of embalming, lord of the necropolis | may he be buried perfectly in his tomb in the (western) necropolis (in) | great old age, may he ascend to the great god of the west, may he unite (with) the land having crossed the firmament, may an invocation offering of bread and beer go forth to him in the West as one honored before the great god | sole companion, lector priest, overseer of Egyptianized Nubians, Djemi, his good name Mesni.

8. **Pillar 3, south face (fig. 103)**

8.1 *ḥtp di nśwt ḥtp di Wśir nb Ḏdw prt-ḫrw t ḥnḳt n.f | m is.f n ẖr(t)-nṯr n bity śmr-wʿty ẖry-ḥbt imy-rꜣ iʿꜣw | imꜣḫw ḫr nṯr ʿꜣ Śꜣbn(i) rn.f nfr Ny-ʿnḫ-Ppy | inn ḫrt ḫꜣśwt nb(t) Ḥr imy-rꜣ ḫꜣśwt nb(t) nt tp-rśy | imy-ib n nb.f śmr-wʿty ẖry-ḥbt imy-rꜣ iʿꜣw Ny-ʿnḫ-Ppy*

an offering that the king gives and an offering that Osiris gives, lord of Busiris, (consisting of) an invocation offering of bread and beer going forth to him | in his tomb in the cemetery (of the king?) sole companion, lector priest, overseer of Egyptianized Nubians | one honored before the great god, Sabni, his good name Nyankh-pepy | who brings the produce of all foreign lands to his lord/Horus, overseer of all foreign lands of the Head of the South(southern region) | favorite/confidant of his lord, sole companion, lector priest, overseer of Egyptianized Nubians Nyankh-pepy

8.2 *ḥm-kꜣ n nb.f irr ḥsst n nb.f ʾIpy*

ka-priest of his lord, he who does what his lord praises, Ipy

9. **Pillar 3, east face (fig. 103)**

ḥtp di nśwt ʾInpw tpy-ḏw.f ḫnty sh-nṯr prt-ḫrw t ḥnḳt n.f m is.f n ḫr(t)-nṯr | ḥ3ty-ʿ imy-r3 šmʿw ḫtmty-bity śmr-wʿty ḫry-ḥbt imy-r3 iʿ3w Ḥrḫwf | ḥry-śšt3 n wḏt-mdwt nbt nt [tp rśy?] imy-ib n nb.f | irr ḥsst n nb.f dd nrw Ḥr m ḫ3św t | inn ḫrt ḫ3św t nb(t) n nb.f imy-r3 ḫ3św t nb nt tp-rśy | [ḫtmty-] bity śmr-wʿty ḫry-ḥbt imy-r3 iʿ3w im3ḫw ḫr nṯr ʿ3 Ḥrḫwf

an offering that the king gives and (an offering that) Anubis (gives), he who is upon his mountain, foremost of the god's booth, (consisting of) an invocation offering of bread and beer going out to him in his tomb in the necropolis | count, overseer of Upper Egypt, sealer of the king of Lower Egypt, sole companion, lector priest, overseer of Egyptianized Nubians, Harkhuf | master of the secret of all the royal decisions of [the head of the south?] favorite/confidant of his lord | he who does what pleases his lord, who places the dread of Horus in foreign lands | he who brings all the produce of the foreign lands to his lord, overseer of all foreign lands of the southern region | [sealer] of the king of Lower Egypt sole companion, lector priest, overseer of Egyptianized Nubians, one honored before the great god, Harkhuf

10. **Pillar 4, South face**

ḥtp di nśwt ḥtp (di) ʾInpw tpy-ḏw.f ḫnty sḥ-nṯr imy-wt nb t3-ḏśr ḳrśt.f | m ḫr(t-)nṯr imnt śmit imntt i3w nfr wrt m im3ḫw ḫr nṯr ʿ3 | nb pt sm3-t3 ḏ3 bi3 iʿ.f n nṯr ʿ3 nb imnt im3ḫw ḫr | Wśir nb Ḏdw prt ḫrw t ḥnḳt n.f m is.f n ḫr(t)-nṯr | n ḥ3ty-ʿ imy-r3 šmʿw ḫtmty-bity smr-wʿty ḫry-ḥbt imy-r3 iʿ3w | im3ḫw ḫr Ptḥ-Skr smr-wʿty ḫry-ḥbt Ḥrḫwf

an offering that the king gives and an offering that Anubis (gives), he who is upon his mountain, foremost of the god's booth in the place of embalming, lord of the necropolis. May he be buried | in the necropolis (in) the western desert in great old age as one honored before the great god | lord of the sky, may he unite with the land having crossed the firmament, may he ascend to the great god, lord of the West (as) one honored before | Osiris, lord of Djedw (Busiris), may an invocation offering of bread and beer go forth to him in his tomb, house in the necropolis | the count, overseer of Upper Egypt, sealer of the king of Lower Egypt, sole companion, lector priest, overseer of Egyptianized Nubians | one honored before Ptah-Sokar, sole companion, lector priest, Harkhuf

11. **Pillar 4, east face (fig. 104)**

ḥtp di nśwt ḥtp (di) ʾInpw tpy-ḏw.f ḫnty sḥ-nṯr prt-ḫrw t ḥnḳt n.f m is.f pr | n ḫr(t)-nṯr (n) ḥ3ty-ʿ imy-r3 šmʿw ḫtmty-bity śmr-wʿty ḫry-ḥbt ỉmy-r3 ỉ῾3w Ḥrḫwf | ḥry-ššt3 n mdt nb(t) nt tp-ršy ỉmy-ỉb n nb.f | ỉrr ḥsst nb.f dd nrw Ḥr m ḫ3św t | ỉnn ỉnwt n ḫkr-nśwt m ḫ3św t nb(t) ỉm3ḫw ḫr nṯr ῾3 | ḫtmty-bỉty śmr-w῾ty ẖry-ḥbt ỉmy-r3 ỉ῾3w Ḥrḫwf

an offering that the king gives and an offering that Anubis (gives), he who is upon his mountain, foremost of the god's booth, (consisting of) an invocation offering of bread and beer going forth to him in his tomb, house | in the necropolis, the count, overseer of Upper Egypt, sealer of the king of Lower Egypt, sole companion, lector priest, overseer of Egyptianized Nubians, Harkhuf | secretary of every word of the Southern Region, favorite of his lord | he who does what pleases his lord, who puts the fear of Horus into all foreign lands | who brings back the products and the royal ornament from all foreign lands, one honored before the great god | sealer of the king of Lower Egypt, sole companion, lector priest, overseer of Egyptianized Nubians, Harkhuf

12. **False door of Harkhuf (fig. 105)**

12.1 Lintel above the stele with offering table scene:

ḥtp dỉ nśwt ḥtp (dỉ) ỉnpw tpy-ḏw.f ḫnty sh-nṯr ỉmy wt | nb t3-ḏśr prt-ḫrw t ḥnḳt n śmr-w῾ty ẖry-ḥbt ỉmy-r3 ỉ῾3w ỉm3ḫw Ḥrḫwf

an offering that the king gives and an offering that Anubis (gives), he who is upon his mountain, foremost of the god's booth in the place of embalming | lord of the necropolis (consisting of) an invocation offering of bread and beer for the sole companion, lector priest, overseer of Egyptianized Nubians, honored one, Harkhuf

12.2 Left outer jamb:

ḥtp dỉ nśwt Wśỉr nb Ḏdw krśt.f m ẖr(t)-nṯr, Ḥrḫwf | ḥ3ty-῾ ỉmy-r3 šm῾w ḫtmty-bỉty śmr-w῾ty ẖry-ḥbt ỉmy-r3 ỉ῾3w Ḥrḫwf

an offering that the king gives and (an offering that) Osiris (gives), lord of Busiris, (may) his burying (be?) in the necropolis, Harkhuf | count, overseer of Upper Egypt, sealer of the king of Lower Egypt, sole companion, lector priest, overseer of Egyptianized Nubians, Harkhuf

12.3 Right outer jamb:

ḥtp dỉ nśwt ḥtp ỉnpw tpy-ḏw.f prt-ḫrw t ḥnḳt n.f m ỉs.f pr n ẖr(t)-nṯr | ḫtmty-bỉty, śmr-w῾ty, ẖry-ḥbt ỉmy-r3 ỉ῾3w ỉm3ḫw Ḥrḫwf

an offering that the king gives and an offering that Anubis (gives), he who is upon his mountain, (consisting of) an invocation offering of bread and beer for him in his tomb, house in the necropolis, sealer of the king of Lower Egypt, sole companion, lector priest, overseer of Egyptianized Nubians, honored one, Harkhuf

12.4 band under the stele with offering table scene:
śmr-wꜥty ẖry-ḥbt imy-rꜣ iꜥꜣw Ḥrḫwf
sole companion, lector priest, overseer of Egyptianized Nubians, Harkhuf

12.5 Middle left jamb:
ḥtp di nśwt prt-ḫrw t ḥnḳt n.f imꜣḫw ḫr Ptḥ-Skr | śmr-wꜥty ẖry-ḥbt imy-rꜣ iꜥꜣw Ḥrḫwf
an offering that the king gives (consisting of) an invocation offering of bread and beer to him, the one honored before Ptah-Sokar | sole companion, lector priest, overseer of Egyptianized Nubians, Harkhuf

12.6 Middle right jamb:
ḫtmty-bity śmr-wꜥty ẖry-ḥbt imy-rꜣ iꜥꜣw | imꜣḫw ḫr Ptḥ-Skr Ḥrḫwf
sealer of the king of Lower Egypt, sole companion, lector priest, overseer of Egyptianized Nubians | one honored before Ptah-Sokar, Harkhuf

12.7 both inner jambs:
sꜣ.f śmśw śmr-wꜥty ẖry-ḥbt imy-rꜣ iꜥꜣw Ḏmi rn.f nfr Mśni
his eldest son, sole companion, lector priest, overseer of Egyptianized Nubians, Djemi, whose good name is Mesni

13. **Subsidiary false door (fig. 106)**

13.1 lintel: *ḥtp di nśwt prt-ḫrw t ḥnḳt n śmr-wꜥty ẖry-ḥbt imy-rꜣ iꜥꜣw*
an offering that the king gives (consisting of) an invocation offering of bread and beer to the sole companion, lector priest, overseer of Egyptianized Nubians

13.2 left outer jamb: *Śꜣbn(i) rn.f nfr Ny-ꜥnḫ-ppy*
Sabni, whose good name is Nyankh-pepy

13.3 right outer jamb: *ḫtmty-bity śmr-wꜥty ẖry-ḥbt Śꜣbn(i)*
sealer of the king of Lower Egypt, sole companion, lector priest, Sabni

13.4 below stele: *śmr-wꜥty ẖry-ḥbt Śꜣbn(i)*
sole companion, lector priest, Sabni

13.5 left inner jamb: *imꜣḫw ḫr nṯr-ꜥꜣ Śꜣbn(i)*
honored before the great god, Sabni

13.6 right inner jamb: *im3ḫw ḫr Ptḥ Ś3bn(i)*
honored before Ptah, Sabni

13.7 offering figure left of false door:
śḏt śnṯr n k3 n nb pn ḥm-k3 ḥss n nb.f ʾIpy
burning incense for the *k3* of this lord, *ka*-priest, one favored by his lord, Ipy

Pepynakht Heqaib1 (35)

As in the tomb of Harkhuf, the façade of Pepynakht Heqaib1's tomb is inscribed with his lengthy autobiography. Edel et al., *Felsgräbernekropole,* I. Abteilung, Band 2, 682–69; Strudwick, *Texts from the Pyramid Age,* 333–5; Sethe, *Urkunden* I, 131–5.

1. **Lintel (fig. 109)**
   ḫnty-š sḫ3 n s3 Mn-ʿnḫ-Nfr-k3-Rʿ ḫtmty-bity śmr-wʿty imy-r3 iʿ3w Ḥḳ3ib | imy-r3 Mn-nfr-Ppy śmr-wʿty ḫry-ḥbt imy-r3 iʿ3w | inn ḫt ḫ3śwt n nb.f Ppynḫt | mty n s3 Ḫʿi-nfr-Mr-n-Rʿ | dd nrw m ḥr (m) ḫ3śwt im3ḫw Ḥḳ3ib
   land tenant and scribe of the phyle of the pyramid "Neferkare is established and living," sealer of the king of Lower Egypt, sole companion, overseer of Egyptianized Nubians, Heqaib | governor of the pyramid of " the perfection of Pepy is established," sole companion, lector priest, overseer of Egyptianized Nubians, he who brings products of the foreign land to his lord, Pepynakht | chief of the phyle of "Merenre's perfection shines," he who places the fear of Horus (in all) foreign lands, honored one, Heqaib
2. **South façade, inscription next to the relief figure of Pepynakht Heqaib (figs 109, 110)**
   ḫnty-š sḫ3 n s3 Mn-ʿnḫ-Nfr-k3-Rʿ śmr-wʿty Ḥḳ3ib | ḥ3ty-ʿ ḫtmty-bity śmr-wʿty ḫry-ḥbt imy-r3 ḫ3śwt | im3ḫw ḫr nṯr ʿ3 Ppy-nḫt
   land tenant and scribe of the phyle of the pyramid "Neferkare is established and living," sole companion, Heqaib | count, sealer of the king of Lower Egypt, sole companion, lector priest, overseer of foreign lands | one honored before the great god, Pepynakht
3. **North façade, inscription next to the relief figure of Pepynakht Heqaib (fig. 109)**
   ḥ3ty-ʿ ḫtmty-bity śmr-wʿty ḫry-ḥbt Ppy-nḫt | śmr-wʿty imy iś iry Nḫn ḥry-tp Nḫb imy-r3 iʿ3w Ḥḳ3ib

count, sealer of the king of Lower Egypt sole companion, lector priest, Pepynakht | sole companion, councillor and guardian of Nekhen (Hierakonpolis) overlord of El-Kab, overseer of Egyptianized Nubians, Heqaib

4. **East wall, south of door (fig. 113)**

   4.1 *ḥm.t-kꜣ Šdt*

   ka-priest(ess) Shedet

5. **East wall, north of door**

   This relief has suffered extensive damage; fragmentary inscriptions were recovered by the Bonn team.

   5.1 *ḥm-kꜣ n(y) śt-ib nb.f imꜣḫw ḫr nb.f 'Inhy*

   ka-priest, favorite of his lord, one honored before his lord, Inhy

   5.2 *ḫrp-sḥ imꜣḫw ḫr nb.f [ḥm-kꜣ ḥs] [y] nb[.f] mr[r] nb.f Śꜣbni rn.f [nfr 'Inh]y*

   director of the (food) hall, one honored before his lord, *ka*-priest, he who does what his lord praises, beloved by his lord, Sabni, his good name Inhy

   5.3 *'Idt (?) irr(t) ḥsst nb.ś (?) | ḥm.t-kꜣ [--] 'Idt*

   Idt, she who does what her lord praises, *ka*-priest, [–] Idt

6. **West wall, over shaft entrance, top panel (fig. 115, top)**

   6.1 *ḫrp-sḥ imy-rꜣ (?) Mḥśḥś*

   director of the (food) hall, overseer of (linen?), Meheshes

   6.2 *ḥm-kꜣ irr [ḥs]t Mry*

   ka-priest, he who is praised (?) Mery

   6.3 *imyt-rꜣ pr-šnʿ Mrit*

   overseer of the *per-shena*, Merit

   6.4 *'Ini*

   Ini

7. **West wall, over shaft entrance, bottom panel (fig. 115, bottom)**

   7.1 *ḫrp-sḥ ḥsy nb.f imꜣḫw Mry*

   director of the (food) hall, one praised by his lord, one honored, Mery

   7.2, 3, 4 no text

8. **West wall, right of false door (fig. 116)**

   8.1 *ḫrp-sḥ n(y) śt-ib nb.f Ny-bꜣ*

   director of the (food) hall, favorite of his lord, Ny-Ba

8.2 *Ḥtp-ty*
Hetepty
8.3 *s3t.ś śmśwt Śnti͗*
her eldest daughter Senti
8.4 *s3t.ś Śṯt-ḥtpy*
her daughter Setjet-hetepy

9. **Pillar 2 (fig. 117)**
no text
10. **False door**
no text

Pepynakht Heqaib2, 35d

FAÇADE

1. **Seated tomb owner approached by subsidiary figure.** Only traces of the outline of the tomb owner's head and shoulders remain visible; the texts were transcribed by the Bonn team.
   1.1 *i͗ry-pꜥt ḥ3ty-ꜥ ḫtmty-bi͗ty śmr-wꜥty ẖry-ḥbt i͗my-r3 ḫ3śwt Ḥḳ3i͗b*
   prince, count, sealer of the king of Lower Egypt, sole companion, lector priest, overseer of foreign lands, Heqaib
   1.2 *ḫrp-sḥ i͗my-r3 pr-šnꜥ Śd*
   director of the (food) hall, overseer of the *per shena*, Sed
2. **Panel of offering figures below tomb owner**
   2.1 small figure at front: no text
   2.2 large male figure: *i͗my-r3 pr-šnꜥ ḫrp-sḥ 3ḫ-ḥpi͗*
   overseer of the *per shena*, director of the (food) hall, Akh-hepy
   2.3 no text
   2.4 *ḥmt.f* [. . .] *ṯ*
   his wife, [. . .]tj
   2.5 *s3.f Ḥḳ3i͗b*
   his son, Heqaib
   2.6 *s3t.f Ḥst*
   his daughter, Heset
   2.7 *s3.f Ḥḳ3i͗b*
   his son, Heqaib
   2.8 *s3t.f Ṯ3wi͗*
   his daughter, Tjawi

Interior

South entrance thickness

3. **Top section (figs. 122, 123, 124)**

3.1 *sḥḏ ḥm(w)-nṯr Mn-nfr-Ppy Ḥḳ3ỉb | sḥḏ ḥm(w)-nṯr Ḫʿỉ-nfr-Mr-n-Rʿ Ḥḳ3ỉb | ḥ3ty-ʿ ḫtmty-bỉty smr-wʿty ḫry-ḥbt Ḥḳ3ỉb | ỉmy-r ḫ3swt ỉm3ḫw nṯr ʿ3 Ḥḳ3ỉb*

inspector of the *netjer*-priests of "the perfection of Pepy is established," Heqaib

inspector of the *netjer*-priests of "Mernere shines in perfection," Heqaib

count, sealer of the king of Lower Egypt, sole companion, lector priest, Heqaib

overseer of foreign lands, one honored (before?) the great god, Heqaib

3.2 *ỉmy-r3 ḥm(w)-k3 n(y) ḏt.f ỉmy-r3 šśr ḫtmw Śntỉ*

overseer of *ka*-priests of his funerary estate, overseer of linen, sealer, Senti

4. **Bottom section (fig. 122, 123, 125)**

4.1 *ḥ3ty-ʿ ḫtmty-bỉty smr-wʿty ḫry-ḥbt ỉmy-r3 ỉʿ3w Ḥḳ3ỉb | ỉm3ḫw ḫr Wsỉr Ppy-nḫt*

count, sealer of the king of Lower Egypt, sole companion, lector priest, overseer of Egyptianized Nubians, Heqaib | one honored before Osiris, Pepynakht

4a. **Offerers a, top register behind bottom figure of Pepynakht Heqaib2 (fig. 131)**

4a.1 *ỉm3ḫw ḫr nṯr ʿ3 ḫrty-nṯr Mśnỉ*

one honored before the great god, stonemason, Mesni

For stonemason title, see Jones, *Index* vol. 2, 793, #2894

4a.2 *ḥmt.f mrt Ḥnwt*

his wife beloved, Henut (or his wife Mery-Henut)

4a.3 *s3t.f mrt.f | ʾIn-nfrt*

his daughter his beloved, Innefret

4b. **Offerers b: bottom register behind the bottom figure of the tomb owner (fig. 132)**

4b.1 *ḥm-k3 ḥry-ḫnt ỉm3ḫw Šm3ỉ | ỉrr ḥsst nb.f mrr(w) nb.f Šm3ỉ*

ka-priest who is head of (i.e., in charge of) the *khent*-box, one honored, Shemai | one who does what his lord praises, beloved of his lord, Shemai

4b.2 *s3.f Ḥḳ3ib*

his son, Heqaib

4c. **Offerer c, in front of Pepynakht Heqaib2, top figure (fig. 126)**

Ḥḳ3ib | ḥm-k3 ḥry-ḫnt mty n s3 ỉrr mrrt nb.f

Heqaib | *ka*-priest who is head of the *khent*, controller of the phyle, he does what his lord loves

4d. **Offerer d, in front of Pepynakht Heqaib2, middle figure (fig. 127)**

ỉmy-r3 ỉswt Ḥtpy

overseer of crews, Hetepy

4e. **Offerer e, in front of Pepynakht Heqaib2, bottom figure, front (fig. 128)**

ỉmy-r3 mś (?) tpy-ʿ r (?) ỉw (tpʿrw?)

overseer of? head of? Iw/Teparw?

4f. **Offerer f, in front of Pepynakht Heqaib2, bottom, rear, under text column (fig. 129)**

ḫrp-sḥ Ḥḳ3ibỉ

director of the (food) hall, Heqaib(i)

4g. **Offerer g, on outer edge, top (fig. 130)**

mrr nb.f ḥss nb.f ḫrp-sḥ Nfr-ʿnỉ (?)

the one who his lord loves, the one who his lord praises, director of the (food) hall, Nefer-any

4h. **Offerer h, on outer edge, bottom**

ḫrp sḥ mrr nb.f św-tp?

director of the food hall, beloved of his lord, Sw-tp? name unclear

North Thickness

5. **Top register (figs. 122, 123, 133)**

5.1 Pepynakht Heqaib

ḥ3ty-ʿ ḫtmty-bỉty śmr-wʿty ḫry-ḥbt | ỉm3ḫw ḫr nṯr ʿ3 nb pt ỉmy-r3 ḫ3śwt Ḥḳ3ib

count, sealer of the king of Lower Egypt, sole companion, lector priest, one honored before the great god, lord of the sky, overseer of foreign lands, Heqaib

5.2 Son

s3.f mry.f ḫtmty-bỉty śmr-wʿty | ḫry-ḥbt ỉm3ḫw ḫr nṯr ʿ3 Nynwnbt (?)

his son, his beloved, sealer of the king of Lower Egypt, sole companion | lector priest, one honored before the great god, Nynw-nebet (?)

5.3 *ḥm-kꜣ ꜥnw*

ka-priest, Anu

6. **Middle register (figs. 122, 123, 134)**

6.1 *ḥꜣty-ꜥ mꜣꜥ ḫtmty-bỉty śmr-wꜥty | ỉmy-rꜣ ỉꜥꜣw Ppy-nḫt rn.f nfr Ḥḳꜣỉb*

count, sealer of the king of Lower Egypt, sole companion, overseer of Egyptianized Nubians, Pepynakht, his good name Heqaib

6.2 *ḫtmty ỉmy-rꜣ śšr ꜥnḫ.n.f*

sealer, overseer of linen, Ankhenef

6.3 *ḥm kꜣ [ḫrp-sḥ] Šmꜣỉ*

ka-priest [director of the (food) hall] Shemai

Cracks in the wall surface have eroded the *ḫrp-sḥ* title, but it was visible when Edel worked in the tomb.

7. **Bottom register (figs 122, 123, 135)**

ḥꜣty-ꜥ ỉmy ỉs mnỉw Nḫn ḥry-tp Nḫb śmr-wꜥty ẖry-ḥbt Ḥḳꜣỉb | ỉmꜣḫw ḫr nṯr ꜥꜣ nb pt Ppy-nḫt

count, councillor and guardian of Nekhen, overlord of El Kab, sole companion, lector priest, Heqaib | one honored before the great god, lord of the sky, Pepynakht

7a. **Bottom register, offerer a, behind Pepynakht Heqaib2, top (fig. 138)**

ỉmy-r pr-šnꜥ Ḏb

overseer of the *per shena*, Djeb (name not certain)

7b. **Bottom register, offerers 7b, behind Pepynakht Heqaib2, middle (fig. 136)**

7b.1 *sḥy-nṯr śḥḏ wt(yw) ỉmꜣsw ḫr nṯr <ꜥꜣ> | Ḫnw ỉrr ḥsst nb.f rꜥ nb*

he who belongs to the divine booth (of Anubis), inspector of embalmers (OR inspector of embalmers in the divine booth of Anubis/place of embalming), one honored by the great god, Khenu, he who does what pleases his lord every day

7b.2 *ḥry sꜣṯ ʾImpy*

libationer, Impy

7c. **Bottom register, offerer 7c, behind Pepynakht Heqaib2, bottom (fig. 137)**

ḫrp-sḥ śḥḏ ḥm(w)-kꜣ ḥssy n nb.f ỉrr mrrt nb.f Š[mꜣỉ]

director of the (food) hall, inspector of *ka*-priests, the one praised by his lord, he who does what his lord loves, Shemai

7d. **Bottom register offerer 7d, in front of Pepynakht Heqaib2, top (fig. 139)**
ẖry-tp nśwt n pr-ꜥꜣ i̓my-rꜣ pr Ḥḳꜣi̓b rn.f nfr Sni̓
royal chamberlain of the great house, overseer of the estate, Heqaib, his good name Seni

7e. **Bottom register, offerer 7e, in front of Pepynakht Heqaib2, middle (fig. 140, top)**
ḥm-kꜣ ḥry-ẖnt Ḥḳꜣi̓b(i̓)
ka-priest who is head of (in charge of) the *khent*-box, Heqaib(i)

7f. **Bottom register offerer 7f, in front of Pepynakht Heqaib2, bottom (fig. 140, bottom)**
ẖrp-sḥ Šmꜣi̓
director of the (food) hall, Shemai

7g. **Bottom register offerer 7g, in front of Pepynakht Heqaib2, along outer edge, top**
ḥm-kꜣ ḥry ẖnt šmꜣi̓
ka-priest who is in charge of the *khent*-box, Shemai

7h. **Bottom register offerer 7h, in front of Pepynakht Heqaib2, along outer edge, bottom (fig. 141)**
ẖrp śh mrrw nb.(f) ḥsy n.f Ḥḳꜣi̓b ꜥnw.f (?)
director of the (food) hall, he who is beloved of his lord, praised by his lord, Hekaib Anwef (?)

East Wall, South half

8. **Panel A (figs. 142, 144)**
Long text across the top
i̓r ḥm-kꜣ nb i̓m.n i̓i̓i̓.ty.fy ḥr wꜣt tn m i̓mi̓ śꜣ i̓ś pn <n> Ḥḳꜣ-i̓ṯi̓.f n.f ẖpš
Each *ka*-priest of us who comes this way as a phyle-member of the tomb of Heqa<ib> may take the cattle-legs to which he is entitled.
   8.1 *ḥm-kꜣ Šmꜣi̓*
   ka-priest Shemai
   8.2 *ẖrp-sḥ Šmꜣi̓*
   director of the (food) hall, Shemai

9. **Panel B**
   9.1 *ẖrp-sḥ śḥḏ n sꜣ Šmꜣi̓*
   director of the (food) hall, inspector of the phyle, Shemai
   9.2 *ẖtmtyt Ḥrb-i̓ši̓ (?)*
   sealer, Hereb-ishy (?)

9.3 *sꜣt.ś mrt Ḥst*
her daughter, beloved, Heset (or Meret-Heset)

10. **Panel C (fig. 143)**
    10.1 no text
    10.2 *mty n sꜣ imy is Ny-bꜣ/ẖnmw*
    controller of the phyle in the tomb, Ny-ba (or Ny-Khnum)
    10.3 *ḥm-kꜣ ḥsw nb.f irr ḥsst nb.f Ny-bꜣ/ẖnmw*
    ka-priest, praised by his lord, he who does what his lord praises, Ny-ba (or Ny-Khnum)
    10.4 *ẖrp-sḥ mry nb.f irr ḥsst nb.f imꜣḫw Ny-bꜣ/ẖnmw*
    director of the (food) hall, beloved of his lord, the one who his lord praised, one honored, Ny-Ba (or Ny-Khnum)
11. **Panel D (fig. 143)**
    Long text over top:
    ẖrp-sḥ ḥsy n nb.f śḥḏ n sꜣ mrr(w) imy-rꜣ rmṯw.f nfr ꜥnwy?
    director of the (food) hall, praised by his lord, inspector of the phyle, one who is beloved, overseer of people/workers, Nefer-anwy
    "Overseer of workers" does not appear in Jones, but Seyfried concurs.
    11.1 *ḥm-kꜣ Nfr-ꜥnwy*
    ka-priest, Nefer-anwy
    11.2 *ḥm-kꜣ Nfr-ꜥnwy irr ḥsst nb.f rꜥ nb*
    ka-priest Nefer-anwy, he who does what his lord praises every day
    11.3 *imy-rꜣ sꜣ irr ḥsst nb(.f) imy-rꜣ rmṯw*
    overseer of the phyle, he who does what his lord praises, overseer of people/workers
12. **Panel E (fig. 143)**
    Framing text:
    ẖrp-sḥ irr ḥsst irr ḥsst imy-rꜣ rmṯw Šmꜣi | śḥḏ n sꜣ irr ḥsst nb.f Šmꜣi
    director of the (food) hall, he who does what is praiseworthy (2X?), overseer of people/workers, Shemai | inspector of the phyle, he who does what his lord praises, Shemai
    12.1 *imy-rꜣ sꜣ m is.f Šmꜣi*
    overseer of the phyle in his tomb, Shemai
    12.2 (figure is erased, presume some titles from frame referred to him?)
    12.3 *ḥm-kꜣ 'Immi*
    ka-priest Imemy

13. **Panel F (fig. 146)**

13.1 *s3b imy-r3 sẖ3 | imy-r3 pr irr ḥsst nb.f rꜥ nb W3ḏ (?)*
overseer of scribes of the judiciary, overseer of the estate, he who does what his lord praises every day, Wadj (?)

13.2 *ḫtmty(t) irr ḥsst nb.ś rꜥ nb (t?) Rꜥbeś?*
sealer, she who does what her lord praises every day, Rabes (?)

13.3 *imy-r3 pr sẖ3 'Ii-n-ḫnt*
overseer of the estate, scribe, Iienkhent

13.4 *sẖ3 Ś3bni*
scribe, Sabni

13.5 unreadable

14. **Panel G (fig. 147)**

14.1 *ḫrp-sḥ ḥs(w).n nb.f irr ḥsst nb.f rꜥ nb ḥsy.f ḥm-k3 ḥry-ḫnt imy-ib n nb.f im3ḫw ḫr nb.f Smn-'Imi | mry nb.f Śmn-imy | di.f śnṯr*
director of the (food) hall, the one whom his lord favored, he who does what his lord favors every day, his favored one | *ka*-priest who is head of (in charge of) the *khent*-box, favorite of his lord, one honored before his lord, Semenimy | beloved of his lord Semenimy | he gives incense

14.2 *s3.f śmśw mry.f 'Ii-n-ḫnt.i*
his eldest son, his beloved, Iienkhenti

14.3 *ḥmt.f mnꜥt(?) W3ḏ-k3w.ś | imyt-ib n nb.ś ḥsyt.f W3ḏ-k3w.ś*
his wife, wet nurse (?) Wadj-kawes, favorite of her lord, the one whom he praised, Wadj-kawes

14.4 *s3t.ś mryt.ś ḫtmty Nb...?*
her dꜥughter, her beloved, śeꜥler, Neb? (Nefer-ꜥnket?)

14.5 *s3.ś mry.ś Ḥḳ3ibi*
her śon, her beloved, ḥeḳꜥibi

14.6 *'Ii-n-ḫnti*
'Iienkhenti

East wall, north half

15a. **Panel I, right half (fig. 149, right)**

15a.1 *imy-r śšr ṯp-ꜥrw*
overseer of linen, Teparw

15a.2 *ḥmt.f Rry (?)*
his wife, Rery (?)

15b. **Panel I, left half (fig. 149, left)**

15b.1 *ḫtmtyt P* (?)
sealer, P? (name unclear)

15b.2 *s3* (*.ś?*) *Śtkỉ* (?)
(her?) daughter, Setki/ her daughter Ki?

16. **Panel H/J (fig. 150)**

16.1 *ḥm-k3 ỉrr ḥsst nb.f Ny-b3*
ka-priest, he who does what his lord favors, Ny-ba

16.2 (woman below) *ḥmt.f Nb* (?)
his wife, Neb–? (name unclear)

16.3 *s3.f ḫrp-sḥ Ḥḳ3ỉb*
his son, director of the (food) hall, Heqaib

16.4 *Ś3bnỉ*
Sabni

16.5 *s3t.f Wỉ*
his daughter Wi

16.6 *Ḥśtỉ*
Heseti

16.7 *ỉmyt-r3 pr-šnʿ Ḥnwt*
overseer of the *per shena*, Henut

17. **Panel K (fig. 151)**

17.1 *ỉmy-r3 pr-šnʿ ỉrr ḥss*(*t*) *nb.f Ḏw-śn?*
overseer of the *per shena*, he who does what his lord praises, Djewsen?

17.2 *ỉmy-r3 ỉswt Ḥḳ3ỉb*
overseer of crews, Heqaib

17.3 *śṯw*
libationer? or Setjew (name?)

17.4 *ḫtmtyt Ḥśt*
sealer, Heset

17.5 *ḫtmtyt Mrty*
sealer Merty

18. **Panel L**

18.1 *sḫ3 ỉmy-r3 pr ỉmy-ỉb nb.f ỉrr ḥsst nb.f ỉm3ḫw ʾIdy*
scribe, overseer of the estate, favorite of his lord, honored, Idy

18.2 *ḥmt.f ʾI3śt*
his wife, Iaset

19. **Panel M (fig. 152)**

19.1 *s3.f Ḥḳ3ỉb*
his son Heqaib

19.2 *ḫrp-sḥ ḥm-kꜣ ỉrr ḥss(t) nb.f ꜥnw*
director of the (food) hall, *ka*-priest, he who does what his lord favors, Anu

19.3 *ḥm kꜣ ꜥnw*
ka-priest, Anu

19.4 *sꜣ.f Śꜣbnỉ*
his son, Sabni

19.5 *ḫtmtyt ḥmt.f Nfr-pnt*
sealer, his wife, Nefer-penet (?)

19.6 *ꞽntỉ*
Inty

19.7 *ḫtmtyt (ꜥr?)-mrt*
sealer, Ar-Meret

20. **Panel N (fig. 153)**

20.1 *ḫrp-sḥ sḥḏ ḥm(w)-kꜣ | ỉr(w) ḥsst nb.f ḥḥw*
director of the (food) hall, inspector of *ka*-priests | he who does what his lord favors, Hehu

20.2 *ḫtmtyt Nfr-wꜥwt*
sealer, Neferwawet

21. **Panel O (fig. 154)**

21.1 *ḫry-tp nśwt n pr ꜥꜣ ỉmy-rꜣ pr Ḥḳꜣỉb rn.f nfr Śnỉ*
royal chamberlain of the great house, overseer of the estate, Heqaib, beautiful name, Seni

21.2 *ḥmt.f Nś-ptḥ rn.ś nfr M-ꜥnḳt (?)*
his wife, Nes-Ptah, beautiful name, M-anket?

21.3 *sꜣ.f mry.f sḫꜣ Ḥḳꜣỉb*
his son, his beloved, scribe, Heqaib

21.4 *sꜣt.f Nfr-(ꜥnw?)*
his daughter, Nefer-anw (?)

Pillar 2/west wall

22. **Pillar 2, north face, partially covered by later wall (fig. 121)**

22.1 *ḫry-tp nśwt n pr ꜥꜣ ỉmy-rꜣ pr Ḥḳꜣỉb rn.f nfr Śnỉ*
royal chancellor of the great house, overseer of the estate, Heqaib, whose good name is Seni

22.2 *ḥmt.f*
his wife

22.3 *sꜣt.f mrt.f Nfr-ꜥnw*
his daughter his beloved Nefer-anw

22.4 *sꜣ.f*
his son

23. **East face, top (scene now lost)**

23.1 *ỉmy-rꜣ śšr ḫtmty štꜣ (?)*
overseer of linen, sealer, Sheta (?)

23.2 *śš Mḳꜣib*
scribe Heqaib

23.3 *ḥm.t.f śbk?*
his wife, Sobek...?

23.4 *sꜣ.t.ś?-ś-ḥtp?*
her daughter, ?-s-hetep?

23.5 *sꜣ.t.ś M...?*
her daughter, M?

24, 24a. **Panel P/Pa, middle of pillar, two registers, top = a, (fig. 156)**

24a.1 *śšmty (? mḏḥ?) [ỉrr ḥsst nb.f] Śnỉ*
butcher? carpenter? he who does what his lord favors, Seni
no other texts

25 **Panel Q, right side of pillar, east face, top**

25.1 *ḥry p-d-ś* (?)
undecipherable

25.2 *Ṯśr* (?)
Tjeser (name?)

26. **Panel R, right side of pillar, east face, bottom (fig. 157)**
No surviving text

27. **Panel S, west wall of passageway to 35e, south (fig. 158)**

27.1 *ỉry bdt (?) Kʿrỉ/ Kʿwrỉ?*
keeper of emmer (?) Kawri? Kari

27.2 *Wśr*
Weser

27.3 *ʾInt*
Int

27.4 *ʾIkỉwỉ*
Ikiwi?

27.5 *ʾIptỉ*
Ipty

28. **Panel T, west wall of passageway to 35e, north (fig. 159)**

28.1 *sꜣ.f Śn-rḥwy*
his son, Senrehwy

28.2 *ḫrp-sḥ ỉrr ḥsst nb.f Śd(ỉ)*
director of the (food) hall, he who does what his lord favors, Sedi

28.3 *ḥm.t.f Mn-nfr-Ppy*
his wife, Mennefer-Pepy

28.4 *Mn-nfr-Ppy*
Mennefer-Pepy

28.5 *sꜣt.ś Ḫwy*
her daughter, Khui

28.6 *sꜣt.ś Kwty*
her daughter, Kwti

28.7 *Kwty*
Kewti

28.8 *ʿnḫy*
Ankhy

28.9 *rḫ ỉb ʿrft*
?

28.10 *Śḫmn*
Sekhemen

28.11 *ʿnḫy*
Ankhi

28.12 *ʿnḫy*
Ankhi

28.13 *Ỉw-nbw*
Iw-nebw

28.14 *Nfr-mśnt*
Nefer-mesnet (?)

28.15 *Mśnỉ*
Mesni

28.16 *Nbw* (?)
Nebw

29. **False door, no texts remain (fig. 120)**

30. **False door niche, south wall**
ḫrp-sḥ n(y) śt-ỉb nb.f ỉrt kꜣ nt Ḥḳꜣỉb rʿ nb Šmꜣỉ
director of the (food) hall, favorite of his lord, he who makes the food of Heqaib every day, Shemai

Sabni2 (35e)

FAÇADE

1. **Lintel panel (figs. 162, 163)**
   Text across bottom of panel:
   ḥȝty-ꜥ ḫtmty-bỉty wḥm mdw (n) Ḥr dd nrw m ḫȝśwt n nb.f Ḥr Śȝbnỉ
   count, sealer of the king of Lower Egypt, he who repeats the word of Horus, he who puts the fear of Horus into the foreign lands, Sabni
   - 1.1 Left side figure of Sabni
     (top) *ḥȝty-ꜥ mꜥȝ ḫtmty-bỉty śmr-wꜥty ẖry-ḥbt ỉnn ḫr(w)t ḫȝśwt nb.f* | *ỉmȝḫw ḫr* [. . .] *Śȝbnỉ*
     true count, sealer of the king of Lower Egypt, sole companion, lector priest, he who brings all foreign products to his lord | one honored before [. . .] Sabni
   - 1.2 right side figure of Sabni
     ḥȝty-ꜥ ḫtmty-bỉty śmr-wꜥty ỉmy-rȝ ỉꜥȝw [*ḥry śšt*]*ȝ nb.f ỉmȝḫw ḫr ỉnpw Śȝbnỉ*
     count, sealer of the king of Lower Egypt, sole companion, overseer of Egyptianized Nubians, secretary? of his lord, one honored before Anubis, Sabni
   - 1.3 *ḫtmtyt Ḥst*
     sealer, Heset
   - 1.4 *śḥḏ ḥm(w)-kȝ ḫrp-sḥ ỉrr ḥsst nb.f Mmỉ*
     inspector of *ka*-priests, director of the (food) hall, he who does what his lord favors, Memi
   - 1.5 *śḥḏ ḥm(w)-kȝ ḫrp-sḥ ỉrr ḥsst nb.f Dwȝ-Śbk*
     inspector of *ka*-priests, director of the (food) hall, he who does what his lord favors, Dwa-Sobek
   - 1.6 *ḫtmtyt Śnt-rꜥw* (?)
     sealer Senet-raw
2. **East jamb, top panel (fig. 264)**
   - 2.1 Two columns of text filling most of the jamb:
     ḥtp dỉ nśwt ỉnpw prt-ḫrw t ḥnḳt n śḥḏ ḥm(w)-nṯr Mn-nfr-Ppy | *ḥtp dỉ nśwt Wśỉr prt-ḫrw t ḥnḳt n śḥḏ ḥm(w)-nṯr Ḫꜥỉ-nfr-Mr-n-Rꜥ* | *ḥȝty-ꜥ ḫtmty-bỉty śmr-wꜥty Śȝbnỉ*
     An offering that the king gives and (an offering that) Anubis (gives), (consisting of) an invocation offering of bread and beer for the inspector of *netjer*-priests of the pyramid

"Pepy's perfection is established," an offering that the king gives and (an offering that) Osiris (gives), to the inspector of *netjer*-priests of the pyramid "Merenra shines in beauty/ perfection" | count, sealer of the king of Lower Egypt, sole companion, Sabni

2.2 *ỉmy-r3 ḥm(w)-k3 m ỉs pw ḫtmty Śnỉ*
overseer of *ka*-priests in this tomb, sealer, Seni

3. **East jamb, bottom panel**
ỉmy-r3 ḥm(w)-k3 m ỉs pw ḫtmw n(y) śt-ỉb nb.f ỉm3ḫw ḫr nb.f Śnỉ
overseer of *ka*-priests in this tomb, sealer, favorite of his lord, one honored before his lord, Seni

4. **West jamb**
ḥ3ty-ʿ ḫtmty-bỉty śmr-wʿty ḫry-ḥbt ỉmy-r3 ḫ3św̓t ỉm3ḫw Ś3bnỉ
count, sealer of the king of Lower Egypt, sole companion, lector priest, overseer of foreign lands, one honored, Sabni

5. **West wall, north end, top (fig. 65)**
Two columns of text
ḥ3ty-ʿ ḫtmty-bỉty ỉmy-r3 šmʿw śmr-wʿty ḫry-ḥbt ḥry-tp ʿ3 n nśwt (n) | ỉmy-r3 pr-šnʿ(w) m Nḫb mḥ-[ỉb] n nśwt n tp-rśy Ś3bnỉ
count, sealer of the king of Lower Egypt, overseer of Upper Egypt, sole companion, lector priest, great overlord of the king, overseer of the *per-shena* of Nekheb, confidant of the king in the Head of the South, Sabni
small dog under chair of Sabni: *Śbn-nb.f šʿbnỉ ỉs hỉs lqrd*

6. **West wall, north end, bottom panel (fig. 166)**

6.1 *s3.f Ś3bnỉ*
his son, Sabni

6.2 *ỉmy-r3 ḥm(w)-k3 n(y) śt-ỉb nb.f Śnỉ*
overseer of *ka*-priests, favorite of his lord, Seni

6.3 text lost to damage

6.4 *ḥmt.f W3ḏw-k3w.ś*
his wife, Wadjkawes

6.5 *s3t.ś*
her daughter

6.6 *s3t.f Ktw*
his daughter, Ketew

7. **West wall, middle section (fig. 167)**

7.1 *ḥ3ty-ʿ ỉmy-r3 šmʿw ḫtmty-bỉty smr-wʿty ḫry-ḥbt ỉmy-r3 ḫ3swt n(y) śt-ỉb nb.f Ś3bnỉ* count, overseer of Upper Egypt, sealer of the king of Lower Egypt, sole companion, lector priest, overseer of foreign lands, favorite of his lord, Sabni

7.2 *ḫrp-sḥ ḥm-kꜣ n(y) śt-ib nb.f ḥḥw*
director of the (food) hall, *ka*-priest, favorite of his lord, Hehu

8. **West wall, south section, top panel (fig. 168, top)**

8.1 *sꜣt.f Nfr-ḥswy.t*
his daughter, Nefer-hesewyt

8.2 *ḥmt.f ḫtmtyt Nfr-wꜥwt*
his wife, sealer, Nefer-wawet

8.3, 8.4 *sꜣ.f Ḥḳꜣib*
his son, Heqaib

8.5, 8.6 *sꜣt.f Ḥst*
his daughter, Heset

8.7 *sꜣt.f Tꜥwi (?)*
his daughter, Tawi

9. **West wall, south section, bottom panel (fig. 168, bottom)**

9.1 *imy-rꜣ iswt ꞽIi-n-ḫnt*
overseer of crews, Iienkhent

9.2 *ḥmt.f ḫtmtyt* []
his wife, sealer

9.3 *sꜣ.ś sꜣb sḫꜣ Śꜣbni*
her son, juridicial scribe, Sabni

9.4 *ḥmt.f mrt.f Śṯt-ḥtp*
his wife, his beloved, Setjet Hetep

Interior chapel program
East entrance thickness

10. **East thickness, main figure (figs. 173, 174)**
ḫtmty-bity śmr-wꜥty imy-rꜣ iꜥꜣw ḫry-ḥbt imꜣḫw ḫr Ḫnmw Śꜣbni | ḥꜣty-ꜥ ḫtmty-bity śmr-wꜥty imꜣḫw ḫr ꞽInpw Śꜣbni
sealer of the king of Lower Egypt, sole companion, overseer of Egyptianized Nubians, lector priest, one honored before Khnum, Sabni | count, sealer of the king of Lower Egypt, sole companion, one honored before Anubis, Sabni

10a. **East thickness, offerer 10a, in front of Sabni2, top**
imy-rꜣ śšr Śni
overseer of linen, Seni

10b. **East thickness, offerer 10b, in front of Sabni2, middle (fig. 277, right)**
ḫrp-sḥ Šmꜣi͗
director of the (food) hall, Shemai

10c. **East thickness, offerer 10c, in front of Sabni2, middle (fig. 277, right)**
ḫrp-sḥ Dwꜣ-Śbk
director of the (food) hall, Dwa-Sobek

10d. **East thickness, offerer 10d, in front of Sabni, at his feet (fig. 175)**
ẖkrt-nśwt wꜥtt Ḫꜥi͗-nfri͗
sole ornamented one of the king, Khai-Nefri

10e. **East thickness, offerer 10e, behind Sabni, bottom register, front (fig. 176)**
sꜣt.f mrt.f špśt nśwt Mri͗t
his daughter, his beloved, noblewoman of the king, Merit

10f. **East thickness, offerers 10f.1–11, registers behind Sabni (figs. 174, 176)**
top register
10f.1 *ḫrp-sḥ Ḥḳꜣi͗b*
director of the (food) hall, Heqaib
10f.2 *ḫrp-sḥ Mmi͗*
director of the (food) hall, Memi
10f.3 no text?
10f.4 *ḫrp-sḥ ꜣḫi͗*
director of the (food) hall, Akhi
middle register
10f.5 *śḥḏ wt(yw) Ḥḳꜣi͗b*
inspector of embalmers, Heqaib
10f.6 *ḥḳꜣ-ḥwt śmr i͗my-rꜣ pr ꞽI͗-n-ḫnt*
chief of the estate, companion, overseer of the estate, Iienkhent
10f.7 *sḫꜣ Śbk-ḥtp*
scribe Sobek-hetep
10f.8 *ḫtmty ꞽIti͗*
sealer Iti

bottom register, behind 10e
10f.9 *śwnw pr ꜥꜣ ꞽIdw*
physician of the palace, Idu

10f.10 *s3b imy-r3 sḫ3 W3ši*
overseer of scribes of the judiciary, Washi
10f.11 *ḫrp-sḥ Mry*
director of the (food) hall, Mery

11. **East thickness, below main scene**
 11.1 *Rdw (rdiw?)*
 Redew/Rediw
 11.2 *ḥry ś3ṯ Nfr-nb?*
 libationer, Nefer-neb
 11.3 *Ḥḳ3ib*
 Heqaib
 11.4 *ḥmt.f imy(t)-r3 pr-šnʿ Śmt-?*
 his wife, overseer of the *per-shena*, Semet-?
 11.5 *Tfrti?*
 Teferti?
 11.6 *iry ḫt (?)*
 custodian?
12. **West entrance thickness, main (figs. 169, 170)**
 12.1 autobiographical text
 ḥ3ty-ʿ śmr-wʿty wḥm-mdw n Ḥr n šmśw.f 3mʿt m Ḥr m ḫ3śwt iw ḥb.n.(i) ḥm n nb(.i) r irt wśḫwy ʿ3wy | m w3w3t r śḫd.t tḫnwy ʿ3wy r 'Iwnw. iw pr.kwi r w3w3t ḥnʿ ṯśwt nt mšʿ 5 iw iʿ3w śḥtp(w).n.(i) ḥr imntt i3btt nt w3w3t r in.t ṯśwt n mšʿ(t) | m ḥtp nn sp di(.i) iti ṯbt p3t nt.i iw ir.n wśḫtwy (tn) r ḥst wi ḥm n nb(.i) Ḥr ink 3ḫ iḳrt rḫ r3.f iw rḫ.kwi r n iʿ n nṯr ʿ3 nb pt.
 count, sole companion, he who repeats the word of Horus to his followers, the jaw (speaker) of Horus in the foreign countries: His Presence my lord sent (me) to build two great boats/barges | in Wawat to send downstream two great obelisks to Heliopolis. I went to Wawat together with five troops of the army. The Egyptianized foreigners (*iʿ3w*) I pacified were on the west and east sides of Wawat (i.e., banks) to bring back the troops of the army | in peace (i.e., safely). Never did I allow to be taken a sandal or a loaf of a man. I made these two barges (so that) his Presence my lord Horus praised me. I am an effective spirit who knows his spells. I know the spell of ascending to the great god lord of the sky.
 framing titles

ḥꜣty-ꜥ ḫtmty-bἰty śmr-wꜥty ἰmy-rꜣ ἰꜥꜣw ḥry śštꜣ n rꜣ-ꜥꜣ rśy Śꜣbnἰ | ḫtmty-bἰty ἰmꜣḫw ḫr nṯr ꜥꜣ nb pt Śꜣbnἰ

count, sealer of the king of Lower Egypt, sole companion, overseer of Egyptianized Nubians, keeper of the secrets of the doorway of the south, Sabni | sealer of the King of Lower Egypt, one honored before the great god, lord of the sky, Sabni

virtues text: along the top of the frame, underneath it in the field with the images

ἰw rdἰ.n(.ἰ) t n ḥḳr ḥ(b)ś n ḥꜣyw ἰw ḏꜣ.n(,ἰ) wn ἰw m ḥꜥw(.ἰ) n sp ἰtἰ ḫ(w)t n(t) rmṯw nn-sp śꜣr(.ἰ) rmṯ nb ḫr ἰšt.f

I gave bread to the hungry, clothing to the naked. I ferried those who were boatless in my boat. Never did I take things of any person, I never deprived a man of his possessions.

12a. **West thickness, offerer 12a, in front of Sabni, top**

ḫrp-sḥ Ḥḳꜣἰb

director of the (food) hall, Heqaib

12b. **West thickness, offerer 12c, in front of Sabni, middle**

ḫrp-sḥ Dwꜣ-Śbk

director of the (food) hall, Dwa-Sobek

12c. **West thickness, offerer 12c, in front of Sabni, at his feet (fig. 172)** (at Sabni's feet)

ḫrp-sḥ Ḥḳꜣἰb

director of the (food) hall, Heqaib

12d. **West. thickness, offerers 12d, 1–15, registers behind Sabni (fig. 170)**

top register

12d.1 *ḫrp-sḥ Ḥḳꜣἰb*

director of the (food) hall, Heqaib

12d.2 *sꜣb ἰmy-rꜣ sḫꜣ ꜥnwἰ*

overseer of scribes of the judiciary, Anwi

12d.3 *ḫtmty Rwdἰ*

sealer, Rewdi

12d.4 *ἰmy-rꜣ śšr Ḥn(ḥn)w?*

overseer of linen, Henu (Henhenu?)

12d.5 *sḫꜣ Ḥḳꜣἰb*

scribe Heqaib

middle register

12d.6 *ḫrp-sḥ Šmꜣỉ*
director of the (food) hall, Shemai

12d.7 *ỉmy-rꜣ śšr Nḥry*
overseer of linen, Nehery

12d.8 *ḫrp-sḥ Ḥḳꜣib*
director of the (food) hall, Heqaib

12d.9 *Ḥpỉ*
Hepi

12d.10 *ꜣṯw*
Atju

bottom register

12d.11 *ẖrty-nṯr Ḥḳꜣib*
stonemason Heqaib

12d.12 *śmr ṯsy / ṯs ḥḳꜣỉ* (?)
companion, Tjesy/Tjes-Heqi?

12d.13 *ẖrty-nṯr Ḥḳꜣib*
stonemason Heqaib

12d.14 *ỉmy-rꜣ pr-šnʿ ꜣḫ-ḥpỉ*
overseer of the *per shena*, Akh-hepi

12d.15 *Ḥwy*
Hwy

13. **West thickness, below main scene (fig. 170, bottom)**
ỉmy-rꜣ ṯs(w)t ʾIi-nfr
overseer of herds, Ii-nefer

Main chapel

14. **East wall, fishing and fowling scene (fig. 180)**

14.1 Text center to left, over fisher
ḥtp dỉ nśwt prt-ḫrw t ḥnḳt n ḥꜣty-ʿ śmr-wʿty Śꜣbnỉ
an offering that the king gives (consisting of) an invocation offering of bread and beer to the count, sole companion, Sabni

14.2 Text center to right, over fowler
ḥtp dỉ nśwt prt-ḫrw t ḥnḳt n ḥꜣty-ʿ Śꜣbnỉ
an offering that the king gives (consisting of) an invocation offering of bread and beer to the count, Sabni

14.3 Seated woman behind fisher (left)
sꜣt.f mrt.f Ḫʿi-nfrỉ
his daughter, his beloved, Khai-nefri

14.4 Seated woman behind fowler (right)
špśt nśwt Śntỉ
noblewoman of the king, Senti

14.5 Priest in front of fisher
ỉmy-rꜣ ḥm(w)-kꜣ ỉmy-rꜣ śšr ḫtmw n(y) śt-ib nb.f Śnỉ
overseer of *ka*-priests, overseer of linen, sealer, favorite of his lord, Seni

14.6 Priest in front of fowler
ỉmy-rꜣ śšr H̱mt-nw
overseer of linen, Khemetnw

15. **Panel U, east wall (fig. 181)**

15.1 *ḫrp-sḥ ỉrr ḥsst n nb.f ꜣḫỉ*
director of the (food) hall, he who does what his lord favors, Akhi

15.2 *ḥmt.f ḫtmtyt Śnt*
his wife, sealer, Senet

15.3 *sꜣ Śbk-ḥtp*
son, Sobek-hetep

15.4 no text

16. **Panel V, north wall (fig. 182)**

16.1 *ḫrp-sḥ Mmỉ*
director of the (food) hall, memi

16.2 *sꜣ.f Śꜣbnỉ*
his son, Sabni

16.3 *ḫtmty nt...?*
sealer of (? unclear)

17. **North wall, bull-watching scene (fig. 183)**

17.1 Text across top
prt-ḫrw t ḥnḳt n ḥꜣty-ꜥ śmr-wꜥty ẖry-ḥbt ỉmy-rꜣ ỉꜥꜣw Śꜣbnỉ | mꜣꜣ wrt
an invocation offering of bread and beer to the count, sole companion, lector priest, overseer of Egyptianized Nubians, Sabni | watching the great ones

17.2 no text

17.3 Offerer: *ḥḳꜣ-ḥwt Ḥḳꜣib*
chief of the estate, Heqaib

18. **Panel W, south wall**

18.1 *ỉmy-rꜣ ṯs(w)t ḫrp-sḥ Mry*
overseer of herds (troops?), director of the (food) hall, Mery

18.2 *sꜣ.f Ḥḳꜣib*
his son, Heqaib

18.3 *ḥmt.f Nwt. . . ?*
his wife, Newt. . . ?

18.4 *sꜣt (. . . ?) Wḏt*
daughter

18.5 no text

18.6 *Śꜣbni͗*
Sabni

19. **West wall, left of false door**
śmr wꜥty i͗my-rꜣ i͗ꜥꜣw ẖry-ḥbt Ḥḳꜣi͗b
sole companion, overseer of Egyptianized Nubians, lector priest, Heqaib

20. **Sabni2 false door**
Refer to Edel et al., *Felsgräbernekropole*, I. Abteilung, Band 2, 822–3.

Table 1. Style Distribution by Tomb, Tomb Owners, and Subsidiary Figures

Style By tomb	A1	A2	RB	Ptd	A	B	C	D	E	Hrkf	Sb2R	Sb2S	other	?	total
Mekhu 25	6	4	0	10	27	0	0	1	0	0	0	0	5	0	53
% of program	11%	8%	0%	19%	51%	0%	0%	2%	0%	0%	0%	0%	9%	0%	
Sabni 26	9	10	0	10	19	0	0	0	0	0	0	0	2	0	50
% of program	18%	20%	0%	20%	38%	0%	0%	0%	0%	0%	0%	0%	4%	0%	
Both 25/26	15	14	0	20	46	0	0	1	0	0	0	0	7	0	
% of program	15%	14%	0%	19%	45%	0%	0%	1%	0%	0%	0%	0%	7%	0%	
Sobekhetep 90	0	10	0	0	4	0	0	0	0	0	0	0	0	0	14
% of program	0%	71%	0%	0%	29%	0%	0%	0%	0%	0%	0%	0%	0%	0%	
IiShemai 98	0	8	0	5	0	0	0	0	0	0	0	0	0	0	13
% of program	0%	62%	0%	38%	0%	0%	0%	0%	0%	0%	0%	0%	0%	0%	
KhwKhnm 102	3	7	0	0	6	0	0	0	0	0	0	0	0	0	16
% of program	19%	44%	0%	0%	38%	0%	0%	0%	0%	0%	0%	0%	0%	0%	
Tjetji 103	1	0	1	0	0	0	4	0	0	0	0	0	3	0	9
% of program	11%	0%	11%	0%	0%	0%	44%	0%	0%	0%	0%	0%	33%	0%	
Khui 34e	0	0	18	0	3	0	0	0	0	0	0	0	0	3	24
% of program	0%	0%	75%	0%	13%	0%	0%	0%	0%	0%	0%	0%	0%	13%	
Khunes 34h	28	17	1	0	12	4	30	0	0	0	0	0	0	2	94
% of program	30%	18%	1%	0%	13%	4%	32%	0%	0%	0%	0%	0%	0%	2%	
Harkhuf 34n	0	0	0	0	0	0	0	0	1	18	0	0	0	0	19
% of program	0%	0%	0%	0%	0%	0%	0%	0%	5%	95%	0%	0%	0%	0%	
Pn1 35	0	0	0	0	0	8	10	0	0	3	0	1	0	0	22
% of program	0%	0%	0%	0%	0%	36%	45%	0%	0%	14%	0%	5%	0%	0%	
PnH2 35d	5	3	0	2	59	15	26	5	19	0	0	1	0	4	139

(*continued*)

Table 1. (continued)

Style By tomb	A1	A2	RB	Ptd	A	B	C	D	E	Hrkf	Sb2R	Sb2S	other	?	total
% of program	4%	2%	0%	1%	42%	11%	19%	4%	14%	0%	0%	1%	0%	3%	
Sabni2 35e	2	7	0	0	39	2	0	0	0	0	10	35	0	0	95
% of program	2%	7%	0%	0%	41%	2%	0%	0%	0%	0%	11%	37%	0%	0%	
total figs	54	66	20	27	169	29	70	6	20	21	10	37	10	9	548
% of total	10%	12%	4%	5%	31%	5%	13%	1%	4%	4%	2%	7%	2%	2%	
Full cemetery															
TO figs	27	10	0	5	15	0	0	0	2	13	5	0	8	0	85
% of TO total	32.1%	11.9%	0.0%	6.0%	17.9%	0.0%	0.0%	0.0%	2.4%	15.5%	6.0%	0.0%	9.5%	0.0%	
Sub figs	27	56	20	22	154	29	70	6	18	8	5	37	2	9	463
% of sub total	5.8%	12.1%	4.3%	4.8%	33.3%	6.3%	15.1%	1.3%	3.9%	1.7%	1.1%	8.0%	0.4%	1.9%	
total figs	54	66	20	27	169	29	70	6	20	21	10	37	10	9	548
% of total figs	9.9%	12.1%	3.7%	4.9%	31.0%	5.3%	12.8%	1.1%	3.7%	3.8%	1.8%	6.8%	1.8%	1.6%	

Table 2. Scene Identification with Figure References and Concordance with Edel, Seyfried, and Vieler

scene ID	Tomb	Wall	Fig. ref	I Abteilung Band, pps	I Abteilung, Sz/Txt #s
MS1 Ramp Stele S Mekhu	Mekhu, Sabni 25–26	ramp S stela	n/a	Band 1, 29–30	Sz 1, Txt 1–2
MS2 Ramp Stele N Sabni	Mekhu, Sabni 25–26	ramp N stela	n/a	Band 1, 30	Sz 2, Txt 3–4
MS3 Mekhu S thickness	Mekhu, Sabni 25–26	Mekhu S ent thickness	n/a	Band 1, 30–31	Sz 3, Txt 5–6
MS4 Mekhu N thickness top	Mekhu, Sabni 25–26	Mekhu N ent thickness	n/a	Band 1, 31–32	Sz 4, Txt 7–8
MS5 Mekhu N thickness bottom	Mekhu, Sabni 25–26	Mekhu N ent thickness, bottom	n/a	Band 1, 32–33	Sz 5, Txt 9–13
MS6 EWall Offs	Mekhu, Sabni 25–26	E wall, right	n/a	Band 1, 33–34	Sz 6, Txt 14–18
MS7 EWall main	Mekhu, Sabni 25–26	E wall main	Plate IV	Band 1, 34–37	Sz 7, part Sec 2–3; Txt 24–26
MS7a EWall inset	Mekhu, Sabni 25–26	E wall, main inset	Plate IV	Band 1, 34–37	Sz 7, sec 2 (part); Txt 20–23
MS8 NWall	Mekhu, Sabni 25–26	N wall	n/a	Band 1, 38–39	Sz 9, Txt 33–35
MS9 SWall	Mekhu, Sabni 25–26	S wall	n/a	Band 1, 37–38	Sz 8, Txt 27–32
MS10 ColE4	Mekhu, Sabni 25–26	Column E4	n/a	Band 1, 41–42	Sz 13; Txt 46–48
MS11 ColE5	Mekhu, Sabni 25–26	Column E5	n/a	Band 1, 42	Sz 14, n/a
MS12 ColM2	Mekhu, Sabni 25–26	Column M2	n/a	Band 1, 42	Sz 15, Txt 49–52
MS13 ColM6	Mekhu, Sabni 25–26	Column M6	Fig. 8	Band 1, 42	Sz 16, Txt 53–54
MS14 ColW2	Mekhu, Sabni 25–26	Column W2	n/a	Band 1, 41	Sz 12, Txt 45
MS15 ColW6	Mekhu, Sabni 25–26	Column W6	Fig. 8	Band 1, 43	Sz 17, Txt 55–58
MS16 WWall sub Fd	Mekhu, Sabni 25–26	West wall, south	n/a	Band 1, 40	Sz 11, Txt 44
MS17 Mekhu Fd	Mekhu, Sabni 25–26	Mekhu false door	n/a	Band 1, 39–40	Sz 10, Txt 36–43
MS18 Sabni SFac	Mekhu, Sabni 25–26	Sabni facade south	n/a	Band 1, 48–49	Sz 18, Txt 60–64
MS19 Sabni NFac	Mekhu, Sabni 25–26	Sabni facade north	n/a	Band 1, 49–58	Sz 19, Txt 59, 65–66
MS20 Sabni Lintel	Mekhu, Sabni 25–26	Sabni entrance lintel	n/a	Band 1, 61–62	Sz 20, Txt 67
MS21 Sabni S thickness top	Mekhu, Sabni 25–26	Sabni S ent thickness, top	n/a	Band 1, 63–64	Sz 21, Txt 70–73

(continued)

Table 2. (continued)

scene ID	Tomb	Wall	Fig. ref	I Abteilung Band, pps	I Abteilung, Sz/Txt #s
MS22 Sabni S thickness bottom	Mekhu, Sabni 25–26	Sabni S ent thickness, bottom	n/a	Band 1, 64	Sz 22, n/a
MS23 Sabni N thickness	Mekhu, Sabni 25–26	Sabni N ent thickness	n/a	Band 1, 64	Sz 23, Txt 74–77
MS24 Sabni PillE6S	Mekhu, Sabni 25–26	Pill E6, Sabni	n/a	Band 1, 69	Sz 28, Txt 97
MS25 Sabni PillE6E	Mekhu, Sabni 25–26	Pill E6, Sabni	n/a	Band 1, 69	Sz 29, Txt 98–100
MS26 Sabni PillW6	Mekhu, Sabni 25–26	Pill W6, Sabni	n/a	Band 1, 70	Sz 30, Txt 101
MS27 Sabni F+F	Mekhu, Sabni 25–26	W wall	Plate V	Band 1, 66–68	Sz 27, Txt 87–96
MS28 Sabni Fd Off1	Mekhu, Sabni 25–26	Sabni false door niche, inner left jamb	Fig. 9	Band 1, 64–65	Sz 24, Txt 78
MS29 Sabni Fd Offs2	Mekhu, Sabni 25–26	Sabni false door niche, outer left jamb	Fig. 9	Band 1, 64–65	Sz 25, Txt 79–80
MS30 Sabni Fd	Mekhu, Sabni 25–26	Sabni false door	Fig. 9	Band 1, 65–66	Sz 26, Txt 81–86
SH1 PillE4	Sobekhetep 90	Pillar E4 north face	n/a	Band 2, 1134–1135	Sz 1, Txt 1–2
SH2 PillE5	Sobekhetep 90	Pillar E5 south face	Fig. 13	Band 2, 1135–1136	Sz 3, Txt 5–10
SH3 PillM5	Sobekhetep 90	Pillar M5 east face	Plate VI	Band 2, 1135	Sz 2, Txt 3–4
SH4 PillM4	Sobekhetep 90	Pillar M4 north face	Plate VIII	Band 2, 1136	Sz 4, Txt 11–15
IiS1 EWall	IiShemai Setka 98	E wall	n/a	Band 2, 1328–1329	Sz 1, Txt 1–3
IiS2 SWall	IiShemai Setka 98	S wall	n/a	Band 2, 1329–1330	Sz 2, Txt 4–7
IiS3 Pill1	IiShemai Setka 98	Pill 1, east face	n/a	Band 2, 1330	Sz 3, Txt 8
IiS4 Pill3	IiShemai Setka 98	Pill 3, east face	Plate VII	Band 2, 1330–1331	Sz 4, Txt 9–11
KK1 PillE2E	Khwin-Khnm 102	Pill E2, east face	n/a	Band 3, 1398	Sz1, Txt 1–2
KK2 PillE2N	Khwin-Khnm 102	Pill E2, north face	Plate XIa	Band 3, 1398–1399	Sz 2, Txt 4–6
KK3 PillE3E	Khwin-Khnm 102	Pill E3, east face	n/a	Band 3, 1399	Sz 3, Txt 7–8
KK4 PillE3S	Khwin-Khnm 102	Pill E3, north face	Plate XIb	Band 3, 1399–1400	Sz 4, Txt 9–10
KK5 PillW2	Khwin-Khnm 102	Pill W2, east face	n/a	Band 3, 1400–1401	Sz 5, Txt 12–14
KK6 PillW3	Khwin-Khnm 102	Pill W3, east face	Plate IX	Band 3, 1401	Sz 6, Txt 15–16
Tj1 PillE1E	Tjetji 103	Col E1, east side top	n/a	Band 3, 1509	n/a, Txt 2–3
Tj2 PillE1N	Tjetji 103	Col E1, north side	n/a	Band 3, 1509	n/a, Txt 1
Tj3 Pill E2S top	Tjetji 103	Col E2 south face top	Fig. 19	Band 3, 1509–1510	Sz 1, Txt 4
Tj3a Pill E2S bot	Tjetji 103	Col E2 south side bottom	Plate XVIc	Band 3, 1509–1510	Sz 1, n/a
Tj4 PillE2E	Tjetji 103	Col E2 east side	Plate X	Band 3, 1510–1511	Sz 2, Txt 5–8
Ku1 Pill E2E top	Khui 34e	Pill E2 east face, top	n/a	Band 1, 465–469	Sz 1, Txt 1–4

Ku2 Pill E2E bot	Khui 34e	Pill E2 east face bottom	Fig. 23	Band 1, 465–471	Sz2, Txt 5–17
Ku3 FD main	Khui 34e	W wall, middle	Fig. 22	Band 1, 472–474	Sz 5–6, Txt 19–24
Ku4 FD secondary	Khui 34e	W wall, south	n/a	Band 1, 471–472	Sz 3–4, Txt 18
Kh1 ent. thick	Khunes 34h	S ent thickness	n/a	Band 1, 543–544	Sz 1, Txt 1–2
Kh2 EWall N	Khunes 34h	E wall, south of ent, north end	n/a	Band 1, 544–545	Sz 2, Txt 3
Kh3 EWall S	Khunes 34h	E wall, south of ent, south end	n/a	Band 1, 545–546	Sz 3, Txt 4–5
Kh4 EWall bottom	Khunes 34h	E wall, south of ent, north end, bottom	n/a	Band 1, 546–547	Sz 4, Txt 6–8
Kh5 SWall E	Khunes 34h	S wall, east end	Fig. 27	Band 1, 547–548	Sz 5, Txt 9–11
Kh6 SWall Middle	Khunes 34h	S wall, middle-east	Fig. 27	Band 1, 549	Sz 6, Txt 12–13
Kh7 SWall W	Khunes 34h	S wall middle to west end	Fig. 27	Band 1, 549–551	Sz 7, Txt 14–15
Kh8 Fd S jamb	Khunes 34h	W wall, south end, left of false door niche	Fig. 31	Band 1, 551–552	Sz 9, n/a
Kh9 Fd S jamb bottom	Khunes 34h	W wall, south end, left of false door niche, bottom	Fig. 31	Band 1, 552	Sz 9, Txt 16–17
Kh10 Fd N jamb	Khunes 34h	W wall, right of false door niche	Fig. 31	Band 1, 552	Sz 10, Txt 18–19
Kh11 Fd Sthick	Khunes 34h	False door niche S thickness	Fig. 31	Band 1, 552–553	Sz 11, Txt 20–21
Kh12 Fd Nthick	Khunes 34h	False door niche N thickness	Fig. 31	Band 1, 553	Sz 12, n/a
Kh13 Khunes FD	Khunes 34h	False door niche, west wall	Fig. 31	Band 1, 563–564	n/a, n/a
Kh14 WWall 1	Khunes 34h	W wall, under cut	Fig. 31	Band 1, 553	Sz 13, n/a
Kh15 WWall 2	Khunes 34h	W wall, under cut	Fig. 31	Band 1, 553–554	Sz 13, Txt 26
Kh16a WWall 3 left	Khunes 34h	W wall, right of cut, top	Fig. 31	Band 1, 553	Sz 13, Txt 24
Kh16b WWall 3 right	Khunes 34h	W wall, right of cut, top	Fig. 31	Band 1, 553	Sz 13, Txt 25
Kh17a WWall 4a	Khunes 34h	W wall, right of cut, bottom	Fig. 31	Band 1, 553	Sz 13, Txt 22
Kh17b WWall 4b	Khunes 34h	W wall, right of cut, bottom	Fig. 31	Band 1, 553	Sz 13, Txt 23
Kh18 WWall 5	Khunes 34h	W wall, north, right of niche	Fig. 31	Band 1, 554	Sz 14, n/a
Kh19 PillE1 top	Khunes 34h	Pill E1, east face, top	Fig. 28	Band 1, 555	Sz 15, Txt 27
Kh20 PillE1 bottom	Khunes 34h	Pill E1, east face, bottom	Fig. 30	Band 1, 555–556	Sz 16, Txt 28–29
Kh21 PillE2E top	Khunes 34h	Pill E2 east face, top	n/a	Band 1, 556	Sz 17, Txt 30–31
Kh22 PillE2E middle	Khunes 34h	Pill E2 east face, middle	n/a	Band 1, 556–557	Sz 18, Txt 32–35
Kh23 PillE2E bottom	Khunes 34h	Pill E2 east face, bottom	n/a	Band 1, 557	Sz 19, Txt 36
Kh24 PillE2N top	Khunes 34h	Pill E2 north face, top	n/a	Band 1, 557	Sz 20, Txt 37
Kh25 PillE2N mid 3	Khunes 34h	Pill E2 north face, middle row	Fig. 29	Band 1, 557–558	Sz 20, Txt 38–40

(*continued*)

Table 2. (continued)

scene ID	Tomb	Wall	Fig. ref	I Abteilung Band, pps	I Abteilung, Sz/Txt #s
Kh26 PillE2N bottom	Khunes 34h	Pill E2 north face, bottom	Fig. 29	Band 1, 557–561	Sz 20, Txt 41 (small)–42 (big), 43x2, 44–45
Kh27 PillE3	Khunes 34h	Pill E3 south face	n/a	Band 1, 561	Sz 21, n/a
Kh28 PillW1	Khunes 34h	Pill W1, east face	n/a	Band 1, 561	Sz 22, Txt 46
Kh29 PillW2 top	Khunes 34h	Pill W2 east face, top	n/a	Band 1, 561–562	Sz 23, Txt 47–50
Kh30 PillW2 bottom	Khunes 34h	Pill W2 east face, bottom	n/a	Band 1, 562	Sz 24, n/a
Kh31 PillW3	Khunes 34h	Pill W3, east face	n/a	Band 1, 562–563	Sz 25, Txt 51–52
An1 Ankhes pillar	Ankhes 34g	Central pillar, east face	n/a	Band 1, 527–528	Sz 1, Txt 1–3
H1 Lintel	Harkhuf 34n	Façade lintel	Fig. 33	Band 1, 620–623	Sz 1, Txt 1
H2 Facade south	Harkhuf 34n	Façade, south side	Fig. 34	Band 1, 624–626	Sz 3, Txt 2–3
H3 Facade north	Harkhuf 34n	Façade, north side	Fig. 33	Band 1, 623–624	Sz 2, Txt 2
H4 Facade letter	Harkhuf 34n	Façade, north side, north end	Fig. 33	Band 1, 626–628	n/a, Txt 6
H5 Facade Off1	Harkhuf 34n	Façade, south side, bottom, left	Fig. 33	Band 1, 625–626	Sz 4, Txt 4
H6 Facade Off2	Harkhuf 34n	Façade, south side, bottom, right	Fig. 33	Band 1, 625–626	Sz 4, Txt 5
H7 Pill1	Harkhuf 34n	Pill 1 north face	n/a	Band 1, 629–630	Sz 5, Txt 7–8
H8 Pill2	Harkhuf 34n	Pill 2 north face	n/a	Band 1, 630	Sz 6, Txt 9
H9 Pill3S	Harkhuf 34n	Pill 3 south face	Plate XII	Band 1, 630	Sz 7, Txt 10–11
H10 Pill3E	Harkhuf 34n	Pill 3 east face	Plate XII	Band 1, 631	Sz 8, Txt 12
H11 Pill4S	Harkhuf 34n	Pill 4 south face	Plate XII	Band 1, 631	Sz 9, Txt 13
H12 Pill4E	Harkhuf 34n	Pill 4 east face	Plate XII	Band 1, 631	Sz 10, Txt 14
H13 Hark Fd	Harkhuf 34n	W wall, north of shaft	n/a	Band 1, 634–635	Scht II, Txt 21–29
H14 Sub Fd	Harkhuf 34n	W wall, south of shaft	n/a	Band 1, 633–634	Scht I, Sz 12, Txt 15–20
Pn1 Lintel	Pepynakht1 35	Façade lintel	n/a	Band 2, 683	Sz 1, Txt 1
Pn2 Facade south	Pepynakht1 35	Façade, south side	Fig. 37	Band 2, 683–689	Sz 3, Txt 2
Pn3 Facade north	Pepynakht1 35	Façade, north side	n/a	Band 2, 683–689	Sz 2, Txt 2
Pn4 EWallS	Pepynakht1 35	E Wall, south of door	n/a	Band 2, 689–690	Sz 4, Txt 3
Pn5 EWallN	Pepynakht1 35	E wall north of door	n/a	Band 2, 690	Sz 5, Txt 4–5
Pn6 WWall Offs1	Pepynakht1 35	W wall over shaft, top	n/a	Band 2, 690–691	Sz 6, Txt 6–9
Pn7 WWall Offs2	Pepynakht1 35	W wall over shaft, bottom	n/a	Band 2, 691	Sz 6, Txt 10

Pn8 WWall Offs3	Pepynakht1 35	W wall, right of false door	Fig. 39	Band 2, 691	Sz 7, Txt 11–14
Pn9 Pill 2	Pepynakht1 35	Pill 2 south face	n/a	Band 2, 691	Sz 8, n/a
Pn10 Fd	Pepynakht1 35	W wall	n/a	Band 2, 692	n/a, n/a
PnH1 Facade upper	Pepynakht Heqaib2 35d	Façade, north, upper	n/a	Band 2, 742	Sz 1, Txt 1–2
PnH2 Facade bottom	Pepynakht Heqaib2 35d	Façade, north, lower	n/a	Band 2, 743–744	Sz 2, Txt 3–9
PnH3 S thickness top	Pepynakht Heqaib2 35d	S ent thickness, top	Fig. 44	Band 2, 744–745	Sz 3, Txt 10–12
PnH4 S thickness bottom	Pepynakht Heqaib2 35d	S ent thickness, bottom	Fig. 46	Band 2, 745–747	Sz 4, Txt 13–26
PnH5 N thickness top	Pepynakht Heqaib2 35d	N ent thickness, top	n/a	Band 2, 748	Sz 5, Txt 27–28
PnH6 N thickness middle	Pepynakht Heqaib2 35d	N ent thickness, middle	Fig. 45	Band 2, 748	Sz 6, Txt 30
PnH7 N thickness bottom	Pepynakht Heqaib2 35d	N ent thickness, bottom	Plate XIII	Band 2, 748–749	Sz 7, Txt 33
PnH8 EWallSA	Pepynakht Heqaib2 35d	E wall S, jamb, top	Fig. 50	Band 2, 764–765	Sz 28, Txt 134–136
PnH9 EWallSB	Pepynakht Heqaib2 35d	E wall S, jamb, bottom	Fig. 50	Band 2, 765	Sz 29, Txt 137–139
PnH10 EWallSC	Pepynakht Heqaib2 35d	E wall S, main, top	Fig. 50	Band 2, 758–760	Sz 24, Txt 110–112
PnH11 EWallSD	Pepynakht Heqaib2 35d	E wall S, main, middle, left	Fig. 50	Band 2, 760–761	Sz 25, Txt 113–116
PnH12 EWallSE	Pepynakht Heqaib2 35d	E wall S, main, middle, right	Fig. 50	Band 2, 761–762	Sz 25, Txt 117–119
PnH13 EWallSF	Pepynakht Heqaib2 35d	E wall S, main, bottom	Plate XV	Band 2, 763–764	Sz 27, Txt 130–133
PnH14 EWallSG	Pepynakht Heqaib2 35d	E wall S, main, under ledge	Fig. 50	Band 2, 762–763	Sz 26, Txt 120–128
PnH15 EWallN I	Pepynakht Heqaib2 35d	E wall, north, right, top	Plate XVII	Band 2, 751	Sz 10, Txt 50–51
PnH16 EWallN H+J	Pepynakht Heqaib2 35d	E wall, north, right, bottom	Plate XIV	Band 2, 750–751	Sz 8.1–8.2, 9, Txt 43–49
PnH17 EWallN K	Pepynakht Heqaib2 35d	E wall, north, middle, top	Fig. 51	Band 2, 751–752	Sz 11, Txt 54–58
PnH18 EWallN L	Pepynakht Heqaib2 35d	E wall, north, middle, middle	Plate XIV	Band 2, 752	Sz 12, Txt 59–60
PnH19 EWallN M	Pepynakht Heqaib2 35d	E wall, north, middle, bottom	Plate XIV	Band 2, 752	Sz 13, Txt 61–67
PnH20 EWallN N	Pepynakht Heqaib2 35d	E wall, north, left, top	Plate XIV	Band 2, 752–753	Sz 14, Txt 68–69
PnH21 EWallN O	Pepynakht Heqaib2 35d	E wall, north, left, bottom	Fig. 52	Band 2, 753	Sz 15, Txt 70–73
PnH22 Pill2N	Pepynakht Heqaib2 35d	Pill E2, north face	n/a	Band 2, 755–756	Sz 18, Txt 95–98
PnH23 Pill2E top	Pepynakht Heqaib2 35d	Pill E2, east face, top (lost)	n/a	Band 2, 756–757	Sz 21, Txt 102–106
PnH24 WWall P	Pepynakht Heqaib2 35d	Pill E2, east face, left, bottom	Fig. 53	Band 2, 757–758	Sz 22, Txt 108
PnH24a WWall P top	Pepynakht Heqaib2 35d	Pill E2, east face, left, bottom	Fig. 53	Band 2, 757–758	Sz 22, Txt 107
PnH25 WWall Q	Pepynakht Heqaib2 35d	Pill E2, east face, right, top	Fig. 53	Band 2, 756	Sz 19, Txt 99–100

(*continued*)

Table 2. (continued)

scene ID	Tomb	Wall	Fig. ref	I Abteilung Band, pps	I Abteilung, Sz/Txt #s
PnH26 WWall R	Pepynakht Heqaib2 35d	Pill E2, east face, right, bottom	Fig. 53	Band 2, 756	Sz 20, n/a
PnH27 WWall S	Pepynakht Heqaib2 35d	W wall of passage, south	Fig. 53	Band 2, 753–754	Sz 16, Txt 74–78
PnH28 WWall T	Pepynakht Heqaib2 35d	W wall of passage, north	Plate XVIII	Band 2, 754–755	Sz 17, Txt 79–94
PnH29 Fd	Pepynakht Heqaib2 35d	False door	n/a	Band 2, 765–766	Sz 30, Txt 140
PnH30 Fd off	Pepynakht Heqaib2 35d	False door niche, south wall	n/a	Band 2, 758	Sz 23, Txt 109
Sb1 Facade Lintel	Sabni (2) 35e	Façade, above entrance	Fig. 54	Band 2, 810–811	Sz 1, Txt 1–6
Sb2 Facade EJamb top	Sabni (2) 35e	Façade, east jamb, top	Fig. 54	Band 2, 811	Sz 2, Txt 7–8
Sb3 Facade EJamb bottom	Sabni (2) 35e	Façade, east jamb, bottom	Fig. 54	Band 2, 811	Sz 3, Txt 9
Sb4 Facade WJamb	Sabni (2) 35e	Façade, west jamb	Fig. 54	Band 2, 811–812	Sz 4, Txt 10
Sb5 WFacade N top	Sabni (2) 35e	Façade, west side, north end, top	Fig. 54	Band 2, 812	Sz 5, Txt 11–12
Sb6 WFacade N bottom	Sabni (2) 35e	Façade, west side, north end, bottom	Fig. 56	Band 2, 812–813	Sz 6, Txt 13–18
Sb7 WFacade middle	Sabni (2) 35e	Façade, west side, middle	Fig. 55	Band 2, 813	Sz 7, Txt 19–20
Sb8 WFacade S top	Sabni (2) 35e	Façade, west side, south, top	Fig. 54	Band 2, 813–814	Sz 7, Txt 21–27
Sb9 WFacade S bottom	Sabni (2) 35e	Façade, west side, south, bottom	Fig. 54	Band 2, 814	Sz 7, Txt 28–31
Sb10 E thickness	Sabni (2) 35e	Sabni2 E ent thickness main	Fig. 58	Band 2, 814–815	Sz 8, Txt 32–33
Sb11 E thickness below	Sabni (2) 35e	Sabni2 E ent thickness, bottom	Fig. 58	Band 2, 815–816	Sz 9, Txt 49–54
Sb12 W thickness	Sabni (2) 35e	Sabni2 W ent thickness, main	Fig. 57	Band 2, 816–818	Sz 10, Txt 55–58
Sb13 W thickness below	Sabni (2) 35e	Sabni2 W ent thickness, bottom	Fig. 57	Band 2, 818–819	Sz 11, Txt 77 (78–79)
Sb14 EWall U	Sabni (2) 35e	E wall, south	Fig. 59	Band 2, 819	Sz 12, Txt 80–83
Sb15 F+F	Sabni (2) 35e	E wall, main	Fig. 60	Band 2, 819–820	Sz 13, Txt 84–85, 86, 89
Sb16 NWall V	Sabni (2) 35e	SE chapel space, N wall, east	n/a	Band 2, 820–821	Sz 14, Txt 90–92
Sb17 NWall Bullfighting	Sabni (2) 35e	Pill E1 south face	Fig. 61	Band 2, 821	Sz 15, Txt 93–94
Sb18 SWall W	Sabni (2) 35e	SE chapel space, S wall	n/a	Band 2, 821–822	Sz 16, Txt 96–101
Sb19 Fd off	Sabni (2) 35e	W wall, left of false door	n/a	Band 2, 822	Sz 17, Txt 102
Sb20 Fd	Sabni (2) 35e	W wall	n/a	Band 2, 822–823	n/a, Txt 103–108

Notes

Introduction

1 Parkinson, *The Tale of Sinuhe and Other Ancient Egyptian Poems*, 38.

2 For studies of titles and the structure of the administration, see especially Helck, *Untersuchungen zu den Beamtentiteln des Ägyptischen Alten Reiches*; Baer, *Rank and Title in the Old Kingdom*; Strudwick, *The Administration of Egypt in the Old Kingdom: The Highest Titles and Their Holders.* Several autobiographical inscriptions appear in the Qubbet el-Hawa cemetery; they are discussed in Chapter 1. The autobiography of Weni is another popular text in this regard: translation in Strudwick, *Texts from the Pyramid Age: Writing from the Ancient World 16*, 352–7; also Eyre, "Weni's Career and Old Kingdom Historiography," 107–24; and Richards, "Text and Context in Late Old Kingdom Egypt: The Archaeology and Historiography of Weni the Elder," 75–102.

3 For example, Fischer, *Dendera in the Third Millennium B.C. Down to the Theban Domination of Upper Egypt*; Kanawati, *Akhmim in the Old Kingdom*; Richards, "Text and Context"; Adams, *Community and Society in Egypt in the First Intermediate Period: An Archaeological Investigation of the Abydos Settlement Site.*

4 For a succinct overview of excavations at Qubbet el-Hawa, see Edel, "Qubbet el-Hawa," in *Lexikon der Ägyptologie*, Band V, 54–5.

5 For a detailed overview of the Bonner mission's work at Qubbet el-Hawa, including all relevant publications, see Edel, Seyfried, and Vieler, *Die Felsgräbernekropole der Qubbet el-Hawa bei Assuan,* I. Abteilung, Band 1, XX–XXIV.

6 Edel et al., *Felsengräber*, 2. Abt.; *Die althieratischen Topfaufschriften.* 1. Bd. *Die Topfaufschriften aus den Grabungsjahren 1960–1963 und 1965.* 1. Teil: *Zeichnungen und hieroglyphische Umschriften*, 2. Teil: *Text* (1970), 2. Bd. *Die Topfaufschriften aus den Grabungsjahren 1968–1970* (1971).

7 Edel et al., *Felsgräbernekropole,* I. Abteilung, 3 Bands.

8 el-Din, "Discovery of a Tomb of the Late Old Kingdom Below the Rock Tombs of Qubbet el-Hawa, Aswan," 31–4.

9 Universidad de Jaén Qubbet el-Hawa project Web site, including bibliography, at http://www.ujaen.es/investiga/qubbetelhawa/index.php.

10 For example see Kanawati, *Governmental Reforms in Old Kingdom Egypt*; Martin-Pardey, *Untersuchungen zur ägyptischen Provinzialverwaltung bis zum Ende des Alten Reiches*, 188–201.

11 References to Harkhuf's autobiography are discussed in Chapter 1. See also, Müller-Wollermann, *Krisenfaktoren im Ägyptischen Staat des Ausgehenden Alten Reichs*; and Eichler, *Untersuchungen zum Expeditionswesen des ägyptischen Alten Reiches.*

12 Stevenson Smith, *A History of Egyptian Sculpture and Painting in the Old Kingdom*, 226–7; Harpur, *Decoration in Egyptian Tombs of the Old Kingdom: Studies in Orientation and Scene Content, Studies in Egyptology*, 35; Fischer, "Administrative Titles of Women in the Old and Middle Kingdoms," 69–79, including a reference to reliefs in the tomb of Tjetji in note 4.

13 Elephantine has a long history, extending before and well after the Old Kingdom period. Work from the site is especially well published, both in a series of monographs, Elephantine 1–34, as well as regular articles in the *MDAIK*, and now seasonal field reports as PDF files on the Deutsches Archäologisches Institut Web page. References relevant to the Old Kingdom areas of the site include: Dreyer, *Der Tempel der Satet: Die Funde der Fühzeit und des Alten Reiches, Elephantine 8*; Ziermann, *Befestigungsanlagen und Stadtentwicklung in der Frühzeit und im frühen Alten Reich, Elephantine 16*; and Ziermann, *Die Baustrukturen der ältern Stadt (Frühzeit und Alten Reiches), Elephantine 28*. For updated field reports, see: http://www.dainst.org/index_54ddb1c8bb1f14a184920017f0000011_en.html.

14 Johnson, "Conceptions of Agency in Archaeological Interpretation," 189–211; Wobst, "Agency in (Spite of) Material Culture," 40–50; Barrett, "A Thesis on Agency," 61–8; idem., "Agency, the Duality of Structure, and the Problem of the Archaeological Record, " 141–64; David, "Intentionality, Agency and an Archaeology of Choice," 67–71.

15 Dobres and Robb, eds., *Agency in Archaeology.*

16 Giddens, *The Constitution of Society: Outline of the Theory of Structuration*; Bourdieu, *Outline of a Theory of Practice.*

17 Wobst, "Agency in (Spite of) Material Culture," 40.

18 DeMarrais, "Figuring the Group," 166.

19 Ibid.

20 As it is described by Barrett, "Agency, the Duality of Structure, and the Problem of the Archaeological Record" 150.

21 Joyce and Lopiparo, "Postscript: Doing Agency in Archaeology," 365–74.

22 Dobres and Robb, "'Doing' Agency: Introductory Remarks on Methodology," 161.

23 Gell, *Art and Agency: An Anthropological Theory.*

24 Winter, "Agency Marked, Agency Ascribed: The Affective Object in Ancient Mesopotamia," 60.

25 Schapiro, "Style (with Bibliography)," 51.

26 Bal and Bryson, "Semiotics and Art History."

27 Moxey, "Semiotics and the Social History of Art," 991.

28 Ibid., 993.

29 N. Bryson, "The Gaze in the Expanded Field," 107.

30 Conkey, "Experimenting with Style in Archaeology: Some Historical and Theoretical Issues," 7.

31 Grosz, *Volatile Bodies: Toward a Corporeal Feminism.*

32 The literature on archaeologies of the body and theories of embodiment is extensive. Some references include Rautman, *Reading the Body: Representations and Remains in the Archaeological Record*; Joyce, "Archaeology of the Body," 139–58; Montserrat, *Changing Bodies, Changing Meanings: Studies on the Human Body in Antiquity.*

33 Lesure, "Linking Theory and Evidence in an Archaeology of Human Agency: Iconography, Style, and Theories of Embodiment," 241–2.

34 For example, Meskell, *Archaeologies of Materiality*; Miller, *Materiality*; Ian Hodder, "Dalrymple Lectures 2007–8, Thing Theory: Toward an Integrated Archaeological

Perspective," 5–6; the recent Clark Colloquium "Art History and Materiality," at The Clark in Williamstown, MA, March 15–16, 2013.

[35] For example, Canuto and Yaeger, eds., *The Archaeology of Communities: A New World Perspective.*

[36] Kolb and Snead, "It's a Small World After All: Comparative Analysis of Community Organization in Archaeology," 611.

[37] Knapp, "The Archaeology of Community on Bronze Age Cyprus: Politiko Phorades in Context," 107.

[38] Ibid.

[39] Yaeger and Canuto, "Introducing an Archaeology of Communities," 6.

[40] Ibid., 5.

[41] Mac Sweeney, *Community Identity and Archaeology: Dynamic Communities at Aphrodisias and Beycesultan*, 20–1.

[42] Frood, "Social Structure and Daily Life: Pharaonic," 474.

[43] For example, Richards, "Conceptual Landscapes in the Egyptian Nile Valley," 83–100; Kemp, *Ancient Egypt: Anatomy of a Civilization*, esp. 261–317.

[44] Regarding perceived connections to local villages, primarily in the New Kingdom, see Meskell, *Private Life in New Kingdom Egypt*, esp. 17–56.

1 People and Place: Historical and Social Context

[1] Ziermann, *Elephantine XVI: Befestigungsanlangen und Stadtentwicklung in der Frühzeit und im frühen Alten Reich*; Müntel, "Stadt und Tempel von Elephantine, 21./22. Grabungsbericht," 103–9.

[2] Dreyer, *Elephantine VIII: Der Tempel der Satet: Die Funde der Frühzeit und des Alten Reiches*, 11–22; Ziermann, *Elephantine XVI*, 18–20, 39–47.

[3] Ziermann, *Elephantine XVI*; esp. 100–28; Ziermann, "Stadt und Tempel von Elephantine, 19./20. Grabungsbericht," 136–41; Müntel and Ziermann, "Stadt und Tempel von Elephantine, 21./22. Grabungsbericht," 105ff.; Seidlmayer, "Town and State in the Early Old Kingdom: A View from Elephantine," 109–12.

[4] von Pilgrim and Müller, *Report on the 9th Season of the Joint Swiss-Egyptian Mission in Syene/Old Aswan (2008/2009).*

[5] Ziermann, *Elephantine XVI,* esp. 27–59.

[6] O'Connor, *Ancient Nubia: Egypt's Rival in Africa*, 11–15.

[7] O'Connor, *Ancient Nubia*, 23–5.

[8] For English translations of all four autobiographies, see Strudwick, *Texts from the Pyramid Age*, *Writing from the Ancient World 16*, 328–40.

[9] Edel, Seyfried, and Vieler, *Die Felsgräbernekropole der Qubbet el-Hawa bei Assuan,* I. Abteilung, Band 1, 621–5; Lichtheim, *Ancient Egyptian Literature, Vol. 1: The Old and Middle Kingdoms*, 23–7.

[10] Strudwick, *Texts from the Pyramid Age*, 134 (52A).

[11] Edel et al., *Felsgräbernekropole*, I. Abteilung, Band 2, 682–8; Breasted, *Ancient Records of Egypt, Volume 1*, 161–4; Strudwick, *Texts from the Pyramid Age*, 332–5.

[12] Edel et al., *Felsgräbernekropole*, I. Abteilung, Band 1, 49–60.

[13] Edel et al., *Felsgräbernekropole*, I. Abteilung, Band 2, 816–17; Habachi, *Sixteen Studies on Lower Nubia*, 20.

[14] el-Dissouky, *Elephantine in the Old Kingdom*, 30–4; Martin-Pardey, *Untersuchungen zur ägyptischen Provinzialverwaltung bis zum Ende des Alten Reiches*, 194–5.

[15] el-Dissouky, *Elephantine*, 31–2; Seidlmayer, "Town and State," 109. Friedman, "Excavating Hierakonpolis: Nubian Cemetery."

16. Seidlmayer, "Town and State," 111–12; Dreyer and Ziermann, "Stadt und Tempel von Elephantine, 15./16. Grabungsbericht," 135–52; Müntel and Ziermann, "Stadt und Tempel," 109–28.

17 Raue, *Who Was Who in Elephantine of the Third Millennium BC?*, 1–14.

18 Seidlmayer, "Town and State," 109.

19 Edel et al., *Felsgräbernekropole,* I. Abteilung, Band I, XXVII–XLI.

20 Moreno García, "L'Organisation Sociale de l'Agriculture dans l'Egypte Pharaonique Pendant l'Ancien Empire (2650–2150 avant J.-C.)," 418–24.

21 Regarding provincial titles during the Old Kingdom, see also Martin-Pardey, *Provinzialverwaltung*.

22 For these two titles see Jones, *An Index of Ancient Egyptian Titles, Epithets, and Phrases of the Old Kingdom*, v.2, 806 (#2947) and 453 (#1698); also, Martin-Pardey, *Provinzialverwaltung*, 109–12.

23 Regarding both honorific and official titles in the Old Kingdom and their ranking, see Helck, *Untersuchungen zu den Beamtentiteln des Ägyptischen Alten Reiches*; Baer, *Rank and Title in the Old Kingdom*; and Strudwick, *The Administration of Egypt in the Old Kingdom*; for a recent catalog of titles (with little commentary), see Jones, *Index of Ancient Egyptian Titles,* 2 volumes.

24 Roth, *Egyptian Phyles in the Old Kingdom*, 77–90; Eyre, "Work and the Organisation of Work in the Old Kingdom," 31. Regarding the integration of provincial elite into the state structure, see Moreno García, "L'Organisation Sociale," 411–50.

25 Eichler, *Untersuchungen zum Expeditionswesen des ägyptischen Alten Reiches*, 234–7.

26 Eichler, *Expeditionswesen*, 163–84; Bell, Johnson, and Whitcomb, "The Eastern Desert of Upper Egypt: Routes and Inscriptions," 27–46.

27 Müller-Wollermann, *Krisenfaktoren im Ägyptischen Staat des Ausgehenden Alten Reichs*, 91.

28 Rock inscription references from Eichler, *Expeditionswesen,* 68 (Nr. 116), 112 (Nr. 258). A related title, "overseer of all foreign lands," is associated with a figure depicted in the funerary temple of Pepy II who has not yet been identified with a tomb owner at Qubbet el-Hawa. Jones, *Index of Ancient Egyptian Titles,* v.1, 185, #697; also Jéquier, *Fouilles à Saqqarah le monument funéraire de Pepi II*, v. 3 pl. 52.

29 Müller-Wollermann, *Krisenfaktoren*, 91.

30 Bell, *Interpreters and Egyptianized Nubians in Ancient Egyptian Foreign Policy: Aspects of the History of Egypt and Nubia*, 74: "The word *iꜥꜣw* developed two distinct meanings: applied to an Egyptian it means 'interpreter', but when applied to a foreigner it means 'Egyptianized Nubian." See also Bell's footnote 1012, which modifies this last statement: "By this translation we intend to refer to the *iꜥꜣw* only as Nubians in Egyptian employ, whether as mercenaries, servants, or in any other capacity."

31 Ibid., 70–1.

32 Goedicke, "The Title in the Old Kingdom," 60–4; Eichler, *Expeditionswesen*, 192–7.

33 Edel, *Die Felsengräber*, II. Abt., Bd. 1, T.2, 90. Eichler, *Expeditionswesen,* 192: "Vielmehr stellen diese j'3w (nubische) Hilfstruppen dar, die zum Expeditionspersonal gehörten und wohl sowohl Arbeiten in den Steinbrüchen, als auch paramilitärische Aufgaben wahrnahmen." "Rather, these represent the '*iꜥꜣw*' Nubian auxiliary troops that were part of the expedition personnel, and probably as well as working in the quarries also took on paramilitary duties."

34 Eichler, *Expeditionswesen,* 197.

35 Edel et al., *Felsgräbernekropole*, I. Abteilung Band 2, 816–17.

36 Strudwick, *Texts from the Pyramid Age*, 330.

37 Ibid.

38 Ibid., 334.

39 Ibid., 336–7; Edel, "Die Grabungen auf der Qubbet el-Hawa, 1975," 193–7.
40 Strudwick, *Texts from the Pyramid Age*, 339; Habachi, *Sixteen Studies*, 20.
41 Eichler, *Expeditionswesen*, 234–7.
42 Eichler, *Expeditionswesen*, 258–68; Müller-Wollermann, *Krisenfaktoren*, 88–91. Both are contra Martin-Pardey, as Eichler makes clear. In addition, this viewpoint is contra Edel to some extent (not made clear by Eichler) in Edel's assertion that Harkhuf's journeys began and ended in Memphis: Edel, "Inschriften des Alten Reiches, V. Die Reiseberichte des *Ḥrw-ḫwỉf* (Herchuf)," 51–75.
43 el-Dissouky, *Elephantine*, 173–6; O'Connor, "The Location of Yam and Kush and Their Historical Implications," 30.
44 Eichler, *Expeditionswesen*, 266–7; Martin-Pardey, *Provinzialverwaltung*, 196–9.
45 For numerous versions of titles beginning *ḥry šštꜣ*, see Jones, *Index*, #2233–366. For a brief discussion of their function, see Strudwick, *Administration*, 207.
46 See el-Dissouky, *Elephantine*, 22ff., for a discussion of the epithets of Elephantine and their meaning in relationship to the location of the town. See also Martin-Pardey, *Provinzialverwaltung*, 188, for a discussion of these titles, and 192(3) regarding the meaning of *tp-rśy*.
47 el-Dissouky, *Elephantine*, 186–7.
48 For variations on the title, see Jones, *Index*, #1672–1679.
49 For comparative ranking see Baer, *Rank and Title*, 231–9.
50 Edel et al., *Felsgräbernekropole*, I. Abteilung, Band 1, LV.
51 Edel et al., *Felsgräbernekropole*, I. Abteilung, Band 1, LV; Band 2, 1348–9.
52 el-Dissouky, *Elephantine*, 188.
53 Ibid., 189–92.
54 Martin-Pardey, *Provinzialverwaltung*, 196.
55 Moreno García, "L'Organisation Sociale," 422–4.
56 Strudwick, *Texts from the Pyramid Age*, 333.
57 The primary debate concerns whether it always designated an official function or whether in some cases it was purely honorific. Kees, "Beiträge zur altägyptischen Provinzialverwaltung und der Geschichte des Feudalismus I: Oberägypten," 85–98; Helck, *Untersuchungen zu den Beamtentiteln*, 109–10; Goedicke, "Zu *ỉmy-rꜣ šmꜥ* und *tp-šmꜥ* im Alten Reich," 1–10; Baer, *Rank and Title*, 281–6; Edel, *Die Felsengraber der Qubbet el-Hawa*, 115–16; Fischer, *Dendera in the Third Millennium B.C. Down to the Theban Domination of Upper Egypt*, 94–9; el-Dissouky, *Elephantine*, 131–2; Martin-Pardey, *Provinzialverwaltung*, 152–70; Kanawati, *Governmental Reforms in Old Kingdom Egypt*; Müller-Wollermann, *Krisenfaktoren*, 96ff.
58 With the exception of *ỉmy-rꜣ šmꜥw* "overseer of Upper Egypt", which may have had official responsibilities attached, though it is clearly a ranking title, as well.
59 Moreno García, "L'Organisation Sociale"; Moreno García, *Hwt et le milieu rural égyptien du IIIe millénaire. Économie, administration et organisation territoriale.*
60 Eyre, "The Village Economy in Pharaonic Egypt," 33–60; Müller-Wollermann, "Das Ägyptische Alte Reich als Beispiel einer Weberschen Patrimonialbürokratie," 25–40; Moreno García, "L'Organisation Sociale," 429–43.
61 Seidlmayer, "Town and State," 119–22, suggests there was a Third Dynasty royal domain on the western island associated with the Step Pyramid that then fell into disuse by the Fourth Dynasty; in the Fifth Dynasty the area became part of the local cemetery.
62 Eichler, *Expeditionswesen*, 265.
63 Anthes, *Die Felseninschriften von Hatnub nach den Aufnahmen Georg Möllers*, Gr. 6; Eyre, "The Organisation of Work," 14.
64 Eyre, Ibid.

65 Strudwick, *Texts from the Pyramid Age*, 354.

66 Regarding military conflict with Nubia, see especially the autobiography of Pepynakht Heqaib1, translation in Strudwick, *Texts from the Pyramid Age*, 333–5. See also O'Connor, "Location of Yam," 44; also discussion by Martin-Pardey, *Provinzialverwaltung*, 191. Mekhu (25) and Tjetji (103) are called "overseers of troops" in rock inscriptions linked to them: see Eichler, *Expeditionswesen*, 221–3.

67 Bell, *Egyptianized Nubians*, 70–2.

68 Friedman, "Excavating Hierakonpolis."

69 A fragment of a papyrus from Elephantine apparently refers to such border-control work, as the writer complains of not having received an "official document" regarding Nubians traveling to Elephantine. See el-Dissouky, *Elephantine*, 186–7, for text and translation, also published in *Hieratische Papyrus aus den königlichen Museen zu Berlin*, Vol. III, pl. VII.

70 Seidlmayer, "Town and State," 108.

71 Martin-Pardey, *Provinzialverwaltung*, 196.

72 Seidlmayer, "Die Ikonographie des Todes," 208–11.

73 For a discussion of the Weber patrimonial household model that is informative here, although not entirely suited, see Schloen, *The House of the Father as Fact and Symbol: Patrimonialism in Ugarit and the Ancient Near East*. Lehner addresses Schloen's work with regard to Egyptian material in "Fractal House of Pharaoh," 275–353; see also Müller-Wollermann, "Das Ägyptische Alte Reich als Beispiel einer Weberschen Patrimonialbürokratie," 25–40. For additional discussion on the nested-household structure of Egyptian villages, see Kemp, *Ancient Egypt*; and Moreno García, "L'Organisation Sociale," 431, where he states, "... ce qui suggère que la famille étendue ait eu une importance plus grande en Egypte que ce que l'on a, en général, admis/ ... which suggests that the extended family in Egypt had been more important than has generally been accepted."

74 Eyre, "The Organisation of Work," 40.

75 Kemp, *Ancient Egypt*, 219. Italics mine. Kemp does not speak specifically of the Old Kingdom; however, he places this analysis "in earlier periods" (i.e., prior to the New Kingdom).

76 Moreno García, "L'Organisation Sociale," 434–7; Eichler, *Expeditionswesen*, 146–7, and Müller-Wollermann, *Krisenfaktoren*, 91.

77 Seidlmayer, "Town and State," 127. Italics mine.

2 Tombs in Context: Description of Cemetery and Overview of Tombs

1 Seidlmayer, "Die Ikonographie des Todes," 205–52.

2 Edel et al, *Felsgräbernekropole,* I. Abteilung, Band I, XXXI. Seyfried and Vieler were responsible for the vast majority of analysis in these volumes, following Edel's passing, but throughout credit is attributed to "Edel et al." [CE: Ok?]

3 Edel et al., *Felsgräbernekropole*, I. Abteilung, Band 1, esp. XXVII-XLV.

4 By "subsidiary" I mean burials of lower status individuals, not sacrifices.

5 Edel et al., *Felsgräbernekropole*, I. Abteilung, Band 1, 21.

6 Edel et al. suggest that posture relates to higher status among the figures in the tomb of Pepynakht Heqaib2, based upon the rank of figures not holding offerings. *Felsgräbernekropole*, I. Abteilung, Band 2, 779. Other figures that hold a hand to their chest include figures leading cattle (in Khwin-Khnum, Khunes, and Sabni2) and figures holding scribal palettes underneath one arm (in Khunes, Pepynakht Heqaib2, and Sabni2).

[7] Moussa and Altenmüller, *Das Grab des Nianchchnum und Chnumhetep.*

[8] N.b. My use of numbers (1) and (2) appended to the two tomb owners named Pepynakht Heqaib and the two tomb owners named Sabni serves only to differentiate them for the purposes of this discussion. No relationship between the two Sabnis has been clarified; the relationship between the two Pepynakht Heqaibs remains uncertain and is discussed in Appendix A.

[9] Several panels executed only in black paint outlines are no doubt preparatory drawings for a scene meant to be carved in relief; they do not comprise their own style category.

[10] Robins, *Proportion and Style in Ancient Egyptian Art*, 64–87.

[11] Edel et al., *Felsgräbernekropole*, I Abteilung, Band I, 30–1.

[12] Edel et al., *Felsgräbernekropole*, I Abteilung, Band I, 49–53. See also Edel, "Die Grabungen auf der Qubbet el-Hawa, 1975," 193–7.

[13] Ibid., 207.

[14] Ibid., 65.

[15] Somehow the detail of the headrest was left off the line drawing of the scene done by the Bonn mission; as a result, Edel et al. do not discuss it, though they do discuss the presence of a headrest in the scene of Khunes: *Felsgräbernekropole*, I Abteilung, Band I, 545–6.

[16] Ibid., 1117–19.

[17] Ibid., Band 2, 1136; for a more in-depth discussion of these texts, see Seyfried, "Dienstpflicht mit Selbstversorgung: die Diener des Verstorbenen im Alten Reich," 41–59.

[18] Edel et al., *Felsgräbernekropole*, Band I, 541–3.

[19] Serrano, "Different Individuals named Khunes in the Cataract Region," 17.

[20] Edel et al., *Felsgräbernekropole*, Band I, 538.

[21] Galán, "Bullfight Scenes in Ancient Egyptian Tombs," 81–96.

[22] Other tombs with a similar arrangement of a raised platform in front of the false door, underneath which the burial shaft extends, include Tjetji (QH103), QH35g, and Snnw (QH105).

[23] Edel et al., *Felsgräbernekropole*, I Abteilung, Band 2, 736–7.

[24] Galan, "Bullfighting," 90–4.

[25] Edel et al., *Felsgräbernekropole*, I Abteilung, Band 2, 905. The combination of rounded columns and squared pillars, as well as smoothed panels in the chapel of 35i, supports this view.

3 Figure, Panel, Program: Form and Meaning

[1] Although de Morgan suggested the possibility of a different mode of decoration intended among the Qubbet el-Hawa tombs, his opinion has not been widely shared. Morgan, *Catalogue des monuments et inscriptions de l'Égypte antique*, 145; de Bissing, "Les Tombeaux d'Assouan," 9; Smith, *A History of Egyptian Sculpture and Painting in the Old Kingdom* (hereinafter *HESPOK*), 214–43; Habachi, *Sixteen Studies on Lower Nubia.*

[2] Habachi, "Elephantine," 1218.

[3] "Die vor der Nische mit einer größeren Menge von Quarzsplittern deponierten Statuettenrohlinge weisen dabei auf eine angegliederte Steinbearbeitungswerkstatt, in der auch Bildhauer tätig waren." Cornelius von Pilgrim, "Stadt und Temple von Elephantine: 25./26./27. Grabungsbericht," 89.

[4] While the architectural evidence for earlier tombs is clear, no earlier texts or images survive. See Edel et al., *Die Felsgräbernekropole* Band I, XLII–XLV.

[5] For the tombs at Hawawish, see Kanawati, *The Rock Tombs of El-Hawawish: The Cemetery of Akhmim.*

6 For example, see the plans of the Sixth Dynasty tomb chapels of Mereruka, Kagemni, and Ankhmahor in Porter and Moss, *Topographical Bibliography of Ancient Egyptian Hieroglyphic Texts, Reliefs, and Paintings*, vol. 3, L, LV, LVI.

7 "Eine weitere Folge dieser Mauerzüge sind die sich daraus ergebenden Wege der Priester, die leicht mäandrierend durch das Halbdunkel der Anlage ziehen mussten." Seyfried, "Dienstpflicht mit Selbstversorgung: Die Diener des Verstorbenen im Alten Reich," 55.

8 For the tomb chapel as a monument of commemoration, see especially Assmann, "Schrift, Tod, und Identität. Das Grab als Vorschule der Literatur im alten Ägypten," 169–99; idem., "Vergeltung und Erinnerung,"; idem., *Das kulturelle Gedächtnis: Schrift, Erinnerung und politische Identität in frühen Hochkulturen*, esp. 29–129; idem., *The Mind of Egypt: History and Meaning in the Time of the Pharaohs*, esp. 66–73.

9 Roth, "The Social Aspects of Death," 53–59; Hartwig, *Tomb Painting and Identity in Ancient Thebes, 1419–1372 BCE.*

10 " *ỉ ꜥnḫw tpyw-tꜣ śwꜣt(y).śn ḥr ỉs pn m ḫd m ḫśftyw ... ỉ rmṯ nb ꜥḳ.t(y).f(y) r ỉs pn m ꜥbw.f ỉw r ỉṯ.t.f.(ỉ) mỉ ꜣpd*," and translation: "O you who live upon earth, who shall pass by this tomb going north or going south … as for any man who enters this tomb unclean, I shall seize him by the neck like a bird," in Lichtheim, *Ancient Egyptian Literature: A Book of Readings, Volume I*, 24.

11 For an overview of the term *Blickpunktbild* and the literature applying it to New Kingdom tombs, see Hartwig, "Institutional Patronage and Social Commemoration in Theban Tomb Painting During the Reigns of Thutmose IV (1419–1410 B.C.) and Amenhotep III (1410–1382 B.C.)," 61–3.

12 Roth, "Social Aspects," 54.

13 The figures from these two sections are not incorporated into this analysis in part because the scenes are very damaged and an accurate count of figures is impossible, and in part because they are atypical scenes among these programs, depicting activities carried out by anonymous figures; their significance is discussed elsewhere.

14 Baines and Yoffee, "Order, Legitimacy, and Wealth in Ancient Egypt and Mesopotamia," 237.

15 Habachi, *Sixteen Studies on Lower Nubia*, 14.

16 Ibid.

17 For an overview of these arguments, see Robins, *The Art of Ancient Egypt*, 81–3; Aldred, *Egyptian Art*, 104–10; Smith, *HESPOK*, 214–43.

18 For ranking lists, see Baer, *Rank and Title in the Old Kingdom*, 231–9; for a brief discussion of this title string, see Strudwick, *The Administration of Egypt in the Old Kingdom*, 311.

19 For example, see Kees, *Studien zur ägyptischen Provinzialkunst*; Smith, *HESPOK*, 214–43.

20 Hartwig, "Institutional Patronage."

21 Edel, *Die Felsengraber der Qubbet el-Hawa bei Assuan, Abteilung 2. Die althieratischen Topfaufschriften*. Bd.1, v.1, 94–114.

22 Ibid., 115.

4 Individuals, Community, Identity: Summation and Interpretation of Program Content

1 For full text translations, see Edel et al., *Felsgräbernekropole*. Author translations are provided in Appendix A.

2 Blackman, *The Rock Tombs of Meir*, v. 4, 19.

3. Khui's titles from the painted panel on the north wall next to his cult place are "sealer of the king of Lower Egypt, sole companion, and lector priest", and Metjnw's titles from the painted panel on the south wall are, "sole companion, lector priest, and expedition leader."

4 Seyfried believes these panels depict two different men named Iienkhenit, one of whom is the overseer and one of whom is the inspector. If correct, the inspector appears alone on the ramp stele with the tomb owner and again on the entrance thickness with his family, while the overseer appears only on the interior east wall panel either with one son and two additional representations of himself, or perhaps with two other sons both also named Iienkhenit, but for some reason not identified as sons. Seyfried, "Dienstflicht," 48–9.

5 Edel first suggested the inscription refers to the *ta-wr phyle* in, "Ein bisher unbeachteter Beleg für 'Kompositum Älterer Bildungsweise,'" 129. This view is supported by Seyfried in Edel et al., *Felsgräbernekropole,* I. Abt, Band 1, 42. Roth discusses the same inscription but is less certain of a phyle designation: Roth, *Egyptian Phyles in the Old Kingdom. The Evolution of a System of Social Organization*, 23.

6 On Sabni's son Mekhu (II), see Edel, "Die Grabungen auf der Qubbet el-Hawa, 1975," 193–7.

7 El-Dissouky, *Elephantine in the Old Kingdom*, 109–10, 127. He agrees that these two Khnumheteps are the same person.

8 Edel suggests Khunes and this scribe are the same two people identified in a rock inscription on Sehel. Edel, "Felsinschriften aus dem Alten Reich auf der Insel Sehel," 132–4.

9 Seyfried, "Dienstpflicht," 51.

10 Seyfried believes some of the figures in this program, in particular a group of four on the lower dado of the north entrance thickness, were a later addition. Edel et al., *Felsgräbernekropole,* I. Abteilung, Band 2, 745.

11 For a comparison of Sabni2's tomb program and the relief on the Middle Kingdom shrine, see Habachi, "Identification of Heqaib and Sabni with Owners of Tombs in Qubbet el-Hawa and Their Relationship with Nubia," 11–27.

12 Seyfried renders the name as Ny-ba, Edel et al., *Felsgräbernekropole,* I. Abteilung, Band 2, 760.

13 A second small, graffiti-like figure scratched into the surface behind this figure was likely not carved at the same time as Shemai; no relationship between them is indicated via text.

14 Roth, *Egyptian Phyles*, 119–44; Eyre, "Work and the Organisation of Work in the Old Kingdom," 11–13.

15 Baer, *Rank and Title*, 231–9.

16 Habachi sees this figure as recarved (*Sixteen Studies on Lower Nubia*, 16–19), but it is carved in raised relief at what appears to be a similar level to the tomb owner, while the figures behind her are in sunk relief. In my opinion the figure is not recarved.

17 Seyfried also suggests the likelihood that this Heqaib is Sabni's son. Edel et al., *Felsgräbernekropole,* I. Abteilung, Band 2, 822–3.

18 Although this title did indicate a professional role in the cult of Hathor, it is possible that the title was also used in a more strictly honorific way; this is likely the case in this cemetery. There is no evidence for a local cult of Hathor, and the absence of reference to the local cult of Satet makes such emphasis on the cult of Hathor all the more unusual. For a discussion of Hathor-cult titles and the archaeological evidence for the cult in the Old Kingdom see Galvin, *The Priestesses of Hathor in the Old Kingdom and First Intermediate Period*, esp. 275–7.

19 The two images of Khnumhetep on his false door in the chapel of Khui have no surviving titles with them, but his titles survive elsewhere in the tomb, as well as the tomb of Tjetji. They are considered titled figures.

[20] Jones, *Index*, 592.

[21] Papazian, *The "Per-Shena": From Palace Estate to Sacred Storehouse. The Structure and Evolution of an Ancient Egyptian Economic Institution.*

[22] Seyfried emphasizes the connection to the household indicated by many of the titles held in the Qubbet el-Hawa programs. See Seyfried, "Dienstpflicht," 50–8.

[23] Baer, *Rank and Title*, 234–9.

[24] Edel, *Die Felsengraber der Qubbet el-Hawa II*, 89

[25] Seyfried discusses some of the recovered evidence of burials in the forecourt of tomb ninety-three in, "Dienstpflicht," 56–7.

[26] The remains of a single mud-brick mastaba were discovered at the foot of Qubbet el-Hawa, near the bottom of the ramp leading up to the tomb of Khunes. Very little of the tomb remained other than the subterranean burial chamber and some pottery offerings. The location and quality of the tomb suggested to the excavators that the owner was of a lower social status than the owners of the rock-cut tombs, and they equated it more closely to the mastabas on Elephantine Island. This status suggests that the owner, named Anu, was more likely a *ka*-cult priest than an elite owner on the level with the other tomb owners. However, the pottery recovered from this burial was inscribed like the pottery from the rock-cut tombs, and Edel determined that this practice was restricted to the elite tomb owners, not including the *ka*-cult priests. Other mastabas may have been constructed at the foot of the Qubbet el-Hawa mountain, but there is no evidence for a large-scale cemetery in this location. The status of the owner of the mastaba and the reasons for the location of this tomb remain unclear. See el-Din, "Discovery of a Tomb of the Late Old Kingdom Below the Rock Tombs of Qubbet el-Hawa, Aswan," 31–34.

[27] Seidlmayer, "Die Ikonographie des Todes," 205–52.

[28] Seidlmayer, "Ikonographie," 210: "Given the total absence of elite cultural features such as decorated and inscribed architectural components, rich grave goods, etc., it is evident that we are dealing with a cemetery of a group of people beneath the ruling classes. The finds from the richest tombs in the cemetery on Elephantine coincide with those from the burials of the 'subordinate functionaries', a level the burials of the adjacent shafts of the rock tombs at Qubbet el-Hawa represent." ["Angesichts des völligen Fehlens elitekultureller Merkmale wie etwa dekorierter und beschrifteter Bauteile, reicher Grabausstattungen etc. ist evident, daß es sich um ein Gräberfeld eines Personenkreises unterhalb der Führungsschicht handelt ... Die Funde der reichsten Gräber des Friedhofs von Elephantine berühren sich mit dem, was von den Bestattungen der "subalternen Funktionäre", bekannt ist, einer Schicht, die etwa die Bestattungen der Nebenschächte der Felsgräber der Qubbet el-Hawa ... repräsentieren."]

[29] Regarding the royal mortuary cults, see Posener-Kriéger, *Les archives du temple funéraire de Néferirkarê-Kakaï*; Roth, *Egyptian Phyles*, 77–90; idem., "The Organization and Functioning of the Royal Mortuary Cults," 133–40.

[30] Roth, "Organization and Functioning," 135–7.

[31] Seyfried discusses several of these texts in "Dienstpflicht," 50–4.

[32] Re: reading of *Rṯnw*, see Edel et al., *Felsgräbernekropole*, I. Abteilung, Band 1, 466. For an alternative translation, see Espinel, "Minima epigraphica," 16. Espinel's translation makes good sense, though it is worth noting that his discussion of the related scene confuses the identity of several of the relevant people. Senti is not Khui's wife but rather Khnumhetep's, and the children belong to the two of them, thus the Hrwemkawes who is identified as his daughter is the daughter of Khnumhetep, both here and in the tomb of Tjetji.

[33] Papazian, *Per Shena*.

[34] Seyfried, "Dienstpflicht," 50–8.

[35] This lack of cult priest titles parallels the lack of god's cult titles in the titularies of the tomb owners, which is unusual for provincial elite of this time. Edel found four inscribed pots with the title "overseer of priests" (*ỉmy-rꜣ ḥm(w) nṯr*). Edel, *Qubbet el-Hawa II*, 89. The exception is the title "priestess of Hathor" discussed in note 22.

[36] Although several of these remain unreadable.

[37] One of these pairs is technically a mother and daughter, PnH15b, but I think originally at least one additional figure was in front of them, probably a father/husband. This figure was carved away and replaced by the current right-hand pair of husband and wife (PnH15a). See Plate XVII.

[38] Assmann, "Preservation and Presentation of Self in Ancient Egyptian Portraiture," 80.

[39] Ibid., 81. Assmann discusses this theme in many other works, including, "Der Literarische Aspect des Ägyptischen Grabes," 97–104; and *Das kulturelle Gedächtnis*, 29–129.

[40] Numerous studies investigate the identity of tomb owners as represented in tomb programs. Assmann has written extensively on the topic, including the works cited in note 39 as well as, "Schrift, Tod, und Identität," 169–99; "Vergeltung und Erinnerung"; "Sepulkrale Selbstthematierisierung im Alten Ägypten," 208–32; and *The Mind of Egypt*, esp. 66–77. Hartwig includes an excellent overview of the issue of identity and tomb programs: *Tomb Painting and Identity*. Additional studies include Fitzenreiter, "Grabdekoration und die Interpretation funerärer Rituale im Alten Reich," 67–140, and idem., "Totenverehrung und soziale Repräsentation im Thebanischen Beamtengrab der 18. Dynastie," 95–130; O'Connor, "Sexuality, Statuary, and the Afterlife; Scenes in the Tomb-Chapel of Pepyankh (Heny the Black). An Interpretive Essay," 621–33, and idem., "Society and Individual in Early Egypt," 21–35.

[41] Bibliography on the topic of identity is extensive. Some relevant sources include: Díaz-Andreu and Lucy, *The Archaeology of Identity*; R. Jenkins, *Social Identity. Key Ideas*; Harris, *The New Art History: A Critical Introduction*, 129–60; Meskell, "Archaeologies of Identity," Assmann, *Das kulturelle Gedächtnis*, 130–62.

[42] Te Velde, "Some Remarks on the Concept 'Person' in the Ancient Egyptian Culture," 83–101.

[43] Te Velde, "Concept 'Person,'" 91.

[44] Díaz-Andreu and Lucy, *The Archaeology of Identity*, 2.

[45] "Individuelle Identität ist das im Bewußtsein des Einzelnen aufgebaute und durchgehaltene Bild der ihn von allen ('signifikanten') Anderen unterscheidenden Einzelzüge. ... Unter einer kollektiven oder Wir-Identität verstehen wir das Bild, das eine Gruppe von sich aufbaut und mit dem sich deren Mitglieder identifizieren." Assmann, *Das kulturelle Gedächtnis*, 131–2.

[46] "Only by naming is a newborn officially 'recognized,' and is integrated into society as a both a biological existence and a 'social existence.'" "Erst durch die Namensgebung wird das Neugeborene offiziell 'anerkannt' und ist neben seiner biologischen Existenz auch als 'sozial existent' in die Gesellschaft integriert." Fitzenreiter, "Grabdekoration," 70.

[47] Te Velde, "Concept 'Person,'" 88.

[48] Fitzenreiter, "Grabdekoration," 92.

[49] Seyfried, "Dienstpflicht," 49–54.

[50] Ibid., 48–9.

[51] Ibid., 50–8.

[52] The problem of the priests of the local cult remains. One assumes they would have been high status enough to be included in this cemetery; however, there is very little evidence of their presence. The inscribed pottery referring to two *ỉmy-rꜣ ḥm(w) nṯr* (mentioned in note 38) analyzed by Edel suggests at least the possibility that priests were in fact included in this group. Edel, *Qubbet el-Hawa II*, 88–9.

53 R. Jenkins, *Social Identity*, 116.

54 "Umgekehrt führt gesteigerte Distinktion nach außen unweigerlich zu gesteigerter Einheit im Innern. Nichts schweißt enger zusammen als die Abschottung gegen eine feindliche Umwelt." Assmann, *Das kulturelle Gedächtnis*, 152.

Conclusion: Monuments of a Community

1 Mitchell, "Showing Seeing: A Critique of Visual Culture," 238.

2 For example, see Robins, *Women in Ancient Egypt*; Richards, *Society and Death in Ancient Egypt*; Meskell, *Archaeologies of Social Life: Age, Sex, Class, Etcetera in Ancient Egypt*; Szpakowska, *Daily Life in Ancient Egypt.*

3 Knapp, "The Archaeology of Community on Bronze Age Cyprus: Politiko Phorades in Context," 107.

4 Frood, "Social Structure and Daily Life: Pharaonic," 474–5.

5 Jeffreys, "Regionality, Cultural, and Cultic Landscapes," 104.

6 Mac Sweeney, *Community Identity and Archaeology: Dynamic Communities at Aphrodisias and Beycesultan,* 20.

7 Jeffreys, "Regionality," 105.

8 von Pilgrim, "Stadt und Temple von Elephantine," *MDAIK* 55, 85–90.

9 von Lieven, "Deified Humans," 2.

10 Varien and Potter, "The Social Production of Communities: Structure, Agency, and Identity," 16.

11 Yaeger and Canuto, "Introducing an Archaeology of Communities," 5.

12 Knapp, "The Archaeology of Community on Bronze Age Cyprus: Politiko Phorades in Context," 107.

Appendix A Chronology and the Two Heqaibs

1 Habachi makes his argument in two places. First and more extensively in: "Identification of Heqaib and Sabni," 11–27; second in his final publication of the shrine: *The Sanctuary of Heqaib.* Discussion of the area of both tombs, as well as each individual tomb, in the final publication assumes the shared identity of the tomb owners: Edel et al., *Felsgräbernekropole,* I. Abteilung, Band 2, 667–77, 678–98, 732–86.

2 Habachi, ibid.

3 Edel et a., *Felsgräbernekropole*, I Abt, Band 2, 667–9.

4 "Surprisingly, Habachi assigned no notes to this large complex." "Diesem großen Bestattungssystem waren überraschenderweise keine Bemerkungen Habachis zuzuordnen." Edel et al., *Felsgräbernekropole*, I Abt, Band 2, 770.

5 Habachi, "Identification of Heqaib and Sabni," 18.

6 Edel et al., *Felsgräbernekropole*, I Abt, Band 2, 693 (36); photograph is Abb. 9, 704.

7 Von Pilgrim, "Stadt und Temple von Elephantine: 25./26./27. Grabungsbericht," 85–90.

8 Edel, *Die Felsengräber der Qubbet el-Hawa bei Assuan. II. Abteilung Band 1.*

9 Edel et al., *Felsgräbernekropole*, I Abt, Band 1, XXVII–XXVIII.

10 Baer, *Rank and Title in the Old Kingdom*, 276.

11 Edel et al., *Felsgräbernekropole*, I Abt, Band 2, 698.

12 Strudwick, *Texts from the Pyramid Age*, 134 (52A).

13 Eichler, *Untersuchungen zum Expeditionswesen*, 355.

14 Kanawati, *Governmental Reforms in Old Kingdom Egypt*, 22.

[15] el-Dissouky, *Elephantine in the Old Kingdom,*109–25.
[16] Fischer, "Administrative Titles of Women in the Old and Middle Kingdoms," 76.
[17] Baer, *Rank and Title*, 115, 293.
[18] Harpur, *Decoration in Egyptian Tombs of the Old Kingdom: Studies in Orientation and Scene Content, Studies in Egyptology*, 282.
[19] Kanawati, *Governmental Reforms*, 140.
[20] Serrano also draws on iconographical analysis by Brovarski of five scenes in the tomb program, but this data seems only to suggest a Sixth Dynasty/reign of Pepy II date, nothing more specific. Alejandro Jimenez Serrano, "Different Individuals Named Khunes in the Cataract Region," 13–23.
[21] Eichler, *Expeditionswesen*, 351.
[22] Ibid., 111.
[23] Serrano, "Different Individuals named Khunes," 14–15.
[24] Edel et al., *Felsgräbernekropole*, I Abt, Band 2, 570, 575.
[25] Ibid., 99.
[26] Edel, "Felsinschriften aus dem Alten Reich," 128.
[27] el-Dissouky, *Elephantine*, 154–5.
[28] Edel, *Felsengräber*, II Abteilung, 115.
[29] Edel et al., *Felsgräbernekropole*, I Abt, Band 1, 49–57; Strudwick, *Texts from the Pyramid Age*, 336–9.
[30] Edel, "Vorbericht über die Arbeiten in den Gräbern der Qubbet el-Hawa bei Assuan." *ZÄS* 93: 48–55.
[31] Edel, *Felsengräber*, II Abteilung, 115–6.
[32] Kanawati, *Governmental Reforms*, 142.
[33] Edel et al., *Felsgräbernekropole*, I Abt, Band 1, 8–20.
[34] Edel, "Vorbericht über die Arbeiten in den Gräbern der Qubbet el-Hawa bei Assuan." *ZÄS* 93, 51.
[35] Edel et al., *Felsgräbernekropole*, I Abt, Band 3, 1442.
[36] Edel, "Vorbericht über die Arbeiten in den Gräbern der Qubbet el-Hawa bei Assuan." *ZÄS* 93, 50; Edel et al., *Felsgräbernekropole*, I Abt, Band 2, 1351.
[37] Baer, *Rank and Title*, 238.
[38] Harpur, *Decoration in Egyptian Tombs*, 282.
[39] Edel et al., *Felsengräber*, II Abteilung, 115–16.

Bibliography

Adams, Matthew Douglas. "The Abydos Settlement Site Project: Investigation of a Major Provincial Town in the Old Kingdom and First Intermediate Period." In *Proceedings of the Seventh International Congress of Egyptologists*, edited by C. J. Eyre, 19–30. Leuven: Uitgeverij Peeters, 1998.

"Community and Society in Egypt in the First Intermediate Period: An Archaeological Investigation of the Abydos Settlement Site." PhD dissertation, University of Pennsylvania, 2005.

Aldred, Cyril. *Egyptian Art in the Days of the Pharaohs 3100–320 BC, World of Art.* London: Thames and Hudson Ltd., 1980.

Allen, James P. *Middle Egyptian. An Introduction to the Language and Culture of Hieroglyphs.* Cambridge: Cambridge University Press, 2000.

Altenmüller, Hartwig. "Geburtsschrein und Geburtshaus." In *Studies in Honor of William Kelly Simpson*, edited by Peter der Manuelian, 27–37. Boston: Museum of Fine Arts, 1996.

Althusser, Louis. "Ideology and Ideological State Apparatuses." In *Lenin and Philosophy and Other Essays*, 123–73. London: New Left Books, 1971.

Andreu, Guillemette. *Egypt in the Age of the Pyramids.* Translated by David Lorton. Ithaca, NY: Cornell University Press, 1997.

Anthes, Rudolf. *Die Felseninschriften von Hatnub nach den Aufnahmen Georg Möllers.* Untersuchungen zur Geschichte und Altertumskunde Aegyptens, Bd. 9. Leipzig: J. C. Hinrichsche, 1928.

Assmann, Jan. *The Mind of Egypt: History and Meaning in the Time of the Pharaohs.* Translated by Andrew Jenkins. New York: Metropolitan Books, 2002.

Das kulturelle Gedächtnis. Schrift, Erinnerung und politische Identität in frühen Hochkulturen. Munich: C. H. Beck, 1999.

"Der Literarische Aspekt des Ägyptischen Grabes und seine Funktion im Rahmen des 'monumentalen Diskurses.'" In *Ancient Egyptian Literature: History and Forms*, edited by Antonio Loprieno, 97–104. Leiden: Brill, 1996.

"Preservation and Presentation of Self in Ancient Egyptian Portraiture." In *Studies in Honor of William Kelly Simpson*, edited by Peter der Manuelian, 55–81. Boston: Museum of Fine Arts, 1996.

"Schrift, Tod und Identität. Das Grab als Vorschule der Literatur im alten Ägypten." In *Schrift und Gedächtnis: Beiträge Archäologie der literarischen Kommunikation*, edited by Aleida Assmann, Jan Assmann, and Christ of Hardmeier, 64–93. Munich: W. Fink, 1983.

"Sepulkrale Selbstthematierisierung im alten Ägypten." In *Selbsthematisierung und Selbstzeugnis: Bekenntnis und Geständnis*, edited by A. Hahn and V. Kapp, 208–32. Frankfurt: Suhrkamp, 1987.

"Vergeltung und Erinnerung." In *Studien zu Sprache und Religion Ägyptens: Zu Ehren von Wolfhart Westendorf*, edited by Friedrich Junge, 687–701. Göttingen: Hubert & Co., 1984.

Assmann, Jan, Günter Burkard, and W. Vivian Davies, eds. *Problems and Priorities in Egyptian Archaeology. Studies in Egyptology*, edited by W. V. Davies. London: KPI Limited, 1987.

Badawy, Alexander. *The Tomb of Nyhetep-Ptah at Giza and the Tomb of 'Ankhm'ahor at Saqqara, University of California Publications: Occasional Papers Number 11: Archaeology*. Berkeley: University of California Press, 1978.

Baer, Klaus. *Rank and Title in the Old Kingdom*. Chicago: University of Chicago Press, 1960.

Baines, John. "On the Status and Purposes of Ancient Egyptian Art." *Cambridge Archaeological Journal* 4, no. 1 (1994): 67–94.

"Theories and Universals of Representation: Heinrich Schäfer and Egyptian Art." *Art History* 8, no. 1 (1985): 1–25.

Baines, John, and Peter Lacovara. "Burial and the Dead in Ancient Egyptian Society." *Journal of Social Archaeology* 2, no. 1 (2002): 5–36.

Baines, John, and Norman Yoffee. "Order, Legitimacy, and Wealth in Ancient Egypt and Mesopotamia." In *Archaic States*, edited by Gary M. Feinman and Joyce Marcus, 199–260. Santa Fe, NM: School of American Research Press, 1998.

Bal, Mieke, and Norman Bryson. "Semiotics and Art History." *The Art Bulletin* 73, no. 2 (1991): 174–208.

Barrett, John C. "Agency, the Duality of Structure, and the Problem of the Archaeological Record." In *Archaeological Theory Today*, edited by Ian Hodder, 141–64. Cambridge: Polity Press, 2001.

"A Thesis on Agency." In *Agency in Archaeology*, edited by Marcia-Anne Dobres and John E. Robb, 61–68. London: Routledge, 2000.

Baud, Michel. "À Propos des Critères Iconographiques Établis par Nadine Cherpion." In *Les Critères de Datation Stylistiques à l'Ancien Empire*, edited by Nicolas Grimal, 31–95. Cairo: IFAO, 1997.

Bell, Lanny. *Interpreters and Egyptianized Nubians in Ancient Egyptian Foreign Policy: Aspects of the History of Egypt and Nubia*. Ann Arbor, MI: University Microfilms, 1976.

Bell, Lanny, J. H. Johnson, and D. Whitcomb. "The Eastern Desert of Upper Egypt: Routes and Inscriptions." *Journal of Near Eastern Studies* 43, 1 (1984): 27–46.

Bintliff, John, ed. *The Annales School and Archaeology*. New York: New York University Press, 1991.

de Bissing, W. "Les Tombeaux d'Assouan." *Annales du Service des Antiquités de l'Égypte* 15 (1915): 1–14.

Blackman, Aylward. *The Rock Tombs of Meir*. Vol. 4. Archaeological Survey of Egypt 25th Memoir. London, Boston: Egypt Exploration Fund, 1953.

Bolshakov, Andrey. "The Moment of the Establishment of the Tomb-Cult in Ancient Egypt." *Altorientalische Forschungen* 18 (1991): 204–18.

Bourdieu, Pierre. *Outline of a Theory of Practice*. Cambridge: Cambridge University Press, 1977.

Breasted, James Henry. *Ancient Records of Egypt. Vol. 1. The First through the Seventeenth Dynasties*. Chicago: University of Illinois Press, 2001.

Brovarski, Edward. "Abydos in the Old Kingdom and First Intermediate Period." In *Hommages à Jean Leclant*, edited by Catherine Berger, Gisèle Clerc, and Nicolas Grimal, 99–121. Cairo: IFAO, 1993.

Brumfiel, Elizabeth M. "On the Archaeology of Choice: Agency Studies as a Research Stratagem." In *Agency in Archaeology*, edited by Marcia-Anne Dobres and John E. Robb, 249–55. London: Routledge, 2000.

Bryson, Norman. "The Gaze in the Expanded Field." In *Vision and Visuality*, edited by Hal Foster, 87–113. Seattle: Bay Press, 1988.

Buchli, Victor. "Interpreting Material Culture: The Trouble with Text." In *Interpreting Archaeology: Finding Meaning in the Past*, edited by Ian Hodder, Michael Shanks, Alexandra Alexandri, Victor Buchli, John Carman, Jonathan Last, and Gavin Lucas, 181–93. London: Routledge, 1995.

Canuto, Marcello A., and Jason Yaeger, eds. *The Archaeology of Communities: A New World Perspective*. London: Routledge, 2000.

Cherpion, Nadine. "La Statuaire Privée d'Ancien Empire: Indices de Datation." In *Les Critères de Datation Stylistiques à l'Ancien Empire*, edited by Nicolas Grimal, 97–142. Cairo: IFAO, 1997.

Conkey, Margaret W. "Experimenting with Style in Archaeology: Some Historical and Theoretical Issues." In *The Uses of Style in Archaeology*, edited by Margaret W. Conkey and Christine A. Hastorf, 5–17. Cambridge: Cambridge University Press, 1990.

Conkey, Margaret W., and Christine A. Hastorf, eds. *The Uses of Style in Archaeology*. Cambridge: Cambridge University Press, 1990.

David, Bruno. "Intentionality, Agency, and an Archaeology of Choice." *Cambridge Archaeological Journal* 14, no. 1 (2004): 67–71.

Davis, Whitney. "Style and History in Art History." In *The Uses of Style in Archaeology*, edited by Margaret W. Conkey and Christine A. Hastorf, 18–31. Cambridge: Cambridge University Press, 1990.

DeMarrais, Elizabeth. "Figuring the Group," *Cambridge Archaeological Journal* 21, no. 2 (2011): 165–86.

de Morgan, Jacques. *Catalogue des monuments et inscriptions de l'Egypte antique.* Vol. 1, *De la frontière de Nubie á Kom Ombos. Series 1, Haute Egypte.* Vienna: Adolphe Holzhuasen, 1894.

der Manuelian, Peter. "Presenting the Scroll: Papyrus Documents in Tomb Scenes of the Old Kingdom." In *Studies in Honor of William Kelly Simpson*, edited by Peter der Manuelian, 561–88. Boston: Museum of Fine Arts, 1996.

ed. *Studies in Honor of William Kelly Simpson.* 2 vols. Boston: Museum of Fine Arts, 1996.

Díaz-Andreu, Margarita, and Sam Lucy, eds. *The Archaeology of Identity.* London: Routledge, 2005.

Dobres, Marcia-Anne, and John E. Robb, eds. *Agency in Archaeology.* London: Routledge, 2000.

"Agency in Archaeology: Paradigm or Platitude?" In *Agency in Archaeology*, edited by Marcia-Anne Dobres and John E. Robb, 3–17. London: Routledge, 2000.

"'Doing' Agency: Introductory Remarks on Methodology." *Journal of Archaeological Method and Theory* 12, no. 3 (2005): 159–66.

Dreyer, Günter. *Der Tempel der Satet: Die Funde der Frühzeit und des Alten Reiches. Elephantine 8.* Archaeologisches Veröffentlichung 39. Mainz: von Zabern, 1986.

Dreyer, Günter, and Martin Ziermann. "Stadt und Tempel von Elephantine, 15./16. Grabungsbericht." *Mitteilungen des Deutschen Archäologischen Instituts, Abteilung Kairo* 44 (1988): 135–52.

Edel, Elmar. "Bericht über die Arbeiten in den Gräbern der Qubbet el Hawa bei Assuan, 1961 und 1962." *Annales du Service des Antiquités de l'Égypte* 60 (1968): 77–94.

"Bericht über die Arbeiten in den Gräbern der Qubbet el Hawa bei Assuan, 1959 und 1960." *Annales du Service des Antiquités de l'Égypte* 57 (1962): 33–41.

"Ein bisher unbeachteter Beleg für ein 'Kompositum älterer Bildungsweise.'" In *Form und Mass: Beiträge zur Literatur, Sprache und Kunst des alten Ägypten. Festschrift für Gerhard Fecht zum 65. Geburtstag am 6. Februar 1987*, edited by J. Osing and G. Dreyer, 124–36. Wiesbaden: Harrassowitz, 1987.

Die Felsengräber der Qubbet el Hawa bei Assuan. Abteilung 2: *Die althieratischen Topfaufschriften.* Bd. 1. *Die Topfaufschriften aus den Grabungsjahren 1960–1963 und 1965.* Teil 1: *Zeichnungen und hieroglyphische Umschriften.* Teil 2: *Text.* Band 2. *Die Topfaufschriften aus den Grabungsjahren 1968–1970.* Wiesbaden: Harrassowitz, 1967–1971.

"Die Grabungen auf der Qubbet El Hawa 1975." In *Actes: 1st International Congress of Egyptology, Cairo, October 2–10, 1976*, edited by Walter F. Reineke, 193–7. Berlin: Akademie-Verlag, 1976.

"Felsinschriften aus dem Alten Reich auf der Insel Sehel." *Mitteilungen des Deutschen Archäologischen Instituts, Abteilung Kairo* 37 (1981): 125–34.

Hieroglyphische Inschriften des Alten Reiches. Vol. 67, *Abhandlungen der Rheinisch-Westfälischen Akademie der Wissenschaften.* Opladen: Westdeutscher Verlag, 1981.

"Inschriften des Alten Reiches V. Die Reiseberichte des Îrw-xwif (Herchuf)." In *Festschrift für Hermann Grapow zum 70. Geburtstag: Ägyptologische Studien*, edited by O. Firchow, 51–75. Berlin: Akademie Verlag, 1955.

"Qubbet el Hawa." In *Lexikon der Ägyptologie.* Band V. Edited by Wolfgang Helck and Eberhard Otto, 54–5. Wiesbaden: Harrassowitz, 1984.

"Vorbericht über die Arbeiten in den Gräbern der Qubbet el Hawa bei Assuan." *Zeitschrift für Ägyptische Sprache und Altertumskunde* 100 (1973): 1–6.

"Vorbericht über die Arbeiten in den Gräbern der Qubbet el Hawa bei Assuan." *Zeitschrift für Ägyptische Sprache und Altertumskunde* 93 (1966): 48–55.

"Zur Familie des Ȯn-Msii nach seinen Grabinschriften auf der Qubbet el Hawa bei Assuan." *Zeitschrift für Ägyptische Sprache und Altertumskunde* 90 (1963): 28–31.

Edel, Elmar, Karl-Joachim Seyfried, and Gerd Vieler, eds. *Die Felsgräbernekropole der Qubbet el-Hawa bei Assuan*, I. Abteilung, 3 Bands. Paderborn: Ferdinand Schöningh, 2008.

Eichler, Eckhard. *Untersuchungen zum Expeditionswesen des ägyptischen Alten Reiches.* Edited by Friedrich Junge and Wolfhart Westendorf, *Göttinger Orientforschungen IV. Reihe: Ägypten.* Wiesbaden: Harrassowitz, 1993.

El-Din, Mohi. "Discovery of a Tomb of the Late Old Kingdom Below the Rock Tombs of Qubbet el Hawa, Aswan." *Mitteilungen des Deutschen Archäologischen Instituts, Abteilung Kairo* 50 (1994): 31–4.

El-Dissouky, Khalid Taha. *Elephantine in the Old Kingdom.* Ann Arbor, MI: University Microfilms, 1969.

Espinel, Andres Diego. "Minima Epigraphica," *Discussions in Egyptology* 59 (2004):7–20.

Eyre, Christopher J. "The Village Economy in Pharaonic Egypt." In *Agriculture in Egypt: From Pharaonic to Modern Times*, edited by Alan K. Bowman and Eugene Rogan, 33–60. Oxford: Oxford University Press, 1999.

"Weni's Career and Old Kingdom Historiography." In *The Unbroken Reed. Studies in the Culture and Heritage of Ancient Egypt in Honour of A. F. Shore*, edited by Christopher Eyre, Anthony Leahy, and Lisa Montagno Leahy, 107–24. London: The Egypt Exploration Society, 1994.

"Work and the Organisation of Work in the Old Kingdom." In *Labor in the Ancient Near East*, edited by Marvin A. Powell, 5–47. New Haven: American Oriental Society, 1987.

Fischer, Henry G. "Administrative Titles of Women in the Old and Middle Kingdoms." In *Varia*, 69–80. New York: Metropolitan Museum of Art, 1976.

Dendera in the Third Millennium B.C. Down to the Theban Domination of Upper Egypt. Locust Valley: J. J. Augustin, 1968.

Egyptian Women of the Old Kingdom and of the Heracleopolitan Period. 2nd ed. New York: Metropolitan Museum of Art, 2000.

"Notes on the Mo'alla Inscriptions and Some Contemporaneous Texts." *Wiener Zeitschrift für die Kunde des Morgenlandes* 57 (1961): 59–77.

Fitzenreiter, Martin. "Grabdekoration und die Interpretation funerärer Riutale im Alten Reich." In *Social Aspects of Funerary Culture in the Egyptian Old and Middle Kingdoms*, edited by Harco Willems, 67–140. Leuven: Uitgeverij Peeters and Department Oosterse Studies, 2001.

"Totenverehrung und soziale Repräsentation im Thebanischen Beamtengrab der 18. Dynastie." *Studien zur Altägyptischen Kultur* 22 (1995): 95–130.

Friedman, Renée. "Excavating Hierakonpolis: Nubian Cemetery." *Archaeology's Interactive Dig*, May 2004, retrieved from http://www.archaeology.org/interactive/hierakonpolis/nubians.html.

Frood, Elizabeth. "Social Structure and Daily Life: Pharaonic." In *A Companion to Ancient Egypt, I*, edited by Alan B. Lloyd, 469–90. Oxford: Blackwell, 2010.

Galán, José. "Bullfight Scenes in Ancient Egyptian Tombs." *Journal of Egyptian Archaeology* 80 (1994): 81–96.

Galvin, Marianne. *The Priestesses of Hathor in the Old Kingdom and First Intermediate Period.* Ann Arbor, MI: University Microfilms, 1981.

Gell, Alfred. *Art and Agency: An Anthropological Theory.* Oxford: Oxford University Press, 1998.

Giddens, Anthony. *The Constitution of Society: Outline of a Theory of Structuration.* Berkeley: University of California Press, 1984.

Goedicke, Hans. "The High Price of Burial." *Journal of the American Research Center in Egypt* 25 (1988): 195–99.

"The Title imy-ra iaAw in the Old Kingdom." *Journal of Egyptian Archaeology* 46 (1960): 60–64.

"Zu imy-rA Sma und tp-Sma im Alten Reich." *Mitteilungen des Instituts für Orientforschung* 4 (1956): 1–10.

Grosz, Elizabeth. *Volatile Bodies: Toward a Corporeal Feminism.* Bloomington: Indiana University Press, 1994.

Habachi, Labib. "Elephantine." In *Lexikon der Ägyptologie.* Band 1, edited by Wolfgang Helck and Eberhard Otto, 1218. Wiesbaden, Germany: Harrassowitz, 1975.

"Identification of Heqaib and Sabni with Owners of Tombs in Qubbet el Hawa and Their Relationship with Nubia." In *Sixteen Studies on Lower Nubia, ASAE 23, Supplement*, 11–27. Cairo: IFAO, 1981.

The Sanctuary of Heqaib. 2 vols. Elephantine 4. Mainz am Rhein: P. von Zabern, 1985.

Harpur, Yvonne. *Decoration in Egyptian Tombs of the Old Kingdom: Studies in Orientation and Scene Content, Studies in Egyptology.* London: KPI, 1987.

Harris, Jonathan. *The New Art History: A Critical Introduction.* London: Routledge, 2001.

Hartwig, Melinda K. "Institutional Patronage and Social Commemoration in Theban Tomb Painting During the Reigns of Thutmose Iv (1419–1410 B.C.) and Amenhotep Iii (1410–1382 B.C.)." PhD dissertation, New York University, 2000.

Tomb Painting and Identity in Ancient Thebes, 1419–1372 BCE, Monumenta Aegyptiaca X. Brussels, Belgium: Fondation Égyptologique Reine Élisabeth, 2004.

Helck, Wolfgang. *Untersuchungen zu den Beamtentiteln des ägyptischen Alten Reiches*. Glückstadt: J.J. Augustin, 1954.

Hendrickx, Stan. "Status Report on the Excavation of the Old Kingdom Rock Tombs at Elkab." In *Atti Sesto Congresso Internazionale di Egittologia*, 255–57. Turin, Italy: Il Comitato Organizzativo, 1992.

Hodder, Ian. *Reading the Past: Current Approaches to Interpretation in Archaeology*. Cambridge: Cambridge University Press, 1986.

"Style as Historical Quality." In *The Uses of Style in Archaeology*, edited by Margaret W. Conkey and Christine A. Hastorf, 44–51. Cambridge: Cambridge University Press, 1990.

ed. *Symbolic and Structural Archaeology, New Directions in Archaeology*. Cambridge: Cambridge University Press, 1982.

"Theoretical Archaeology: A Reactionary View." In *Symbolic and Structural Archaeology*, edited by Ian Hodder, 1–16. Cambridge: Cambridge University Press, 1982.

"Dalrymple Lectures 2007–8, Thing Theory: Toward an Integrated Archaeological Perspective." *Scottish Archaeological Journal* 28, no. 2 (2006): 5–6.

Isbell, William H. "What We Should be Studying: The 'Imagined Community' and the 'Natural Community.'" In *The Archaeology of Communities: A New World Perspective*, edited by Marcello A. Canuto and Jason Yaeger, 243–66. London: Routledge, 2000.

Jeffreys, David. "Regionality, Culture and Cultic Landscapes." In *Egyptian Archaeology*, edited by Willeke Wendrich, 102–18. West Sussex: Wiley-Blackwell, 2010.

Jenkins, Michael R. "Notes on the Tomb of Setka at Qubbett El-Hawa, Aswan." *Bulletin of the Australian Center for Egyptology* 11 (2000): 67–81.

Jenkins, Richard. *Social Identity. Key Ideas*, edited by Peter Hamilton. London: Routledge, 1996.

Jéquier, Gustave. *Fouilles à Saqqarah: Le Monument Funéraire de Pepi II*. Vol. 3. Cairo: IFAO, 1936.

Johnson, Matthew H. "Conceptions of Agency in Archaeological Interpretation." *Journal of Anthropological Archaeology* 8 (1989): 189–211.

Jones, Dilwyn. *An Index of Ancient Egyptian Titles, Epithets and Phrases of the Old Kingdom*. 2 vols., *BAR International Series 866*. Oxford: Archaeopress, 2000.

Joyce, Rosemary A. "Archaeology of the Body." *Annual Review of Anthropology*, v. 34 (2005): 139–58.

Joyce, Rosemary A., and Jeanne Lopiparo. "Postscript: Doing Agency in Archaeology," *Journal of Archaeological Method and Theory* 12, no. 3 (2005): 365–374.

Junge, Friedrich. "Stadt und Tempel von Elephantine VI: Holzrelief der 6. Dynastie." *Mitteilungen des Deutschen Archäologischen Intituts, Abteilung Kairo* 32 (1976): 141–43.

Kadish, Gerald E. "Old Kingdom Egyptian Activity in Nubia: Some Reconsiderations." *Journal of Egyptian Archaeology* 52 (1966): 23–33.

Kamil, Jill. *Aswan and Abu Simbel: History and Guide.* Cairo: The American University in Cairo Press, 1993.

Kanawati, Naguib. *Akhmim in the Old Kingdom.* Sydney: Australian Center for Egyptology, 1992.

The Egyptian Administration in the Old Kingdom: Evidence on Its Economic Decline. Warminster, England: Aris & Phillips Ltd., 1977.

"El-Hagarsa and Its Mummies." *Bulletin of the Australian Center for Egyptology* 4 (1993): 29–40.

Governmental Reforms in Old Kingdom Egypt. Warminster, England: Aris and Phillips, 1980.

The Rock Tombs of El-Hawawish: The Cemetery of Akhmim. 10 vols. Sydney: Australian Center for Egyptology, 1980–1989.

Kees, Herman. "Beiträge zur altägyptischen Provinzialverwaltung und der Geschichte des Feudalismus I: Oberägypten." *Nachrichten der Akademie der Wissenschaften in Gottingen* (1932): 85–98.

Studien zur aegyptischen Provinzialkunst. Leipzig: J. C. Hinrichs, 1921.

Kemp, Barry J. *Ancient Egypt: Anatomy of a Civilization.* London: Routledge, 1989.

"Double Review of 'The House of the Father as Fact and Symbol: Patrimonialism in Ugarit and the Ancient Near East': An Egyptian Perspective." *Cambridge Archaeological Journal* 13, no. 1 (2003): 124–28.

Knapp, A. Bernard. "The Archaeology of Community on Bronze Age Cyprus: Politiko Phorades in Context." *American Journal of Archaeology* 107 (2003): 559–80.

Kolb, Michael J., and James E. Snead. "It's a Small World after All: Comparative Analyses of Community Organization in Archaeology." *American Antiquity* 62, no. 4 (1997): 609–28.

Kus, Susan. "Matters Material and Ideal." In *Symbolic and Structural Archaeology*, edited by Ian Hodder, 47–62. Cambridge: Cambridge University Press, 1982.

Lehner, Mark. "Fractal House of Pharaoh." In *Dynamics in Human and Primate Societies: Agent-Based Modeling of Social and Spatial Processes*, edited by Timothy Kohler and George Gumerman, 275–353. New York: Oxford University Press, 2000.

Lesure, Richard G. "Linking Theory and Evidence in an Archaeology of Human Agency: Iconography, Style, and Theories of Embodiment." *Journal of Archaeological Method and Theory* 12, no. 3 (2005): 237–55.

Lichtheim, Miriam. *Ancient Egyptian Literature: A Book of Readings.* 2 vols. *Vol. 1. The Old and Middle Kingdoms.* Berkeley: University of California Press, 1975.

Limme, Luc, Stan Hendrickx, and Dirk Huyge. "Elkab: Excavations in the Old Kingdom Rock Necropolis." *Egyptian Archaeology* 11 (1997): 3–6.

Mac Sweeney, Naoíse. *Community Identity and Archaeology: Dynamic Communities at Aphrodisias and Beycesultan.* Ann Arbor: University of Michigan Press, 2011. Retrieved from http://muse.jhu.edu/ (accessed April 12, 2013).

Malek, Jaromír. "The Old Kingdom." In *The Oxford History of Ancient Egypt*, edited by Ian Shaw, 89–117. Oxford: Oxford University Press, 2000.

Marcus, Joyce. "Toward an Archaeology of Communities." In *The Archaeology of Communities: A New World Perspective*, edited by Marcello A. Canuto and Jason Yaeger, 231–42. London: Routledge, 2000.

Martin-Pardey, Eva. *Untersuchungen zur ägyptischen Provinzialverwaltung bis zum Ende des Alten Reiches.* Edited by Arne Eggebrecht, *Hildesheimer Ägyptologische Beiträge.* Hildesheim: Gebrüder Gerstenberg, 1976.

Meskell, Lynn. "Archaeologies of Identity." In *Archaeological Theory Today*, edited by Ian Hodder, 187–213. Cambridge: Polity Press, 2001.

ed. *Archaeologies of Materiality.* Oxford: Blackwell, 2005.

Archaeologies of Social Life: Age, Sex Class, et cetera in Ancient Egypt. Oxford: Blackwell, 1999.

"An Archaeology of Social Relations in an Egyptian Village." *Journal of Archaeological Method and Theory* 5, no. 3 (1998): 209–43.

Private Life in New Kingdom Egypt. Princeton: Princeton University Press, 2002.

Metropolitan Museum of Art, ed. *Egyptian Art in the Age of the Pyramids.* New York: Metropolitan Museum of Art, 1999.

Miller, Daniel, ed. *Materiality.* Durham, NC: Duke University Press, 2005.

Mitchell, W. J. T. "Showing Seeing: A Critique of Visual Culture." In *Art History, Aesthetics, Visual Studies*, edited by Michael Ann Holly and Keith Moxey, 231–250. Williamstown: Sterling and Francine Clark Art Institute, 2002.

Montserrat, Dominic, ed. *Changing Bodies, Changing Meanings: Studies on the Human Body in Antiquity.* London: Routledge, 1998.

Moreno Garcia, Juan Carlos. "Acquisition de Serfs durant la Première Période Intermédiaire: Une Étude d'Histoire Sociale dans l'Egypte du IIIe Millénaire." *Revue d'Égyptologie* 51 (2000): 123–39.

"Administration Territoriale et Organisation de L'Espace en Egypte au Troisième Millénaire Avant J.-C. (II): swnw." *Zeitschrift für Ägyptische Sprache und Altertumskunde* 124 (1997): 116–30.

"Administration Territoriale et Organisation de L'Espace en Egypte au Troisième Millénaire Avant J.-C. (III-IV): nwt mAwt et Hwt-aAt." *Zeitschrift für Ägyptische Sprache und Altertumskunde* 125 (1998): 38–55.

"Administration Territoriale et Organisation de L'Espace en Egypte au Troisième Millénaire Avant J.-C. (V): gs-pr." *Zeitschrift für Ägyptische Sprache und Altertumskunde* 126 (1999): 116–31.

"Administration Territoriale et Organisation de L'Espace en Egypte au Troisième Millénaire Avant J.-C.: grgt et le titre a(n)D-mr grgt." *Zeitschrift für Ägyptische Sprache und Altertumskunde* 123 (1996): 116–38.

"De l'Ancien Empire à La Première Période Intermédiare: l'Autobiographie de Qar d'Edfou, Entre Tradition et Innovation." *Revue d'Égyptologie* 49 (1998): 151–60.

Îwt *et le milieu rural égyptien du IIIe millénaire. Économie, administration et organisation territoriale.* Paris: H. Champion, 1995.

"J'ai Rempli Les Pâturages de Vaches Tachetées...Betail, Économie Royale et Idéologie en Égypte, de L'Ancien au Moyen Empire." *Revue d'Égyptologie* 50 (1999): 241–57.

"L'Organisation Sociale de l'Agriculture dans l'Egypte Pharaonique Pendant l'Ancien Empire (2650–2150 Avant J.-C.)." *Journal of the Economic and Social History of the Orient* 44, no. 4 (2001): 411–50.

"La Population mrt: Une Approche du Problème de la Servitude dans l'Egypte du IIIe Millénaire." *Journal of Egyptian Archaeology* 84 (1998): 71–83.

Moussa, Ahmed, and Hartwig Altenmüller. *Das Grab des Nianchchnum und Chnumhotep.* Mainz am Rhein, Germany: Zabern, 1977.

Moxey, Keith. "Semiotics and the Social History of Art." *New Literary History*, 22, no. 4 (1991): 985–99.

Müller-Wollermann, Renate. "Das ägyptische Alte Reich als Beispiel einer Weberschen Patrimonialbürokratie." *Bulletin of the Egyptological Seminar* 9 (1987/88): 25–40.

Krisenfaktoren im ägyptischen Staat des ausgehenden Alten Reichs. Tübingen, Germany: Eberhard-Karls-Universität, 1986.

"Zur Lokalisierung von Orten in Mittelägypten." In *Proceedings of the Xixth International Congress of Papyrology, Cairo 2–9 September 1989*, edited by A. H. S. El Mosalamy, 713–21. Cairo: Ain Shams University, 1992.

Müntel, Sven. "Stadt und Tempel von Elephantine, 21./22. Grabungsbericht." *Mitteilungen des Deutschen Archäologischen Intituts, Abteilung Kairo* 50 (1994): 103–09.

Müntel, Sven, and Martin Ziermann. "Stadt und Tempel von Elephantine, 21./22. Grabungsbericht." *Mitteilungen des Deutschen Archäologischen Intituts, Abteilung Kairo* 51 (1995): 109–28.

Newberry, Percy E. "A Sixth Dynasty Tomb at Thebes." *Annales du Service des Antiquités de l'Égypte* 4 (1903): 97–100.

O'Connor, David B. *Ancient Nubia: Egypt's Rival in Africa.* Philadelphia: University Museum, 1993.

"The Locations of Yam and Kush and Their Historical Implications." *Journal of the American Research Center in Egypt* 23 (1986): 27–50.

"Political Systems and Archaeological Data in Egypt: 2600–1780 B.C." *World Archaeology* 6 (1974): 15–37.

"Sexuality, Statuary and the Afterlife: Scenes in the Tomb-Chapel of Pepyankh (Heny the Black). An Interpretive Essay." In *Studies in Honor of William Kelly Simpson*, edited by Peter der Manuelian, 621–33. Boston: Museum of Fine Arts, 1996.

"Society and Individual in Early Egypt." In *Order, Legitimacy, and Wealth in Ancient States*, edited by Mary Van Buren and Janet Richards, 21–35. Cambridge: Cambridge University Press, 2000.

Papazian, Hratch. *The "Per-Shena": From Palace Estate to Sacred Storehouse. The Structure and Evolution of an Ancient Egyptian Economic Institution*, October 15, 1999. Retrieved from http://oi.uchicago.edu/research/research-archives-library/dissertations/dissertation-proposals/shena-palace-estate-sacred.

Parkinson, Richard. *Reading Ancient Egyptian Poetry: Among other Histories.* West Sussex, UK: Wiley-Blackwell, 2009.

The Tale of Sinuhe and Other Ancient Egyptian Poems. Oxford: Clarendon Press, 1997.

Pearson, Michael Parker. "Tombs and Territories: Material Culture and Multiple Interpretations." In *Interpreting Archaeology: Finding Meaning in the Past*, edited by Ian Hodder, Michael Shanks, Alexandra Alexandri, Victor Buchli, John Carman, Jonathan Last, and Gavin Lucas, 205–09. London: Routledge, 1995.

Peden, Alexander J. *The Graffiti of Pharaonic Egypt: Scope and Roles of Informal Writings (c. 3100–332 B.C.).* Leiden: Brill, 2001.

Porter, Bertha, and Rosalind Moss. *Topographical Bibliography of Ancient Egyptian Hieroglyphic Texts, Reliefs, and Paintings*, 2nd ed. Revised by Jaromir Malek. Vol. 3, Fasc.1. Oxford: University Press, 1978.

Posener-Kriéger, Paule. *Les archives du temple funéraire de Néferirkarê-Kakaï (Les Papyrus d'Abousir): Traduction et Commentaire.* Cairo: Institut Français d'Archéologie Orientale du Caire, 1976.

Preucel, Robert, and Ian Hodder. "Material Symbols." In *Contemporary Archaeology in Theory: A Reader*, edited by Robert Preucel and Ian Hodder, 299–314. Oxford: Blackwell, 1996.

"Process, Structure and History." In *Contemporary Archaeology in Theory: A Reader*, edited by Robert Preucel and Ian Hodder, 205–19. Oxford: Blackwell, 1996.

Ranke, Hermann. *Die ägyptischen Personennamen.* 2 vols. Glückstadt, Germany: J. J. Augustin, 1935.

Raue, Dietrich. "Who Was Who in Elephantine of the Third Millennium BC?" *The British Museum Studies in Ancient Egypt and the Sudan* 9 (2008): 1–14.

Rautman, Alison E., ed. *Reading the Body: Representations and Remains in the Archaeological Record.* Philadelphia: University of Pennsylvania Press, 2000.

Richards, Janet. *Society and Death in Ancient Egypt: Mortuary Landscapes of the Middle Kingdom*. Cambridge, UK: Cambridge University Press, 2005.

"Conceptual Landscapes in the Egyptian Nile Valley." In *Archaeologies of Landscape*, edited by Wendy Ashmore and A. Bernard Knapp, 83–100. London: Blackwell, 1999.

"Modified Order, Responsive Legitimacy, Redistributed Wealth: Egypt, 2260–1650 BC." In *Order, Legitimacy, and Wealth in Ancient States*, edited by Mary Van Buren and Janet Richards, 36–45. Cambridge: Cambridge University Press, 2000.

"Text and Context in Late Old Kingdom Egypt: The Archaeology and Historiography of Weni the Elder." *Journal of the American Research Center in Egypt* 39 (2002): 75–102.

Robins, Gay. *The Art of Ancient Egypt*. Cambridge, MA: Harvard University Press, 1997.

.*Proportion and Style in Ancient Egyptian Art*. Austin: University of Texas Press, 1994.

Women in Ancient Egypt. Cambridge, MA: Harvard University Press, 1993.

Roccati, Alessandro. *La Littérature Historique Sous L'Ancien Empire Égyptien*. Paris: Les Éditions du Cerf, 1982.

Rössing, Friedrich. "Wirtschaftliche und gesellschaftliche Entwicklung im Übergang vom Alten zum Mittleren Reich: Über den menschen Selbst als Geschichtsquelle." In *Problems and Priorities in Egyptian Archaeology*, edited by Jan Assmann, Günter Burkard, and W. Vivian Davies, 141–48. London: KPI Limited, 1987.

Roth, Ann Macy. *Egyptian Phyles in the Old Kingdom. The Evolution of a System of Social Organization, Studies in Ancient Oriental Civilization 48*, edited by Thomas A. Holland. Chicago: The Oriental Institute of the University of Chicago, 1991.

"The Organization and Functioning of the Royal Mortuary Cults of the Old Kingdom in Egypt." In *The Organization of Power: Aspects of Bureaucracy in the Ancient Near East*, edited by McGuire Gibson and Robert D. Biggs, 133–40. Chicago: The Oriental Institute of the University of Chicago, 1991.

"The Social Aspects of Death." In *Mummies and Magic: the Funerary Arts of Ancient Egypt*, edited by Sue D'Auria, Peter Lacovara, and Catherine H. Roehrig, 52–9. Boston: Museum of Fine Arts, 1998.

Russell, Lynette. "Drinking from the Penholder: Intentionality and Archaeological Theory." *Cambridge Archaeological Journal* 14, no. 1 (2004): 64–7.

Säve-Söderbergh, Torgny. *The Old Kingdom Cemetery at Hamra Dom (el-Qasr wa es-Saiyad)*. Stockholm: The Royal Academy of Letters, History and Antiquities, 1994.

Schapiro, Meyer. "On Some Problems in the Semiotics of Visual Art: Field and Vehicle in Image-Signs." In *Theory and Philosophy of Art: Style, Artist, and Society*, 1–32. New York: George Braziller, Inc., 1994.

"Style (with Bibliography)." In *Theory and Philosophy of Art: Style, Artist, and Society*, 51–102. New York: George Braziller, Inc., 1994.
Schloen, J. David. *The House of the Father as Fact and Symbol: Patrimonialism in Ugarit and the Ancient Near East.* Winona Lake, IN: Eisenbrauns, 2001.
Seidlmayer, Stephan Johannes. "Die Datierung Dekorierter Gräber des Alten Reiches-ein Problem der Methode." In *Archäologie und Korrespondenzanalyse: Beispiele, Fragen, Perspektiven*, edited by Johannes Müller and Andreas Zimmermann, 17–51. Espelkamp, Germany: Verlag Marie Leidorf, 1997.
"The First Intermediate Period." In *The Oxford History of Ancient Egypt*, edited by Ian Shaw, 118–47. Oxford: Oxford University Press, 2000.
"Die Ikonographie des Todes." In *Social Aspects of Funerary Culture in the Egyptian Old and Middle Kingdoms*, edited by Harco Willems, 205–52. Leuven, Belgium: Uitgeverij Peeters and Departement Oosterse Studies, 2001.
"Town and State in the Early Old Kingdom: A View from Elephantine." In *Aspects of Early Egypt*, edited by Jeffrey Spencer, 108–1217. London: British Museum Press, 1996.
"Vom Sterben der kleinen Leute: Tod und Bestattung in der sozialen Grundschicht am Ende des Alten Reiches." In *Grab und Totenkult im Alten Ägypten*, edited by Heike Guksche, Eva Hofmann, and Martin Bommas, 60–74. Munich: C. H. Beck, 2003.
"Wirtschaftliche und gesellschaftliche Entwicklung im Übergang vom Alten zum Mittleren Reich: Ein Beitrag zur Archäologie der Gräberfelder der Region Qau-Matmar in der Ersten Zwischenzeit." In *Problems and Priorities in Egyptian Archaeology*, edited by Jan Assmann, Günter Burkard, and W. Vivian Davies, 175–218. London: KPI Limited, 1987.
Serrano, Alejandro Jimenez. "Different Individuals Named Khunes in the Cataract Region." *Zeitschrift für Ägyptische Sprache und Altertumskunde* 140 (2013) 13–23.
Seyfried, Karl-Joachim. "Dienstpflicht mit Selbstversorgung: die Diener des Verstorbenen im Alten Reich." In *Grab und Totenkult im Alten Ägypten*, edited by Heike Guksch, Eva Hofmann, and Martin Bommas, 41–59. Munich: C. H. Beck, 2003.
Shanks, Michael, and Ian Hodder. "Processual, Postprocessual and Interpretive Archaeologies." In *Interpreting Archaeology: Finding Meaning in the Past*, edited by Ian Hodder, Michael Shanks, Alexandra Alexandri, Victor Buchli, John Carman, Jonathan Last, and Gavin Lucas, 3–29. London: Routledge, 1995.
Shanks, Michael, and Christopher Tilley. *Re-Constructing Archaeology. Theory and Practice.* Edited by Colin Renfrew and Jeremy Sabloff. 2nd ed. *New Studies in Archaeology.* London: Routledge, 1992.
Social Theory and Archaeology. Albuquerque: University of New Mexico Press, 1988.

Simpson, William Kelly. "A Late Old Kingdom Letter to the Dead from Nag' ed-Deir N3500." *Journal of Egyptian Archaeology* 56 (1970): 58–64.

Smith, William Stevenson. *A History of Egyptian Sculpture and Painting in the Old Kingdom.* 1st ed. London: Oxford University Press, 1946.

Smither, Paul C. "An Old Kingdom Letter Concerning the Crimes of Count Sabni." *Journal of Egyptian Archaeology* 28 (1942): 16–19.

Spanel, Donald. "Two Studies on Beni Hasan and Bersheh." Unpublished manuscript, 2003.

Stone, Elizabeth C. "Double Review of 'The House of the Father as Fact and Symbol: Patrimonialism in Ugarit and the Ancient Near East': A Mesopotamian Perspective." *Cambridge Archaeological Journal* 13, no. 1 (2003): 121–24.

Strudwick, Nigel. *The Administration of Egypt in the Old Kingdom: The Highest Titles and Their Holders. Studies in Egyptology*, edited by W. V. Davies. London: KPI, 1985.

Texts from the Pyramid Age, Writings from the Ancient World 16. Atlanta: Society of Biblical Literature, 2005.

Szpakowska, Kasia. *Daily Life in Ancient Egypt: Recreating Lahun.* Oxford, UK: Blackwell Publishing, 2008.

Te Velde, Herman. "Some Remarks on the Concept 'Person' in the Ancient Egyptian Culture." In *Concepts of Person in Religion and Thought*, edited by Hans G. Kippenberg, Yme B. Kuiper, and Andy F. Sanders, 83–101. Berlin: Mouton de Gruyter, 1990.

Thomas, Julian. "Archaeologies of Place and Landscape." In *Archaeological Theory Today*, edited by Ian Hodder, 165–86. Cambridge: Polity Press, 2001.

Tilley, Christopher. "Interpreting Material Culture." In *The Meanings of Things: Material Culture and Symbolic Expression*, edited by Ian Hodder, 185–94. London: Unwin Hyman, 1989.

"Mind and Body in Landscape Research." *Cambridge Archaeological Journal* 14, no. 1 (2004): 77–80.

"Social Formation, Social Structures, and Social Change." In *Symbolic and Structural Archaeology*, edited by Ian Hodder, 26–38. Cambridge: Cambridge University Press, 1982.

Traunecker, Claude. "De l'Hiérophanie au Temple: Quelques Réflexions." *Orientalia Lovaniensia Analecta* 39 (1991): 303–17.

Trigger, B. G., Barry J. Kemp, David O'Connor, and Alan B. Lloyd. *Ancient Egypt: A Social History.* Cambridge: Cambridge University Press, 1983.

Van Buren, Mary, and Janet Richards. "Introduction: Ideology, Wealth, and the Comparative Study of 'Civilizations.'" In *Order, Legitimacy, and Wealth in Ancient States*, edited by Mary Van Buren and Janet Richards, 3–12. Cambridge: Cambridge University Press, 2000.

Van Walsem, René. "The Interpretation of Iconographic Programmes in Old Kingdom Elite Tombs of the Memphite Area. Methodological and Theoretical (Re)Considerations." In *Proceedings of the Seventh International*

Congress of Egyptologists, edited by C. J. Eyre, 1197–203. Leuven, Belgium: Uitgeverij Peeters, 1998.

Varien, Mark D., and James M. Potter. "The Social Production of Communities: Structure, Agency, and Identity." In *The Social Construction of Communities: Agency, Structure, and Identity in the Prehispanic Southwest*, edited by Mark D. Varien and James M. Potter, 1–18. Plymouth, MA: Altamira Press, 2008.

von Lieven, Alexandra. "Deified Humans." In *UCLA Encyclopedia of Egyptology*, edited by Jacco Dielmann, Willeke Wendrich, Elizabeth Frood, and John Baines. Los Angeles: University of California Los Angeles, 2010. Retrieved from http://escholarship.org/uc/item/3kk97.

von Pilgrim, Cornelius. "Stadt und Temple von Elephantine: 25./26./27. Grabungsbericht: IV. Palast und früheste Kultstätte des Heqaib im Siedlungsbereich südlich des späten Chnumtempels." *Mitteilungen des Deutschen Archäologischen Instituts, Abteilung Kairo* 55 (1999): 85–90.

von Pilgrim, Cornelius, and Wolfgang Müller, *Report on the 9th Season of the Joint Swiss-Egyptian Mission in Syene/Old Aswan (2008/2009)*, Swiss Institute of Architectural and Archaeological Research on Ancient Egypt, Cairo, 2010. Retrieved from http://www.swissinst.ch/downloads/Report%209th%20Season_2008–2009.pdf.

Wiessner, Polly. "Style and Changing Relations between the Individual and Society." In *The Meanings of Things: Material Culture and Symbolic Expression*, edited by Ian Hodder, 56–62. London: Unwin Hyman, 1989.

Wildung, Dietrich. "La Haute Égypte: Un Style Particulier de La Statuaire de L'Ancien Empire?" In *L'Art de L'Ancien Empire Égyptien. Actes Du Colloque Organisé au Musée du Louvre par le Service Culturel les 3et 4 Avril 1998*, edited by Christiane Ziegler and Nadine Palayret, 335–53. Paris: La Documentation Française, 1999.

Wilson, John A. "Funeral Services of the Egyptian Old Kingdom." *Journal of Near Eastern Studies* 3, no. 4 (1944): 201–18.

Winter, Irene. "Agency Marked, Agency Ascribed: The Affective Object in Ancient Mesopotamia." In *Art's Agency and Art History*, edited by Robin Osborne and Jeremy Tanner, 42–69. Oxford: Blackwell, 2007.

Witkin, Robert W. *Art and Social Structure*. Cambridge: Polity Press, 1995.

Wobst, H. Martin. "Agency in (Spite of) Material Culture." In *Agency in Archaeology*, edited by Marcia-Anne Dobres and John E. Robb, 40–50. London: Routledge, 2000.

Wylie, Alison. *Thinking from Things: Essays in the Philosophy of Archaeology*. Berkeley: University of California Press, 2002.

Yaeger, Jason, and Marcello A. Canuto. "Introducing an Archaeology of Communities." In *The Archaeology of Communities: A New World Perspective*, edited by Marcello A. Canuto and Jason Yaeger, 1–15. London: Routledge, 2000.

Ziermann, Martin. *Befestigungsanlangen und Stadtentwicklung in der Frühzeit und im frühen Alten Reich. Elephantine 16:* Archaeologisches Veröffentlichungen 87. Mainz, Germany: von Zabern, 1993.

"Stadt und Tempel von Elephantine, 19./20. Grabungsbericht," *Mitteilungen des Deutschen Archäologischen Instituts, Abteilung Kairo* 49 (1993): 136–41.

Index

Abu, 19–20, 38, 223
Abydos, 17
administration
  of expeditions, 4, 20–30
  provincial, 23, 27, 30–36, 214, 237
  Qubbet el-Hawa tomb owners' roles in, 21–37, 176–177, 199
aesthetics, 10
agency theory, 7–15, 17, 173, 209–210
agriculture, 5–6
  administration of 25, 31–34
  at Elephantine 19, 24
  See also scene types, agriculture
Akhmim, 139
Amarna, 17
Ankhes (wife of Khunes)
  description of her chapel and program, 96–97
  in the tomb of Khunes, 91, 187
archaeology,
  at Elephantine, 2–3
  at Qubbet el-Hawa, 2–4
  theoretical discussions, 7–17, 48, 209–211
art history, 10–14
artisans/artists, 45, 47, 160, 164
  at Elephantine, 135
  in the tomb of Mekhu, 70, 181
  in the tomb of Pepynakht Heqaib1, 107
  in the tomb of Pepynakht Heqaib2, 112–113, 154–155
  in the tomb of Sabni2, 128
  role in tombs 7–9, 11, 45, 47, 51, 56, 63, 107, 133–142, 147–148, 157, 160–178, 209–211, 218, 221
Assmann, Jan, 208, 210–215
Aswan, 2, 22, 38–39, 220, 231
audience, 45–46, 62–64, 69, 138–140, 221
autobiographies, 2, 4, 19, 31, 225
  of Harkhuf, 21, 27, 43, 97–98, 174
  of Khnumhetep, 200
  of Pepynakht Heqaib1, 21, 27, 43, 105, 174, 226–231
  of Sabni1, 21, 27, 43, 62, 234–235
  of Sabni2, 21, 27, 127
  of Weni, 33

Baer, Klaus, 231–232, 236–237
Baines, John, 160
barges 21, 127, 230
beer
  as offering, 123
  in titles, 186, 199, 203–204
  See also scenes, making beer
birds, 74
  as offerings, 52–55, 119, 123, 157
  catching, 91, 140–141
Bell, Lanny, 26
Bonner Ägyptologisches Institut, 3
border, 2, 22, 28–30, 32, 34, 214–215
Bourdieu, Pierre, 7, 15
Bryson, Norman, 12
Budge, E. A. Wallis, 2
burial
  chambers, 43, 73, 87, 90, 97–99, 111, 139, 228
  elite 1, 23
  intrusive, 41
  subsidiary, 42, 60, 64, 67, 181–182, 199–208, 221
Byblos, 203

Canuto, Marcello A., 15–16, 222
carpenter 194
Cecil, Lady William 2
cemetery 38–41
  as analytic context 5–10, 16
  on Elephantine 34, 39
  in the landscape 5, 14
  Memphite 1
children
  of elite tomb owners 197, 207
  of subsidiary figures 85, 119, 126, 182, 188, 196, 200, 213
columns, rock-cut
  in the tomb of Khunes 87
  in tomb of Mekhu 43–44, 59–65, 139, 154, 163, 182–183

columns, rock-cut (*cont.*)
in the tomb of Pepynakht Heqaib2 43, 102, 107–109, 111, 124
in the tomb of Tjetji 78–81, 146, 185–186, 232
community
of Elephantine 6–8, 12, 16–17, 32–39, 42–43, 62, 217–223
and locality 15–18
and environment 19–20
elite tomb owners' role in 32–37
identity of 15–17, 36–37
and tomb programs 44–48, 133–142, 166–178
titles held by 197–204
names and relationships of 205–215
of artists 51, 135–136, 165–166
Conkey, Margaret 13
Coptic remains 38, 81–83, 86–88, 90–91, 97, 111–112

Dahshur 33
Deir el-Gebrawi 30
DeMarrais, Elizabeth 8
Díaz-Andreu, Margarita 209
Djaw 30
Djemi 99, 101, 190, 198
Dobres, Marcia-Anne 7, 9
drawing 14, 122, 151, 170, 233

earthquake 86–87
Edel, Elmar 26, 28, 233
and Qubbet el-Hawa excavations 3–4, 84, 102, 111–112, 174–177, 191, 195, 199, 228, 230
on pottery from Qubbet el-Hawa 29, 201, 225, 229, 234–237
Edel, Seyfried, Vieler 41–43, 58, 61–62, 65, 87, 90–91, 97, 104–105, 226, 231
Edfu 30, 220
Eichler, Eckhard 25–26, 28, 32, 231–233, 236
El-Amin, Osama Fahmi 4
El-Dissouky, Mohammed 28–30, 232–233, 236
Elephantine
Island 5, 13, 19–20, 24
townsite 3, 6, 21–22, 28–31, 41, 139, 226–227
See also community, of Elephantine
embalmer 198
embodied agents 14, 48, 217–223
excavation 4–6, 22, 41–42, 84, 102, 228
expeditions 19–22, 219
administration of 4, 23, 28, 30–36
titles relating to 25–26, 28–29, 200
in autobiographies 27, 85, 97, 234
Eyre, Christopher 35

false doors 43–44, 57, 136–140, 208, 221
family
and patronage 171–172
groups on panels 205–208, 211–214

figures, offering
descriptions of 49–57, 166
disposition of in programs 138–140
as thematic focus 141–142, 208–214
style of 142–159, 167–178
significance of inscriptions with 179–208
forecourts 42
views from 41
and subsidiary burials 201–202, 221, 227, 233–234
fortress 20–21
funerary cult. *See* mortuary cult

Gell, Alfred 10–11
German Archaeological Institute 6
Giddens, Anthony 7, 9
Giza 1, 221
goods, luxury 22, 27, 36
Grenfell, Francis 2
grid 49, 150

Habachi, Labib 3, 102–103, 131, 160–164, 192, 226–229, 236
habitus 7, 223
Harkhuf
dating of 230–232
description of tomb and program 46, 97–102, 135–136, 156, 174, 189–190, 200
as related to tomb of Pepynakht Heqaib1 102–105
See also autobiographies, of Harkhuf
See also styles, Harkhuf
Harpur, Yvonne 232, 236
Hartwig, Melinda 169–171
Hathor 184–185, 188, 198–200
Hatnub 32
Hawawish 137, 139
headrest 66, 77, 91
Heliopolis 230
Heqaib, Sanctuary of at Elephantine 3, 226–227
Hierakonpolis 33

identity
and tombs at Qubbet el-Hawa 6, 208–215
and pottery offerings 3
and style 166, 170–171
and landscape 19–21, 218–223
See also community, identity of
Ii-Shemai Setka
description of tomb and program 71–74, 144, 150, 172, 175–177, 184, 206–207
dating of tomb 174–175, 232–236
incense
burning 53, 56, 168–169, 184, 193, 198, 212
burners 53, 55
individuals
in archaeology theory 7–8, 12, 15
and identity 208–217

inscriptions, rock 20, 25, 32, 80, 123, 155, 187, 223, 228, 231–236
Irtjet 25, 27

Jeffreys, David 217–219
Joyce, Rosemary A. 9

ka-cult. *See* mortuary cult, private
ka-priests
  and image style 168–170
  burials of 201–202
Kemp, Barry 35
Khufu 221
Khunes
  description of tomb and program 86–96, 136–137, 187–189
  dating of tomb 175–176, 232–237
  damage to tomb 86–88
Khui
  description of tomb and program 80–86, 146–147, 149, 159, 163, 168, 177, 186–187, 200, 203, 207
  dating of tomb 175–176, 230–232, 234
Khwti 64, 181, 200
Khwin-Khnum
  description of tomb and program 44, 74–78, 129, 144, 146, 149, 167, 172–177, 185
  dating of tomb 225–226, 232–237
king 1, 8, 17, 161, 209
  interest in Elephantine 19, 21–23, 27–29, 31–32, 34–36, 127, 197, 230, 234
  See also mortuary cults, royal
Knapp. A. Bernard 15, 216, 223
Kolb, Michael J. 15
Kom Ombo 30
Kubanaya 22, 33

landscape 13–15, 17
  local 19–20, 38–39, 222–223
locality 15–17
Lopiparo, Jeanne 9
Lorton, David 29
Lucy, Sam 209
Luxor 17, 32, 44

Mac Sweeney, Naoíse 16, 218
Martin-Pardey, Eva 28, 30, 34
mastabas
  mud-brick at Qubbet el-Hawa 4
  in cemetery on Elephantine Island 39, 202
material culture 12–14, 133, 173, 216–217, 220–223
  provincial 2
  and context 5–6, 22
  and agency 7–11
Mekhu
  description of tomb and program 58–67, 136, 138–141, 143–146, 154, 163–164, 180–182, 206
  in autobiography of Sabni1 21, 27
  dating of tomb 174–177, 225, 229, 232–237
Memphis 19, 36
  and expedtions 27–28, 31
Merenre 21, 24, 162, 227, 229–231
  inscription at Satet temple 21, 231
  in titles 24, 162, 227–229
Moreno García, Juan Carlos, 31–32
mortuary cults
  royal 202–203
    titles related to 24, 32, 227, 229, 233
  private 70, 202–203, 219–220
    and tomb forecourts 42
    and tomb programs 137–138, 208, 211
    titles in 168, 182, 198–199
  See also titles, mortuary cult
  See also *ka*-priests
Moxey, Keith 11, 13
Müller-Wollermann, Renate 26, 28

nomarch 23, 29, 31, 34, 199, 237
Nubia
  Egyptian relationship with 4
  and Elephantine 16, 19–23, 25, 27–29, 31–33, 35–37, 62, 97, 105, 214–215, 219, 231, 234
  "Egyptianized" 26

O'Connor, David 28
obelisk stele 43, 59, 68, 75, 78–79, 109

paleography 50, 153
panels, system of
  formal aspects of 44–48, 134–140, 211–212
  and figure groupings 205–210
patronage
  in the community 35
  of tomb programs and artists 165–172, 222
  of subsidiary figures 204
Pepy I
  titles in mortuary cult of 24, 162, 227, 229
  rock inscriptions dated to 232–233
Pepy II
  titles in mortuary cult of 24, 176, 227
  letter to Harkhuf 31, 98
  tomb chronology and reign of 229–237
Pepynakht Heqaib1
  description of tomb and program 56, 102–107, 143, 148, 152–153, 157–158, 171–177, 190–191, 201
  and Pepynakht Heqaib2 225–229
  dating of tomb 236–237
  See also autobiographies, of Pepynakht Heqaib1
Pepynakht Heqaib2
  description of tomb and program 42–44, 48, 56–57, 102–104, 107–123, 137, 143, 147, 149, 151–157, 160, 162, 166, 171–177, 191–195, 201, 207
  Habachi and 162–164
  and Pepynakht Heqaib1 225–229

Pepynakht Heqaib2 (*cont.*)
relationship of tomb to tomb of Sabni2 123–124, 126, 131
dating of tomb 173–177, 236–237
per-shena 198–199, 203
phyle 182, 189, 194
plaster 88, 90–91, 97
portico 43, 107, 109
pottery, offerings at Qubbet el-Hawa 3, 29, 201, 225, 233–237
programs, text and image
nature of 44–48, 133–142, 159
thematic focus of 179–180, 197–199
See also style, use in programs and styles at Qubbet el-Hawa

Qar 30

ramp
of Ii-Shemai Setka 72
of Khunes 86–87
of Mekhu and Sabni1 58–59, 62
of Sobekhetep 67
of Tjetji 78
Raue, Dietrich 22
Retjenw 203
"reversion of offerings" texts 70, 74, 184, 202–203, 212
Robb, John E. 7, 9
Robins, Gay 49
Roth, Ann Macy 202

Sabni1
description of tomb and program, 58–67, 136, 143–146, 148, 182–183
dating of, 161–162, 173–177, 225–236
See also autobiographies, of Sabni1
Sabni2
description of tomb and program, 102–104, 123–132, 139, 147–148, 157–158, 161–162, 195–197
dating of, 173–177, 236–237
See also autobiographies, of Sabni2
Saqqara 1, 30, 47, 221
sarcophagi 58, 177, 235
Satet, temple of 21–22, 135, 204, 219, 231
scene types
fishing and fowling 46, 66, 77, 91, 129–131, 140, 161–162, 179, 183, 187–188, 195, 234
agriculture 46, 63, 123, 140–141, 179, 181, 207, 234
leading animals 74, 77, 96, 119–120, 122, 129, 147, 193
bull fighting 46, 95, 131–132, 140, 189
making beer 46, 85, 91, 141, 146, 186
other, 90–92
Schapiro, Meyer, 11
Schiaparelli, Ernesto, 2
scribes, 189, 194, 196, 214
Sehel Island, 233
Seidlmayer, Stephan, 6, 22, 36, 202
serdab, 90, 93
Serrano, Alejandro Jimenez, 4, 87, 233
Setju, 27
Seyfried, Karl-Joachim, 3, 29, 58, 139, 190, 204, 213, 228–229
Sinai, 25
Sirenput I, 43, 132
Snead, James, 15
Sobekhetep
description of tomb and program, 67–71, 183–184
dating of tomb, 174–175, 232–237
statue niches, 66, 79
stele, obelisk. *See* obelisk stele
style, 11–15, 217
and agency, 10
use in programs, 47–48, 159–178, 221–222
styles in Qubbet el-Hawa tomb programs, 48–50
Harkhuf, 56–57, 99–101, 105, 158
Painted, 57, 64, 143–145
Raised A1, 51–52, 142–143
Raised A2, 52, 145–146
Raised B, 52–53, 146–147
Sabni2 Raised, 57, 127–128, 147–148
Sabni2 Sunken, 57, 128–129, 157–158
Sunken A, 53–54, 148–151
Sunken B, 54, 151–152
Sunken C, 54–55, 152–153
Sunken D, 55–56, 153–154
Sunken E, 56, 112–115, 154–157

titles
elite, 23–31
of subsidiary figures, 199–204
Tjetji
description of tomb and program, 78–81, 185–186
Khnumhetep and, 163, 168, 200, 203, 213
dating of tomb, 175–177, 230–234
Tjetjw, 30
trade, 19, 22–23, 26–27, 30, 33, 35–36

Universidad de Jaén, 4, 87

Vieler, Gerd, 3, 58, 228–229
visuality, 11–12, 18

Wadi Hammamat, 25, 231
walls, mud-brick, 62, 64–65, 79, 81, 97, 138
Wawat, 21, 25, 27, 127, 230
Weni, 33, 231
Winter, Irene, 10–11
Wobst, H. Martin, 7
women,
images of in different styles, 50, 52–54, 119, 121, 157
titles held by, 195, 198

Yaeger, Jason, 15–16, 222
Yam, 25, 27